ENCYCLOPEDIA OF DEPRESSION

ENCYCLOPEDIA OF DEPRESSION

Volume 2
[M–Z]

Linda Wasmer Andrews

GREENWOOD

AN IMPRINT OF ABC-CLIO, LLC
Santa Barbara, California • Denver, Colorado • Oxford, England

Copyright 2010 by ABC-CLIO, LLC

All rights reserved. No part of this publication may be reproduced, stored in a retrieval system, or transmitted, in any form or by any means, electronic, mechanical, photocopying, recording, or otherwise, except for the inclusion of brief quotations in a review, without prior permission in writing from the publisher.

Library of Congress Cataloging-in-Publication Data

Andrews, Linda Wasmer.
  Encyclopedia of depression / Linda Wasmer Andrews.
     p. cm.
  Includes bibliographical references and index.
  ISBN 978-0-313-35378-9 (vol. 1 : alk. paper) — ISBN 978-0-313-35379-6 (vol. 1 ebook) — ISBN 978-0-313-35380-2 (vol. 2 : alk. paper) — ISBN 978-0-313-35381-9 (vol. 2 ebook) — ISBN 978-0-313-35366-6 (set : alk. paper) — ISBN 978-0-313-35367-3 (set, ebook)
  1. Depression, Mental—Encyclopedias. I. Title.
  RC537.A567 2010
  616.85'27003—dc22   2010001363

ISBN: 978-0-313-35366-6
EISBN: 978-0-313-35367-3

14 13 12 11 10   1 2 3 4 5

This book is also available on the World Wide Web as an eBook.
Visit www.abc-clio.com for details.

Greenwood
An Imprint of ABC-CLIO, LLC

ABC-CLIO, LLC
130 Cremona Drive, P.O. Box 1911
Santa Barbara, California 93116-1911

This book is printed on acid-free paper ∞

Manufactured in the United States of America

The information published in this volume or any related e-book, Web site, or database is provided for informational purposes only and is not intended to supplement or replace the advice of a trained medical professional. The information provided here should never be used for the purpose of diagnosing or treating a medical or health condition. Readers should consult their own physicians before making any decisions or taking any actions that might affect their health.

For Victor,
My personal antidepressant

CONTENTS

Volume 1

Volume 2

LIST OF ENTRIES

QUICK REFERENCE

Use this outline as a quick study guide to depression. Items in **bold font** are titles of entries in this encyclopedia. Items not in bold font are addressed in the higher-level entries under which they fall.

DEPRESSION

1. **Mood Disorders**
   a. **Major Depression**
      i. **Atypical Depression**
      ii. **Catatonic Depression**
      iii. **Chronic Depression**
      iv. **Melancholic Depression**
      v. **Postpartum Depression**
      vi. **Psychotic Depression**
      vii. **Recurrent Depression**
      viii. **Seasonal Affective Disorder**
   b. **Dysthymia**
   c. **Depressive Disorder Not Otherwise Specified**
   d. **Bipolar Disorder**
      i. Bipolar Episodes
         1. **Mania**
         2. Hypomania
         3. Depression
         4. **Mixed Episode**
      ii. **Bipolar I**
         1. **Rapid Cycling** Bipolar Disorder
      iii. **Bipolar II**
   e. **Cyclothymia**
   f. **Bipolar Disorder Not Otherwise Specified**
   g. **Mood Disorder Due to a General Medical Condition**
   h. **Substance-Induced Mood Disorder**
2. Symptoms of **Major Depression**
   a. **Depressed Mood**

c. **Relaxation Techniques**
d. **Self-Help**
e. **Social Support**

OTHER CONDITIONS WITH DEPRESSIVE SYMPTOMS

1. **Adjustment Disorder With Depressed Mood**
2. Complicated **Grief**
3. **Dementia Syndrome of Depression**
4. **Depressive Personality Disorder**
5. **Minor Depression**
6. **Mixed Anxiety-Depressive Disorder**
7. **Premenstrual Dysphoric Disorder**
8. **Schizoaffective Disorder**

TOPICAL GUIDE

Use this guide as a starting point for exploring a dozen lesser-known but wholly fascinating aspects of depression.

What Are Some Controversial Social Issues Related to Depression?

Environmental toxins—*See:* **Pollution**
Ethnic disparities—*See:* **Ethnicity**
Insurance coverage—*See:* **Insurance Parity**
Managed care—*See:* **Managed Care**
Pharmaceutical advertising—*See:* **Serotonin Norepinephrine Reuptake Inhibitors**
Psychologist prescribing—*See:* **Clinical Psychologist**
Residential treatment centers—*See:* **Continuum of Care**
Stigma of mental illness—*See:* **Stigma**

What Are Some Key Laws and Legal Cases Related to Mental Illness?

Americans with Disabilities Act—*See:* **Americans with Disabilities Act**
Andrea Yates case—*See:* **Postpartum Depression**
Individuals with Disabilities Education Act—*See:* **Individuals with Disabilities Education Act**

Kenneth Donaldson case—*See:* **Hospitalization**
Section 504 of the Rehabilitation Act—*See:* **Individuals with Disabilities Education Act**
Wellstone-Domenici Mental Health Parity and Addiction Equity Act—*See:* **Insurance Parity**

Who Are Some Eminent Poets and Authors Who Suffered from Depression?

Emily Dickinson—*See:* **Seasonal Affective Disorder**
Herman Melville—*See:* **Bipolar Disorder**
John Keats—*See:* **Melancholia**
William Styron—*See:* **Styron, William**
Numerous authors—*See:* **Mood Disorders**
Numerous poets—*See:* **Creativity**

Who Are Some Other Famous Depression Sufferers?

Abraham Lincoln—*See:* **Mental Health**
Brooke Shields—*See:* **Postpartum Depression**
Marie Osmond—*See:* **Postpartum Depression**

Søren Kierkegaard—*See:* **Creativity**
Thomas Eagleton—*See:*
   Electroconvulsive Therapy
Numerous others—*See:* **Mood Disorders**

What Are Some Emerging Treatments for Depression?

Acceptance and commitment therapy—
   See: **Acceptance and Commitment Therapy**
Dialectical behavior therapy—*See:*
   Dialectical Behavior Therapy
Mindfulness-based cognitive therapy—
   See: **Mindfulness-Based Cognitive Therapy**
St. John's wort—*See:* **St. John's Wort**
Transcranial magnetic stimulation—*See:*
   Transcranial Magnetic Stimulation
Vagus nerve stimulation—*See:* **Vagus Nerve Stimulation**
Wake therapy—*See:* **Wake Therapy**

What Are Some Experimental Treatment Approaches for Depression?

Agomelatine—*See:* **Agomelatine**
Cingulotomy—*See:* **Cingulotomy**
Dawn simulation—*See:* **Dawn Simulation**
Deep brain stimulation—*See:* **Deep Brain Stimulation**
Ketamine-like compounds—*See:* **Ketamine**
Magnetic seizure therapy—*See:* **Magnetic Seizure Therapy**
Negative ion therapy—*See:* **Negative Ion Therapy**

What Are Some Lifestyle Choices That Help Manage Depression?

Alcohol moderation—*See:* **Alcohol**
Caffeine moderation—*See:* **Caffeine**
Diet—*See:* **Diet**
Exercise—*See:* **Exercise**
Sleep—*See:* **Sleep Disturbances**

Smoking cessation—*See:* **Smoking**
Stress management—*See:* **Stress Management**

What Are Some Important Nutrients for Healthy Brain Function?

Antioxidants—*See:* **Diet**
Folate—*See:* **Folate**
Omega-3 fatty acids—*See:* **Omega-3 Fatty Acids**
Vitamin B12—*See:* **Vitamin B12**

What Are Some Complementary Approaches That Might Be Helpful for Depression?

Acupuncture—*See:* **Acupuncture**
Dietary supplements—*See:* **Dietary Supplements**
Herbal Remedies—*See:* **Herbal Remedies**
Meditation—*See:* **Meditation**
Music therapy—*See:* **Music Therapy**
Relaxation techniques—*See:* **Relaxation Techniques**
Spirituality—*See:* **Spirituality and Religion**
Traditional Chinese Medicine—*See:* **Traditional Chinese Medicine**
Yoga—*See:* **Yoga**

What Are Some Culture-Specific Syndromes That Are Similar to Depression?

Shenjing shuairuo—*See:* **Cultural Factors**
Susto—*See:* **Susto**
Numerous syndromes—*See:* **Cultural Factors**

What Are Some Notable Books about Depression?

Darkness Visible—*See:* **Styron, William**
Listening to Prozac—*See:* **Fluoxetine**

M

MAGNETIC SEIZURE THERAPY. Magnetic seizure therapy (MST) is an experimental treatment for depression that uses strong, rapidly alternating magnetic fields to induce a brief seizure. It was developed as a gentler alternative to **electroconvulsive therapy** (ECT), which also triggers a seizure that alters electrochemical processes in the brain. ECT is the most effective and fastest-acting treatment currently available for severe depression, but its use is limited by the risk of side effects, including memory loss and temporary confusion. MST aims to build on what is good about ECT while reducing such side effects by controlling the seizure more precisely.

Another goal of MST is to enhance effectiveness, because ECT does not work equally well for everyone. By giving researchers more control, MST may help them pinpoint which aspects of the seizure are most beneficial. Theoretically, this could lead to more focused and individualized treatment. Preliminary studies have yielded promising results, but further research is needed to confirm the safety and effectiveness of MST.

Treatment Procedure. MST is a high-intensity version of **transcranial magnetic stimulation** (TMS), a treatment that uses rapid pulses of magnetic fields to stimulate brain cells. Before MST, anesthesia is administered to keep the patient unconscious and pain-free during the procedure. A muscle relaxant also is administered to prevent violent physical convulsions during the seizure.

During MST, a special electromagnetic coil is placed against the patient's scalp. The electromagnet produces short bursts of powerful magnetic fields, which pass through the hair, skin, and skull and penetrate about two centimeters (a little less than an inch) into the brain. This stimulation is focused on brain areas thought to be involved in mood regulation.

The strong magnetic pulses produce electrical currents. The result is a seizure—a sudden change in electrical activity—in that part of the brain. Since the first human test of MST in 2000, researchers have been refining the technology to improve effectiveness. However, it is still experimental and not available outside of research settings.

Comparison to ECT. Seizures produced by MST differ from those caused by ECT in crucial ways. In a nutshell, MST uses magnetic fields to stimulate the brain, and ECT uses electricity. Because the scalp and skull divert the flow of electricity, the effects of ECT are spread over a wide area of the brain.

In contrast, magnetic fields pass unimpeded through the scalp and skull, so they can be aimed more precisely at a specific brain area. And because magnetic fields do not penetrate very deeply into brain matter, their effects are limited to the cortex—the outermost part of the brain.

Better control with MST improves the ability to target areas of the brain that may be involved in ECT's benefits, such as the **prefrontal cortex**. It also limits the unwanted impact on other parts of the brain that may be responsible for ECT's side effects, such as the temporal lobes.

In research to date, MST caused milder side effects that ECT. Patients also experienced less confusion and recovered more quickly right after treatment. However, in early studies, the effectiveness of MST was also less than that of ECT, limiting its practical usefulness. It remains to be seen whether recent technological advances will narrow the effectiveness gap. If so, MST could be an appealing alternative to the older treatment.

Risks and Side Effects. Although MST is designed to be a gentler option than ECT, it still requires anesthesia and causes a seizure, so it is not risk-free. Preliminary research suggests that common aftereffects of ECT—such as muscle aches, jaw pain, nausea, and memory problems—are lessened with MST, but it is still possible that some might occur. In addition, possible side effects of the magnetic stimulation procedure include scalp discomfort, headache, lightheadedness, tingling, or twitching of facial muscles and discomfort from noise made by the MST device.

See also: Brain Stimulation; Treatment of Depression; Treatment-Resistant Depression

Bibliography

Electroconvulsive Therapy. Mayo Clinic, July 11, 2008, http://www.mayoclinic.com/health/electroconvulsive-therapy/MY00129.

Kirov, George, Klaus P. Ebmeier, Allan I. F. Scott, Maria Atkins, Najeeb Khalid, Lucy Carrick, et al. "Quick Recovery of Orientation After Magnetic Seizure Therapy for Major Depressive Disorder." *British Journal of Psychiatry* 193 (2008): 152–155.

Lisanby, Sarah H., and Angel V. Peterchev. "Magnetic Seizure Therapy for the Treatment of Depression." *Advances in Biological Psychiatry* 23 (2007): 155–171.

Lisanby, Sarah H., Bruce Luber, Thomas E. Schlaepfer, and Harold A. Sackeim. "Safety and Feasibility of Magnetic Seizure Therapy (MST) in Major Depression: Randomized Within-Subject Comparison with Electroconvulsive Therapy." *Neuropsychopharmacology* 28 (2003): 1852–1865.

Moore, Heidi W. "A Novel Convulsive Therapy for Depression." *NeuroPsychiatry Reviews* (September 2004).

Transcranial Magnetic Stimulation. Mayo Clinic, July 26, 2008, http://www.mayoclinic.com/health/transcranial-magnetic-stimulation/MY00185.

MAINTENANCE TREATMENT. Treatment for depression falls into three stages: acute, continuation, and maintenance. During the maintenance phase, the aim is to prevent a future **recurrence**—a new episode of depression after a period of wellness.

After six months of sustained remission, during which symptoms are resolved to the level of healthy individuals, people are often said to have achieved **recovery**. But that does not necessarily mean they should stop treatment. Many people find that taking **antidepressants** even after recovering helps them maintain improvements and stay well for the long haul.

Not everyone with depression needs maintenance treatment. The risks and costs of long-term medication must be weighed against the likelihood that depression will recur. Maintenance treatment might not be necessary for someone who has fully recovered after a single episode of moderate depression.

For someone who has had two bouts of depression, whose depression was especially severe, or whose symptoms have not completely gone away, maintenance treatment might be considered. For someone who has had three or more bouts of depression, whose depression is part of bipolar disorder, or whose symptoms were very long-lasting, maintenance treatment is usually recommended. Once on maintenance medication, people usually see their prescribing doctor for monthly or quarterly visits.

Long-term **psychotherapy** for maintenance purposes has not been as well studied or widely advocated. But studies to date show that, for people at very high risk for recurrence, ongoing psychotherapy sessions may improve the odds of staying well. Sessions may be scheduled as infrequently as once a month. Both **cognitive-behavioral therapy** and **interpersonal therapy** have been adapted for maintenance use.

See also: Acute Treatment; Continuation Treatment

Bibliography

Dombrovski, Alexandre Y., Jill M. Cyranowski, Benoit H. Mulsant, Patricia R. Houck, Daniel J. Buysse, Carmen Andreescu, et al. "Which Symptoms Predict Recurrence of Depression in Women Treated with Maintenance Interpersonal Psychotherapy?" *Depression and Anxiety* 25 (2008): 1060–1066.

Fava, Giovanni A., Chiara Rafanelli, Silvana Grandi, Sandra Conti, and Piera Belluardo. "Prevent of Recurrent Depression with Cognitive Behavioral Therapy: Preliminary Findings." *Archives of General Psychiatry* 55 (1998): 816–820.

Kupfer, David J. "Acute Continuation and Maintenance Treatment of Mood Disorders." *Depression* 3 (1995): 137–138.

U.S. Department of Health and Human Services. *Mental Health: A Report of the Surgeon General.* Rockville, MD: U.S. Department of Health and Human Services, 1999.

Vos, Theo, Michelle M. Haby, Jan J. Barendregt, Michelle Kruijshaar, Justine Corry, and Gavin Andrews. "The Burden of Major Depression Avoidable by Longer-Term Treatment Strategies." *Archives of General Psychiatry* 61 (2004): 1097–1103.

MAJOR DEPRESSION. Major depression—also known as major depressive disorder—is a mental disorder that involves being in a low mood nearly all the time and/or losing interest or enjoyment in almost everything. These feelings last for at least two weeks, are associated with several other symptoms, and lead to serious problems getting along in everyday life.

Everyone feels down in the dumps now and then, but major depression is more than just a short-term case of the blues. It is a disabling illness that touches every facet of people's lives, including how they feel, think, and behave. Unlike normal **sadness** or **grief**, major depression is long-lasting. Without treatment, it can hang on for months or even years. Major depression also makes it very hard to function at home, work, and school. In fact, of all medical illnesses, it is the leading cause of disability in the United States and many other developed nations.

Major depression is a common problem. According to the Substance Abuse and Mental Health Services Administration, eight percent of U.S. adults say they have experienced at least one bout of major depression within the past year, and 15 percent say they have experienced the disorder at some point in their lives. Fortunately, major depression is also one of the most treatable mental disorders. With proper treatment, most people with the disorder improve, often within weeks, and get back to their daily lives.

Criteria for Diagnosis. The symptoms of major depression are defined by the ***Diagnostic and Statistical Manual of Mental Disorders, Fourth Edition, Text Revision***

Mild, Moderate, or Severe?

Mental health professionals decide how severe major depression is based on how many symptoms a particular person has and the degree to which these symptoms impair the person's life.

Mild Depression

A person has only five or six of the symptoms listed under Criteria for Diagnosis. The person is able to get along in daily life, but it takes more effort than usual to accomplish everyday tasks.

Moderate Depression

A person may have a few more symptoms than what is seen in mild depression. These symptoms are bad enough to interfere with the person's ability to do everything he or she needs to do.

Severe Depression

A person has nearly all the listed symptoms. These symptoms make it almost impossible to accomplish major life tasks, such as going to work or school and taking care of children. In some cases, a person may develop **psychotic depression**, which is marked by distorted beliefs or perceptions that are seriously out of touch with reality.

(*DSM-IV-TR*), a diagnostic guidebook published by the American Psychiatric Association and widely used by mental health professionals from many disciplines. According to the *DSM-IV-TR*, people with major depression have symptoms that last for at least two weeks. These symptoms cause serious distress or significant problems in everyday life.

People with major depression experience a low mood and/or a loss of interest or pleasure in once-enjoyed activities (the first two symptoms listed below). In addition, they must have several other symptoms from the following list, for a minimum total of five symptoms.

Low Mood. People with a **depressed mood** feel sad, empty, helpless, or hopeless for most of the day, nearly every day. Some have **crying** spells. In **children** and **adolescents**, the mood sometimes seems irritable rather than sad or dejected. Depressed adults also may have a short temper or get easily frustrated.

Loss of Interest or Pleasure. People with this symptom—also known as **anhedonia**—are unable to take interest or find pleasure in activities they used to enjoy. They may give up hobbies or withdraw from social activities. Those who previously were sexually active may notice a drastic decline in desire.

Changes in Eating Habits. Many people with major depression lose their appetite and feel as if they have to force themselves to eat. Adults may lose weight without meaning to, and growing children may fail to gain weight as expected. At the other end of the spectrum, some people with depression have an increased appetite or a craving for sweets, which can lead to putting on unwanted pounds.

Changes in Sleep Habits. Major depression can lead to **sleep disturbances**. The most common is insomnia, which refers to difficulty falling or staying asleep. Often, people wake up in the middle of the night or too early in the morning and are unable to get back to sleep. At the other extreme, some people with depression develop hypersomnia, which refers to oversleeping or excessive daytime sleepiness.

Changes in Activity Level. Major depression can produce changes in behavior that are apparent to others. Psychomotor agitation refers to restless activity—such as pacing, fidgeting, or hand-wringing—that goes along with an inner feeling of tension. Psychomotor retardation refers to slowed-down movements and speech.

Changes in Energy Level.   People with major depression may feel tired nearly all the time, or they may feel as if all their energy has been sapped. Even the smallest tasks seem to require a herculean effort. Simple, everyday chores, such as showering and dressing, may seem exhausting and take much longer than normal.

Changes in Thinking Ability.   People with major depression may have trouble concentrating or making decisions. In other cases, they may become unusually forgetful. Those with intellectually demanding jobs often have trouble keeping up with the workload. Students may experience a sudden drop in grades.

Feelings of Worthlessness.   Some people with major depression have low self-esteem. Others feel excessive guilt over minor failings or blame themselves for untoward events that are beyond their control. At times, the self-blame can reach quite irrational proportions; for example, blaming themselves for world hunger.

Thoughts of Death.   A preoccupation with death and **suicide** is another common feature of major depression. Suicidal behavior ranges from occasional thoughts of death ("my family would be better off if I were dead"), to more frequent thoughts, to specific suicide plans, to actual suicide attempts. Anything more than the occasional, passing thought of death is a warning sign that should be taken seriously. People who find themselves contemplating suicide should call a doctor, mental health clinic, or suicide hotline immediately rather than simply waiting for the thoughts to pass.

One Disorder, Multiple Forms

In a very real sense, there are as many forms of depression as there are people with the disorder. No two individuals are depressed in exactly the same way. Nevertheless, general similarities exist among certain subgroups of people with depression. Below are some clusters of symptoms that often occur together.

	Defining Characteristic	**Other Symptoms**
Atypical Depression	The person's mood is highly sensitive to good or bad news.	Increased appetite, sleeping too much, sensation of heaviness, hypersensitivity to rejection.
Catatonic Depression	Severe reductions in movement and responsiveness, extreme overactivity, and/or bizarre behavior.	Extreme negativity, purposeless imitation.
Melancholic Depression	A near-complete absence of the ability to feel pleasure or react to positive events.	Distinctive mood quality, morning worsening, early awakening, changes in activity level, loss of appetite, excessive guilt

Course of the Illness.   Major depression can strike at any age from early childhood to late adulthood. It most often starts during the teens or early twenties, however. Many people feel just mildly depressed or anxious at first. This phase can last for weeks to months before they sink into full-blown major depression.

Once major depression sets in, it generally lasts for at least four months if left untreated. With proper treatment, however, the vast majority of people with major depression feel better before long and are able to get back to their usual activities. Many begin to rebound emotionally within two to four weeks, although it might take up to 12 weeks for the full effects of treatment to be felt.

About 60 percent of people who have recovered from a first episode of major depression go on to have another episode later. The risk of a **recurrence**—in other words, a repeat bout of the illness—just goes up with subsequent episodes. After three episodes, the odds of a fourth rise to 90 percent.

Over the course of their lifetime, people who don't get treatment average five to seven bouts of depression, and the episodes tend to get worse each time. The good news is that treatment can brighten this outlook substantially. If started early, treatment may keep depression from ever becoming severe or long-lasting, and it also may interrupt the downward spiral into frequent recurrences.

Causes and Risk Factors. Anyone of either sex and any age or **ethnicity** can develop major depression. Those with a family history of depression or suicide are at increased risk. But although major depression seems to run in some families, it also can occur in people whose family tree is depression-free. On the flip side, some people with numerous relatives who suffered from depression do not become depressed themselves. At most, then, certain people may inherit a genetic predisposition to become depressed more readily than others.

Stressful life events may trigger depression in some vulnerable individuals. Certain personality traits—such as having low self-esteem and being overly dependent, self-critical, or pessimistic—may play a role as well. Having a serious medical condition—such as Alzheimer's disease, cancer, heart disease, or human immunodeficiency virus (HIV)—also increases the risk of depression.

The Gender Divide. **Women** are twice as likely as men to become depressed. This two-to-one ratio exists regardless of ethnic group or economic status in the United States, and it also has been observed in countries around the world.

The reasons for the gender gap are still being studied. During childhood, boys and girls seem to have about the same risk of depression. The rate of depression starts to diverge around puberty, when sex hormone levels are changing rapidly. As adults, some women seem to be more vulnerable to depression at times when their sex **hormones** are in flux, such as right after giving birth. Therefore, it is likely that hormones play a role in the gender divide. But other factors may be involved, too. For instance, some stresses and pressures—such as the trauma of rape or domestic violence and the demands of being a single parent—may impact women more than men as a group.

Depression across the Lifespan. Children, adolescents, and **older adults** may react a little differently to major depression than younger adults do. Children are especially likely to be cranky rather than sad, withdraw from their classmates, and complain about feeling sick when no obvious cause can be found. Depressed children also may have a drop in grades, refuse to go to school, or develop behavior problems. Many also have unhealthy fears and worries, such as constantly worrying that a parent will become sick or be killed in an accident.

Many adolescents with major depression begin struggling with **substance abuse**, turning to alcohol or illegal drugs in a desperate attempt to reduce their suffering. Anxiety remains a common problem at this age. Some teens also get into frequent trouble at home or school or with the law. Others develop **eating disorders**, which are characterized by serious disturbances in eating behavior.

Older adults with major depression often are more willing to talk about their physical symptoms than their emotional ones. Changes in mental functioning—such confusion, distractibility, and memory problems—also may be particularly prominent in this age group.

Treatment of Major Depression. The main treatments for major depression are **antidepressants** and **psychotherapy**. For mild to moderate cases of major depression, psychotherapy alone is sometimes enough. But in adults with more severe symptoms, psychotherapy usually is combined with medication. In adolescents with major depression, a combination of both treatments also seems to work the best and may help keep depression from coming back.

People whose depression is very severe may be too ill to take part effectively in psychotherapy. For them, the initial treatment may be medication or **electroconvulsive therapy** (ECT), which involves passing a carefully controlled electrical current through a person's brain to induce a brief seizure. ECT is thought to alter some of the electrochemical processes that play a role in brain functioning. Once these individuals start to feel better, they may be able to take full advantage of psychotherapy.

Even people with the most severe depression can be helped by treatment. Major depression is a real illness that causes very real suffering, but it does not have to just be endured. Help is out there for those who seek it.

See also: Clinical Depression; Diagnosis of Depression; Environmental Factors; Genetic Factors; Mood Disorders; Personality Factors; Treatment of Depression; Unipolar Depression

Further Information. Depression and Bipolar Support Alliance, 730 N. Franklin Street, Suite 501, Chicago, IL 60610, (800) 826-3632, www.dbsalliance.org, www .peersupport.org, www.facingus.org.

Families for Depression Awareness, 395 Totten Pond Road, Suite 404, Waltham, MA 02451, (781) 890-0220, www.familyaware.org.

National Alliance for Research on Schizophrenia and Depression, 60 Cutter Mill Road, Suite 404, Great Neck, New York 11021, (516) 829-0091, www.narsad.org.

Bibliography

American Psychiatric Association. *Diagnostic and Statistical Manual of Mental Disorders.* 4th ed., text rev. Washington, DC: American Psychiatric Association, 2000.

Depression (Major Depression). Mayo Clinic, February 14, 2008, http://www.nimh.nih.gov/health/ publications/depression/complete-publication.shtml.

Depression. National Institute of Mental Health, March 20, 2008, http://www.nimh.nih.gov/health/ publications/depression/complete-publication.shtml.

Frances, Allen, Michael B. First, and Harold Alan Pincus. *DSM-IV Guidebook.* Washington DC: American Psychiatric Press, 1995.

Harvard Medical School. *Understanding Depression.* Boston: Harvard Health Publications, 2003.

Jamison, Kay Redfield. *Touched with Fire: Manic-Depressive Illness and the Artistic Temperament.* New York: Free Press, 1993.

Let's Talk Facts About Depression. American Psychiatric Association, November 2006, http://www.healthyminds.org/multimedia/depression.pdf.

Major Depression. National Alliance on Mental Illness, http://www.nami.org/Content/Content Groups/Helpline1/Major_DepressioD.htm.

Melville, Herman. *Melville: Pierre, Israel Potter, The Piazza Tales, The Confidence-Man, Uncollected Prose, Billy Budd.* New York: Library of America, 1984.

The NSDUH Report: Depression Among Adults. Substance Abuse and Mental Health Services Administration Office of Applied Studies, March 17, 2006, http://www.oas.samhsa.gov/2k5/ depression/depression.htm.

MANAGED CARE. Managed care plans are health insurance plans that contract with health care providers and facilities to provide services for a prearranged fee. The managed care organization controls costs by negotiating reduced fees and discouraging overuse of expensive services. The term "managed behavioral health care" is often applied to managed care plans that focus specifically on services for mental disorders and **substance abuse**.

There are three main types of managed care plans: health maintenance organizations (HMOs), preferred provider organizations (PPOs), and point-of-service (POS) plans. All these plans enter into contractual arrangements with health care professionals and facilities, which together form a provider network. Individuals covered by a managed care plan are referred to as members.

Under most circumstances, HMOs only pay for services from providers within their network, and one provider coordinates most of a member's care. Although this option offers the least freedom of choice in selecting a health care provider, the out-of-pocket costs for members are usually low. PPOs allow members to see either in-network or out-of-network providers. However, members have to foot more of the bill themselves if they go outside the network. POS plans are hybrids that let members choose between the HMO option and the PPO option each time they seek care. POS plans are gaining in popularity due to the flexibility they afford.

Cost-Containment Strategies. Managed care developed as a way of curtailing health care expenses. One managed care strategy for controlling costs is utilization review, a formal review of health care services to determine whether payment for them will be authorized or denied. In making this determination, managed care companies look at two factors: whether the service is covered under the member's insurance plan and whether the service is "medically necessary." To meet the latter standard, the service must be deemed both medically appropriate and essential for the member's health.

When payment is denied, it is usually on the grounds of medical necessity. As a result, this is a frequent point of contention between members and their health insurance plans. It is not unusual for a situation to arise in which a member's insurance benefits indicate that 18 treatment visits are covered, and the treatment provider believes that services are needed. Yet the managed care company says it will not pay for the treatment because it is not considered medically necessary.

In this scenario, the treatment provider has a vested interest in providing moneymaking services, and the managed care company has a vested interest in containing costs. The health plan member is caught in the middle of this economic tug of war. To help protect the member's rights, certain safeguards are built into the system—most notably, an appeals process that can be used to contest treatment denials.

Other strategies that managed care companies use to keep costs in check include gatekeepers, prior authorization, and formularies. Gatekeepers are primary care providers or local agencies charged with coordinating and managing the health care needs of a member. Generally, the gatekeeper must approve a referral for specialty care, such as visits to a psychiatrist, before these services will be covered. Prior authorization requires the health care provider to get approval from the managed care company before furnishing a service, such as psychiatric hospitalization. Formularies are lists of medications that restrict reimbursement to certain drugs in a therapeutic class or require higher copayments (the amount members must pay out of pocket) for more expensive medications.

The overall impact of managed care remains controversial. On one hand, economists estimate that treatment of depression costs at least $12 billion a year in the United States. Keeping those costs from skyrocketing even higher benefits society as a whole.

On the other hand, mental health advocates and treatment providers note that restricting access to appropriate care may cost society much more in the long run. In economic terms, inadequately treated depression may lead to lost productivity at work and expensive medical complications. In human terms, the cost in unnecessary suffering is incalculable. Balancing the push-pull between cost containment and effective treatment is the central challenge facing managed care, today and tomorrow.

See also: Economic Impact; Insurance Parity

Further Information.   Center for Studying Health System Change, 600 Maryland Ave S.W., Suite 550, Washington, DC 20024, (202) 484-5261, www.hschange.com.

National Committee for Quality Assurance, 1100 13th Street N.W., Suite 1000, Washington, DC 20005, (202) 955-3500, www.ncqa.org.

Bibliography

Dealing with Treatment Denials. Mental Health America, http://www.nmha.org/go/help/how-to-pay -for-treatment/dealing-with-treatment-denials.
Diagnosing and Treating Depression in a Managed Care Environment: Concerns, Perceptions, and Misperceptions. Supplement to *Managed Care* (February 2004).
Evans, Dwight L., and Linda Wasmer Andrews. *If Your Adolescent Has Depression or Bipolar Disorder: An Essential Resource for Parents.* New York: Oxford University Press, 2005.
Managed Care Glossary. National Mental Health Information Center, September 2002, http:// mentalhealth.samhsa.gov/publications/allpubs/Mc98–70/default.asp.
Managed Care. National Library of Medicine, http://www.nlm.nih.gov/medlineplus/managedcare .html.
Managed Care: A National Overview. National Alliance on Mental Illness, http://www.nami.org/ Template.cfm?Section=Issue_Spotlights&template=/ContentManagement/ContentDisplay.cfm &ContentID=34786.
Managed Health Care Plans. American Heart Association, http://www.americanheart.org/presenter .jhtml?identifier=4663.
Muszynski, Irvin L. "Formularies Are Latest Managed Care Strategy." *Psychiatric News* 38 (2003): 13.
Wang, Philip S., and Ronald C. Kessler. "Global Burden of Mood Disorders." In *The American Psychiatric Publishing Textbook of Mood Disorders,* by Dan J. Stein, David J. Kupfer and Alan F. Schatzberg, eds., 55–67. Washington, DC: American Psychiatric Publishing, 2006.

MANIA.   Mania refers to an excessively high, grandiose, or irritable **mood** that is disruptive enough to cause serious problems in daily life and relationships. Drastic changes in energy level and behavior go along with the manic mood. In the most familiar form of **bipolar disorder**, bouts of mania alternate with bouts of **major depression**, leading to extreme ups and downs that are quite different from the normal mood fluctuations that everybody goes through.

Left untreated, mania can lead to wildly irrational thinking, dangerous risk taking, or nonstop activity and sleeplessness. In some people, it also leads to extreme **irritability** or angry outbursts. Not surprisingly, such erratic behavior can create severe problems at home, work, or school and put a serious strain on personal relationships.

In some cases, the symptoms of mania get so severe that the person must be hospitalized to prevent harm to self or others. In other cases, the symptoms reach psychotic proportions, causing delusions (false personal beliefs that have no basis in reality, but that remain unchanged even in the face of strong evidence to the contrary) or hallucinations (false sensory impressions, in which the person sees, hears, tastes, smells, or feels something that is not really there).

Polar Opposites

Perhaps the earliest medical theory about the relationship between mania and **melancholia** (depression) was put forth by ancient Greek physician Aretaeus of Cappadocia in the second century:

> If black bile be determined upwards toward the stomach and diaphragm, it forms melancholy . . . It is a lowness of spirit without fever; and it appears to me that melancholy is the commencement of mania. For in those who are mad, the understanding is turned sometimes to anger and sometimes to joy, but in the melancholics—to sorrow and despondency only.

Fortunately, treatment for bipolar disorder can help keep moods from veering back and forth so uncontrollably. With help from medications and **psychotherapy**, people with bipolar disorder can learn to manage their moods instead of letting the moods control them.

Criteria for Diagnosis. Each period of mania is referred to as an episode. During a manic episode, people experience an excessively high, grandiose, or irritable mood that lasts for at least a week. (This time requirement is waived if the symptoms are severe enough to necessitate hospitalization.) The mood causes marked problems getting along in daily life or relating to other people, leads to hospitalization, or gives rise to psychotic symptoms.

When the person's mood is high or grandiose, at least three of the following symptoms must be present. When it is only irritable, at least four symptoms are required.

Inflated Self-Esteem. Most people in the grips of mania have an exaggerated sense of their own importance. Many feel as if they are uniquely talented, intelligent, or wise. This belief may lead them to embark upon lofty ventures, from composing a symphony to curing a disease, for which they lack any expertise. Taken to an extreme, such grandiose ideas can become delusional. For example, people may be falsely convinced that they have a special relationship with a movie star or sports figure.

Decreased Sleep. People with mania almost invariably have a decreased need for sleep. Unlike people with insomnia, who wake up tired and feel worn out the next day, those with mania may wake up bursting with energy after sleeping only a few hours. In severe cases, people may go for days on end without sleep and still not feel tired.

Unusual Talkativeness. People with mania may feel an inner pressure to keep talking, as if there are so many important things to say and not enough time to say them. Their speech is often loud and rapid-fire, and it may contain a barrage of jokes and amusing asides. If the person's mood is more irritable, their speech may be filled with hostile remarks and angry tirades.

Racing Thoughts. No matter how fast the words pour out, people with mania typically feel as if their thoughts are racing even faster. As a result, they often jump quickly from one topic to another when speaking.

Easy Distractibility. People with mania may be unable to filter out irrelevant stimuli when trying to concentrate on the task at hand. As a result, they get distracted easily and lose track of what they are trying to do.

Increased Activity. During a manic episode, people with mania often over-schedule activities and projects to an extreme degree. This almost always gives rise to increased socializing, often with little regard for how intrusive or demanding their behavior may be. Other people pace or fidget restlessly.

Risky Behavior. The manic pursuit of thrills can lead to risky behavior without concern for the possible consequences. For example, people who normally would not behave this way might drive at dangerous speeds, have sexual encounters with strangers, or spend money carelessly during a manic episode.

Over-the-Top Behavior. People in the throes of mania often do not realize that they are ill. But to other people, their behavior seems like a drastic departure from how they act at other times. They may gesture more flamboyantly, dress more provocatively, or travel impulsively without telling anyone where they are going. People who are normally very conscientious may run up large gambling debts, commit ethical breaches at work, or get into trouble with the law. Abuse of alcohol or other drugs frequently increases, which may worsen or prolong the episode. When the manic mood has an irritable edge, people may become hostile and threatening. Some even become physically violent or suicidal.

Mania can be extremely disruptive and even dangerous without treatment. Fortunately, effective treatments are available. Staying on treatment after the mania has passed can help keep the mood swings under control and reduce the risk of having frequent, worsening episodes.

See also: Mixed Episode

Bibliography

American Psychiatric Association. *Diagnostic and Statistical Manual of Mental Disorders.* 4th ed., text rev. Washington, DC: American Psychiatric Association, 2000.

"Aretaeus of Cappadocia." *Encyclopedia Britannica Online,* 2008, http://www.britannica.com/EBchecked/topic/33531/Aretaeus-of-Cappadocia.

Bipolar Disorder. National Institute of Mental Health, April 3, 2008, http://www.nimh.nih.gov/health/publications/bipolar-disorder/complete-publication.shtml.

Frances, Allen, Michael B. First, and Harold Alan Pincus. *DSM-IV Guidebook.* Washington, DC: American Psychiatric Press, 1995.

Stone, Michael H. "Historical Aspects of Mood Disorders." In *The American Psychiatric Publishing Textbook of Mood Disorders,* by Dan J. Stein, David J. Kupfer and Alan F. Schatzberg, eds., 3–15. Washington, DC: American Psychiatric Publishing, 2006.

MARRIAGE AND FAMILY THERAPIST. Marriage and family therapists are mental health professionals who diagnose and treat mental, emotional, and interpersonal problems in the context of close relationships. The mode of treatment used by marriage and family therapists is **psychotherapy**. Typical treatment goals include changing destructive behaviors and perceptions, resolving interpersonal conflicts, and improving communication between partners or family members.

Marriage and family therapists don't just focus on **relationship issues**, though. They also treat a wide range of mental disorders, including depression. Relationship conflict and **stress** may trigger or worsen the symptoms of these disorders. As the symptoms get worse, in turn, they may put added strain on the relationship. Marriage and family therapists help people break this cycle, feel better, and lead more satisfying lives.

About half of the treatment provided by marriage and family therapists takes place in a one-on-one setting. The other half is provided in **couples therapy** or **family therapy**. In the latter case, the couple or family, rather than any particular individual, is the "patient." Whatever form therapy takes, it is typically short term in nature. The average treatment takes 12 sessions, with two-thirds of cases completed within 20 sessions.

Training and Credentials. Marriage and family therapists generally have a master's degree or higher and at least two years of clinical experience. Students in master's, doctoral, and postgraduate programs that prepare marriage and family therapists come from a variety of educational backgrounds, including psychology, social work, nursing, pastoral counseling, and education.

Marriage and Family Therapy in Action. There are an estimated 48,000 marriage and family therapists in the United States and Canada. The American Association for Marriage and Family Therapy, with more than 24,000 U.S. and Canadian members, is the major professional society representing the field in those countries.

Forty-eight states require licensure or certification for marriage and family therapists. In addition to having the requisite education and post-degree experience, applicants in most states are required to take a licensing exam. The Association of Marital and Family Therapy Regulatory Boards is the organization for state boards that regulate the profession.

See also: Diagnosis of Depression; Treatment of Depression

Further Information. American Association for Marriage and Family Therapy, 112 S. Alfred Street, Alexandria, VA 22314, (703) 838-9808, www.aamft.org.

Association of Marital and Family Therapy Regulatory Boards, 1843 Austin Bluffs Parkway, Colorado Springs, CO 80918, (719) 388-1615, www.amftrb.org.

Bibliography

Bureau of Labor Statistics. "Counselors," in *Occupational Outlook Handbook, 2006–07 Edition.* Washington, DC: U.S. Department of Labor, 2005.

Frequently Asked Questions on Marriage and Family Therapists. American Association for Marriage and Family Therapy, 2002, http://www.aamft.org/faqs/index_nm.asp.

MEDITATION. Meditation involves focusing the mind intently on a particular thing or activity, while becoming relatively oblivious to everything else. Some meditation techniques trace their roots back to Eastern religious or spiritual practices. Today, however, people often use meditation in a secular context for inducing relaxation, reducing **stress**, and enhancing health and well-being. In addition, meditation is sometimes used to help decrease symptoms of depression.

A growing body of research supports the health benefits of meditation. But because many of the studies were not well designed, it is impossible to draw firm conclusions from them. Keeping that caveat in mind, some research suggests that meditation may help alleviate not only depression, but also **anxiety disorders**, **substance abuse**, binge-eating disorder, allergies, asthma, **chronic pain**, high blood pressure, and a host of other medical conditions.

There are several different forms of meditation, all aimed at focusing attention on one thing while freeing the mind of other distractions. The focal point can be a special word, a particular object, a repetitive activity, or even the simple act of breathing. Rather than actively trying to suppress other thoughts, the meditator passively lets them come and go without judgment, gently bringing attention back to the focal point. Most meditation techniques also emphasize finding a quiet spot to practice, assuming a comfortable position, and taking deep, even breaths to promote relaxation.

Meditation works partly by decreasing activity in the sympathetic **nervous system**, which mobilizes the body during stress, and increasing activity in the parasympathetic nervous system, which counteracts the body's stress response. Research has shown that sympathetic activity tends to be more pronounced in people who are depressed than in those who are not. Regular meditation also may improve the mind's ability to pay attention—an essential skill for regulating mood and getting along in everyday life.

Types of Meditation. People do meditation to increase relaxation, enhance general well-being, or cope with mental or physical illness. Below are two types of meditation that are commonly used for health purposes.

Mantra Meditation. In mantra meditation, the focus is on a mantra—a special word, phrase, or sound that is repeated, either silently or aloud, to keep distracting thoughts from entering the mind. The goal is to achieve a state of pure, relaxed awareness. Transcendental Meditation, a modern variation derived from Hindu traditions, was introduced in 1958 by Indian guru Maharishi Mahesh Yogi (ca. 1918–2008).

Mindfulness Meditation. Mindfulness meditation, rooted in Buddhist practices, involves fully focusing on whatever is being experienced from moment to moment, without reacting to or judging that experience. This technique is a core feature of **mindfulness-based cognitive therapy**, a treatment approach specifically designed to help people who have recovered from depression avoid a recurrence in the future.

See also: Relaxation Techniques; Spirituality and Religion; Stress Management

Breathe!

Deep breathing exercises are meditation pared down to its most basic elements. The focal point is the breath going in and out. Because such mini-meditations can elicit the relaxation response, they may help control stress and depression.

To practice a breathing exercise, find a quiet spot to sit or lie down. Rest a hand on your abdomen, just below the navel. Inhale through your nose as you slowly count to four, feeling your belly push out slightly against your hand as the air enters. Hold for a second. Then exhale through your mouth as you slowly count to four, feeling your belly fall back slightly toward your spine as the air exits. Repeat five to ten times.

Further Information. Center for Mindfulness in Medicine, Health Care and Society, University of Massachusetts Medical School, 55 Lake Avenue North, Worcester, MA 01655, (508) 856-2656, www.umassmed.edu/cfm.

Transcendental Meditation Program, (888) 532-7686, www.tm.org.

Bibliography

Andrews, Linda Wasmer. *Stress Control for Peace of Mind.* New York: Main Street, 2005.

Meditation: An Introduction. National Center for Complementary and Alternative Medicine, February 2009, http://nccam.nih.gov/health/meditation/overview.htm.

Meditation: Take a Stress-Reduction Break Wherever You Are. Mayo Clinic, April 21, 2009, http://www .mayoclinic.com/health/meditation/HQ01070.

Ospina, Maria B., Kenneth Bond, Mohammad Karkhaneh, Lisa Tjosvold, Ben Vandermeer, Yuanyuan Liang, et al. *Meditation Practices for Health: State of the Research.* Evidence Report/ Technology Assessment No. 155. Rockville, MD: Agency for Healthcare Research and Quality, 2007.

Relax in a Hurry. Benson-Henry Institute for Mind Body Medicine, http://www.mbmi .org/basics/mstress_RIAH.asp.

Ruthven, Malise. "Maharishi Mahesh Yogi." *Guardian.co.uk* (February 6, 2008).

Stress and Your Health. National Women's Health Information Center, August 1, 2005, http:// womenshealth.gov/faq/stress-your-health.cfm.

MELANCHOLIA.   Melancholia is a condition, first described by the ancient Greeks, which predated the modern concept of depression. From classical antiquity through the nineteenth century, descriptions of melancholia took on various forms and diverse connotations. Yet one common thread persisted: an emphasis on distressing **sadness**, despondency, and anxiety.

The Latinized term "melancholia" derives from the Greek roots *melas* and *khole*, meaning "black bile." This terminology is based on the theory of humors, which posits that everything is composed of four fundamental elements in nature: earth, air, fire and water. The elements, in turn, correspond to four body fluids and their associated temperaments: earth-black bile-melancholic, air-blood-sanguine, fire-yellow bile-choleric and water-phlegm-phlegmatic.

The fact that all four temperaments survive as adjectives in the English language attests to the lasting influence of the humoral theory. Black bile itself has proved less durable. The substance, once believed to be secreted by the spleen or kidneys, is not analogous to any body fluid known to modern science.

Ancient Greek View.   The ancient Greeks were not the first to suggest that nature was composed of four elements. Earlier versions of that idea existed in Egypt, India, and China. But the Greeks elaborated the theory into the version that became the direct-line ancestor of Western medicine.

Greek physician Hippocrates (ca. 460 BC–ca. 375 BC) is credited with the first unequivocal statement attributing melancholia—excessive black bile—to dysfunction of the brain. According to Hippocrates, those with a melancholic **temperament** were prone to despondency, sleeplessness, irritability, restlessness, and an aversion to food—symptoms remarkably similar to current diagnostic criteria for depression.

Yet melancholia was always a broader concept than **major depression** or **dysthymia**. It encompassed any disorder arising from a presumed excess of black bile. In later medical writings, such as those of the Greek physician Galen (129–ca. 216) and the Persian physician Avicenna (980–1037), the term was applied to a wide range of disorders, including **epilepsy** and **stroke**.

One of Galen's contemporaries, Greek physician Aretaeus of Cappadocia (ca.150–ca. 200), is credited with the first coherent theory linking the mood extremes of melancholia and **mania**—a theory that anticipated current thinking about **bipolar disorder**. Over time, melancholia gradually came to be associated with not only depressive symptoms, but also manic ones.

Love, Genius, and Melancholy.   In the late thirteenth century, love emerged as an important concept in Arab medicine, and it was thought that pining over the object of unrequited love could at times turn into lovesickness—a dangerously obsessive longing characterized by melancholia and despair. Later, the association between melancholia and delusional thinking about a particular subject reemerged as another major theme in Western medicine.

From Renaissance times onward, the term melancholia was increasingly applied not only to a mental malady, but also to a normal state of sadness and dejection. Perhaps the most famous artistic representation of this state was an engraving titled *Melencolia I*, created by German artist Albrecht Dürer (1471–1528) in 1514. This allegorical composition depicts a winged personification of melancholia sitting dejectedly, surrounded by an array of symbolic objects. It has been interpreted by some as a spiritual self-portrait of the artist.

In the 1600s, a cultural and literary movement marked by fascination with melancholy—the English word for melancholia—arose in England. Perhaps the zenith of the movement was William Shakespeare's character Hamlet, known as the melancholy Dane. In *As You Like*

It, Shakespeare (1564–1616) provides a catalog of melancholic states that is ironic, yet nevertheless instructive about his view of the concept: "I have neither the scholar's melancholy, which is emulation, nor the musician's, which is fantastical, nor the courtier's, which is proud, nor the soldier's, which is ambitious, nor the lawyer's, which is politic, nor the lady's, which is nice, nor the lover's, which is all these: but it is a melancholy of mine own, compounded of many simples, extracted from many objects, and indeed the sundry's contemplation of my travels, in which my often rumination wraps me in a most humorous sadness" (IV.I.10–20).

"Like a Weeping Cloud"

The melancholic state was idealized in English Romantic poetry of the early nineteenth century. These poets celebrated mental suffering, which they believed could help the individual feel more deeply, think more sharply, and approach the sublime. In "Ode to Melancholy," John Keats (1795–1821), himself a depression sufferer, described the melancholic experience this way:

> But when the melancholy fit shall fall
> Sudden from heaven like a weeping cloud,
> That fosters the droop-headed flowers all,
> And hides the green hill in an April shroud . . .

By the nineteenth century, it was clear that melancholia had become so broadly and vaguely defined that it had outlived its usefulness as a specific medical diagnosis. In the mid-1800s, the word "depression" entered the medical lexicon. Today, medical use of the term melancholia survives only in a severe subtype of major depression, known as **melancholic depression**. Yet the rich history behind the word lives on, informing contemporary views of depression and influencing current criteria for diagnosis.

See also: Burton, Robert; Goethe, Johann Wolfgang von; Historical Perspective

Bibliography

Davison, Kenneth. "Historical Aspects of Mood Disorders." *Psychiatry* 5 (2006): 115–118.

Evans, G. Blakemore, ed. *The Riverside Shakespeare*. Boston: Houghton Mifflin, 1974.

"History 1450–1789," in *Encyclopedia of the Early Modern World*. Farmington Hills, MI: Gale Group, 2004.

Keats, John. *The Poetical Works of John Keats*. 1884. Bartleby.com, http://www.bartleby.com/126/48.html.

Melencolia I. Metropolitan Museum of Art, http://www.metmuseum.org/toah/hd/durr/ho_43.106.1.htm.

Radden, Jennifer, ed. *The Nature of Melancholy: From Aristotle to Kristeva*. New York: Oxford University Press, 2000.

Stone, Michael H. "Historical Aspects of Mood Disorders." In *The American Psychiatric Publishing Textbook of Mood Disorders*, by Dan J. Stein, David J. Kupfer, and Alan F. Schatzberg, eds., 3–15. Washington, DC: American Psychiatric Publishing, 2006.

MELANCHOLIC DEPRESSION. Melancholic depression is a subtype of **major depression** that, at its lowest point, is marked by a near-complete absence of the ability to feel pleasure. Even when something much desired happens, the person's mood may brighten little, if at all. Because these symptoms are so pronounced, there is some debate about whether melancholic depression is actually a distinct subtype or just another way of describing severe depression.

The word "melancholic" comes from two Greek words, *melas* and *khole,* meaning "black bile." The term dates back to a theory that held sway in ancient Greece and continued to influence medicine in Europe through the Middle Ages. According to this theory, the human body contained four basic fluids, called humors, that determined a person's emotional and physical makeup. One of the humors was **melancholia** (black bile); the others were blood, phlegm, and choler (yellow bile).

The perfectly healthy person possessed the ideal proportion of the four humors. Many people had an excess of one humor or another, however, which affected their temperament and physical health. Those with an excess of black bile were thought to have a melancholic temperament, with an inclination toward feeling dejected.

Research has shown that melancholic depression is often associated with overactivity of the **hypothalamic-pituitary-adrenal axis**. This body system—comprised of the **hypothalamus**, pituitary glands, and adrenal gland along with the substances they secrete—plays a central role in the body's **stress** response. In many people with melancholic depression, the body stays keyed up even when nothing stressful is happening.

Some symptoms of melancholic depression—such as waking up early, lack of appetite, and loss of interest in sex—may stem from the body staying in this constant state of high alert. Many people with melancholic depression also feel intense anxiety, another feature that could be related to an overly prolonged stress response. In addition, they may focus on thoughts of unworthiness and **pessimism** while finding it hard to concentrate on anything else, much like someone in danger would focus single-mindedly on the threat.

Criteria for Diagnosis.   Melancholic depression is a variant of major depression. All forms of major depression involve being in a low mood nearly all the time or losing interest or enjoyment in almost everything. These feelings last for at least two weeks, are associated with several other symptoms, and lead to serious problems getting along in everyday life.

Along with meeting the diagnostic criteria for major depression, people with melancholic depression, when at their lowest point, experience a near-total loss of the capacity to feel pleasure or lack of reaction to positive events (the first two symptoms listed below). In addition, they have three or more other symptoms from the following list.

Loss of Pleasure.   People with this symptom—also known as **anhedonia**—have a profound inability to feel pleasure from activities they once enjoyed. They may give up hobbies or withdraw from social activities. Those who previously were sexually active may notice a drastic decline in desire.

Lack of Reaction.   People with this symptom do not feel much better, even temporarily, when something good happens. Rather than getting a boost from positive events, their mood stays consistently depressed.

Distinctive Mood Quality.   The mood experienced during melancholic depression often has a distinctive quality that sets it apart from other periods of sadness or episodes of non-melancholic depression. For instance, it is different from the feelings experienced after the death of a loved one.

Morning Worsening.   Melancholic depression may be worse in the morning than at other times of day, a pattern that repeats on a regular basis.

Early Awakening.   People with melancholic depression may awaken too early—at least two hours before their usual wake-up time.

Changes in Activity Level. This form of depression almost always produces marked changes in activity level. Some people develop psychomotor agitation—restless behavior that goes along with an inner feeling of tension. Others develop psychomotor retardation—slowed-down movements and speech.

Loss of Appetite. Another common symptom is loss of appetite. In some cases, this leads to a significant weight loss.

Excessive Guilt. Those with melancholic depression often are plagued by excessive or inappropriate feelings of guilt.

Causes and Risk Factors. Melancholic depression is most often seen in people with severe depression. Some have symptoms of **psychotic depression**, developing distorted beliefs or perceptions that are seriously out of touch with reality. Melancholic depression also is more likely to occur in people with depression who require psychiatric **hospitalization** than in those who are treated outside the hospital.

There is no single lab test that can diagnose melancholic depression in clinical practice. In scientific studies, though, melancholic symptoms are often associated with elevated concentrations of a stress hormone called **cortisol** in the blood, urine, and saliva. People with melancholic depression also may show abnormal patterns of electrical activity in the brain during sleep, as measured by **electroencephalography** (EEG).

Treatment of Melancholic Depression. People with melancholic depression are particularly likely to respond well to **antidepressants**. These medications are designed to relieve the symptoms of depression and keep them from returning.

Many with severe melancholic depression also get good results from **electroconvulsive therapy** (ECT). The latter treatment involves passing a carefully controlled electrical current through the person's brain, which induces a brief seizure that is thought to alter some of the electrochemical processes involved in brain functioning. Modern ECT is painless and relatively safe, and it works faster than other depression treatments.

Once the worst symptoms begin to lessen, **psychotherapy** also may be helpful. Melancholic depression tends to be associated with severe symptoms. But with proper treatment, most people begin to feel better and get back to their normal lives, often in a matter of weeks.

Bibliography

American Psychiatric Association. *Diagnostic and Statistical Manual of Mental Disorders.* 4th ed., text rev. Washington, DC: American Psychiatric Association, 2000.

Dinan, Timothy G., and Lucinda V. Scott. "Anatomy of Melancholia: Focus on Hypothalamic-Pituitary-Adrenal Axis Overactivity and the Role of Vasopressin." *Journal of Anatomy* 207 (2005): 259–264.

Frances, Allen, Michael B. First, and Harold Alan Pincus. *DSM-IV Guidebook.* Washington DC: American Psychiatric Press, 1995.

Radden, Jennifer, ed. *The Nature of Melancholy: From Aristotle to Kristeva.* New York: Oxford University Press, 2000.

Wong, Ma-Li, Mitchel A. Kling, Peter J. Munson, Samuel Listwak, Julio Licinio, Paolo Prolo, et al. "Pronounced and Sustained Central Hypernoradrenergic Function in Major Depression with Melancholic Features: Relation to Hypercortisolism and Corticotropin-Releasing Hormone." *Proceedings of the National Academy of Sciences of the USA* 97 (2000): 325–330.

MELATONIN. Melatonin is a hormone produced by the pineal gland in the brain that has a mild drowsiness-inducing effect. It helps the body know when to go to sleep and when to wake up. Changes in the daily timing of melatonin production may be a factor in

seasonal affective disorder (SAD), a form of **major depression** in which symptoms start and stop around the same time each year, typically beginning in fall or winter and subsiding in spring.

The secretion of melatonin follows a daily rhythm that is governed by the body's internal "clock," which is located in a pair of pinhead-sized brain structures called the suprachiasmatic nucleus (SCN). When light reaches the retina of the eye, a signal travels along the optic nerve to the SCN. From there, a message is sent to the pineal gland, which switches off production of melatonin in response. Production of melatonin switches back on once darkness falls, helping people feel drowsy.

Melatonin does not control sleep by itself, but it does play a key role. The hormone also helps regulate other body functions that are tied to the sleep-wake cycle. These include body temperature, hormone secretion, urine production, and changes in blood pressure.

Connection to SAD. At one time, it was thought that people with SAD might have an overabundance of melatonin. Among other things, this could account for oversleeping, a common symptom. In general, though, studies have not found a difference between the amounts of melatonin secreted by people with SAD and those without the disorder. On the other hand, some research indicates that people with SAD may experience changes in the daily timing of melatonin secretion, compared to those without depression.

There is also some evidence that taking melatonin supplements at the right time each day might help relieve the symptoms of SAD. In one study, researchers tracked sleep, activity level, melatonin, and depression symptoms in 68 people with SAD who took either low doses of melatonin or a placebo (dummy pill) in the morning or afternoon during the winter month when their symptoms were most troublesome.

Previous research in healthy individuals had shown that the optimal interval between the time when the pineal gland begins secreting melatonin and the middle of sleep is about six hours. The majority of people with SAD in this study had a shorter-than-usual interval, indicating that their body's daily rhythms were delayed due to the late winter dawn. For them, taking melatonin supplements in the afternoon was beneficial, and the closer they got to the ideal six-hour interval, the more their mood improved. For the minority of people who had longer-than-usual intervals, taking melatonin in the morning was helpful. Although these results are intriguing, further research is needed before any firm conclusions can be drawn.

Melatonin Supplements. Melatonin supplements are sold without a prescription. In studies, people have taken 0.5 to 50 milligrams of melatonin nightly. But the optimal dose for safety and effectiveness has not been established.

Some people have reported side effects such as drowsiness, headache, stomachache, or a hung-over feeling. Also, high doses of melatonin can build up in the body, and the long-term effects are unknown. In addition, there is limited information about how melatonin might interact with other medications. Given the lack of safety data, many experts recommend talking to a doctor before trying melatonin supplements. This may be doubly important for people with SAD, because taking the wrong amount on the wrong schedule could potentially make symptoms worse rather than better.

See also: Agomelatine; Circadian Rhythms; Hormones

Bibliography

Brain Basics: Understanding Sleep. National Institute of Neurological Disorders and Stroke, May 21, 2007, http://www.ninds.nih.gov/disorders/brain_basics/understanding_sleep.htm.

Lam, Raymond W., and Anthony J. Levitt, eds. *Canadian Consensus Guidelines for the Treatment of Seasonal Affective Disorder.* Clinical & Academic Publishing, 1999.

Lewy, Alfred J., Bryan J. Lefler, Jonathan S. Emens, and Vance K. Bauer. "The Circadian Basis of Winter Depression." *Proceedings of the National Academy of Sciences of the USA* 103 (2006): 7414–7419.

Melatonin. American Academy of Family Physicians, May 2008, http://familydoctor.org/online/famdocen/home/articles/258.html.

Natural Standard Research Collaboration. *Melatonin.* Mayo Clinic, February 1, 2008, http://www.mayoclinic.com/health/melatonin/NS_patient-melatonin.

Properly Timed Light, Melatonin Lift Winter Depression by Syncing Rhythms. National Institute of Mental Health, May 1, 2006, http://www.nimh.nih.gov/science-news/2006/properly-timed-light-melatonin-lift-winter-depression-by-syncing-rhythms.shtml.

Questions and Answers About Melatonin. Society for Light Treatment and Biological Rhythms, 1994, http://www.websciences.org/sltbr/melfaq.htm.

Srinivasan, Venkataramanujan, Marcel Smits, Warren Spence, Alan D. Lowe, Leonid Kayumov, Seithikurippu R. Pandi-Perumal, et al. "Melatonin in Mood Disorders." *World Journal of Biological Psychiatry* 7 (2006): 138–151.

MEN. Men are half as likely as women to experience depression—but that does not mean male depression is rare. In fact, according to government statistics, about five percent of American men have experienced **major depression** within the past year. When men do become depressed, they may develop different symptoms and rely on different coping methods than women. Men are also four times more likely than women to die by **suicide**.

Male depression—the ailment British prime minister Winston Churchill (1874–1965) nicknamed his "black dog"—is not always easy to recognize. Feelings of sadness, worthlessness, and excessive guilt are classic symptoms of depression. But rather than reporting such feelings, many men with depression say they are bothered mainly by fatigue, irritability, sleep problems, and loss of interest in work or hobbies.

Men, more than women, may be reluctant to talk about what they are going through and hesitant to seek professional help. Instead, they may turn to **alcohol** or drugs in a vain effort to suppress their feelings, or they may become angry, frustrated, irritable, discouraged, or occasionally even violent. Some men throw themselves into a workaholic routine. Others try to escape their feelings through gambling, reckless driving, unsafe sex, or other risky behavior.

Because of such differences, some researchers have questioned whether the standard diagnostic criteria for depression truly capture the male experience. When men do seek help, they might be at risk for misdiagnosis if their symptoms do not match the ones treatment providers have been taught to look for.

Even after depression is diagnosed, men may resist treatment if they believe it makes them seem weak or vulnerable. Some may think they should be able to tough out depression on their own. Others may worry they will lose the respect of family and friends or damage their reputation at work. Yet depression is an illness, not a character flaw, and getting treatment for it is a powerful step. With effective treatment, men can take charge of their symptoms, improve their mood, and reclaim their life again.

Bibliography

Male Depression: Understanding the Issues. Mayo Clinic, November 15, 2008, http://www.mayoclinic.com/health/male-depression/MC00041.

Melin, Gabrielle J. *Depression in Men Less Frequent Than Women.* Mayo Clinic, October 23, 2008, http://www.mayoclinic.com/health/depression-in-men/MY00347.

Men and Depression. National Institute of Mental Health, April 1, 2009, http://www.nimh.nih .gov/health/publications/men-and-depression/index.shtml.

MENOPAUSE.   Menopause is an important transition in a woman's life. The years around menopause are also a time when **women** who are prone to depression may be vulnerable to a **recurrence**. Technically speaking, menopause refers to the end of menstrual periods, and perimenopause refers to the two to eight years leading up to that point, during which women may have symptoms such as hot flashes, sleep problems, and mood swings.

Typically, perimenopause starts at about age 47, but the timing varies from woman to woman. Those who have previously experienced **major depression** or **postpartum depression** (depression that begins soon after childbirth) are especially likely to become depressed when they enter perimenopause. Women who have suffered from **premenstrual dysphoric disorder** (severe, cyclic moodiness in the week before menstrual periods begin) are also at increased risk. But even women who have never been depressed before are almost twice as likely to develop major depression when they reach perimenopause as other women of the same age who are not perimenopausal yet.

Time of Transition.   Menopause is a literal change of life. Physiologically, hormone levels tend to fluctuate erratically. These hormonal changes can directly affect brain circuits that help regulate mood. At the same time, they can affect brain centers that help control body temperature, leading to hot flashes and night sweats (hot flashes that occur during sleep). The **stress** caused by having unpredictable hot flashes and not getting enough sleep, in turn, may indirectly contribute to depression.

Psychologically, some midlife women have concerns about body image, aging, sexuality, or an "empty nest" that add to their emotional distress. In those predisposed to depression, stress may trigger or worsen an episode.

It is worth noting that most women navigate the menopausal transition smoothly. Although mild sadness or irritability is not uncommon, severe, long-lasting depression is never normal. Menopausal women who become depressed can benefit from treatment just like women do at any other stage of life.

Treatment of Menopausal Depression.   **Antidepressants** and **psychotherapy** are the mainstays of treatment for depression. There is some evidence that a group of antidepressants called **serotonin-norepinephrine reuptake inhibitors** may help relieve hot flashes as well, although to a lesser extent than hormone replacement therapy.

Conversely, hormone replacement therapy including **estrogen** can reduce hot flashes and improve sleep, and it may also decrease depression in some perimenopausal women, although not as consistently as antidepressants. However, treatment with estrogen has been linked to an increased risk of breast cancer, heart disease, stroke, blood clots, and urinary incontinence, so the possible benefits must be carefully weighed against the potential side effects.

Some doctors prescribe both an antidepressant and estrogen for perimenopausal women with hard-to-treat depression. When an antidepressant alone is not enough, adding estrogen may enhance the effectiveness of treatment and reduce the time it takes to feel better. To be on the safe side, women who opt to take estrogen should be sure to get all their recommended health screenings, including tests that detect early signs of cancer and cardiovascular disease.

Further Information.   American College of Obstetricians and Gynecologists, 409 12th Street S.W., P.O. Box 96920, Washington, D.C. 20090, (202) 638-5577, www.acog.org.

National Institute on Aging, Building 31, Room 5C27, 31 Center Drive, MSC 2292, Bethesda, MD 20892, (301) 496-1752, www.nia.nih.gov.

National Women's Health Information Center, (800) 994-9662, www.womenshealth.gov.

North American Menopause Society, P.O. Box 94527, Cleveland, OH, 44101, (440) 442-7550, www.menopause.org.

Bibliography

Depression in Women: Understanding the Gender Gap. Mayo Clinic, September 6, 2008, http://www .mayoclinic.com/health/depression/MH00035.

Kahn, David A., Margaret L. Moline, Ruth W. Ross, Lori L. Altshuler, and Lee S. Cohen. "Depression During the Transition to Menopause: A Guide for Patients and Families." *Postgraduate Medicine* (March 2001): 114–115.

Menopause and Mental Health. National Women's Health Information Center, May 29, 2008, http://womenshealth.gov/menopause/mental.

Nelson, Heidi D., Kimberly K. Vesco, Elizabeth Haney, Rongwei Fu, Anne Nedrow, Jill Miller, et al. "Nonhormonal Therapies for Menopausal Hot Flashes: Systematic Review and Meta-analysis." *JAMA* 17 (2006): 2057–2071.

Parry, Barbara L. "Perimenopausal Depression." *American Journal of Psychiatry* 165 (2008): 23–27.

Stewart, Donna E., Danielle E. Rolfe and Emma Robertson. "Depression, Estrogen, and the Women's Health Initiative." *Psychosomatics* 45 (2004): 445–447.

Wise, Dana D., Angela Felker, and Stephen M. Stahl. "Tailoring Treatment of Depression for Women Across the Reproductive Lifecycle: The Importance of Pregnancy, Vasomotor Symptoms, and Other Estrogen-Related Events in Psychopharmacology." *CNS Spectrums* 13 (2008): 647–655, 658–662.

MENTAL HEALTH. Mental health is a state of emotional well-being and good behavioral adjustment. People who are mentally healthy are able to form constructive relationships and cope effectively with challenge and adversity. It is easy to take mental health for granted unless something goes awry. Yet this salutary state of mind lays the foundation for thinking, learning, communicating, and making contributions to society.

Mental health implies the absence of an active **mental illness**, such as **major depression**, **bipolar disorder**, or schizophrenia. Yet mental health is more than just the lack of distress and dysfunction. It also connotes the presence of emotional awareness, psychological resilience, personal growth, and positive self-esteem.

Defining Mental Health. Most of us have a vague sense of what constitutes mental health. Pinning down a specific definition is no easy task, however. In a 1999 report titled *Mental Health*, the U.S. Surgeon General defined it as "a state of successful performance of mental function, resulting in productive activities, fulfilling relationships with other people, and the ability to adapt to change and to cope with adversity."

According to the World Health Organization's Web site, mental health is "a state of well-being in which every individual realizes his or her own potential, can cope with the normal stresses of life, can work productively and fruitfully, and is able to make a contribution to her or his community."

One problem with attempting to define mental health in scientific terms is that there is not a strong evidence base for choosing what to include. Considerable research has been done on identifying the characteristics of various mental illnesses. The same effort has not yet been applied to identifying the characteristics that make up psychological well-being.

Historical Perspectives. As a general rule, both medicine and psychology have focused more on illness than on health. There have been some notable exceptions to this rule, however. U.S. psychologist Carl Rogers (1902–1987) described the fully functioning person as having certain qualities, such as being open to experience, living in the here and now, trusting one's own judgment, being creative, and feeling free to make choices and take responsibility for them.

U.S. psychologist Abraham Maslow (1908–1970) used the term self-actualization to describe the self-fulfillment that comes from realizing one's personal potential. Maslow believed that optimal health is achieved through the full use of talents and capabilities. But for most people, the achievement of this state is delayed as they go about meeting the more basic needs of physical survival, safety, love, and belonging.

Those who achieve self-actualization tend to have certain qualities in common, according to Maslow. These qualities include an ability to differentiate the honest and authentic from the dishonest and fake, a tendency to treat difficulties as problems in need of solutions, and a belief that the journey is often more important than the destination in life. Self-actualizers also tend to be comfortable with solitude, enjoy a few deep personal relationships, value their autonomy, resist pressure to conform, accept themselves and others, display a non-hostile sense of humor, be spontaneous and unpretentious, show humility and respect, be guided by strong ethics and a social conscience, and have the ability to view even the most ordinary things with a sense of awe.

More recently, U.S. psychologist **Martin E. P. Seligman** (1942–) proposed a new field he calls positive psychology, which focuses on the scientific study of strengths and virtues that enable people to thrive. Positive psychology puts a premium on pleasant emotions, including contentment with the past, happiness in the present, and hope for the future. It also stresses personally and socially desirable traits, such as courage, compassion, resilience, creativity, curiosity, integrity, self-knowledge, moderation, self-control, wisdom, and the capacity for love and work.

Cultural Dimensions. One problem with listing traits that comprise mental health is that any such list is inevitably influenced by cultural values. One culture might consider hearing voices to be a symptom of mental illness, for example, while another might view it as a sign of psychological giftedness.

Yet whatever the specific components of mental health might be, there is a general consensus that they have a wide-ranging impact. Mental health is the springboard for emotional, cognitive,

The Lincoln Conundrum

Sixteenth president Abraham Lincoln (1809–1865) was the picture of mental health by many definitions. He personified virtues such as loyalty, honesty, wisdom, humor, and courage. And he was indisputably successful at realizing his potential, putting his principles into action, and making great contributions to society. In fact, Lincoln was among an august group of historical high-achievers that Maslow studied when developing his theory. To Maslow, it was obvious that Lincoln exemplified self-actualization.

Yet Lincoln also suffered from episodes of deep depression off and on throughout his adult life. In his book *Lincoln's Melancholy* (2005), U.S. essayist and author Joshua Wolf Shenk makes a convincing argument that Lincoln's depression actually helped spur his personal growth and fuel his history-shaping achievements. The implication: Lincoln's mental illness in some way helped give rise to his mental health.

The paradox of Lincoln illustrates the complex relationship between mental health and mental illness. The boundary between the two states is not nearly as clear-cut as might be supposed, and it is quite possible for elements of both to coexist within the same person. Lincoln may be an extreme example, but on a less exalted level, it is likely that we all are a complex mix of functional and dysfunctional qualities.

behavioral, and social functioning in any culture. Without sound mental health, a person is unable to achieve optimal happiness and make the most out of life.

Bibliography

Boeree, C. George. *Abraham Maslow.* Shippensburg University, http://webspace.ship.edu/cgboer/maslow.html.

Boeree, C. George. *Carl Rogers.* Shippensburg University, http://webspace.ship.edu/cgboer/rogers.html.

Positive Psychology Center Home Page. University of Pennsylvania, http://www.ppc.sas.upenn.edu.

Shenk, Joshua Wolf. *Lincoln's Melancholy: How Depression Challenged a President and Fueled His Greatness.* Boston: Houghton Mifflin, 2005.

U.S. Department of Health and Human Services. *Mental Health: A Report of the Surgeon General.* Rockville, MD: U.S. Department of Health and Human Services, 1999.

Viney, Wayne, and D. Brett King. *A History of Psychology: Ideas and Context.* Boston: Allyn and Bacon, 1998.

What Is Mental Health? World Health Organization, September 3, 2007, http://www.who.int/features/qa/62/en/index.html.

MENTAL HEALTH AMERICA. Mental Health America (formerly the National Mental Health Association) is a national, nonprofit group dedicated to helping all people live mentally healthier lives. Members of the 320 affiliates across the United States include mental health consumers, family members, advocates, and treatment providers. The organization's goal is to educate the public about ways to preserve and strengthen **mental health** as well as to support those with **mental illness** and **substance abuse** problems.

Mental Health America traces its roots back to 1909, when U.S. businessman and mental health advocate Clifford Beers (1876–1943) founded the National Committee for Mental Hygiene. Inspired by his personal struggles with manic depression (now called **bipolar disorder**), Beers became a prominent figure in early twentieth-century efforts to reform the treatment of and attitudes toward mental illness. The aim of his organization was to improve conditions for people living with mental illness and promote greater public awareness of mental health.

Today those remain the core themes at Mental Health America. Local affiliates provide public education, **support groups**, and rehabilitation and housing services. They also strive to influence public policy at the national, state, and local level, advocating to protect the rights of individuals with mental illness and improve access to care. Among the events sponsored by Mental Health America are an annual conference and Mental Health Month, observed every year in May.

Further Information. Mental Health America, 2000 N. Beauregard Street, 6th Floor Alexandria, VA 22311, (800) 969-6642, www.nmha.org.

Bibliography

"Beers, Clifford (1876–1943)," in *Gale Encyclopedia of Psychology.* 2nd ed. Farmington Hills, MI: Gale Group, 2001.

History of the Organization and Movement. November 11, 2006, http://www.nmha.org/index.cfm?objectId=DA2F000D-1372–4D20-C8882D19A97973AA.

Mental Health Month: Get Connected. Mental Health America, May 9, 2008, http://www.nmha.org/go/may.

We Are Mental Health America! Mental Health America, November 17, 2006, http://www.nmha.org/go/about-us.

MENTAL HEALTH COUNSELOR.   Counselors help people cope with a wide range of personal, family, educational, and occupational problems. Mental health counselors diagnose and treat mental and emotional disorders and promote psychological well-being. They typically put a practical, problem-solving spin on **psychotherapy**. The focus is on short-term, solution-focused treatment. There is also an emphasis on not only treating disorders, but also fostering growth.

In addition to providing psychotherapy, mental health counselors may advise people on how to handle problems of daily living. Some provide other psychological interventions as well. Examples include **substance abuse** treatment and crisis intervention, which helps people cope with the immediate aftermath of a traumatic event.

Training and Credentials.   Licensed mental health counselors have a master's degree or above, plus at least two years of supervised post-degree experience. Some also choose to apply for professional credentials from the National Board for Certified Counselors. To qualify as a National Certified Counselor (NCC), applicants must have the requisite education and experience as well as pass a national exam. To qualify as a Certified Clinical Mental Health Counselor (CCMHC), applicants must hold the NCC credential and meet additional requirements.

Mental Health Counseling in Action.   Mental health counselors work in a variety of settings, including private practice, community agencies, hospitals, employee assistance programs, and substance abuse treatment centers. The American Counseling Association, with nearly 45,000 members, is the world's largest association for professional counselors. The American Mental Health Counselors Association is the national organization for those who specialize in the mental health field.

All states except California license or certify mental health counselors for private practice. In addition to meeting the requirements for education and experience, candidates must pass a licensure or certification exam. The American Association of State Counseling Boards is the organization for state boards that regulate the profession.

See also: Diagnosis of Depression; Treatment of Depression

Further Information.   American Association of State Counseling Boards, 5999 Stevenson Avenue, Alexandria, VA 22304, (703) 212-2239, www.aascb.org.

American Counseling Association, 5999 Stevenson Avenue, Alexandria, VA 22304, (800) 347-6647, www.counseling.org.

American Mental Health Counselors Association, 801 N. Fairfax Street, Suite 304, Alexandria, VA 22314, (800) 326-2642, www.amhca.org.

National Board for Certified Counselors, P.O. Box 77699, Greensboro, NC 27417, (336) 547-0607, www.nbcc.org.

Bibliography

Bureau of Labor Statistics. "Counselors," in *Occupational Outlook Handbook, 2006–07 Edition.* Washington, DC: U.S. Department of Labor, 2005.
Why Use a Mental Health Counselor? American Mental Health Counselors Association, 2004, http://www.amhca.org/why.

MENTAL ILLNESS.   Mental illness is an umbrella term that encompasses a wide range of brain-based disorders affecting thoughts, feelings, or behavior. To be considered mental illnesses, such disorders must cause serious distress or lead to a reduced capacity to get along in daily life. In practical terms, this means that people with mental illness may have trouble coping with **stress**, handling their emotions, maintaining healthy relationships, or keeping up with their responsibilities at home, work, or school. Serious mental illnesses that include a **depressed mood** as one of their symptoms include **major depression**, **bipolar disorder**, and **schizoaffective disorder**.

In the past, the subject of mental illness often was shrouded in mystery, fear, and shame. Today, people with mental illness and their families still battle prejudice and **stigma**. Nevertheless, great strides have been made in demystifying the subject. Most people now understand that mental illness is not a character flaw or sign of personal weakness. Instead, it is a brain disorder just as asthma is a lung disease.

In fact, the distinction between mental and physical illness is somewhat arbitrary. "Mental" illnesses can have a biological component. For instance, depression is associated with changes in several **neurotransmitters**, chemicals that act as messengers within the brain. Likewise, "physical" illnesses can have a psychological component. For instance, long-term psychological stress increases the risk of heart disease and stroke, raises blood sugar levels, heightens the perception of pain, and decreases the body's ability to heal wounds and fight off infections.

Without treatment, the toll on the individual and the cost to society are staggering. Consequences of untreated mental illness include not only unnecessary suffering, but also missed work, unemployment, homelessness, **substance abuse**, **suicide**, and the waste of human potential. The economic cost of untreated mental illness in the United States is estimated to exceed $100 billion each year.

Fortunately, mental illness is treatable. Medication, **psychotherapy**, peer **support groups**, and community support services are just some of the treatment options that can help relieve symptoms and promote **recovery**. With appropriate treatment, even those with the most serious mental illnesses usually are able to enjoy richer, more satisfying lives.

What's a "Mental Disorder"?

A wide array of mental, emotional, and behavioral conditions are cataloged in the *Diagnostic and Statistical Manual of Mental Disorders, Fourth Edition, Text Revision* (*DSM-IV-TR*), a diagnostic guidebook published by the American Psychiatric Association and used by mental health professionals from many disciplines. The *DSM-IV-TR* defines the term "mental disorder" extremely broadly, applying it to any behavioral or psychological set of symptoms that is associated with distress, dysfunction, or an increased risk of death, pain, disability, or significant loss of freedom. Some of the included conditions fall within the scope of what is usually called a mental illness; others do not. Below are the various categories of mental disorders described in the *DSM-IV-TR*.

	Definition	**Examples**
Developmental Disorders	Mental, emotional, or behavioral conditions that are usually first diagnosed in infancy, childhood, or adolescence	**Attention-deficit hyperactivity disorder**, **conduct disorder**, **learning disorders**, autism, mental retardation, Tourette's syndrome

What's a "Mental Disorder"? (cont.)

	Definition	Examples
Cognitive Disorders	Mental disorders characterized by a cognitive deficit that is a significant change from the person's previous level of functioning	Alzheimer's and other forms of dementia, amnesia
Mental Disorders Due to a General Medical Condition	Mental symptoms that are the direct physiological consequence of a general medical condition	**Mood disorder due to a general medical condition**, other medically-related mental disorders, or personality changes
Substance-Related Disorders	Mental symptoms that are related to the use of alcohol or other drugs, side effects of medication or exposure to toxic chemicals	**Substance abuse** and addiction
Psychotic Disorders	Mental disorders that are characterized by delusions, hallucinations, disorganized speech, and/or bizarre behavior	Schizophrenia, schizoaffective disorder
Mood Disorders	Mental disorders in which the dominant feature is a disturbance in mood	Major depression, **dysthymia**, bipolar disorder, **cyclothymia**
Anxiety Disorders	Mental disorders that are characterized by excessive fear or worry that is recurrent or long-lasting	**Generalized anxiety disorder**, **post-traumatic stress disorder**, obsessive-compulsive disorder, panic disorder, phobias
Somatoform Disorders	Physical symptoms that suggest a general medical condition but for which no physical explanation can be found	Chronic pain with a psychological component, hypochondriasis
Factitious Disorders	Physical or psychological symptoms that are intentionally produced or faked in order to assume the sick role	Ganser syndrome (feigned psychological illness), Munchausen syndrome (feigned physical illness)
Dissociative Disorders	An abnormal separation in the usually integrated mental functions of conscious awareness, memory, identity, or perception	Amnesia due to psychological causes, dissociative identity disorder (multiple personality disorder)

What's a "Mental Disorder"? (cont.)

	Definition	Examples
Sexual and Gender Identity Disorders	Disturbances in sexual desire or response that cause emotional distress, interpersonal problems, or harm to others	Problems with sexual arousal or orgasm, sexual pain with a psychological component, pedophilia, exhibitionism
Eating Disorders	Disturbances in eating behavior, such as severely restricting what is eaten or adopting a pattern of binging and purging	Anorexia, bulimia
Sleep Disorders	**Sleep disturbances** due to abnormalities in the body's sleep-wake cycle, another mental disorder, a general medical condition or drug use	Insomnia, narcolepsy, sleep apnea, sleepwalking
Impulse-Control Disorders	Behavioral disorders characterized by the failure to resist an impulse do something that is harmful to oneself or others	Gambling addiction, kleptomania (compulsive stealing), pyromania (compulsive fire-setting)
Adjustment Disorders	A psychological response to a stressful situation that leads to more distress than would normally be expected or causes problems in daily life	**Adjustment disorder with depressed mood**, other types of adjustment disorder (for example, with anxiety or conduct problems)
Personality Disorders	A pervasive, long-lasting pattern of thinking, feeling, and behaving that deviates from cultural expectations and leads to distress or dysfunction	**Borderline personality disorder**, other types of personality disorder (for example, antisocial, narcissistic, dependent or paranoid)

Causes and Risk Factors.   About one in five individuals in the United States has a diagnosable mental illness during any given year. "Severe and persistent mental illness"—a term sometimes used for the most disabling and long-lasting conditions—affects about three percent of the population.

Anyone of any age can have a mental illness. However, many mental illnesses are especially insidious because they strike during the prime of life, often during adolescence or young adulthood. Late life is another time when people are particularly vulnerable.

Mental illness encompasses a wide range of complex conditions with multiple causes. Some mental illnesses may be primarily genetic in cause, and others primarily environmental. Most of the time, though, the cause is probably an interaction between nature and nurture. Whatever the source, the result may be a change in **brain physiology** that in turn leads to a change in how the person thinks, feels, and behaves.

Help and Hope. A century ago, little was known about how to treat mental illness effectively. Today, the best treatments help a large majority of people with even the most serious conditions enjoy an improved quality of life, and the prospects for the coming decades are brighter still.

Mental illnesses are currently classified based on the symptoms they produce. One problem with this approach is that the same symptom may have very different biological causes in different people. As scientific knowledge grows, it may become possible to classify mental illnesses based on their underlying causes rather than their external manifestations. And that, in turn, may lead to a new generation of treatments that target individual changes in brain functioning with ever-increasing accuracy.

See also: Environmental Factors; Genetic Factors; Historical Perspective; Mental Health

Bibliography

American Psychiatric Association. *Diagnostic and Statistical Manual of Mental Disorders.* 4th ed., text rev. Washington, DC: American Psychiatric Association, 2000.

Defining Mental Illness: An Interview with a Mayo Clinic Specialist. Mayo Clinic, August 17, 2006, http://www.mayoclinic.com/print/mental-illness/HQ01079.

Let's Talk Facts About What Is Mental Illness? American Psychiatric Association, November 2006, http://healthyminds.org/factsheets/LTF-WhatIsMentalIllness.pdf.

What Is Mental Illness: Mental Illness Facts. National Alliance on Mental Illness, 2008, http://www.nami.org/Content/NavigationMenu/Inform_Yourself/About_Mental_Illness/About_Mental_Illness.htm.

MIGRAINE. A migraine is a type of headache characterized by pulsing or throbbing pain in one area of the head. The pain can be excruciating, sidelining the sufferer for hours or even days at a time. Often the headaches are accompanied by extreme sensitivity to light and sound as well as nausea and vomiting. Depression is a common co-occurring disorder. In fact, people who get migraines are more than twice as likely to develop depression as the general population.

Forecast: Headache Ahead

Some people have migraines that are preceded by auras. These are sensory warning signs, such as seeing flashing lights or zig-zag lines, developing temporary blind spots, or feeling a tingling sensation in an arm or leg. Other people have nonsensory feelings that predict a migraine from several hours to a day in advance. Depression is sometimes part of this premonitory state, which also may include feelings of irritability or elation, intense energy, thirst, drowsiness, and a craving for sweets.

The relationship between depression and migraine seems to cut both ways. Having migraines increases the risk of developing depression, and vice versa. On one hand, having recurring bouts of intense pain creates **stress**, which might trigger or worsen depression in those predisposed to mood problems. It is also possible that the unpredictability of many migraine attacks could foster a sense of helplessness, which might contribute to depression as well.

On the other hand, depression is sometimes expressed through physical symptoms, including **chronic pain**. To some extent, this may be due to a psychological reaction that converts emotional pain into physical suffering. But in the case of depression and migraine, the two conditions also may connected by shared physiological causes.

The Depression Connection. Some researchers believe that migraines result from functional changes in a major pain pathway called the trigeminal nerve system. These changes may be linked to abnormalities in brain chemicals, including **serotonin**. Among serotonin's many jobs in the body are helping regulate mood and helping direct pain messages going through the trigeminal pathway.

During a migraine, serotonin levels drop. According to one theory, this causes the trigeminal nerve to release other substances, which travel to the meninges, the brain's outer covering. There the substances make blood vessels swollen and inflamed, which produces pain.

Cortical Spreading Depression. A newer theory links migraine pain to tiny areas of stroke-like brain damage. The damage is related to a phenomenon called cortical spreading depression (CSD; "depression" in this case refers not to mood, but rather to reduced function). A neuron is a cell in the brain or another part of the **nervous system** that is specialized to send, receive, and process information. In CSD, a slow-moving wave of potassium ions causes many **neurons** to signal at once, followed by a period when normal activity ceases in the area. CSD occurs not only in migraines, but also in strokes and traumatic brain injuries.

At least in animals, recent studies show that CSD can cause oxygen deprivation, swelling of neurons, and loss of the tiny projections on neurons that receive information. CSD also irritates the trigeminal nerve. These effects seem to be temporary. But if there are numerous CSD waves, the neuronal damage might build up and lead to lasting problems with brain function. This is an active area of research, and time will tell what relevance it might have for depression.

Treatment Considerations. Medications used to treat migraines fall into two categories: those that help relieve the pain once it starts and those that help prevent future attacks. Among the most widely used preventive medications are **tricyclic antidepressants**.

Other widely prescribed types of **antidepressants** generally are not as effective for preventing migraines. However, they may still be used specifically to treat depression. **Psychotherapy** may help reduce depression as well. Because stress can both trigger migraine attacks and make depression worse, learning **stress management** and **relaxation techniques** may be helpful for both conditions.

See also: Neurological Disorders; Physical Illness; Stroke

Further Information. American Headache Society, 19 Mantua Road, Mount Royal, NJ 08061, (800) 255-2243, www.americanheadachesociety.org, www.achenet.org.

National Headache Foundation, 820 N. Orleans, Suite 217, Chicago, IL 60610, (888) 643-5552, www.headaches.org.

National Institute of Neurological Disorders and Stroke, P.O. Box 5801, Bethesda, MD 20824, (800) 352-9424, www.ninds.nih.gov.

Bibliography

Breslau, N., R. B. Lipton, W. F. Stewart, L. R. Schultz, and K. M. A. Welch. "Comorbidity of Migraine and Depression: Investigating Potential Etiology and Prognosis." *Neurology* 60 (2003): 1308–1312.

Headache: Hope Through Research. National Institute of Neurological Disorders and Stroke, September 16, 2008, http://www.ninds.nih.gov/disorders/headache/detail_headache.htm.

Is It Just a Headache? Study Links Migraine to Brain Damage in Mice. National Institute of Neurological Disorders and Stroke, November 16, 2007, http://www.ninds.nih.gov/news_and _events/news_articles/news_story_migraine_hypoxia.htm.

Kececi, H., S. Dener, and E. Analan. "Co-morbidity of Migraine and Major Depression in the Turkish Population." *Cephalalgia* 23 (2003): 271–275.

Migraine. Mayo Clinic, June 6, 2007, http://mayoclinic.com/health/migraine-headache/DS00120.

Migraine Headaches: Ways to Deal with the Pain. American Academy of Family Physicians, June 2007, http://familydoctor.org/online/famdocen/home/common/brain/disorders/127.html.

Molgat, Carmen V., and Scott B. Patten. "Comorbidity of Major Depression and Migraine: A Canadian Population-Based Study." *Canadian Journal of Psychiatry* 50 (2005): 832–837.

NINDS Migraine Information Page. National Institute of Neurological Disorders and Stroke, July 31, 2008, http://www.ninds.nih.gov/disorders/migraine/migraine.htm.

Sheftell, Fred D., and Susan J. Atlas. "Migraine and Psychiatric Comorbidity: From Theory and Hypotheses to Clinical Application." *Headache* 42 (2002): 934–944.

Takano, Takahiro, Guo-Feng Tian, Weiguo Peng, Nanhong Lou, Ditte Lovatt, Anker J. Hansen, et al. "Cortical Spreading Depression Causes and Coincides with Tissue Hypoxia." *Nature Neuroscience* 10 (2007): 754–762.

Zwart, J.- A., G. Dyb, K. Hagen, K. J. Ødegård, A. A. Dahl, G. Bovim, et al. "Depression and Anxiety Disorders Associated with Headache Frequency: The Nord-Trøndelag Health Study." *European Journal of Neurology* 10 (2003): 147–152.

MINDFULNESS-BASED COGNITIVE THERAPY. Mindfulness-based cognitive therapy (MBCT) is a treatment program that fuses two different approaches: **cognitive therapy** and mindfulness. Cognitive therapy is a treatment that helps people recognize and change self-defeating thought patterns. Mindfulness is a practice derived from Buddhism that involves focusing attention, fully and non-judgmentally, on whatever the person is experiencing from moment to moment. The fusion of these two approaches is designed to help people who have recovered from depression stay well and avoid another bout of the illness.

MBCT is based on the premise that, while people are depressed, their low mood generally occurs alongside negative thinking and physical fatigue. An association is learned between the mood and these symptoms. Once the mood gets back to normal, the mental and physical symptoms subside as well. But if the low mood returns, it will tend to trigger the other symptoms—and the stronger the previously learned association, the more powerful this effect is apt to be. Negative thoughts take hold of the mind, sluggishness takes hold of the body, and full-blown depression may result.

This cycle helps explain why the risk of **recurrence** rises dramatically after each bout of depression. At least 60 percent of people who have recovered from a first episode of **major depression** will go on to have a second. After a second episode, the risk of having a third is 70 percent, and after a third episode, the risk of having a fourth goes up to 90 percent.

Proponents of MBCT stress that the best way to stay depression-free is to respond to mild dips in mood before they can set off other symptoms. The goal of the approach is to teach people the skills they need to become more aware of changes in their mood, mind, and body—and to manage these changes before they spiral out of control.

Mindfulness and Depression. Mindfulness has been part of Buddhist tradition for millennia. It was introduced into Western medicine by U.S. scientist and **meditation** teacher Jon Kabat-Zinn (1944–), who founded a mindfulness-based Stress Reduction Clinic at the University of Massachusetts Medical School in 1979. The focus of mindfulness is on experiencing thoughts, feelings, and sensations as they arise, without judging or reacting to them. By applying mindfulness to everyday life, people can learn to handle daily ups and downs with greater calm and acceptance.

For people who are at risk for a repeat episode of depression, mindfulness helps them accept distressing moods, thoughts, or sensations without becoming overly alarmed. This attitude helps keep an occasional bad day from setting off a chain of events that leads to another bout of depression.

The Process at a Glance. MBCT typically is taught in eight weekly group meetings that more closely resemble classes than group therapy.

The Zen of Sitting

To see how mindfulness works, take a few minutes to focus intently on the act of sitting in your chair. You might become aware of the slight tension in your shoulder muscles or the little ache in your lower back. You might feel your feet pressing against the floor or your bottom sinking into the seat cushion. If you're wearing short sleeves, you might notice the coolness of plastic armrests or the scratchiness of chair fabric against your skin. In other words, you become totally absorbed in what you're experiencing here and now—which reduces your concern about what happened yesterday or might happen tomorrow.

Up to 12 people who have recently recovered from depression make up each group. The first four class sessions mainly address learning to focus attention, and the last four address watching for and coping with mood shifts.

Along with mindfulness meditation, the classes include exercises from cognitive therapy that elucidate the link between thinking and feeling. Participants learn specific strategies they can use when a depressed mood threatens to take hold of their mind. Homework is assigned to help participants keep practicing mindfulness at home.

Benefits for Depression. Both mindfulness and cognitive therapy are well-established approaches. However, the melding of the two into a program specifically designed to prevent the recurrence of depression is still relatively new. An initial evaluation of the program published in 2000 included 145 people in recovery from major depression, who were randomly assigned either to simply continue standard treatment or to receive standard treatment plus MBCT. For participants who had experienced three or more previous episodes of depression, 66 percent of those who got treatment as usual had symptoms reemerge within the next 60 weeks, compared to only 37 percent of those who received MBCT. For those who had experienced only two previous episodes, however, MBCT did not provide any added benefit.

The researchers speculated that one reason for this difference might be that as depression goes on, succeeding episodes are increasingly less likely to be triggered by stressful external events and more likely to be triggered by negative thought patterns. A follow-up study supported this idea. Specifically, it found that MBCT was most effective for people with major depression who have experienced three or more previous episodes, the first of which occurred relatively early in their lives. MBCT also was most beneficial for preventing recurrences that did not appear to be related to stressful external events.

One major advantage of this approach is that it is inexpensive compared to traditional one-on-one therapy. More research is still needed to sort out exactly which clients the approach is most likely to help. But based on studies to date, it seems that MBCT probably is effective at reducing the high risk of recurrence among people who have had several bouts of past depression.

See also: Recurrent Depression; Relaxation Techniques; Treatment of Depression

Further Information. Mindfulness-Based Cognitive Therapy, www.mbct.com.

Bibliography

Coelho, Helen F., Peter H. Canter, and Edzard Ernst. "Mindfulness-Based Cognitive Therapy: Evaluating Current Evidence and Informing Future Research." *Journal of Consulting and Clinical Psychology* 75 (2007): 1000–1005.

Ma, S. Helen, and John D. Teasdale. "Mindfulness-Based Cognitive Therapy for Depression: Replication and Exploration of Differential Relapse Prevention Efforts." *Journal of Consulting and Clinical Psychology* 72 (2004): 31–40.

Meditation for Health Purposes. National Center for Complementary and Alternative Medicine, June 2007, http://nccam.nih.gov/health/meditation/overview.htm.

Mindfulness Based Cognitive Therapy and the Prevention of Relapse in Depression. University of Oxford Centre for Suicide Research, http://cebmh.warne.ox.ac.uk/csr/mbct.html.

Segal, Zindel V., J. Mark G. Williams, and John D. Teasdale. *Mindfulness-Based Cognitive Therapy for Depression: A New Approach to Preventing Relapse.* New York: Guilford Press, 2002.

Teasdale, John D., Zindel V. Segal, J. Mark G. Williams, Valerie A. Ridgeway, Judith M. Soulsby, and Mark A. Lau. "Prevention of Relapse/Recurrence in Major Depression by Mindfulness-Based Cognitive Therapy." *Journal of Consulting and Clinical Psychology* 68 (2000): 615–623.

Williams, Mark, John Teasdale, Zindel Segal, and Jon-Kabat Zinn. *The Mindful Way Through Depression: Freeing Yourself From Chronic Unhappiness.* New York: Guilford Press, 2007.

MINNESOTA MULTIPHASIC PERSONALITY INVENTORY. The Minnesota Multiphasic Personality Inventory (MMPI) is among the most popular tests in the world for assessing personality. It can also be used to screen for general mental illness in adults and **adolescents**. The original version of the MMPI was published in 1942 by two professors at the University of Minnesota, psychologist Starke Rosecrans Hathaway (1903–1984), and psychiatrist John Charnley McKinley (1891–1950). An updated version, the MMPI-2, was introduced in 1989.

When Hathaway and McKinley first set out to develop their test, they cast a wide net for ideas. In addition to reviewing previous tests, they also culled ideas from psychology texts, folk customs, and religious and political lore. The test developers wound up with several hundred true-false items, which they gave to both a normative sample (people without psychiatric diagnoses) and criterion groups (people with diagnoses such as depression and schizophrenia). After analyzing the responses, they retained items that showed a significant difference between the criterion groups and normative sample. They also identified sets of items that reflected the typical response patterns of people with various mental characteristics. Reponses on these item sets were tallied to give people scores on 10 clinical scales.

Hathaway and McKinley built three validity scales into their test as well. These scales were intended to detect a suspect pattern of responses, which might indicate that the test taker was lying, careless, or overly eager to please by giving the "right" answer. For example, the Lie scale contains items that are somewhat negative, but that apply to most people, such as "I gossip a little at times." A "false" answer on several such items might call the test taker's honesty into question.

The original MMPI contained 550 items and 10 clinical scales: Depression, Hypochondriasis, Hysteria, Psychopathic Deviate, Masculinity-Femininity, Paranoia, Psychasthenia (anxiety), Schizophrenia, Hypomania, and Social Introversion. To supplement these 10 scales, researchers have introduced numerous other scales based on various clusters of MMPI items.

The multiphasic, or many-faceted, test soon assumed something akin to mythic status. A treasure trove of information was amassed from many thousands of studies using the

MMPI. Yet the test was not without its problems, the most glaring of which was the lack of representative norms. The original normative sample was composed of about 1,500 individuals, half of whom were friends and relatives who happened to be visiting patients at University of Minnesota hospitals. The resulting sample was far from representative of the United States as a whole.

Updating a Classic. A second version of the MMPI, developed in the 1980s, was intended to address this shortcoming. The normative sample for the MMPI-2 was comprised of 2,600 adults of all ages from across the United States, who were matched to the national population on age, gender, minority group, social class, and education. The group was 19 percent non-white.

For the second version, 14 percent of the original test items were rewritten to correct for grammatical errors and make the language more contemporary, nonsexist, and readable. Some items that might offend modern test takers were removed, and other items dealing with drug abuse, suicide, marriage, work, and Type A behavior were added. In total, the MMPI-2 contains 567 true-false items, including 394 that are identical to original test items. The test retains the same 10 clinical scales. It also includes the three original validity scales along with a handful of new ones.

In addition, the MMPI-2 includes a number of clinical subscales (also called Harris-Lingoes scales), content scales, content component scales, and supplementary scales. These four types of scales focus on specific symptoms or areas of interest. Several relate to symptoms of depression. For instance, there are clinical subscales for Subjective Depression, Psychomotor Retardation, Physical Malfunctioning, Mental Dullness, and Brooding. There is also a content scale called Depression, and there are content component scales for Lack of Drive, **Dysphoria**, Self-Depreciation, and Suicidal Ideation.

The developers of the first MMPI had recommended its use for adolescents as well as adults. But researchers soon noticed that adolescents as a group scored higher on the clinical scales than adults, which raised questions about the test's appropriateness for that age group. When the second version of the MMPI was being devised, the test developers opted to create a new test for adolescents ages 14 to 18, dubbed the MMPI-A. The 478 true-false items on this test are similar to those on the MMPI-2, but some items were deleted, others were rewritten, and still others are new.

The MMPI-2 and MMPI-A each take about 60 to 90 minutes to complete. Both tests can be given in a printed test booklet, on audiotape, or via computer. The items are presented in a mostly random order, although the first few are intended to be relatively non-threatening. The items included in the basic clinical and validity scales are among the first 370 presented on the MMPI-2 and the first 350 of the MMPI-A.

Why Are There Two Depression Scales?

The MMPI-2 contains a clinical scale called Depression and a content scale called Depression. What is the difference?

MMPI-2 clinical scales were developed by testing psychiatric patients with various forms of depression. The clinical scale for Depression measures discomfort and dissatisfaction with life, as evidenced by symptoms such as poor morale, hopelessness, unhappiness, low self-esteem, withdrawal, and slowed-down movements and speech.

MMPI-2 content scales are based on sets of test items with similar content. The content scale for Depression measures only one facet of the illness: self-reported depressive thoughts.

Pros and Cons of the MMPI-2. The MMPI-2 clinical scales each have relatively low internal consistency, a gauge of how consistently the items within each scale measure a single thing. At the same time, correlations among the different clinical scales are relatively high. This calls into question exactly what the individual scales are measuring. For example, high scores on the Schizophrenia scale are often found not only in people with schizophrenia, but also in those with **major depression, borderline personality disorder,** and some **anxiety disorders.**

Given this overlap, the MMPI-2 alone is not enough to diagnose a specific mental disorder. When combined with other information, however, it can be useful for identifying general mental illness, exploring major issues, and helping devise the best treatment plan for a particular individual's personality.

The MMPI-2 has been used for other purposes, too, such as forensic evaluation, neurological assessment, and employment screening. Given the range of information it provides, especially on the various extra scales, the MMPI-2 is among the most versatile of all psychological tests.

MMPI-2 Restructured Form. The MMPI-2 is still published and widely used. However, a restructured form of the test, called the MMPI-2 RF, was introduced in 2008. In this latest version, the 10 older clinical scales are replaced by nine restructured clinical scales: Demoralization, Somatic Complaints, Low Positive Emotions, Cynicism, Antisocial Behavior, Ideas of Persecution, Dysfunctional Negative Emotions, Aberrant Experiences, and Hypomanic Activation.

The normative sample for the MMPI-2 RF consists of 2,276 adults drawn from the MMPI-2 group. The new test has been shortened to 338 items. It takes about 25 to 50 minutes to complete.

According to the publisher, the MMPI-2 RF is meant to be an adjunct to its predecessor, not a replacement for it. The MMPI-2, building on the original MMPI, is among the best researched psychological tests of all time. Time will tell whether the MMPI-2 RF can live up to the high standard of utility and adaptability set by earlier versions of the test.

See also: Diagnosis of Depression

Bibliography

Cohen, Ronald Jay, and Mark E. Swerdlik. *Psychological Testing and Assessment: An Introduction to Tests and Measurement.* 5th ed. Boston: McGraw-Hill, 2002.

Delman, Howard M., Delbert G. Robinson, Craig A. Kimmelblatt, and Joanne McCormack. "General Psychiatric Symptoms Measures." In *Handbook of Psychiatric Measures,* 2nd ed., by A. John Rush Jr., Michael B. First, and Deborah Blacker, eds., 61–82. Washington, DC: American Psychiatric Publishing, 2008.

Millon, Theodore. *Masters of the Mind: Exploring the Story of Mental Illness from Ancient Times to the New Millennium.* New York: John Wiley and Sons, 2004.

MMPI-2 (Minnesota Multiphasic Personality Inventory-2). Pearson, 2008, http://www.pearsonassessments.com/mmpi2.aspx.

MMPI-2 RF (Minnesota Multiphasic Personality Inventory-2 Restructured Form). Pearson, 2008, http://www.pearsonassessments.com/mmpi2_rf.aspx.

MINOR DEPRESSION. Minor depression is a term that is sometimes used for a depressive episode that has the same kinds of symptoms as **major depression**, but fewer of them. Although relatively mild, the symptoms are present almost all the time for at least two weeks, so they are more than just a passing blue mood. Over time, even this low level of depression can chip away at a person's motivation, optimism, and self-esteem, and make it harder to bounce back from stressful situations.

Minor depression is not yet a formally recognized disorder in the ***Diagnostic and Statistical Manual of Mental Disorders, Fourth Edition, Text Revision***, a diagnostic guide published by the American Psychiatric Association and used by mental health professionals from many disciplines. At present, individuals with minor depression may be given the nonspecific diagnosis of "**depressive disorder not otherwise specified**." Minor depression is being considered for inclusion as a distinct entity in the manual's next edition, however. The condition seems to be fairly common, affecting an estimated three percent to 10 percent of the U.S. population at some point in their lives.

Because the symptoms of minor depression are mild, friends, family, and even doctors may regard them as no big deal. But the condition is less "minor" than it might seem. In the short term, it predisposes people to sleep problems, weight gain, and a run-down feeling. In the long term, it increases the risk of full-fledged major depression. Almost 30 percent of young adults with minor depression go on to develop major depression within the next 15 years.

Criteria for Diagnosis. Like people with major depression, those with minor depression have one or both of two core symptoms: (1) a low mood nearly all the time and (2) loss of interest or enjoyment in almost everything. At the same time, they may experience associated problems: (3) weight gain or weight loss, (4) trouble sleeping or oversleeping, (5) restless activity or slowed-down movements, (6) constant tiredness or lack of energy, (7) feelings of worthlessness or inappropriate guilt, (8) difficulty concentrating or making decisions, and (9) recurring thoughts of death or **suicide**. The symptom list is the same for both conditions. The difference is that minor depression involves a total of two to four symptoms, and major depression involves five or more.

To qualify as minor depression, the condition must cause some distress or disruption in daily life. It also must occur in someone who has never had major depression before. (When just a few symptoms hang on after a person starts to get better from major depression, it is considered a **partial remission**—in other words, an incomplete recovery.)

Dysthymia is another form of depression that is less intense than major depression. However, the symptoms of dysthymia must be present for at least two years. In contrast, the symptoms of minor depression must be present for a minimum of only two weeks. So minor depression is not only milder than major depression, but also briefer than dysthymia.

Treatment of Minor Depression. There is some debate about whether minor depression needs to be treated. The symptoms of minor depression often begin after a stressful event, such as getting divorced, losing a job, or having a medical illness. Some people consider the symptoms to be a normal reaction to a difficult situation and assume that they will usually get better on their own in time.

Other people argue that minor depression is a scaled-down version of major depression, not simply a normal response to **stress**. If left untreated, minor depression may worsen and become major. In this view, treatment is helpful not only for relieving current symptoms, but also for preventing more severe future ones.

Many mental health professionals take the middle ground, recommending treatment if minor depression starts getting worse or is bad enough to cause serious problems in a person's home, work, school, or social life. The main treatment options are **psychotherapy** and **antidepressants**. One type of psychotherapy that has proved beneficial is **cognitive-behavioral therapy**, which targets self-defeating thoughts and maladaptive behaviors.

When medication is prescribed, a group of antidepressants known as **selective serotonin reuptake inhibitors** may lead to moderate improvement.

Bibliography

Ackerman, Ronald T., and John W. Williams Jr. "Rational Treatment Choices for Non-major Depressions in Primary Care: An Evidence-Based Review." *Journal of General Internal Medicine* 17 (2002): 293–301.

American Psychiatric Association. *Diagnostic and Statistical Manual of Mental Disorders.* 4th ed., text rev. Washington, DC: American Psychiatric Association, 2000.

Banazak, Deborah A. "Minor Depression in Primary Care." *Journal of the American Osteopathic Association* 100 (2000): 783–787.

Williams, John W. Jr., James Barrett, Tom Oxman, Ellen Frank, Wayne Katon, Mark Sullivan, et al. "Treatment of Dysthymia and Minor Depression in Primary Care: A Randomized Controlled Trial in Older Adults." *JAMA* 284 (2000): 1519–1526.

MIXED ANXIETY-DEPRESSIVE DISORDER.   Mixed anxiety-depressive disorder (MADD) is a term that is sometimes used to describe a mixture of anxiety and depression symptoms that do not meet the full criteria for any other disorder. It is one of the proposed new diagnoses being considered for inclusion in the next edition of the *Diagnostic and Statistical Manual of Mental Disorders*, a diagnostic guide published by the American Psychiatric Association and used by mental health professionals from many disciplines.

It is a well-established fact that anxiety and depression often go hand in hand. More than half of people with **major depression** or **dysthymia** (a milder but quite long-lasting form of depression) also have an anxiety disorder, and vice versa. When people meet all the criteria for major depression, an anxiety disorder, or both, that is the diagnosis given. MADD is intended for situations in which symptoms fall short of this threshold, yet still cause real distress or disruption in daily life.

Defining the Problem.   MADD was introduced as a formal diagnosis in *The International Statistical Classification of Diseases and Related Health Problems, Tenth Edition* (*ICD-10*), a classification system for diseases developed by the World Health Organization. The tenth—and latest—edition was endorsed by the 43rd World Health Assembly in 1990. According to the *ICD-10*, a diagnosis of MADD should be given "when symptoms of anxiety and depression are both present, but neither is clearly predominant, and neither type of symptom is present to the extent that justifies a diagnosis if considered separately."

Inclusion of the disorder in the *ICD-10* also propelled it into the ***Diagnostic and Statistical Manual of Mental Disorders, Fourth Edition, Text Revision*** (*DSM-IV-TR*). The latter strives to be as compatible as possible with the international system, so MADD was included in an appendix of conditions warranting further study.

However, using the provisional diagnostic criteria presented in the *DSM-IV-TR*, the need for elevating MADD to the status of a full-fledged disorder is still debatable. It is estimated that MADD as defined in the *DSM-IV-TR* occurs in less than one percent of the general population. It is possible that most people with both depression and anxiety already meet the criteria for another mood or anxiety disorder, which would exclude a diagnosis of MADD. However, it is also possible that the provisional criteria for MADD simply need some tweaking to ensure that they are not leaving out people who would benefit from being diagnosed with the disorder.

Criteria for Diagnosis. The defining characteristic of MADD is **dysphoria**, an unpleasant **mood** characterized by feelings such as sadness, anxiety, or irritability. *DSM-IV-TR* criteria require that this mood either lasts continuously or comes and goes over a period of at least one month. During that time, four or more of the following symptoms are present: (1) trouble concentrating or a problem with one's mind going blank, (2) difficulty falling or staying asleep, or restless sleep that is not refreshing, (3) low energy or unexplained fatigue, (4) irritability, (5) worry, (6) a state of constant alertness, (7) **crying** easily, (8) anticipating the worst, (9) hopelessness, and (10) low self-esteem or feelings of worthlessness.

The symptoms of MADD are serious enough to cause emotional distress or lead to work, school, or social problems. To be diagnosed with MADD, a person must have never had **major depression**, **dysthymia**, **generalized anxiety disorder**, or **panic disorder**. The person also must not currently meet the requirements for having any other mood or anxiety disorder.

Treatment of MADD. One type of **psychotherapy** with proven effectiveness for treating both depression and anxiety is **cognitive-behavioral therapy** (CBT). In CBT, people learn to recognize and change maladaptive thought and behavior patterns that are contributing to their symptoms.

Antidepressants—especially those classified as **selective serotonin reuptake inhibitors** or **serotonin-norepinephrine reuptake inhibitors**—also are commonly prescribed for both depression and **anxiety disorders**. People with anxiety are particularly sensitive to side effects such as jitteriness when they first start taking antidepressants. To minimize problems, antidepressants may be started at a low dose and gradually increased to a therapeutic level.

Bibliography

American Psychiatric Association. *Diagnostic and Statistical Manual of Mental Disorders.* 4th ed., text rev. Washington, DC: American Psychiatric Association, 2000.

Klein, Daniel N., Stewart A. Shankman, and Brian R. McFarland. "Classification of Mood Disorders." In *The American Psychiatric Publishing Textbook of Mood Disorders,* by Dan J. Stein, David J. Kupfer, and Alan F. Schatzberg, eds., 17–32. Washington, DC: American Psychiatric Publishing, 2006.

Malyszczak, Krzysztof, and Tomasz Pawlowski. "Distress and Functioning in Mixed Anxiety and Depressive Disorder." *Psychiatry and Clinical Neuroscience* 60 (2006): 168–173.

Means-Christensen, Adrienne J., Cathy D. Sherbourne, Peter P. Roy-Byrne, Marin C. Schulman, Jennifer Wu, David C. Dugdale, et al. "In Search of Mixed Anxiety-Depressive Disorder: A Primary Care Study." *Depression and Anxiety* 23 (2006): 183–189.

Simon, Naomi M., and Jerrold F. Rosenbaum. "Anxiety and Depression Comorbidity: Implications and Intervention." *Medscape Psychiatry and Mental Health* 8 (2003): http://www.medscape.com/viewarticle/451325.

The International Statistical Classification of Diseases and Related Health Problems. 10th ed., 2007 version. World Health Organization, http://www.who.int/classifications/apps/icd/icd10online.

Weisberg, Risa B., Kristin M. Maki, Larry Culpepper, and Martin B. Keller. "Is Anyone Really M.A.D.? The Occurrence and Course of Mixed Anxiety-Depressive Disorder in a Sample of Primary Care Patients." *Journal of Nervous and Mental Disease* 193 (2005): 223–230.

MIXED EPISODE. A mixed episode is a bout of **bipolar disorder** in which a person simultaneously experiences the symptoms of both **mania** (an excessively high mood) and **major depression** (an excessively low mood) nearly every day for at least one week. The person may be very sad and hopeless while at the same time feeling highly energized. Common features of a mixed state include restlessness, trouble sleeping, changes in appetite, thoughts of **suicide**, and psychotic symptoms.

Mixed episodes occur in two different contexts. For some people, they are simply a transitional state during the switchover from mania to depression, or vice versa. For others, however, they are the primary form that mood episodes take. A history of having at least one mixed episode qualifies someone for a diagnosis of **bipolar I**, the classic form of bipolar disorder.

Mania is accompanied by prominent symptoms of depression about 31 percent of the time. When mixed episodes occur, bipolar disorder may be more challenging to treat. That just makes it all the more important to seek treatment early and maintain it long-term. In general, bipolar disorder is better controlled if treatment is continuous rather than off and on.

Bibliography

American Psychiatric Association. *Diagnostic and Statistical Manual of Mental Disorders.* 4th ed., text rev. Washington, DC: American Psychiatric Association, 2000.

Bipolar Disorder. National Institute of Mental Health, April 3, 2008, http://www.nimh.nih.gov/health/publications/bipolar-disorder/complete-publication.shtml.

Frances, Allen, Michael B. First, and Harold Alan Pincus. *DSM-IV Guidebook.* Washington, DC: American Psychiatric Press, 1995.

Klein, Daniel N., Stewart A. Shankman, and Brian R. McFarland. "Classification of Mood Disorders." In *The American Psychiatric Publishing Textbook of Mood Disorders,* by Dan J. Stein, David J. Kupfer and Alan F. Schatzberg, eds., 17–32. Washington, DC: American Psychiatric Publishing, 2006.

MONOAMINE HYPOTHESIS. Monoamines are a type of **neurotransmitters**, naturally occurring chemicals that act as messengers within the brain. A monoamine contains one amine group (NH_2) formed by a metabolic change in certain amino acids, the building blocks of proteins. There are two kinds of monoamines: (1) catecholamines, which include **norepinephrine**, epinephrine, and **dopamine**, and (2) indoleamines, which include **serotonin**. The monoamine hypothesis states that depression is caused by an imbalance in one or more of these brain chemicals.

The hypothesis ushered in a new era of research, with scientists striving to understand mental disorders in terms of the biological functioning of the **nervous system**. Thousands of studies looked at monoamine function in people with depression. Yet attempts to find direct support for the hypothesis have so far led to contradictory results rather than conclusive evidence.

Nevertheless, the development of new types of **antidepressants** that affect monoamines in various ways revolutionized the treatment of depression. The effectiveness of these medications for many people is indirect evidence for the role of monoamines. The fact that the medications do not work equally well for everyone may partly reflect individual differences in monoamine defects. Such differences could explain why across-the-board problems with monoamine function have been so hard to find. As more is learned about the role of monoamines, scientists may one day be able to single out subgroups of people with depression who have specific monoamine defects—and thus are most likely to benefit from taking a particular antidepressant.

It also seems increasingly clear that monoamine abnormalities are only part of the depression story. Much recent research has focused on the role of **hormones** and neurotrophic factors, substances that promote nerve cell growth and survival. But monoamines still are a subject of great interest half a century after the monoamine hypothesis was formulated.

Historical Perspective. The groundwork for the monoamine hypothesis was laid by a series of scientific discoveries in the mid-twentieth century. The first involved a blood pressure medication called reserpine, which often caused depression as a side effect. In the mid-1950s, U.S. biochemist Bernard B. Brodie (1907–1989) and his colleagues at the National Institutes of Health (NIH) found that reserpine led to a profound depletion in the brain's stores of norepinephrine and serotonin. Also, in both animals and humans, the depressive symptoms brought on by resperine could be reversed by a compound that gave rise to catecholamines. These findings suggested that there was a link between monoamines and depression.

Around the same time, scientists noticed that iproniazid, a medication used to treat tuberculosis, had an unexpected side effect: It made some people very cheerful, even mildly manic at times. Further research showed that isoniazid blocks an enzyme, called **monoamine oxidase**, that breaks down monoamines in the brain. As a result, monoamine levels stay higher. This discovery led to the development of a group of antidepressants called **monoamine oxidase inhibitors**, which are still prescribed occasionally.

Serendipity also played a role in the discovery of a second, more important group of antidepressants, called **tricyclic antidepressants** (TCAs), which remain in use today. Trying to devise an improved form of an early schizophrenia medication, scientists developed a drug called imipramine. Although imipramine did not help schizophrenia, an observant Swiss psychiatrist named Roland Kuhn (1912–2005) noted that it did work unexpectedly well for relieving depression. This led to the development of numerous other TCAs, which dominated the drug treatment of depression for the next three decades.

Another NIH scientist named **Julius Axelrod** (1912–2004), who was later awarded the Nobel Prize in Physiology or Medicine, had been studying **reuptake**, the process by which a neurotransmitter is absorbed back into the brain cell that originally released it. This process helps control how much neurotransmitter is available for use by the brain. Axelrod and his colleagues found that imipramine blocked the reuptake of norepinephrine, increasing the brain's available supply.

A similar reuptake system for serotonin was soon found. Researchers also learned that TCAs inhibited the reuptake not only of norepinephrine, but also of serotonin. Taken together, these findings indicated that depression might be due to a monoamine deficiency, and the monoamine hypothesis was born.

Testing the Hypothesis. For a time, it seemed as if science might be on the brink of explaining the physiology of depression once and for all. Unfortunately, the results of later studies on monoamine function were not as clear-cut as scientists had hoped.

Some studies measured substances in urine or cerebrospinal fluid that are produced by the metabolism of monoamines. Others looked at brain scans or postmortem brain samples for changes in monoamines or monoamine-related molecules. The results of these studies were inconsistent. On the whole, though, they suggest that monoamines do indeed play a role in depression, although the role may not be as straightforward or all-encompassing as once believed.

When researchers examined the cerebrospinal fluid of people with severe depression, they found that those with the lowest levels of serotonin were more likely to die by **suicide** than those with normal levels. Also, in a recent **brain imaging** study, scientists found elevated levels of monoamine oxidase throughout the brain in people with **major depression**.

Another set of experiments involved people who were given a drink that caused a rapid drop in blood levels of **tryptophan**, an amino acid that is a building block in serotonin production. In depressed individuals who were being treated with serotonin-boosting antidepressants, most who had only partially recovered from depression had an immediate relapse. The relapse was reversed by eating a tryptophan-rich meal.

Current Viewpoint. All in all, the monoamine hypothesis has stood the test of time relatively well. It did not wind up offering a single, simple answer to the question of what causes depression. But it did open up a very fruitful avenue of research that is still yielding fresh insights today.

The hypothesis led to the development of several new types of antidepressants that affect one or more monoamines in a variety of ways. Almost every compound that has been developed for the purpose of blocking serotonin or norepinephrine reuptake has turned out to be an effective antidepressant—a testament to the power of monoamines.

See also: Causes of Depression

Bibliography

Belmaker, R. H., and Galila Agam. "Major Depressive Disorder." *New England Journal of Medicine* 358 (2008): 55–68.

Belmaker, Robert H. "The Future of Depression Psychopharmacology." *CNS Spectrum* 13 (2008): 682–687.

Cahn, Charles. "Roland Kuhn, 1912–2005." *Neuropsychopharmacology* 31 (2006): 1096.

Carlson, Neil R. *Physiology of Behavior.* 8th ed. Boston: Allyn and Bacon, 2004.

DePaulo, J. Raymond Jr. *Understanding Depression: What We Know and What You Can Do About It.* New York: John Wiley and Sons, 2002.

Iversen, Leslie. "The Monoamine Hypothesis of Depression." In *Biology of Depression: From Novel Insights to Therapeutic Strategies,* by Julio Licinio and Ma-Li Wong, eds., 71–86. Weinheim, Germany: Wiley-VCH, 2005.

Kalat, James W. *Biological Psychology.* 7th ed. Belmond, CA: Wadsworth/Thomson Learning, 2001.

Meyer, Jeffrey H., Nathalie Ginovart, Anahita Boovariwala, Sandra Sagrati, Doug Hussey, Armando Garcia, et al. "Elevated Monoamine Oxidase A Levels in the Brain: An Explanation for the Monoamine Imbalance of Major Depression." *Archives of General Psychiatry* 63 (2006): 1209–1216.

Moore, Polly, Hans-Peter Landolt, Erich Seifritz, Camellia Clark, Tahir Bhatti, John Kelsoe, et al. "Clinical and Physiological Consequences of Rapid Tryptophan Depletion." *Neuropsychopharmacology* 23 (2000): 601–622.

Narvaez, Alfonso A. "Bernard B. Brodie, 81, a Pioneer In Drug Therapy Research, Dies." *New York Times,* March 2, 1989.

Nobel Laureate Axelrod, Neuroscience Pioneer. National Institute of Mental Health, June 26, 2008, http://www.nimh.nih.gov/science-news/2004/nobel-laureate-axelrod-neuroscience-pioneer.shtml.

MONOAMINE OXIDASE. Monoamine oxidase is an enzyme that breaks down and inactivates a group of chemicals called monoamines. This group includes three brain chemicals—**serotonin**, **norepinephrine**, and **dopamine**—that tend to be abnormal in depression. A class of **antidepressants** called **monoamine oxidase inhibitors** works by blocking the activity of monoamine oxidase, which causes levels of these three chemicals to rise.

There are two main forms of monoamine oxidase in the human body: MAO-A and MAO-B. To have an antidepressant effect, a medication must block MAO-A, the form that metabolizes serotonin and norepinephrine in the brain. All MAOIs currently used as anti-depressants also block brain MAO-B, the form that metabolizes dopamine.

See also: Monoamine Hypothesis

Bibliography

Stahl, Stephen M., and Angela Felker. "Monoamine Oxidase Inhibitors: A Modern Guide to an Unrequited Class of Antidepressants." *CNS Spectrums* 13 (2008): 855–870.

VandenBos, Gary R., ed. "Monoamine Oxidase (MAO)" and "Monoamine Oxidase Inhibitors (MAOIs; MAO Inhibitors)," in *APA Dictionary of Psychology.* Washington, DC: American Psychological Association, 2007.

MONOAMINE OXIDASE INHIBITORS.   Monoamine oxidase inhibitors (MAOIs) are the oldest class of **antidepressants**, dating back to the 1950s. These medications are still occasionally used to treat depression today. But because MAOIs can cause serious side effects and safety issues, they are usually prescribed only after other treatments have been tried first without success.

There are currently four MAOIs approved for treating depression: isocarboxazid, phenelzine, selegiline, and tranylcypromine. Scientists believe they work by blocking the activity of an enzyme called **monoamine oxidase**, which breaks down a group of chemicals called monoamines. This group includes three brain chemicals—**serotonin**, **norepinephrine**, and **dopamine**—which tend to be abnormal in depression. By increasing brain levels of these chemicals, MAOIs may provide a mood boost.

MAOIs have a long history of use as a treatment for depression. In general, their effectiveness is comparable to that of other antidepressants. When first-choice medications fail to work, MAOIs may be especially helpful for people with **atypical depression**, whose mood tends to be highly reactive to good or bad outside events.

MAOI Antidepressants

	Brand Names
Isocarboxazid†	Marplan
Phenelzine†	Nardil
Selegiline†	Emsam
Tranylcypromine†	Parnate

† FDA approved for treating depression

Use and Precautions.   One major drawback is that people taking MAOIs have to restrict what they eat. Some foods naturally contain an amino acid called tyramine, which helps regulate blood pressure. Tyramine can also be produced by the bacterial breakdown of foods as they age. MAOIs block the metabolism of tyramine, which can lead to a spike in blood pressure and potentially a **stroke**.

A partial list of foods high in tyramine includes aged cheese, tap beer, dried or smoked fish and poultry, broad bean pods, sauerkraut, tofu, and soy foods. A doctor or dietitian can provide a complete list of foods to avoid. In addition, the doctor might advise eating only fresh foods—skipping the leftovers and any foods that are past their freshness date.

An MAOI called selegiline, sold under the brand name Emsam, may offer an alternative to following a special diet. Unlike other antidepressants, which are taken by mouth,

The "Cheese Effect"

The dangerous connection between MAOIs and tyramine was discovered by an alert British pharmacist, whose wife was taking an MAOI. The pharmacist noticed that she got a severe headache whenever she ate aged cheese, which turns out to be high in tyramine. Doctors dubbed it the "cheese effect," even though that is something of a misnomer. Only aged cheeses, such as Stilton, are especially high in tyramine. Most processed cheeses contain just small amounts.

this one comes in the form of a skin patch that is applied once a day to the thigh, torso, or upper arm. The medication is then absorbed through the skin into the bloodstream. At its lowest strength (6 mg), the patch can be used without dietary restrictions. People using higher strength patches still need to watch what they eat, though.

It can take three to six weeks, or sometimes longer, to feel the full benefits of an MAOI. Once people start feeling better, they should still continue taking their medication for as long as prescribed to help keep symptoms from coming back. Stopping an MAOI abruptly can lead to symptoms such as nausea, vomiting, and tiredness. To prevent this problem, it is important to take the medication exactly as directed. When it is time to stop, a doctor can explain how to taper it off gradually and safely.

Risks and Side Effects. MAOIs can also cause a number of other unwanted effects. Possible side effects include drowsiness, constipation, nausea, diarrhea, fatigue, dry mouth, dizziness, lightheadedness upon standing, low blood pressure, decreased urination, sexual problems, muscle twitching, increased appetite, weight gain, sleep problems, blurred vision, headache, restlessness, shakiness, weakness, and sweating.

Certain medications, including many decongestants, can interact with MAOIs to raise blood pressure dangerously high. To be on the safe side, people on MAOIs should check with their doctor before taking any new prescription medication, over-the-counter medicine, or dietary supplement.

Serotonin syndrome is a rare but potentially life-threatening drug reaction that can occur when serotonin levels build up to dangerously high levels in the body. This most often occurs when people combine two drugs that each raise serotonin levels. To avoid this problem, people on MAOIs should be sure to tell their doctor about any other prescription medications, over-the-counter medicines, or herbal supplements they are taking.

Antidepressants may save lives by reducing depression and thus decreasing the risk of **suicide**. In a small number of **children**, **adolescents**, and young adults, though, taking antidepressants may actually lead to worsening mood symptoms or increased suicidal thoughts and behavior. Patients taking MAOIs—or parents of younger patients—should be alert for any suicidal thoughts and actions or unusual changes in mood and behavior. If such symptoms occur, they should contact their doctor right away.

See also: Antidepressant Discontinuation Syndrome; Antidepressants and Suicide; Monoamine Hypothesis; Treatment of Depression

Bibliography

FDA Approves Emsam (Selegiline) as First Drug Patch for Depression. Food and Drug Administration, February 28, 2006, http://www.fda.gov/NewsEvents/Newsroom/PressAnnouncements/2006/ucm108607.htm.

Gitlin, Michael J. "Pharmacotherapy and Other Somatic Treatments for Depression." In *Handbook of Depression*. 2nd ed., by Ian H. Gotlib and Constance L. Hammen, eds., 554–585. New York: Guilford Press, 2009.

Hall-Flavin, Daniel K. *MAOIs and Diet: Is It Necessary to Restrict Tyramine?* Mayo Clinic, September 3, 2008, http://www.mayoclinic.com/health/maois/HQ01575.

Isocarboxazid. National Library of Medicine, September 1, 2008, http://www.nlm.nih.gov/medlineplus/druginfo/meds/a605036.html.

Medication Information Sheet. Depression and Bipolar Support Alliance, May 4, 2006, http://www.dbsalliance.org/site/PageServer?pagename=about_treatment_medinfosheet.

Mental Health Medications. National Institute of Mental Health, July 28, 2009, http://www.nimh.nih.gov/health/publications/mental-health-medications/complete-index.shtml.

Monoamine Oxidase Inhibitors (MAOIs). Mayo Clinic, December 10, 2008, http://www.mayoclinic.com/health/maois/MH00072.

Rao, T. S. Sathyanarayana, and Vikram K. Yeragani. "Hypertensive Crisis and Cheese." *Indian Journal of Psychiatry* 51 (2009): 65–66.

MONTGOMERY-ÅSBERG DEPRESSION RATING SCALE. The Montgomery-Åsberg Depression Rating Scale (MADRS) is an interview-based test administered by a health care provider. It assesses the severity of symptoms in people who have already been diagnosed with **major depression**. The MADRS was introduced in 1978 by British psychiatrist Stuart A. Montgomery and Swedish psychiatrist Marie Åsberg. Their primary goal was to develop a scale that would be highly sensitive to differentiating the effect of treatment from the placebo effect, a response to an inactive substance (such as a sugar pill) or nonspecific intervention.

In well-controlled treatment studies, one group of participants is given a placebo to see how much of any observed improvement is due to the expectation of getting better rather than to the treatment itself. To show that a treatment is effective, researchers have to demonstrate that it leads to a positive change over and above that caused by the placebo effect. The MADRS is useful for gauging this type of change in symptom severity.

The MADRS is designed to be used by both mental health professionals and health care providers without specific mental health training. A high correlation has been reported between scores obtained by psychiatrists and non-psychiatrist doctors evaluating the same patients.

The MADRS consists of a 10-item checklist that takes about 15 minutes to complete. For each item, a series of sentences are presented that describe a particular symptom of depression in increasing order of severity. A nine-item self-report version, designed to be filled out by patients themselves, has also been developed.

Pros and Cons of the MADRS. Studies have shown that the MADRS has acceptable reliability, the extent to which results are consistent and repeatable, as well as good validity, the degree to which it actually measures what it purports to measure. Research has found that the self-rated version does as well as the popular **Beck Depression Inventory** at discriminating between symptoms of depression and anxiety, and it does a better job at differentiating between mood symptoms and underlying personality traits.

One problem with the original MADRS is that it doesn't specify the timeframe over which symptoms have occurred. Yet timeframe may be an important indicator of symptom severity. For instance, poor sleep for a week indicates a more serious sleep problem than poor sleep for two nights. The self-rated version of the MADRS addresses this problem by asking people to report how they have felt during the past three days.

See also: Diagnosis of Depression

Bibliography

Åsberg, M., S. A. Montgomery, C. Perris, D. Schalling, and G. Sedvall. "A Comprehensive Psychopathological Rating Scale." *Acta Psychiatrica Scandinavica* 271 (1978): 5–27.

Dew, Mary Amanda, Galen E. Switzer, Larissa Myaskovsky, Andrea F. DiMartini, and Marianna I. Tovt-Korshynska. "Rating Scales for Mood Disorders." In *The American Psychiatric Publishing Textbook of Mood Disorders,* by Dan J. Stein, David J. Kupfer and Alan F. Schatzberg, eds., 69–97. Washington, DC: American Psychiatric Publishing, 2006.

Montgomery, S. A., and M. Asberg. "A New Depression Scale Designed to Be Sensitive to Change." *British Journal of Psychiatry* 134 (1979): 382–389.

Yonkers, Kimberly A., and Jacqueline A. Samson. "Mood Disorders Measures." In *Handbook of Psychiatric Measures,* 2nd ed., by A. John Rush Jr., Michael B. First, and Deborah Blacker, eds., 499–528. Washington, DC: American Psychiatric Publishing, 2008.

MOOD. A mood is a general predisposition to respond emotionally in a certain way that lasts for hours, days, or even much longer. Common examples of moods include depression, elation, anger, and anxiety. When moods—especially depression or exaggerated elation—become seriously distressing or dysfunctional, they are known as **mood disorders**.

Moods are closely related to emotions. However, an **emotion** is a more short-lived and specific response to a personally meaningful situation. In contrast, a mood is longer lasting and more wide ranging. One way to think of the difference: Emotions fluctuate like the weather, but moods are more sustained and pervasive, like the climate.

Euthymia is the medical term for a relatively tranquil mood in the normal range that is neither excessively low nor excessively high. It can be distinguished from **dysphoria** and euphoria. Dysphoria is an unpleasant mood characterized by feelings such as sadness, **irritability**, or anxiety. An exaggerated degree of dysphoria is the hallmark of **major depression**, which involves feeling sad or dejected almost all the time or losing interest in almost everything.

Euphoria is a pleasant mood characterized by feelings such as happiness and well-being. An exaggerated degree of euphoria that is out of proportion to real-life circumstances is the hallmark of **mania**, which involves feelings that are overly high or wildly unrestrained.

See also: Depressed Mood

Bibliography

American Psychiatric Association. *Diagnostic and Statistical Manual of Mental Disorders.* 4th ed., text rev. Washington, DC: American Psychiatric Association, 2000.

Frances, Allen, Michael B. First, and Harold Alan Pincus. *DSM-IV Guidebook.* Washington, DC: American Psychiatric Press, 1995.

MOOD DISORDER DUE TO A GENERAL MEDICAL CONDITION. A "mood disorder due to a general medical condition" is a pronounced and long-lasting disturbance in **mood** that is the direct physiological consequence of a general medical illness. The disorder may take the form of depression (an overly low mood), **mania** (an overly high mood), or a mixture of both. A variety of medical conditions can give rise to such symptoms, including **Parkinson's disease, stroke, vitamin B12** deficiency, thyroid disease, and **cancer** of the pancreas.

It is no simple matter to determine which cases of depression are physiologically caused by another medical illness. Take the example of **diabetes**. Some studies indicate that people with diabetes are twice as likely to develop depression as those without the disease. The link could be physiological, because the same stress **hormones** that help regulate blood sugar may play a role in regulating mood. But the link could also be psychological, because having a chronic disease can create considerable **stress** in someone's life.

To get to the root of the problem, health care professionals must become disease detectives. They look for clues that the depression is the direct physiological result of another medical ailment. Typically, depression due to a general medical condition arises soon after the start of the medical illness. The severity of the mood symptoms may follow the course of the medical illness as it gets better or worse. Sometimes the depression has uncommon features. For instance, an older adult with no personal or family history of mood disorders might suddenly become deeply depressed.

If a person's depression seems to be caused by another medical illness, getting treatment for that illness is obviously critical. However, getting **psychotherapy** and/or taking **antidepressants** to treat the depression may be just as important. Research shows that such approaches still help, although finding the best treatment plan for a particular individual may be a bit more challenging once other medical problems are in the picture.

Criteria for Diagnosis. The symptoms of a mood disorder due to a general medical condition are defined by the ***Diagnostic and Statistical Manual of Mental Disorders, Fourth Edition, Text Revision*** (*DSM-IV-TR*), a diagnostic guidebook published by the American Psychiatric Association and used by mental health professionals from many disciplines. According to the *DSM-IV-TR*, this type of mood disorder is characterized by a prominent and persistent disturbance in mood. Evidence that the mood problems are directly due to the physiological effects of another medical illness can be found in the person's health history, physical exam, or lab tests.

The mood disturbance is serious enough to cause distress or problems in daily life. It can take four forms: depressive features, major depression-like episode, manic features, or mixed features.

Depressive Features. Depression is the dominant mood. However, the full criteria are not met for an episode of **major depression**.

Major Depression-like Episode. All the criteria for an episode of major depression are met, except that the root cause is another medical illness.

Manic Features. Mania dominates, characterized by an overly high, grandiose, or irritable mood.

Mixed Features. Symptoms of both depression and mania are present, but neither is dominant.

Treatment Considerations. Psychotherapy and medication are the standard treatments for depression, and depression caused by a medical illness is no exception. Theoretically, the exact type of therapy or antidepressant that works best might be affected by the underlying medical problem. In fact, this is the rationale for distinguishing depression due to a general medical condition from other forms of depression. Unfortunately, relatively little research has been done to pinpoint the most effective treatments when depression is caused by one medical condition or another. This is an area in which more research is sorely needed.

See also: Hypothyroidism; Mood Disorders; Neurological Disorders; Physical Illness

Bibliography

American Psychiatric Association. *Diagnostic and Statistical Manual of Mental Disorders.* 4th ed., text rev. Washington, DC: American Psychiatric Association, 2000.

Boland, Robert. "Depression in Medical Illness (Secondary Depression)." In *The American Psychiatric Publishing Textbook of Mood Disorders,* by Dan J. Stein, David J. Kupfer, and Alan F. Schatzberg, eds., 639–652. Washington, DC: American Psychiatric Publishing, 2006.

MOOD DISORDERS. Mood disorders are mental disorders in which the dominant feature is a disturbance in **mood**. A mood is a general predisposition to respond emotionally in a certain way that lasts for hours, days, or even much longer. When depression, elation, anger, or anxiety is pervasive and sustained, it can be considered a mood. However, the term "mood disorder" traditionally is reserved for people with a disturbed mood that is characterized by depression or out-of-control elation. Disorders that fall within this category include **major depression**, **dysthymia**, **bipolar disorder**, and **cyclothymia**.

Major depression involves being in a sad or irritable mood nearly all the time and/or losing interest or enjoyment in almost everything. In major depression, these feelings last for at least two weeks, are associated with several other symptoms, and lead to serious problems getting along in everyday life. Dysthymia is major depression's less intense cousin. It involves being mildly depressed most of the day. These feelings occur more days than not for at least two years and are associated with other symptoms. Although the symptoms of dysthymia are milder, they can still cause a lot of misery because they hang around for such a long time.

Bipolar disorder is a mood disorder in which periods of depression alternate with periods of **mania**, an overly high mood. Mania is a classic case of too much of a good thing. Elation is exaggerated to the point where it can lead to wildly irrational thinking, dangerous risk taking, or out-of-control bouts of nonstop activity and sleeplessness. Cyclothymia involves cycling between milder periods of depression and mania. Although the symptoms are more subdued, the pattern lasts for at least a year, with any intermittent periods of normal mood lasting no longer than two months at a time.

Everyone has ups and downs in mood, but mood disorders go well beyond these normal fluctuations. They last a long time and cause serious distress or significant problems. With proper treatment, however, most people with even the most severe mood disorders can enjoy fruitful and fulfilling lives.

Who's Who of Mood Disorders

Mood disorders are serious illnesses, but they are not insurmountable obstacles to a successful life. Nothing proves that point more effectively than the roster of eminent individuals who are believed to have suffered from mood disorders. The list below is just the tip of the iceberg.

	Born	**Died**	**Nationality**	**Occupation**
Abraham Lincoln	1809	1865	U.S.	Politician
Art Buchwald	1925	2007	U.S.	Humorist
Charles Dickens	1812	1870	British	Author
Charlie Parker	1920	1955	U.S.	Musician
Cole Porter	1891	1964	U.S.	Songwriter
Edvard Munch	1863	1944	Norwegian	Painter
Ernest Hemingway	1899	1961	U.S.	Author
Eugene O'Neill	1888	1953	U.S.	Playwright
F. Scott Fitzgerald	1896	1940	U.S.	Author
Friedrich Nietzsche	1844	1900	German	Philosopher
George Frideric Handel	1685	1759	German-born British	Composer

Who's Who of Mood Disorder (cont.)

	Born	**Died**	**Nationality**	**Occupation**
Georgia O'Keeffe	1887	1986	U.S.	Painter
Hans Christian Andersen	1805	1875	Danish	Author
Ingmar Bergman	1918	2007	Swedish	Film director
Irving Berlin	1888	1989	Russian-born U.S.	Composer
Isaac Newton	1642	1727	British	Physicist and mathematician
Jackson Pollock	1912	1956	U.S.	Painter
John Stuart Mill	1806	1873	British	Philosopher and economist
Julian Huxley	1887	1975	British	Biologist
Mark Twain (Samuel Clemens)	1835	1910	U.S.	Author
Martin Luther	1483	1546	German	Theologian
Michelangelo	1475	1564	Italian	Sculptor and painter
Noel Coward	1899	1973	British	Playwright, actor, and composer
Paul Gauguin	1848	1903	French	Painter
Pyotr Tchaikovsky	1840	1893	Russian	Composer
Ralph Waldo Emerson	1803	1882	U.S.	Philosopher and author
Robert Schumann	1810	1856	German	Composer
Sergey Rachmaninoff	1873	1943	Russian	Composer and musician
Søren Kierkegaard	1813	1855	Danish	Philosopher
Tennessee Williams	1911	1983	U.S.	Playwright
Vincent van Gogh	1853	1890	Dutch	Painter
Virginia Woolf	1882	1941	British	Author
William Faulkner	1897	1962	U.S.	Author
William James	1842	1910	U.S.	Psychologist and philosopher
Winston Churchill	1874	1965	British	Politician

What Are Affective Disorders? Affect, used as a noun, refers to any experience of feeling or emotion. In the third edition of the *Diagnostic and Statistical Manual of Mental Disorders* (*DSM-III*), published in 1980, the conditions mentioned above were grouped together in a category called affective disorders. Rather confusingly, though, an affective disorder was defined in the manual as "a disturbance in mood, accompanied by a full or partial manic or depressive syndrome, that is not due to any other physical or mental disorder." So although the name of the category emphasized affect, the definition emphasized mood. A revised version of the manual (*DSM-III-R*) published in 1987 redressed this inconsistency. It kept the same definition, but rechristened the category mood disorders—the name in use today.

The term "affective disorder" is no longer used to designate a *DSM* category, but it still turns up in other contexts. It has survived in the names of **seasonal affective disorder** and **schizoaffective disorder**. And it is sometimes used as an umbrella term covering both mood disorders and **anxiety disorders**. Because these disorders often exist side by side and cause overlapping symptoms, it frequently makes sense to discuss them together, and calling them affective disorders makes that easier.

See also: Creativity

Further Information.   International Society for Affective Disorders, www.isad.org.uk.

Bibliography

American Psychiatric Association. *Diagnostic and Statistical Manual of Mental Disorders.* 3rd ed. Washington, DC: American Psychiatric Association, 1980.

American Psychiatric Association. *Diagnostic and Statistical Manual of Mental Disorders.* 3rd ed., rev. Washington, DC: American Psychiatric Association, 1987.

American Psychiatric Association. *Diagnostic and Statistical Manual of Mental Disorders.* 4thed., text rev. Washington, DC: American Psychiatric Association, 2000.

Frances, Allen, Michael B. First, and Harold Alan Pincus. *DSM-IV Guidebook.* Washington, DC: American Psychiatric Press, 1995.

Jamison, Kay Redfield. *Touched with Fire: Manic-Depressive Illness and the Artistic Temperament.* New York: Free Press, 1993.

U.S. Department of Health and Human Services. *Mental Health: A Report of the Surgeon General.* Rockville, MD: U.S. Department of Health and Human Services, 1999.

MOOD STABILIZERS.   Mood stabilizers are medications that help keep moods on a more even keel. The medications are typically prescribed for **bipolar disorder**, a mental disorder characterized by extreme shifts in mood, energy, and ability to function. People with bipolar disorder alternate between an excessively high mood (**mania**) and an excessively low one (depression). Mood stabilizers can help get mania under control, and some can also help prevent the next bout of mania or depression.

In addition, mood stabilizers are sometimes prescribed for people with **major depression** who do not get enough relief from antidepressant medication alone. Adding a mood stabilizer to the antidepressant may boost its effectiveness.

There are two main types of mood-stabilizing medication. **Lithium**, the first and best-known type, is in a class by itself. It is highly effective, but the dosage must be calibrated carefully. **Anticonvulsants**, the second type, were originally developed to prevent seizures, but they help control moods as well. Different anticonvulsants vary in their effectiveness for treating bipolar disorder. The evidence is strongest for carbamazepine, valproic acid (also called divalproex sodium), and lamotrigine.

Treatment with a mood stabilizer works best when it is continuous, rather than on and off. Because bipolar disorder is a chronic condition that can be managed but not cured, people may need to keep taking medication for the rest of their lives. Those who discontinue their medication are at high risk for having symptoms return or seeing minor episodes turn into full-blown mania or depression. Even with non-stop medication, some mood episodes may still occur, but mood stabilizers can help reduce their frequency and severity.

Mood stabilizers can cause a number of unwanted side effects. In rare cases, these effects can be serious or even life-threatening. In addition, mood stabilizers can interact with numerous other drugs. To minimize the risks, it is important to take the medication exactly as directed.

See also: Pharmacotherapy

Bibliography

Bipolar Disorder: Treatments and Drugs. Mayo Clinic, January 4, 2008, http://www.mayoclinic.com/
health/bipolar-disorder/DS00356/DSECTION=treatments-and-drugs.
Medication Information Sheet. Depression and Bipolar Support Alliance, May 4, 2006, http://www
.dbsalliance.org/site/PageServer?pagename=about_treatment_medinfosheet.
Mental Health Medications. National Institute of Mental Health, July 28, 2009, http://www
.nimh.nih.gov/health/publications/mental-health-medications/complete-index.shtml.
*Treating Bipolar Disorder, Nerve Pain, and Fibromyalgia: The Anticonvulsants—Comparing Effective-
ness, Safety, and Price.* Consumer Reports, September 2007, http://www.consumerreports.org/
health/best-buy-drugs/anticonvulsants.htm.

MULTIPLE SCLEROSIS.   Multiple sclerosis (MS) is a disease of the central **nervous system** in which communication between the brain and the rest of the body is disrupted. Depression is common, affecting about 50 percent to 60 percent of people with MS to some degree.

Left untreated, depression can take much of the fun out of life. Being depressed also makes it harder for people with MS to stick to their treatment plan. In addition, the risk of **suicide** among those with MS is up to seven times higher than in the population at large.

Sadly, about one-third of people with MS who have **major depression** or suicidal thoughts are never treated for these problems. Yet depression in MS, like depression in general, is quite treatable with **antidepressants**, **psychotherapy**, or both. With proper care for depression, most people can feel better and enjoy richer, more satisfying lives.

The Depression Connection.   In MS, the body mistakenly attacks proteins in the myelin sheath, the fatty covering that insulates nerve fibers in the brain and spinal cord. This leads to **inflammation** and injury to the sheath and ultimately damage to the nerves it surrounds. The damage can slow or block the transmission of nerve signals that control various bodily functions. Symptoms vary widely, based on the site of the affected nerves. In addition to depression, they may include muscle weakness, vision problems, shaking, lack of coordination, unsteady gait, fatigue, dizziness, slurred speech, tingling or pain, periods of uncontrollable laughing or crying, and problems with bladder function.

Such symptoms range from mild to severe. In the worst cases, they can be permanently disabling, leaving a person unable to walk, speak, or write. The unpredictability of the disease and its potential for causing serious disability can contribute to **stress** and depression.

The connection between MS and depression seems to be more than just psychological, however. Depression may result from the MS disease process itself, if damage occurs in areas of the brain that are involved in regulating emotions. There is also some evidence that depression may be associated with MS-related changes in the **immune system**. Research has found an association between depression and the production of inflammation-promoting proteins by certain immune cells.

Medications used to treat MS may play a role as well. Beta interferons, medications that help regulate the immune system, are sometimes prescribed to help manage MS flare-ups. These medications reduce levels of **serotonin**, a brain chemical linked to depression. Some doctors suspect that the medications might trigger or worsen depression in susceptible individuals, although research on the subject has yielded conflicting results.

Diagnostic Challenges.   Depression and MS have several symptoms in common. Both can cause fatigue, restless activity, slowed-down movements, sleep problems, and trouble concentrating. As a result, patients and even doctors may not recognize depression for what it is at first.

To diagnose depression, health care professionals look for a low mood or loss of interest and enjoyment that persists for weeks or months. The mood hangs on even when something good happens. But often the depressive symptoms are at their worst during MS flare-ups.

Treatment Considerations. MS is a highly variable disease, and treatment depends on the form it takes for a particular individual. For some with mild or infrequent symptoms, a wait-and-see approach may be advised. For others, medications may help control symptoms or delay the worsening of disability. Physical and occupational therapy also can help people stay as active as possible.

When depression is diagnosed, **cognitive-behavioral therapy** can help people learn to cope with illness and manage stress better. Antidepressants are often prescribed as well. Some of these medications may also reduce other MS-related symptoms, including fatigue, pain, bladder control problems, and episodes of uncontrollable laughing or crying.

See also: Mood Disorder Due to a General Medical Condition; Neurological Disorders; Physical Illness

Further Information. Multiple Sclerosis Association of America, 706 Haddonfield Road, Cherry Hill, NJ 08002, (800)532-7667, www.msassociation.org.

Multiple Sclerosis Foundation, 6350 N. Andrews Avenue, Fort Lauderdale, FL 33309, (800) 225-6495, www.msfocus.org.

National Institute of Neurological Disorders and Stroke, P.O. Box 5801, Bethesda, MD 20824, (800) 352-9424, www.ninds.nih.gov.

National Multiple Sclerosis Society, 700 Broadway, Suite 810, Denver, CO 80203, (800) 344-4867, www.nationalmssociety.org.

Bibliography

Boland, Robert. "Depression in Medical Illness (Secondary Depression)." In *The American Psychiatric Publishing Textbook of Mood Disorders,* by Dan J. Stein, David J. Kupfer, and Alan F. Schatzberg, eds., 639–652. Washington, DC: American Psychiatric Publishing, 2006.

Bourdette, Dennis. "Depression Is a Treatable Cause of Suffering Among Multiple Sclerosis Patients and Can Result in Suicide." *Neurology* 59 (2002): 6–7.

Depression. National Multiple Sclerosis Society, http://www.nationalmssociety.org/about-multiple -sclerosis/symptoms/depression/index.aspx.

Depression and Multiple Sclerosis. National Multiple Sclerosis Society, 2007, http://www .nationalmssociety.org/multimedia-library/brochures/managing-specific-issues/download .aspx?id=53.

Mohr, David C., and Darcy Cox. "Multiple Sclerosis: Empirical Literature for the Clinical Health Psychologist." *Journal of Clinical Psychology* 57 (2001): 479–499.

Mohr, David C., Donald E. Goodkin, Janeen Islar, Stephen L. Hauser, and Claude P. Genain. "Treatment of Depression Is Associated with Suppression of Nonspecific and Antigen-Specific TH1 Responses in Multiple Sclerosis." *Archives of Neurology* 58 (2001): 1081–1086.

Multiple Sclerosis. Mayo Clinic, December 6, 2006, http://www.mayoclinic.com/health/multiple -sclerosis/DS00188.

Multiple Sclerosis: Hope Through Research. National Institute of Neurological Disorders and Stroke, August 13, 2008, http://www.ninds.nih.gov/disorders/multiple_sclerosis/detail_multiple _sclerosis.htm.

MUSIC THERAPY. Music therapy is a treatment approach in which a specially trained professional uses music to enhance the psychological, physical, mental, and/or social well-being of clients. This approach is sometimes used in addition to **psychotherapy** or

antidepressants to help treat depression. Although research is limited, the available evidence suggests that music therapy plus standard care can lead to a greater mood boost than standard care alone.

Listening to music has the power to evoke strong emotions. Many people have noticed this, for instance, when they hear the song that was playing during their first kiss or a hymn that was sung at a loved one's funeral. Playing music also can be a mode of expression for some people who have trouble putting their feelings into words. Music therapy makes use of both listening to music and playing it, depending on the abilities and needs of the client.

The overall goal of music therapy is to harness the power of music for therapeutic purposes. This approach has been applied to the treatment of a wide range of mental and physical health conditions—not only depression, but also developmental disabilities, learning disorders, Alzheimer's disease, **substance abuse** problems, brain injuries, chronic pain, and childbirth.

Historical Roots. The notion that music can be healing has been around for millennia. Ancient Greek philosophers Plato (428/427 BC–348/347 BC) and Aristotle (384 BC–322 BC) both mention it in their writings.

The modern field of music therapy began after World Wars I and II, when amateur and professional musicians played for ailing veterans at hospitals around the country. It soon became evident that the musicians needed special training to work with veterans who had suffered both physical and emotional trauma. In response to this need, the first music therapy degree program was founded at Michigan State University in 1944.

The Process at a Glance. Both instrumental and vocal music are used in music therapy. Clients take part in activities such as listening to recordings, playing instruments, writing songs, and discussing lyrics. The type of music is individualized to suit each person's needs and preferences, and the nature and extent of the response is based on factors such as the familiarity and predictability of the music as well as feelings of relaxation and security associated with it. No musical ability or training is required to participate in the therapy.

Music therapy differs from simple entertainment or recreation because it is guided by a trained professional who can help the client work toward specific therapeutic goals. Music therapists must complete an approved college program including an internship. Those who meet educational and clinical training standards are granted the RMT, CMT, or ACMT designation by the National Music Therapy Registry. Some music therapists also sit for a national exam offered by the Certification Board for Music Therapists. Those who pass receive the board-certified credential (MT-BC).

Music therapists often are part of an interdisciplinary team that might also include a psychotherapist and/or physician. They work in a variety of settings, including psychiatric and medical hospitals, rehabilitation centers, outpatient clinics, community mental health centers, drug and alcohol programs, nursing homes, schools, and private practice.

The Brain's Response to Music. The exact mechanism by which music has its positive effects is still unknown. However, **brain imaging** studies have shown that music activates specific pathways in several areas of the brain that are associated with emotional behavior, including the **hypothalamus**, **hippocampus**, **amygdala**, and **prefrontal cortex**.

In addition, several brain chemicals seem to be involved in the perception and emotional processing of music. **Dopamine**, which is thought to play a key role in the natural response to pleasant stimuli, may be involved in the enjoyment of music. This could be significant, because levels of dopamine seem to fall during depression in people with bipolar disorder. Music also may promote the release of **endorphins**, protein-like compounds that have natural pain-relieving and mood-elevating effects.

Benefits for Depression. A recent review looked at five small studies in which music therapy was used as a treatment for depression. Four reported a greater reduction in symptoms of depression among people who received music therapy plus standard care, compared to those who received a treatment that did not involve music. The fifth study did not find this effect, however. More and larger studies are needed before any firm conclusions can be drawn.

In the meantime, music therapy by a trained professional has few risks for those who choose to try it. Many people find music relaxing, and some studies have found that music therapy can reduce heart rate, blood pressure, and breathing rate—physiological functions that increase during **stress**. Research also suggests that music therapy may decrease insomnia and anxiety—two common problems among people with depression.

Further Information. American Music Therapy Association, 8455 Colesville Road, Suite 1000, Silver Spring, MD 20910, (301) 589-3300, www.musictherapy.org.

Certification Board for Music Therapists, 506 East Lancaster Avenue, Suite 102, Downingtown, PA 19335, (800) 765-2268, www.cbmt.org.

Bibliography

Boso, Marianna, Pierluigi Politi, Francesco Barale, and Enzo Emanuele. "Neurophysiology and Neurobiology of the Musical Experience." *Functional Neurology* 21 (2006): 187–191.

Frequently Asked Questions About Music Therapy. American Music Therapy Association, 1999, http://www.musictherapy.org/faqs.html.

Maratos, A. S., C. Gold, X. Wang, and M. J. Crawford. "Music Therapy for Depression (Review)." *Cochrane Database of Systematic Reviews* 1 (2008): art. no. CD004517.

Music Therapy. American Cancer Society, March 26, 2007, http://www.cancer.org/docroot/ETO/content/ETO_5_3X_Music_Therapy.asp?sitearea=ETO.

N

NATIONAL ALLIANCE FOR RESEARCH ON SCHIZOPHRENIA AND DEPRESSION.

NATIONAL ALLIANCE FOR RESEARCH ON SCHIZOPHRENIA AND DEPRESSION. The National Alliance for Research on Schizophrenia and Depression (NARSAD) is a charitable organization dedicated to research on a wide range of mental illnesses. It was formed in 1981 by three leading mental health organizations: the National Alliance for the Mentally Ill (now the **National Alliance on Mental Illness**), the National Mental Health Association (now **Mental Health America**), and the National Depressive and Manic Depressive Association (now the **Depression and Bipolar Support Alliance**). By combining the forces of these three large groups, NARSAD immediately became a prominent private research organization in the mental health field.

As its name implies, NARSAD funds research on schizophrenia and depression. However, it also now supports research on other mental disorders, including **bipolar disorder**, **anxiety disorders**, **attention-deficit hyperactivity disorder**, and autism. To emphasize its broader mission, the organization later adopted a new business name: NARSAD, The World's Leading Charity Dedicated to Mental Health Research.

Since its inception, NARSAD has given over $234 million and more than 3,400 grants to researchers. The resulting research has increased scientific understanding of brain development and function. NARSAD has also provided continuing support as research findings were applied to developing new diagnostic and treatment approaches.

Some current NARSAD projects are using the latest advances from the human genome project to explore the relationship between genetics, the environment, and **mental illness**. Others are using sophisticated **brain imaging** techniques to view the brain at work. Such research today carries the promise of a brighter tomorrow for people with depression and other mental disorders.

Further Information. National Alliance for Research on Schizophrenia and Depression, 60 Cutter Mill Road, Suite 404, Great Neck, New York 11021, (516) 829-0091, www.narsad.org.

Bibliography

History and Accomplishments. National Alliance for Research on Schizophrenia and Depression, http://www.narsad.org/about/history.

What We Do. National Alliance for Research on Schizophrenia and Depression, http://www.narsad.org/about/whatwedo.

NATIONAL ALLIANCE ON MENTAL ILLNESS.   The National Alliance on Mental Illness (NAMI) is the largest grassroots organization in the United States for people with **mental illness** and their families. Founded in 1979, it now has 1,200 local affiliates spanning all 50 states, the District of Columbia, Puerto Rico, the Virgin Islands, and Canada. These local affiliates usually start out as **support groups** that seek to become part of the NAMI network as they grow. NAMI also operates a state organization in every state as well as a national office.

NAMI originally stood for National Alliance for the Mentally Ill. The organization's corporate name was changed to simply NAMI in 1997 due to concerns that the full name was not person-first language—in other words, language that recognizes that individuals with disabilities are people first and not defined by their condition. Thus, saying "people with mental illness" is considered more appropriate than saying "the mentally ill." In 2005, the meaning of the NAMI acronym was changed to its current form to remove any stigmatizing association with the name.

In addition to support groups, NAMI offers a variety of educational programs that help mental health consumers and their families gain knowledge and skills needed for living successfully with mental illness. The organization also sponsors a telephone helpline that serves over 4,000 callers per month. Signature programs include NAMIWalks, in which thousands of individuals from across the country walk to raise money and awareness, and In Our Own Voice, in which people with mental illness make presentations about what is involved in **recovery**. StigmaBusters is another NAMI program that responds to inaccurate and hurtful media portrayals of mental illness.

NAMI advocates for state and federal legislation as well as private-sector policies aimed at advancing research, fighting discrimination, and promoting mental health services and supports. NAMI Action Centers advocate for causes that are of special interest to specific groups. They include the Child and Adolescent Action Center, the Multicultural Action Center, and the Law and Criminal Justice Action Center.

See also: Stigma

Further Information.   National Alliance on Mental Illness, 2107 Wilson Boulevard, Suite 300, Arlington, VA 22201, (800) 950-6264, www.nami.org.

Bibliography

About NAMI. National Alliance on Mental Illness, http://www.nami.org/Template.cfm?Section =About_Nami.

Frequently Asked Questions. National Alliance on Mental Illness, http://www.nami.org/Template .cfm?Section=Frequently_Asked_Questions&Template=/ContentManagement/Contentdisplay .cfm&ContentID=14425.

NAMI at the Local, State and National Levels. National Alliance on Mental Illness, http://www.nami .org/template.cfm?section=state_and_local_organizations.

NATIONAL DEPRESSION SCREENING DAY.   National Depression Screening Day is an annual event held during Mental Illness Awareness Week each October. The event was launched in 1991 by Screening for Mental Health, a nonprofit organization that pioneered large-scale screening for mental health problems. On National Depression Screening Day, health care providers, workplaces, colleges, and military bases around the United States offer free, anonymous screenings. The event educates people about the symptoms of depression and warning signs of suicide.

In 2007, over 1,700 sites participated in National Depression Screening Day. About 86,000 people attended related events, and more than 17,000 people were screened. Another 19,000 screenings were completed online. Participants learned how to identify signs of depression and access treatment for themselves or loved ones. Mental health professionals were available to speak with participants at no cost and with no appointment necessary.

Further Information.   Screening for Mental Health, One Washington Street, Suite 304, Wellesley Hills, MA 02481, (781) 239-0071, mentalhealthscreening.org.

Bibliography

National Depression Screening Day (NDSD) Presents Stops a Suicide Today. Screening for Mental Health, http://mentalhealthscreening.org/events/ndsd.

National Depression Screening Day. Mental Health America, November 16, 2006, http://www.nmha .org/go/depression-screening-day.

NATIONAL INSTITUTE OF MENTAL HEALTH.   The National Institute of Mental Health (NIMH) is one of the National Institutes of Health, the primary federal agency for conducting and supporting medical research in the United States. The specific mission of the NIMH is to reduce the burden of mental illness and behavioral disorders through research on the mind, the brain, and behavior.

About 500 scientists work for the NIMH's internal research program. Although guided by a rigorous peer review system, these scientists are given unique flexibility to follow up quickly on new findings. A dual focus on basic research and clinical trials encourages interdisciplinary studies. The NIMH also supports more than 2,000 research grants and contracts at institutions across the country and overseas.

To assess the current state of the science and plot a course for future action, the NIMH convened nine workgroups in 2001. These workgroups—composed of scientific experts, NIMH staff, and representatives of consumer and advocacy organizations—were charged with developing strategic plans for key research areas. *Breaking Ground, Breaking Through: The Strategic Plan for Mood Disorders Research* (2003) addressed six core topics related to **mood disorders**: brain science, genetics, behavior, treatment, prevention, and the mental health care system. It also noted special research needs for five segments of the population: **women**, **children**, **older adults**, members of racial and ethnic minority groups, and individuals who simultaneously have a mood disorder and another **physical illness**.

Further Information.   National Institute of Mental Health, 6001 Executive Boulevard, Room 8184, MSC 9663, Bethesda, MD 20892, (866) 615-6464, www.nimh .nih.gov.

Bibliography

About NIMH. National Institute of Mental Health, April 3, 2008, http://www.nimh.nih.gov/about/ index.shtml.

National Institute of Mental Health. *Breaking Ground, Breaking Through: The Strategic Plan for Mood Disorders Research.* Bethesda, MD: National Institute of Mental Health, 2003.

NEGATIVE ION THERAPY. Negative ion therapy is an experimental treatment for **seasonal affective disorder** (SAD), a form of **major depression** in which symptoms start and stop around the same time each year, typically beginning in fall or winter and subsiding in spring. Negative ions are charged particles that are always circulating in the air, and natural concentrations tend to be higher in the summer than in the winter. In negative ion therapy, a small electronic device produces charged air particles in an effort to mimic summer conditions.

The machine used for this treatment switches on automatically an hour to hour and a half before the person's wake-up time. The charged air particles it emits are imperceptible to the senses, and the exact route by which these particles might activate the brain remains unknown.

Natural levels of negative ions vary widely. They tend to be higher in humid environments, vegetated areas, and at the seashore, and lower in dry environments, urban areas, and heated or air-conditioned rooms. Studies of negative ion therapy indicate that relatively high concentrations may be needed to achieve any positive effects. (The level of ions infused into the air by some ordinary air purifiers may be too low.)

Benefits for Depression. Preliminary research suggests that treatment with high levels of negative ions can help relieve symptoms of SAD. In one study, 99 people with SAD were randomly assigned to receive three weeks of high-density negative ion therapy, low-density negative ion therapy, or various treatments using artificial light. High-density ionization worked about as well as either bright **light therapy** or **dawn simulation**, and significantly better than low-density ionization, indicating that it was an effective treatment.

One big advantage to negative ion therapy is that it can be done while the person sleeps, requiring no special effort beyond setting up the machine. Unlike dawn simulation, in which a timer gradually turns on a lamp during the final hour or two of sleep, it does not disturb a bed partner. But controlled research on negative ion therapy is still limited. More research is needed before it can be deemed a proven treatment.

Bibliography

DeAngelis, Tori. "Promising New Treatments for SAD." *Monitor on Psychology* (February 2006).

Frequently Asked Questions at CET. Center for Environmental Therapeutics, 2007, http://www.cet .org/q-and-a.htm.

Goel, Namni, Michael Terman, Jiuan Su Terman, Mariana M. Macchi, and Jonathan W. Stewart. "Controlled Trial of Bright Light and Negative Air Ions for Chronic Depression."

Terman, M., and J. S. Terman. "Treatment of Seasonal Affective Disorder with a High-Output Negative Ionizer." *Journal of Alternative and Complementary Medicine* 1 (1995): 87–92.

Terman, Michael, and Jiuan Su Terman. "Controlled Trial of Naturalistic Dawn Simulation and Negative Air Ionization for Seasonal Affective Disorder." *American Journal of Psychiatry* 163 (2006): 2126–2133.

Terman, Michael, and Jiuan Su Terman. "Light Therapy for Seasonal and Non-seasonal Depression: Efficacy, Protocol, Safety, and Side Effects." *CNS Spectrums* 10 (2005): 647–663.

Terman, Michael, Jiuan Su Terman, and Donald C. Ross. "A Controlled Trial of Timed Bright Light and Negative Air Ionization for Treatment of Winter Depression." *Archives of General Psychiatry* 55 (1998): 875–882.

NERVOUS SYSTEM. The nervous system is a complex network of cells, tissues, and organs that regulate the body's response to internal and external stimuli. It includes the brain, spinal cord, and nerves. When something goes wrong, it may affect sbasic bodily functions, such as movement, speech, breathing, and swallowing. Or it may cause problems with core mental functions, such as mood, learning, memory, and perception. The physiological roots of mental disorders, including depression, are grounded in a malfunction of this system.

The nervous system is organized into two major divisions: the central nervous system (CNS) and the peripheral nervous system (PNS). The CNS, which consists of the brain and spinal cord, is the main information-processing center of the body. The PNS, which consists of nerve tissue located outside the brain and spinal cord, carries information from the sense organs to the CNS and from the CNS to the voluntary muscles and glands.

Components of the CNS.   The brain is the body's command center. Much more complex than even the most sophisticated supercomputer, the human brain contains as many as 100 billion information-transmitting cells, called **neurons**. In most cases, these cells work together with marvelous efficiency to direct all the body's physical and mental activities. But as would be expected with any system this complicated, glitches sometimes occur. Depending on the nature, location, and extent of the problem, the result can be myriad forms of dysfunction and disease, including depression.

The brain is organized into three sections: forebrain, midbrain, and hindbrain. The largest section is the forebrain, which is responsible for all forms of conscious experience, including perception, emotion, thought, and planning. The forebrain also controls the pituitary gland and helps regulate sleep, appetite, and the activities of internal organs. The hindbrain helps control bodily activities such as breathing, heart rate, blood pressure, muscle tone, and the coordination of muscle movement. The midbrain is the main pathway for sensory and movement impulses passing between the forebrain and hindbrain, and it also coordinates visual and auditory reflexes.

The spinal cord is a thick cord of nerve tissue that extends from the hindbrain through the spinal column. It transmits information to and from the brain and the rest of the body. Sensory impulses received from the peripheral nerve endings are carried up the spinal cord to the brain, and movement impulses received from the brain are carried down the spinal cord to the peripheral nerve endings.

Divisions of the PNS.   The PNS has two main divisions: somatic and autonomic. The somatic nervous system connects the CNS to voluntary muscles and provides sensory feedback about movement. The autonomic nervous system (ANS) connects the CNS to internal organs responsible for involuntary bodily functions, such as circulation, breathing, and digestion. The ANS is itself comprised of two branches: sympathetic and parasympathetic.

The sympathetic nervous system mobilizes the body's energy and resources during times of **stress** and arousal. The parasympathetic nervous system, in contrast, conserves energy and resources when the body is relaxed. Studies have found that several markers of sympathetic activity tend to more pronounced in people with depression than in those who are not depressed. These markers include elevated blood levels of the hormone **norepinephrine**, higher heart rates, exaggerated heart rate responses to stress, and reduced beat-to-beat variability in the heart's rhythm.

Cells of the Nervous System.   The basic functional unit of the nervous system is the neuron, a cell that is specialized to send, receive, and process information. There are three types of **neurons**: sensory, motor, and interneurons. Sensory neurons detect environmental stimuli, such as light, sound, taste, or pressure. Motor neurons stimulate muscles to contract or relax and glands to release **hormones**. Interneurons act as a link between the other two types. Communication is lightning fast. It takes only milliseconds to pass a message from a sensory neuron through several interneurons to a motor neuron.

Although neurons are the stars of the nervous system, they are greatly outnumbered by **glial cells**, which have supporting roles. Some glia form myelin, an insulating sheath that surrounds certain axons, the fiber-like extensions on neurons that send messages. Other glia remove debris after neurons are injured or die. And still others direct the growth of axons during development or assist communication between neurons.

Role of Neurotransmitters. When a neuron is first activated, it sends an electrical signal from the cell body down an axon. Once the signal reaches the end of the axon, however, it faces a challenge. A tiny gap called a synapse exists between each neuron and its neighbor. Although a synapse is only about 20 millionths of a millimeter wide, the electrical signal is unable to get across. To cross the gap, a different delivery method is required.

That is where chemical messengers, called **neurotransmitters**, come into play. There are numerous types of neurotransmitters, each with a distinct chemical shape. To deliver its message, a neurotransmitter must dock at a specialized site, called a receptor, on the receiving cell. **Receptors** are designed to accept a specific type of neurotransmitter. Think of the receptor as a lock and the neurotransmitter as a key. The message can only be delivered if the two fit together properly.

Once a neurotransmitter matches up with a receptor, the message is transmitted to next cell's receiving branches, called dendrites. There it acts like an on or off switch in the receiving cell. If the message is excitatory, it tells the cell to switch on and keep relaying the signal. If the message is inhibitory, it tells the cell to switch off and suppress the signal. Either way, a message is received.

Three neurotransmitters have been singled out as key players in depression. **Serotonin** not only influences mood, but also helps regulate sleep, appetite, and sexual drive. Norepinephrine, which functions as a neurotransmitter as well as a hormone, is involved in the body's stress response and helps regulate arousal, sleep, and blood pressure. **Dopamine**, which is essential for movement, also influences motivation and the perception of reality.

Other Important Substances. Various other natural substances also affect how the nervous system works. Neurotrophic factors are small proteins in the brain needed for the growth and survival of specific groups of neurons. Scientists are currently exploring the role that one such substance, called **brain-derived neurotrophic factor**, may play in the development of depression.

Hormones carry chemical messages in the **endocrine system**, just as neurotransmitters do in the nervous system. These two sets of chemical messengers interact in complex ways to influence mental and physical functioning. Researchers are now studying how interactions within the **hypothalamic-pituitary-adrenal axis** may contribute to depression. This network is comprised of the **hypothalamus**, pituitary gland, and adrenal glands along with the substances they secrete.

See also: Brain Anatomy; Brain Physiology; Neurological Disorders

Further Information. American Academy of Neurology, 1080 Montreal Avenue, Saint Paul, MN 55116, (800) 879-1960, www.aan.com.

National Institute of Neurological Disorders and Stroke, P.O. Box 5801, Bethesda, MD 20824, (800) 352-9424, www.ninds.nih.gov.

Society for Neuroscience, 1121 14th Street N.W., Suite 1010, Washington, DC 20005, (202) 962-4000, www.sfn.org.

Bibliography

Brain Facts: A Primer on the Brain and Nervous System. 6th ed. Washington, DC: Society for Neuroscience, 2008.

Carney, Robert M., Kenneth E. Freedland, and Richard C. Veith. "Depression, the Autonomic Nervous System, and Coronary Heart Disease." *Psychosomatic Medicine* 67 (2005): S29–S33.

Information About the Brain. National Institute of Neurological Disorders and Stroke, http://science.education.nih.gov/supplements/nih4/Self/guide/info-brain.htm.

Taylor, Shelley E. *Health Psychology.* 4th ed. Boston: McGraw-Hill, 1999.

NEUROLOGICAL DISORDERS.   Neurological disorders affect the brain, spinal cord, and/or nerves. Taken together, these components of the **nervous system** control the workings of the body. When a disorder strikes, it can affect basic bodily functions, such as movement, speech, breathing, and swallowing. It also can cause problems with mood, learning, memory, and perception. Depression is common in many neurological disorders.

More than 600 neurological diseases have been identified, and it is estimated that one person in five has some type of damage to the nervous system. Major types of neurological disorders include (1) neurological conditions caused by faulty genes (such as Huntington's disease), (2) birth defects that lead to lifelong problems with the nervous system (such as spina bifida), (3) conditions that cause progressive deterioration of the nervous system (such as **Alzheimer's disease**), (4) problems with the blood vessels that supply the brain (such as a **stroke**), (5) trauma to the nervous system (such as traumatic brain injury), (6) conditions that cause seizures (such as **epilepsy**), (7) infections that affect the nervous system (such as meningitis), and (8) cancer that affects the nervous system (such as a brain tumor).

The Depression Connection.   In a "**mood disorder due to a general medical condition**," a general medical illness is the direct physiological cause of a pronounced, long-lasting disturbance in mood. Below are examples of neurological disorders that sometimes give rise to symptoms of depression.

Alzheimer's Disease.   Alzheimer's disease is an age-related brain disorder that leads to a progressive decline in memory and mental function as well as changes in personality and behavior. Up to 40 percent of people with Alzheimer's suffer from depression.

Brain Tumor.   A brain tumor is an abnormal mass of cells growing in the brain. Such tumors can be either cancerous or benign. Depending on a tumor's size, type, and location, it can produce a wide variety of symptoms, including mood changes.

Epilepsy.   In epilepsy, the normal pattern of electrical charges passing between nerve cells is disrupted by short bursts of high-intensity electrical activity. Prevalence estimates vary depending on how depression is defined, but when standardized methods are used, about 29 percent of people with epilepsy have **major depression**.

Huntington's Disease.   Huntington's disease is a genetic disorder in which certain nerve cells in the brain waste away. The disease can affect movement, thought, behavior, and emotions. About 40 percent to 50 percent of those with Huntington's experience depression.

Migraine.   A **migraine** is a type of headache characterized by intense pulsing or throbbing pain in one area of the head. Often the pain is accompanied by extreme sensitivity to light and sound as well as nausea and vomiting. People who get migraines are more than twice as likely to develop depression as the general population.

Multiple Sclerosis. **Multiple sclerosis** is a disease of the central nervous system in which communication between the brain and the rest of the body is disrupted. About 50 percent to 60 percent of people with MS experience depression to some degree.

Parkinson's Disease. **Parkinson's disease** is a degenerative disorder characterized by trembling of the face and limbs, stiffness of the limbs and trunk, slowed movement, and impaired balance. Up to 60 percent of people with Parkinson's have depressive symptoms.

Stroke. A stroke occurs when blood flow to part of the brain is interrupted, depriving brain tissue of vital oxygen and nutrients. About one-third of stroke survivors have serious problems with depressive symptoms during the post-stroke period.

Traumatic Brain Injury. A traumatic brain injury results when normal brain function is disrupted by a sudden blow or jolt to the head or a penetrating head wound. Such injuries can lead to a wide range of symptoms, including changes in thinking, sensation, language, or emotions. Depression is one possible consequence.

See also: Physical Illness

Further Information. American Academy of Neurology, 1080 Montreal Avenue, Saint Paul, MN 55116, (800) 879-1960, www.aan.com.

National Institute of Neurological Disorders and Stroke, P.O. Box 5801, Bethesda, MD 20824, (800) 352-9424, www.ninds.nih.gov.

Society for Neuroscience, 1121 14th Street N.W., Suite 1010, Washington, DC 20005, (202) 962-4000, www.sfn.org.

Bibliography

American Psychiatric Association. *Diagnostic and Statistical Manual of Mental Disorders.* 4th ed., text rev. Washington, DC: American Psychiatric Association, 2000.

Boland, Robert. "Depression in Medical Illness (Secondary Depression)." In *The American Psychiatric Publishing Textbook of Mood Disorders,* by Dan J. Stein, David J. Kupfer, and Alan F. Schatzberg, eds., 639–652. Washington, DC: American Psychiatric Publishing, 2006.

Bourdette, Dennis. "Depression Is a Treatable Cause of Suffering Among Multiple Sclerosis Patients and Can Result in Suicide." *Neurology* 59 (2002): 6–7.

Brain Basics: Know Your Brain. National Institute of Neurological Disorders and Stroke, May 1, 2007, http://www.ninds.nih.gov/disorders/brain_basics/know_your_brain.htm.

Depression. Parkinson's Disease Foundation, http://www.pdf.org/en/depression_pd.

Depression and Alzheimer's. Alzheimer's Association, http://www.alz.org/living_with_alzheimers _depression.asp.

Depression and Epilepsy. Epilepsy Foundation, http://www.epilepsyfoundation.org/answerplace/ Medical/related/Depression/epilepsy.cfm.

Hackett, Maree L., Chaturangi Yapa, Varsha Parag, and Craig S. Anderson. "Frequency of Depression After Stroke: A Systematic Review of Observational Studies." *Stroke* 36 (2005): 1330–1340.

Kaplan, Harold I., and Benjamin J. Saddock. *Pocket Handbook of Clinical Psychiatry.* 2nd ed. Baltimore: Williams and Wilkins, 1996.

Molgat, Carmen V., and Scott B. Patten. "Comorbidity of Major Depression and Migraine: A Canadian Population-Based Study." *Canadian Journal of Psychiatry* 50 (2005): 832–837.

Neurologic Diseases. National Library of Medicine, October 16, 2008, http://www.nlm.nih.gov/ medlineplus/neurologicdiseases.html.

Paulsen, Jane S., Carissa Nehl, Karin Ferneyhough Hoth, Jason E. Kanz, Michelle Benjamin, Rachel Conybeare, et al. "Depression and Stages of Huntington's Disease." *Journal of Neuropsychiatry and Clinical Neuroscience* 17 (2005): 496–502.

Traumatic Brain Injury: Hope Through Research. National Institute of Neurological Disorders and Stroke, September 15, 2008, http://www.ninds.nih.gov/disorders/tbi/detail_tbi.htm.

What You Need to Know About Brain Tumors. National Cancer Institute, March 31, 2003, http://www.cancer.gov/cancertopics/wyntk/brain.

NEURONS.   Neurons are nerve cells that send, receive, and process information. They are the basic functional units of the **nervous system**. All sensations, thoughts, memories, feelings, and movements are the result of signals that pass through neurons. A breakdown in the signaling process lies at the core of mental and neurological disorders, including depression.

The human brain contains as many as 100 billion neurons. Within each one, information is carried by electrical impulses. But to be passed from one neuron to the next, the message has to cross a tiny gap, called a synapse. To get across this gap, it must be carried by chemical messengers, called **neurotransmitters**.

There are three main types of neurons: sensory, motor, and interneurons. Sensory neurons detect environmental stimuli, such as light, sound, taste, or pressure. Motor neurons stimulate muscles to contract or relax and glands to release **hormones**. Interneurons link the other two types. Within these three main types, there are hundreds of different subtypes, each with its own specific communication abilities.

Parts of a Neuron.   A neuron is composed of three parts: a cell body, an axon, and dendrites.

Cell Body.   The cell body contains the nucleus, which controls the cell's activities and houses the cell's genetic material. Also within the cell body is cytoplasm, the term for living material outside the nucleus.

Axon.   The axon is the fiber-like sending extension of a neuron. It looks like a tail extending from the cell body, often splitting into many smaller branches. Each branch ends in a tiny sac called a terminal, where neurotransmitters are stored. Some axons are very short, such as those that send messages from one neuron to another less than a hair's breadth away. Others are very long, such as those that carry signals from the brain all the way down the spinal cord. Many axons are covered with an insulating sheath that helps nerve signals travel faster.

A neuron's ability to generate an electrical impulse depends on there being a difference in charge between the inside and outside of the cell. When a neuron is activated, it temporarily reverses the electrical state of its internal membrane from negative to positive. This change in electrical state, called an action potential, generates an impulse, which then races down the membrane of the axon at speeds up to several hundred miles per hour. The high speed means that a neuron may be able to fire many impulses in a single second.

Once the electrical impulse reaches the end of the axon, it triggers the release of neurotransmitters from the terminals. Neurotransmitters then cross the synapse and bind to **receptors**, specialized sites on the receiving cell.

Dendrites.   Dendrites are a neuron's receiving extensions, which look like the branches on a tree. Once a neurotransmitter fits into a matching receptor on a dendrite, it changes the receiving cell's membrane and triggers a response. Depending on the message carried by the neurotransmitter, it might switch on an action potential or switch off neurotransmitter release in the receiving cell.

Neuronal Life Cycle.   Most of a person's neurons are already formed at birth. But to some extent, neurogenesis—the creation of new neurons—is a lifelong process. Neurogenesis occurs in areas of the brain that are rich in neural stem cells, which have the potential to generate to all the different types of nervous system cells. One such area that seems to play an important role in depression is the dentate gyrus of the **hippocampus**.

Once a neuron is created, it must travel to the part of the brain where it will do its work, a process known as migration. Scientists think that only about a third of neurons complete the journey successfully.

After a neuron reaches its destination, it must begin its work. This is the last in a series of steps by which the cell becomes specialized to perform specific tasks, a process known as differentiation. As the neuron settles in, it develops an axon and dendrites and starts communicating with its neighbors.

Neurons are the longest-lived cells in the body. Nevertheless, large numbers die during migration and differentiation. Others are killed or take abnormal turns as the result of a neurological injury or illness.

In depression, a malfunction in neuronal communication leads to mental, physical, and behavioral symptoms. It comes as no surprise that a system this complex would develop occasional glitches. The real marvel is that such a vast network works so efficiently for most purposes most of the time.

See also: Brain Physiology; Neuroplasticity; Second Messengers

Bibliography

Brain Basics: Know Your Brain. National Institute of Neurological Disorders and Stroke, May 1, 2007, http://www.ninds.nih.gov/disorders/brain_basics/know_your_brain.htm.

Society for Neuroscience. *Brain Facts: A Primer on the Brain and Nervous System.* 6th ed. Washington, DC: Society for Neuroscience, 2008.

The Life and Death of a Neuron. National Institute of Neurological Disorders and Stroke, December 8, 2005, http://www.ninds.nih.gov/disorders/brain_basics/ninds_neuron.htm.

NEUROPEPTIDE Y.   Neuropeptide Y (NPY) is a neurotransmitter—a chemical messenger in the **nervous system**—that affects appetite, weight control, and emotional responses. After a stressful encounter, it also helps the body recover from **stress** and return to its normal state. Several lines of research have linked low levels of NPY to depression and anxiety.

People with depression tend to have decreased levels of NPY in their cerebrospinal fluid, and lower NPY levels are associated with a higher risk of coexisting anxiety or **suicide** attempts. Postmortem studies of key brain areas also have found decreased concentrations of NPY in people who died by suicide. On the flip side, NPY levels tend to rise in depressed individuals who are treated with **electroconvulsive therapy**.

NPY seems to play a crucial role in helping people bounce back from stress. In general, more resilient people have greater increases in blood NPY levels during a stressful event as well as a quicker recovery afterward. This may help explain why a deficiency in NPY is linked to depression, because stress can trigger or worsen a depressed mood.

See also: Neurotransmitters

Bibliography

Gene Variants Affect Human Stress Resilience. National Institutes of Health, April 7, 2008, http://www.nih.gov/news/research_matters/april2008/04072008stress.htm.

Morgan, Charles A. III, Ann M. Rasmusson, Sheila Wang, Gary Hoyt, Richard L. Hauger, and Gary Hazlett. "Neuropeptide-Y, Cortisol, and Subjective Distress in Humans Exposed to Acute Stress: Replication and Extension of Previous Report." *Biological Psychiatry* 52 (2002): 136–142.

Sajdyk, Tammy J. "Neuropeptide Y Receptors as Therapeutic Targets in Anxiety and Depression." *Drug Development Research* 65 (2005): 301–308.

NEUROPLASTICITY. Neuroplasticity refers to the brain's ability to modify connections between cells to better cope with new circumstances. These adaptive changes may be a response to recent patterns of use or disuse in brain cells. Or they may be adaptations to new injuries in the **nervous system**. Research indicates that long-lasting **stress** disrupts the process of neuroplasticity, and this disruption may contribute to depression. Conversely, the loss of neuroplasticity may be blocked or reversed by depression treatments, which help restore the brain's adaptability.

The brain is a marvel of anatomic and chemical complexity. But without neuroplasticity, it would be static. Neuroplasticity is what makes new learning and memories possible. To create a memory, for instance, a person's brain forms new connections between brain cells. It also prunes away some old connections and strengthens or weakens others.

It is estimated that the human brain contains from 100 trillion to a quadrillion synapses, tiny gaps between brain cells across which chemical messages are exchanged. Although genes lay the groundwork for this vast network of connection points, information from the environment is constantly changing it. This is where nature and nurture interact to influence both **mental health** and mental disorders such as depression.

Effects of Chronic Stress. Stress and depression often go hand in hand. Prolonged stress has a number of adverse effects on neuroplasticity as well. For example, in part of the brain called the **hippocampus**, animal studies have shown that stress impairs synaptic plasticity—a change in the functional properties of synapses as a result of use. This type of plasticity is an important component of memory formation in the hippocampus. Impaired function in the hippocampus also is characteristic of **major depression**, and memory problems are a common symptom.

In the hippocampus, prolonged exposure to the stress hormone **cortisol** can cause brain cells to pull back their dendrites—tiny, branchlike extensions that receive messages transmitted across a synapse. And in another part of the brain called the cortex, long-term stress reduces the dendrites' length and complexity.

On one hand, then, depression may be associated with a stress-related loss of neuroplasticity. On the other hand, depression treatments may halt or even reverse this loss. In animals, **antidepressants** have been shown to increase the number of synapses as well as the length and complexity of dendrites in key regions of the brain.

See also: Prefrontal Cortex

Bibliography

Pittenger, Christopher, and Ronald S. Duman. "Stress, Depression, and Neuroplasticity: A Convergence of Mechanisms." *Neuropsychopharmacology* 33 (2008): 88–109.
Society for Neuroscience. *Brain Facts: A Primer on the Brain and Nervous System.* 6th ed. Washington, DC: Society for Neuroscience, 2008.
U.S. Department of Health and Human Services. *Mental Health: A Report of the Surgeon General.* Rockville, MD: U.S. Department of Health and Human Services, 1999.

NEUROSCIENCE. Neuroscience is the scientific discipline that studies the **nervous system** as it relates to mood, emotion, thought, and behavior. This burgeoning field is a hybrid of biology, chemistry, physics, anatomy, physiology, and psychology. Using specialized tools, neuroscientists examine molecules, nerve cells, neural networks, and brain regions. Their goal is to understand how the nervous system normally develops and functions as well as what goes wrong in **mental illness** and **neurological disorders**.

Within the field of neuroscience, there are several subspecialties. Molecular biologists, using tools such as antibodies and gene probes, isolate and describe genes that make the proteins required by nerve cells in order to work properly. Neuroanatomists, using tools such as special dyes that detect specific chemicals and mark certain nerve cells, study the structure and organization of the nervous system.

Developmental neuroscientists explore how the brain grows and changes over the lifespan. Cognitive neuroscientists study mental functions, such as learning and memory, in both animals and humans. For human research, they may use sophisticated **brain imaging** techniques to observe the brain in action and map routes of neural processing.

Behavioral neuroscientists investigate the physiological processes underlying animal and human behavior. Among other tools, they use microelectrodes to measure electrical activity in nerve cells. Clinical neuroscientists apply basic science research to the diagnosis, treatment, and prevention of various disorders, including depression. The cutting-edge research being done in neuroscience labs around the country today may well lead to the groundbreaking advances of tomorrow.

Further Information. Dana Foundation, 745 Fifth Avenue, Suite 900, New York, NY 10151, (212) 223-4040, www.dana.org.

Society for Neuroscience, 1121 14th Street N.W., Suite 1010, Washington, DC 20005, (202) 962-4000, www.sfn.org.

Bibliography

Society for Neuroscience. *Brain Facts: A Primer on the Brain and Nervous System.* 6th ed. Washington, DC: Society for Neuroscience, 2008.

What Is Neuroscience? Society for Neuroscience, http://www.sfn.org/index.cfm?pagename= whatIsNeuroscience.

NEUROTRANSMITTERS. Neurotransmitters are naturally occurring chemicals that act as messengers within the brain. Depression is thought to involve abnormalities in certain neurotransmitters, and **antidepressants** are believed to work by normalizing the levels of these brain chemicals.

Neurons are nerve cells that send, receive, and process information. Within each neuron, this information is carried in electrical signals. But to be passed from one neuron to another, the message has to cross a tiny gap, called a synapse. To get across this gap, it must be converted into chemical form, which is where neurotransmitters come in.

At one time, it was believed that neurotransmitter imbalances might offer a global explanation for all depression. This did not turn out to be the case. Researchers are increasingly exploring the roles played by other natural substances, such as **hormones** and neurotrophic factors (substances that promote nerve cell growth and survival). Nevertheless, neurotransmitters remain a subject of great interest and an important piece of the whole depression puzzle.

Transmitting a Message. When a neuron is activated, it sends an electrical signal from the cell body down a fiber-like sending extension, called an axon. At the end of the axon, neurotransmitters are stored. The signal releases certain neurotransmitters into the gap between the neuron and its neighbor.

There are numerous types of neurotransmitters, each with a distinct chemical shape. To deliver its message, a neurotransmitter must dock at a specialized site, called a receptor, on the receiving cell. **Receptors** are designed to accept a specific type of neurotransmitter. Think of the receptor as a lock and the neurotransmitter as a key. The message can only be delivered if the two fit together properly. Each neurotransmitter has multiple receptors that it binds to, however, like a master key that fits more than one lock. Various receptors have different actions, which helps explain how the same neurotransmitter can have several different effects on brain function.

Once a neurotransmitter matches up with an appropriate receptor, its message is transmitted to next cell's receiving branches, called dendrites. There it acts like an on or off switch for the receiving cell. If the neurotransmitter is excitatory, it tells the cell to switch on and keep passing the signal along. If the neurotransmitter is inhibitory, it tells the cell to switch off and suppress the signal.

In addition to receptors on the receiving cell, there are autoreceptors on the sending cell. These sites tell the sending cell how much of the neurotransmitter has been released. They are part of a sophisticated feedback loop that controls neurotransmitter levels.

Inactivating the Messenger.   After a message has been delivered, the neurotransmitter remains in the synapse, waiting to be disposed of. One way the brain can do this is by returning the neurotransmitter to the sending neuron for recycling. A protein complex, called a **transporter**, carries the neurotransmitter back into the axon that originally released it. The process by which it is reabsorbed into the sending axon is called **reuptake**.

The brain also can use enzymes to break down and inactivate a neurotransmitter. For example, **monoamine oxidase** is an enzyme that breaks down certain neurotransmitters called monoamines, which are thought to be important in depression.

The Depression Connection.   Most of the time, the brain's chemical messages are delivered with remarkable smoothness and efficiency. But for people with depression, something seems to go awry, and the delicate balance among the various neurotransmitters is upset.

In some cases, receptors may be either too sensitive or not sensitive enough to a neurotransmitter, leading to a response that is either excessive or inadequate. In other cases, the sending cell may release too little of a neurotransmitter or the transporter may bring it back too soon, before it has had a chance to deliver its message.

Monoamines.   Monoamines are a group of neurotransmitters that contain one amine group (NH_2) formed by a metabolic change in certain amino acids, the building blocks of proteins. These neurotransmitters are the targets of the various types of antidepressants currently on the market.

Serotonin.   This neurotransmitter not only influences mood, but also helps regulate sleep, appetite, and sexual drive. Studies have found low levels of serotonin in some severely depressed or suicidal individuals. **Selective serotonin reuptake inhibitors**, a widely prescribed group of antidepressants, increase the brain's supply of this neurotransmitter. Most other types of antidepressants also increase serotonin's availability.

Norepinephrine.   This neurotransmitter, which also functions as a hormone, is involved in the body's **stress** response and helps regulate arousal, sleep, and blood pressure. Medications that boost norepinephrine have a long track record of effectiveness for many people with depression. Several types of antidepressants fall into this category, including **tricyclic antidepressants** and **serotonin-norepinephrine reuptake inhibitors**.

Dopamine.   This neurotransmitter, which is essential for movement, also influences motivation, the perception of reality, and the ability to experience pleasure. Dopamine levels seem to fall during depression and rise during **mania** in people who cycle back and forth between the two extremes. Depression also is a side effect of certain diseases (such as Parkinson's disease) and medications (such as the blood pressure drug reserpine) that reduce the brain's dopamine supply. Types of antidepressants that give dopamine a boost include **norepinephrine-dopamine reuptake inhibitors** and **monoamine oxidase inhibitors**.

Amino Acids and Peptides.   Amino acids are acids that contain an amine group (NH_2), and peptides are chains of amino acids. Both types of substances can function as neurotransmitters.

Gamma-Amino-Butyric Acid (GABA).   This amino acid has an inhibitory effect, making brain cells less excitable. GABA also may help quell anxiety. Researchers have found low levels of GABA in some depressed individuals.

Glutamate.   This is another amino acid that has been implicated in depression. Excessive glutamate activity may interfere with healthy brain function. Research has shown that people with depression tend to have high levels of glutamate in some regions of the brain.

Endorphins.   Endorphins are peptides with mood-elevating and pain-relieving properties. Researchers have found that some people with depression have abnormal patterns of endorphin activity.

Neuropeptide Y.   This peptide affects appetite, weight control, and emotional responses. It also helps the body bounce back from stress. Studies have linked depression to low levels of neuropeptide Y.

Substance P.   This peptide helps transmit and amplify pain signals to and from the brain. Research indicates that excessive amounts of substance P may be released during states of emotional distress.

See also: Brain Physiology; Monoamine Hypothesis; Nervous System

Bibliography

DePaulo, J. Raymond Jr. *Understanding Depression: What We Know and What You Can Do About It.* New York: John Wiley and Sons, 2002.

Evans, Dwight L., and Linda Wasmer Andrews. *If Your Adolescent Has Depression or Bipolar Disorder: An Essential Resource for Parents.* New York: Oxford University Press, 2005.

Harvard Medical School. *Understanding Depression.* Boston: Harvard Health Publications, 2003.

Kalat, James W. *Biological Psychology.* 7th ed. Belmont, CA: Wadsworth/Thomson Learning, 2001.

McNally, Leah, Zubin Bhagwagar, and Jonas Hannestad. "Inflammation, Glutamate and Glia in Depression: A Literature Review." *CNS Spectrums* 13 (2008): 501–510.

Medication Information Sheet. Depression and Bipolar Support Alliance, May 4, 2006, http://www.dbsalliance.org/site/PageServer?pagename=about_treatment_medinfosheet.

Society for Neuroscience. *Brain Facts: A Primer on the Brain and Nervous System.* 6th ed. Washington, DC: Society for Neuroscience, 2008.

NORADRENERGIC AND SPECIFIC SEROTONERGIC ANTIDEPRESSANTS. Noradrenergic and specific serotonergic **antidepressants** (NaSSAs) are antidepressant medications with a unique mode of action. Most antidepressants block the reabsorption of key brain chemicals, such as **serotonin** and **norepinephrine**, after they have been released. But NaSSAs cause more of the chemicals to be released in the first place. So far, the only NaSSA medication available in the United States is mirtazapine, which is sold in the United States under the brand name Remeron.

NaSSAs prevent a couple of chemical messengers—norepinephrine and epinephrine—from binding with alpha-2 **receptors** on brain cells. Normally, one job of these receptors is to receive messages telling the cell when it is time to stop releasing serotonin and more norepinephrine. But NaSSAs keep the message from going through, so the cell keeps pumping out norepinephrine and serotonin, which in turn may give mood a lift.

NaSSAs also target certain types of serotonin receptors, but not others. Blocking the action of these particular receptors may help relieve both depression and anxiety. But NaSSAs affect other kinds of receptors as well, which accounts for side effects such as drowsiness, increased appetite, and weight gain.

There is some confusion over the best name for this category. Because mirtazapine has a four-ring molecular structure, it is structurally a tetracyclic antidepressant. But its mode of action is different enough from other tetracyclic and **tricyclic antidepressants** that mirtazapine is generally placed in a class by itself. Although NaSSA is an awkwardly long label, it seems to be the most descriptive term for this drug.

The effectiveness of mirtazapine for treating depression is comparable to that of other antidepressants. Due to the potential for troubling side effects, mirtazapine is not considered a first-choice treatment. But because different people vary in their response to different antidepressants, it may be a good choice for some who are not helped by other medications. In addition, mirtazapine's most common side effect—drowsiness—may actually be a plus for people with depression who have insomnia.

Use and Precautions. Mirtazapine is usually taken once a day at bedtime. In addition to regular tablets, it also comes in the form of special disintegrating tablets, which are made to dissolve on the tongue.

Several studies have shown that mirtazapine starts working faster than the most widely prescribed class of antidepressants, called **selective serotonin reuptake inhibitors** (SSRIs). With mirtazapine, people may start feeling some benefits in as little as a week or two. That is an important advantage, because the delay between starting an antidepressant and feeling its benefits not only extends suffering, but also makes it more likely that people will give up on treatment too soon. There is also evidence that younger users may be at increased risk for **suicide** during the delay period.

Even after depression lifts, most people need to stay on medication for at least six to nine months, and sometimes for years, to help keep symptoms from coming back. People should not quit taking mirtazapine without talking to their doctor first.

Risks and Side Effects. The greatest drawback to mirtazapine is its side effects. More than half of users experience drowsiness. Weight gain is another common problem, and people tend to gain more on mirtazapine than on most SSRIs. Other possible side effects include increased appetite, dry mouth, dizziness, thirst, muscle or joint aches, constipation, and higher cholesterol.

Serotonin syndrome is a rare but potentially life-threatening drug reaction that can occur when serotonin levels build up to dangerously high levels in the body. This most often occurs when people combine two drugs that each raise serotonin levels. To avoid this problem, people taking mirtazapine should be sure to tell their doctor about any other prescription medications, over-the-counter medicines, or herbal supplements they are using.

Antidepressants may save lives by reducing depression and thus decreasing the risk of suicide. In a small number of **children**, **adolescents**, and young adults, however, taking antidepressants may actually lead to worsening mood symptoms or increased suicidal thoughts and behavior. Patients taking mirtazapine—or parents of younger patients—should be alert for any suicidal thoughts and actions or unusual changes in mood and behavior. If such symptoms occur, they should contact their doctor right away.

See also: Antidepressants and Suicide; Treatment of Depression

Bibliography

Antidepressant Medicines: A Guide for Adults with Depression. Agency for Healthcare Research and Quality, August 2007, http://effectivehealthcare.ahrq.gov/repFiles/AntidepressantsConsumerGuide.pdf.

Antidepressants: Comparing Effectiveness, Safety, and Price. Consumer Reports, 2009, http://www.consumerreports.org/health/resources/pdf/best-buy-drugs/Antidepressants_update.pdf.

Hartmann, Peter M. "Mirtazapine: A Newer Antidepressant." *American Family Physician* (January 1, 1999).

Medication Information Sheet. Depression and Bipolar Support Alliance, May 4, 2006, http://www.dbsalliance.org/site/PageServer?pagename=about_treatment_medinfosheet.

Mirtazapine. National Library of Medicine, September 1, 2008, http://www.nlm.nih.gov/medlineplus/druginfo/meds/a697009.html.

Shelton, Richard C., and Natalie Lester. "Selective Serotonin Reuptake Inhibitors and Newer Antidepressants." In *The American Psychiatric Publishing Textbook of Mood Disorders,* by Dan J. Stein, David J. Kupfer, and Alan F. Schatzberg, eds., 263–280. Washington, DC: American Psychiatric Publishing, 2006.

Tetracyclic Antidepressants. Mayo Clinic, December 10, 2008, http://www.mayoclinic.com/health/mental-health/MH00069.

Thompson, Chris. "Onset of Action of Antidepressants: Results of Different Analyses." *Human Psychopharmacology* 17 (2002): S27–S32.

Watanabe, Norio, Ichiro M. Omori, Atsuo Nakagawa, Andrea Cipriani, Corrado Barbui, Hugh McGuire, et al. "Mirtazapine Versus Other Antidepressants in the Acute-Phase Treatment of Adults with Major Depression: Systematic Review and Meta-analysis." *Journal of Clinical Psychiatry* 69 (2008): 1404–1415.

NOREPINEPHRINE. Norepinephrine—also known as noradrenaline—has a dual role in the body as both a neurotransmitter and a hormone. This means it acts as a chemical messenger within both the **nervous system** and the **endocrine system**, respectively. It is involved in the body's **stress** response and helps regulate arousal, sleep, and blood pressure. Several types of **antidepressants** increase the availability of norepinephrine. Because these medications are effective for many people with depression, scientists once reasoned that depression must be caused by low levels of norepinephrine. However, they now know that the situation is more complicated than that.

Many studies have looked at blood, urine, or cerebrospinal fluid levels of norepinephrine or the chief product of its metabolism, called 3-methoxy-4-hydroxyphenylglycol (MHPG). But when scientists compared levels found in people with depression to those of healthy individuals, the results were inconsistent and often showed no difference, perhaps because of problems with how the studies were done.

Nevertheless, some studies do suggest a complex link to depression. For example, in one set of studies, researchers gave people a drug that depleted their levels of norepinephrine and **dopamine**, a related neurotransmitter. Individuals with depression who were being successfully treated with a norepinephrine-boosting antidepressant often experienced a temporary relapse. In contrast, currently depressed individuals who were not on medication did not get worse. And healthy volunteers with no personal or family history of depression did not develop depressive symptoms.

Such studies are suggestive. But perhaps the best argument for norepinephrine's influence is rooted in anatomy. The norepinephrine system originates deep inside the brain and fans out over almost the whole organ. This suggests a system with far-reaching impact on thoughts, feelings, and behavior.

Transmitting a Message. To convey a message from one brain cell to another, norepinephrine is first released by a sending cell into the synapse—the tiny gap between a cell and its neighbor. After crossing the gap, norepinephrine binds with a matching receptor on the receiving cell. Scientists have identified three groups of adrenergic **receptors**: alpha-1, alpha-2, and beta. These receptors bind to and react with norepinephrine and epinephrine—another chemical that doubles as both a neurotransmitter and a stress hormone.

Once norepinephrine has delivered its message, it is carried back into the cell that originally released it by a protein complex called a norepinephrine **transporter**. The process by which it is reabsorbed into the sending cell is called **reuptake**. Some antidepressants, such as **tricyclic antidepressants** and **serotonin and norepinephrine reuptake inhibitors**, block the reuptake of norepinephrine. This keeps more of it available for use by the brain, which may enhance the sending of nerve impulses.

The whole system is dynamic. The density and sensitivity of adrenergic receptors and the number of norepinephrine transporters is increased or decreased based on how much norepinephrine is present. Postmortem studies of brain tissue from **suicide** victims or depressed individuals have found increased adrenergic receptors and decreased norepinephrine transporters in part of the brain where many norepinephrine-producing cells are concentrated. Such changes are typical of adjustments the brain might make to compensate for low levels of norepinephrine.

See also: Axelrod, Julius; Hormones; Monoamine Hypothesis; Neurotransmitters; Second Messengers

Bibliography

Belmaker, R. H., and Galila Agam. "Major Depressive Disorder." *New England Journal of Medicine* 358 (2008): 55–68.

Delgado, Pedro L., and Francisco A. Moreno. "Neurochemistry of Mood Disorders." In *The American Psychiatric Publishing Textbook of Mood Disorders,* by Dan J. Stein, David J. Kupfer, and Alan F. Schatzberg, eds., 101–116. Washington, DC: American Psychiatric Publishing, 2006.

Klimek, Violetta, Craig Stockmeier, James Overholser, Herbert Y. Meltzer, Sheila Kalka, Ginny Dilley, et al. "Reduced Levels of Norepinephrine Transporters in the Locus Coeruleus in Major Depression." *Journal of Neuroscience* 17 (1997): 8451–8458.

Ordway, Gregory A., Jane Schenk, Craig A. Stockmeier, Warren May, and Violetta Klimek. "Elevated Agonist Binding to α_2-Adrenoceptors in the Locus Coeruleus in Major Depression." *Biological Psychiatry* 53 (2003): 315–323.

Serotonin and Norepinephrine Reuptake Inhibitors (SNRIs). Mayo Clinic, December 10, 2008, http://www.mayoclinic.com/health/antidepressants/MH00067.

Tricyclic Antidepressants. Mayo Clinic, December 10, 2008, http://www.mayoclinic.com/health/antidepressants/MH00071.

NOREPINEPHRINE-DOPAMINE REUPTAKE INHIBITORS. Norepinephrine-dopamine reuptake inhibitors (NDRIs) are antidepressant medications that increase the brain's supply of **norepinephrine** and **dopamine**, two chemical messengers that help regulate mood. Research indicates that depression is associated with abnormalities in these brain chemicals.

NDRIs block the **reuptake**, or reabsorption, of norepinephrine and dopamine back into the cells that originally released them. In addition, NDRIs may enhance the release of these chemicals in the first place. Consequently, a larger amount of the chemicals is available for use by the brain, and that may enhance the transmission of chemical messages from one brain cell to another.

So far, the only antidepressant of this type available in the United States is bupropion. Sold under the brand name Wellbutrin, it is approved by the Food and Drug Administration as a treatment for **major depression**. An extended-release once-a-day form, called Wellbutrin XL, also is approved for the prevention of future episodes of **seasonal affective disorder**. In addition, bupropion is marketed under the brand name Zyban as a quit-**smoking** medication.

When bupropion hit the U.S. market in 1985, it ushered in a new generation of **antidepressants**. Although these second-generation medications were no more effective than their predecessors, they caused fewer serious side effects. The arrival of newer antidepressants, marked by bupropion's introduction, represented a major advance in the **treatment of depression**.

Use and Precautions. Bupropion is a tablet that comes in three forms: regular (usually taken two or three times a day), sustained-release (usually taken twice a day), and extended-release (usually taken once a day in the morning). For seasonal affective disorder, people typically start taking bupropion in early fall, continue through the winter, and stop in the early spring.

Symptoms relating to sleep, appetite, and energy level may improve within the first week or two—a sign that the medication is working. However, it may take four weeks or longer to feel the full benefits of bupropion. Even after depression lifts, most people with nonseasonal depression need to stay on medication for at least several months, and sometimes for years, to help keep symptoms from coming back.

Bupropion is the only antidepressant in current use that has little or no effect on **serotonin**, another brain chemical involved in depression. Because of its unique mode of action, bupropion is sometimes combined with another antidepressant when that medication alone does not provide enough relief.

Risks and Side Effects. One major advantage of bupropion is that it is less likely to cause sexual problems as a side effect than **selective serotonin reuptake inhibitors**, the most widely used type of antidepressant. Another plus for many is that people on bupropion tend to lose a little weight—about two to three pounds, on average.

Other side effects are usually mild and short-lived, although some can be more serious or long-lasting. Possible side effects include loss of appetite, headache, dry mouth, skin rash, sweating, ringing in the ears, anxiety, agitation, shakiness, stomachache, constipation, dizziness, trouble sleeping, muscle pain, nausea, vomiting, faster heartbeat, sore throat, frequent urination, and increased blood pressure.

There is also a small chance that bupropion might trigger a seizure, especially in those with certain risk factors, such as previous seizures, **eating disorders**, or a head injury. The medication generally is not prescribed for people with these conditions. Drinking alcohol or using illicit drugs while taking bupropion should also be avoided. People who are dependent on alcohol or drugs and who want to stop should seek medical help, because quitting abruptly may lead to a seizure.

Antidepressants may save lives by reducing depression and thus decreasing the risk of suicide. In a small number of **children**, **adolescents**, and young adults, however, taking antidepressants may actually lead to worsening mood symptoms or increased suicidal thoughts and behavior. Patients taking mirtazapine—or parents of younger patients—should be alert for any suicidal thoughts and actions or unusual changes in mood and behavior. If such symptoms occur, they should contact their doctor right away.

See also: Antidepressants and Suicide

Bibliography

Antidepressant Medicines: A Guide for Adults with Depression. Agency for Healthcare Research and Quality, August 2007, http://effectivehealthcare.ahrq.gov/repFiles/AntidepressantsConsumerGuide .pdf.

Antidepressants: Comparing Effectiveness, Safety, and Price. Consumer Reports, 2009, http://www .consumerreports.org/health/resources/pdf/best-buy-drugs/Antidepressants_update.pdf.

Bupropion. National Library of Medicine, September 1, 2008, http://www.nlm.nih.gov/medlineplus/ druginfo/meds/a695033.html.

Medication Information Sheet. Depression and Bipolar Support Alliance, May 4, 2006, http://www .dbsalliance.org/site/PageServer?pagename=about_treatment_medinfosheet.

Norepinephrine and Dopamine Reuptake Inhibitors (NDRIs). Mayo Clinic, December 10, 2008, http://www.mayoclinic.com/health/antidepressants/MH00068.

Shelton, Richard C., and Natalie Lester. "Selective Serotonin Reuptake Inhibitors and Newer Antidepressants." In *The American Psychiatric Publishing Textbook of Mood Disorders,* by Dan J. Stein, David J. Kupfer, and Alan F. Schatzberg, eds., 263–280. Washington, DC: American Psychiatric Publishing, 2006.

Wellbutrin (Bupropion). National Alliance on Mental Illness, March 2009, http://www.nami .org/Template.cfm?Section=About_Medications&template=/ContentManagement/ContentDisplay .cfm&ContentID=7388.

O

OBSESSIVE-COMPULSIVE DISORDER. The defining features of **obsessive-compulsive disorder** (OCD) are recurrent, uncontrollable thoughts (obsessions) and actions (compulsions). The most common mental disorder coexisting with OCD is depression. Prevalence estimates vary widely, but researchers have reported that up to two-thirds of people with OCD may develop depression at some point in their lives.

Obsessions are intrusive, upsetting thoughts that keep coming back despite efforts to push them away. Because the thoughts cause so much anxiety, people try to counteract them with some physical or mental act, which is where compulsions come into play. Compulsions are ritualistic actions that people feel driven to perform in an effort to reduce the anxiety produced by an obsession.

Typical obsessions involve frequent, exaggerated thoughts about being diseased, dirty, or sinful, or doing abhorrent things. Examples of common compulsions include repetitively washing one's hands, cleaning, checking the locks, putting objects in order, counting, or silently saying a phrase. Such obsessions and rituals control people with OCD rather than the other way around, preoccupying their thoughts and consuming time that could otherwise have been spent doing more productive things.

OCD affects about 2.2 million U.S. adults, striking men and women in roughly equal numbers. It usually starts in childhood, adolescence, or early adulthood. Compared to those with OCD alone, people whose OCD is combined with **major depression** tend to have more severe and longer-lasting OCD symptoms as well as a greater number of hospitalizations and **suicide** attempts.

Although adding depression to the mix makes treatment a bit more complicated, both disorders usually respond well to medication and/or **psychotherapy**. With appropriate treatment, most people are able to feel better, reduce their obsessions and compulsions, and regain control of their lives.

Criteria for Diagnosis. The symptoms of OCD are defined by the ***Diagnostic and Statistical Manual of Mental Disorders, Fourth Edition, Text Revision*** (*DSM-IV-TR*), a diagnostic guidebook published by the American Psychiatric Association and widely used by mental health professionals from many disciplines. People with OCD have obsessions and compulsions that cause serious distress, take up more than an hour a day, or interfere with daily activities. Most adults with the disorder recognize that their obsessive thoughts and compulsive behaviors are excessive or unreasonable, but they feel powerless to stop. Children may not realize that their behavior is out of the ordinary, however.

Treatment of OCD

When people have OCD and depression simultaneously, both conditions need to be addressed during treatment. Below are some of the main treatment options for OCD.

Psychotherapy

Cognitive-behavioral therapy (CBT) helps people identify maladaptive thought and behavior patterns and replace them with more adaptive ones. One offshoot of CBT developed specifically for treating OCD is called exposure and response prevention. The exposure part of the treatment involves confronting thoughts and situations that provoke obsession-related distress. The response-prevention part involves voluntarily refraining from using compulsions to reduce distress during these encounters.

Medication

SSRIs, a widely prescribed class of antidepressants, can help relieve symptoms of anxiety as well as depression. SSRIs are considered a first-choice treatment for OCD. If these medications do not provide enough relief, a tricyclic antidepressant called clomipramine may be used instead.

Obsessions. Obsessions are recurring, unwanted thoughts, impulses, or mental images that intrude into people's minds and cause great distress or anxiety. These thoughts are more than just excessive worries about real-life problems. Typical themes include being very fearful of dirt or disease, having repeated doubts, and keeping things orderly or symmetrical. Some people experience disturbing aggressive impulses or mental images of distressing sexual scenes. Despite efforts to ignore or suppress such thoughts, the obsessions keep coming back time and again.

Compulsions. Compulsions are ritualistic behaviors (for example, washing and cleaning, arranging objects in order, checking something repeatedly) or mental acts (for example, counting, repeating words silently) that people feel driven to do over and over in response to an obsession or according to rigid rules. The rituals are aimed at reducing distress or preventing some calamity from occurring. However, they are either clearly excessive or not connected in a realistic way to what they are intended to prevent. At best, the rituals provide only temporary relief from the anxiety caused by obsessions.

Relationship to Depression. Shared **genetic factors** may help explain why OCD and major depression occur together so often. Major depression is more common in the close family members of people with OCD than in the family members of those without the disorder.

Biological and **environmental factors** may play central roles as well. When people have both OCD and major depression, the OCD usually comes first. Obsessions and compulsions can be very demoralizing and disruptive to everyday life, and the **stress** created by them may trigger depression in some people. It is also possible that abnormalities in brain function and chemistry associated with OCD could render the brain itself more vulnerable to the development of other disorders, including depression.

There is some evidence that depression in people with OCD may differ somewhat from garden-variety depression. Both people with OCD plus depression and those with major depression alone are prone to experiencing a low mood, loss of interest in most activities, lack of energy, trouble concentrating, and suicidal thoughts. But those with OCD plus depression are less likely to have difficulty sleeping and changes in appetite, and they are more likely to experience inner tension and **pessimism**.

These differences in symptoms may derive from differences in **brain physiology**. For instance, researchers have found that people with major depression alone tend to have increased metabolic activity in the thalamus, a structure inside the brain that acts as a relay station for sensory input, filtering out important information from the mass of incoming signals. In contrast, people with both major depression and OCD tend to have decreased activity in the thalamus.

The response to **antidepressants** also differs, suggesting that there may be underlying differences in brain chemistry as well. **Selective serotonin reuptake inhibitors** (SSRIs), antidepressants that increase the available supply of a chemical called serotonin in the brain, can help relieve symptoms of both OCD and depression. But higher doses may be needed when OCD is present, compared to the doses needed to treat major depression by itself. Other types of antidepressants that work well for people with major depression alone do not seem to be as effective for those with OCD.

See also: Anxiety Disorders; Comorbidity

Further Information.   Obsessive-Compulsive Foundation, P.O. Box 961029, Boston, MA 02196, (617) 973-5801, www.ocfoundation.org.

Bibliography

American Psychiatric Association. *Diagnostic and Statistical Manual of Mental Disorders.* 4th ed., text rev. Washington, DC: American Psychiatric Association, 2000.

Anxiety Disorders. National Institute of Mental Health, 2007, http://www.nimh.nih.gov/health/publications/anxiety-disorders/summary.shtml.

Fineberg, Naomi A., Hannelie Fourie, Tim M. Gale, and Thanusha Sivakumaran. "Comorbid Depression in Obsessive Compulsive Disorder (OCD): Symptomatic Differences to Major Depressive Disorder." *Journal of Affective Disorders* 87 (2005): 327–330.

Fineberg, Naomi A., Sanjaya Saxena, Joseph Zohar, and Kevin J. Craig. "Obsessive-Compulsive Disorder: Boundary Issues." *CNS Spectrums* 12 (2007): 359–364, 367–375.

Foa, Edna B., and Linda Wasmer Andrews. *If Your Adolescent Has an Anxiety Disorder: An Essential Resource for Parents.* New York: Oxford University Press, 2006.

Hong, Jin Pyo, Jack Samuels, O. Joseph Bienvenu III, Paul Cannistraro, Marco Grados, Mark A. Riddle, et al. "Clinical Correlates of Recurrent Major Depression in Obsessive-Compulsive Disorder." *Depression and Anxiety* 20 (2004): 86–91.

Obsessive-Compulsive Disorder (OCD). Mayo Clinic, December 21, 2006, http://www.mayoclinic.com/health/obsessive-compulsive-disorder/DS00189.

Practice Guideline for the Treatment of Patients with Obsessive-Compulsive Disorder. American Psychiatric Association, July 2007, http://www.psychiatryonline.com/pracGuide/pracGuideTopic_10.aspx.

When Unwanted Thoughts Take Over: Obsessive Compulsive Disorder. National Institute of Mental Health, June 26, 2008, http://www.nimh.nih.gov/health/publications/when-unwanted-thoughts-take-over-obsessive-compulsive-disorder/summary.shtml.

OLDER ADULTS.   Many people think depression is a normal part of getting older, but that is a myth. Depression at any age is a disorder that can—and should—be treated. In fact, the consequences of leaving it untreated may be especially harsh for older adults. Along with causing emotional suffering, depression can contribute to disability and worsen symptoms of **physical illness.** In addition, the **suicide** rate among people ages 65 and older is 14 per 100,000 individuals, higher than the rate of 11 per 100,000 in the population at large.

Late-life depression is a common problem. Researchers estimate that from one percent to five percent of older adults living independently in the community suffer from **major**

depression. However, that figure rises to 13.5 percent among those who require home health care.

When someone becomes depressed late in life, it is often a **recurrence** of earlier depression. But at times, depression arises for the first time in an older adult. In such cases, it is often the result of another medical illness, which can make the depression both harder to recognize and more difficult to manage.

Not only the depressed individual, but also friends, family, and sometimes health professionals may regard depression as a natural response to late-life problems, such as illness, **grief**, or financial **stress**. Couple that with the fact that today's seniors grew up at a time when mental illness was often seen as a sign of being "crazy" or weak. Such lingering attitudes contribute to low rates of diagnosis and treatment in older adults.

Yet there is a bright side to the picture, too. Contrary to the stereotype, depression is not an inevitable part of aging. With appropriate treatment, most older adults with depression, like their younger counterparts, can begin to feel better and get more enjoyment out of life.

Geriatric Risk Factors. Several factors may put older adults at increased risk for depression. Age-related health challenges can give rise to stress. And stress, in turn, may trigger depression in vulnerable individuals. Beyond that, some medical conditions—such as **stroke** and **Parkinson's disease**—cause changes in the brain that may contribute to depression directly.

For other conditions, the link to depression may be less direct, but just as powerful in the long run. Consider age-related physical disabilities, for example. Impairments in physical mobility, sight, and hearing may be both stressful and socially isolating, and those effects may feed a tendency toward depression.

Several medications commonly taken by this age group can cause or worsen mood symptoms as a side effect. These include certain blood pressure-lowering medications, antiulcer medications, Parkinson's medications, muscle relaxants, and corticosteroids.

On a psychological level, late life, like any other stage, brings its own set of changes and challenges. Some people must adjust to major life changes, such as a retirement or move. Others must adapt to new roles, such as becoming a caregiver or care recipient. At times, the stress associated with such changes may lead to depression or make it worse.

One very stressful event that many face is the death of a loved one—a trauma that becomes more likely as people get older. **Grief** is a natural and even healthy response to such a profound loss. The symptoms of grief resemble those of depression, and they may be severe and disruptive in the short term, but they usually start to lift after several weeks. In some cases, though, grief may deepen into full-blown, long-term depression.

Diagnostic Issues. Depression in older adults is identified using the same diagnostic criteria as those used for younger individuals. Applying the criteria may be more complicated, though, because many classic symptoms of depression can also occur as a result of medical illness or the normal aging process. Examples include changes in appetite, sleep patterns, and energy level. Because such symptoms are tricky to interpret, doctors may be slower to recognize depression in older patients.

Another factor that adds to the challenge is the frequent co-occurrence of late-life depression and age-related mental decline. A self-report questionnaire called the **Geriatric Depression Scale** can help distinguish depressed from nondepressed individuals among those with mild to moderate dementia. But a different approach may be required for those with advanced **Alzheimer's disease**, in whom both psychological self-awareness and language skills are often seriously impaired. In this situation, mental health professionals rely more heavily on nonverbal cues and secondhand reports from caregivers.

Treatment Considerations. The upshot is that late-life depression tends to be under-diagnosed and therefore under-treated. When left untreated, it may contribute to problems with functioning in everyday life, poor adherence to treatment for other conditions, worsening of coexisting medical illnesses, and an increased risk of premature death. Yet once treatment enters the picture, most older adults with depression

> **Depression and Dementia**
>
> Depression that appears for the first time late in life is often followed within a few years by dementia, a significant impairment in memory and mental abilities caused by Alzheimer's disease or blood flow problems in the brain. According to one theory, depression in this case is actually an early symptom of dementia. But another theory states that depression at any age is simply a risk factor for dementia disorders. It turns out that a history of depression even years earlier increases the risk of developing dementia later in life.

can be helped by **psychotherapy**, **antidepressants**, or a combination of both.

If antidepressants are prescribed, **selective serotonin reuptake inhibitors** (SSRIs) are often first-choice treatments. Two SSRIs—citalopram and sertraline—are especially recommended for older adults. These two medications are not only generally effective and well tolerated, but also less likely to cause harmful interactions with other drugs. However, depending on the individual, several other antidepressants may be safe and effective as well.

If psychotherapy is used, research has shown that three approaches may be effective treatments for late-life depression. **Cognitive-behavioral therapy** helps people identify and change maladaptive patterns of thought and behavior. **Interpersonal therapy** helps people address the interpersonal triggers for depressive symptoms. **Problem-solving treatment** helps people learn strategies for solving everyday problems associated with depression.

Research has shown that the effectiveness of psychotherapy for older adults with depression is comparable to that for younger individuals. It is also similar to the effectiveness of antidepressants. For optimal results, a combination of psychotherapy and antidepressants is often recommended.

Once an episode of late-life depression has ended, there is a 50 percent to 90 percent chance of a recurrence within two to three years. Continuing treatment even after recovering may help older adults stay well and prevent many future episodes. In one study, people age 70 and older who had gotten better after their initial treatment for depression were less likely to have a recurrence if they stayed on their medication for another two years.

See also: Mood Disorder Due to a General Medical Condition

Further Information. American Association for Geriatric Psychiatry, 7910 Woodmont Avenue, Suite 1050, Bethesda, MD 20814, (301) 654-7850, www.aagponline.org, www.gmhfonline.org.

American Geriatrics Society, 350 Fifth Avenue, Suite 801, New York, NY 10118, (212) 308-1414, www.americangeriatrics.org.

Bibliography

Alexopoulos, George G., Ira R. Katz, Charles F. Reynolds III, and Ruth Ross. The *Expert Consensus Guideline Series: Depression in Older Adults—A Guide for Patients and Families.* Comprehensive Neuroscience, 2001, http://www.psychguides.com/Geriatric%20Depression%20LP%20Guide.pdf.

Blazer, Dan G., and Celia F. Hybels. "Depression in Later Life: Epidemiology, Assessment, Impact, and Treatment." In *Handbook of Depression.* 2nd ed., by Ian H. Gotlib and Constance L. Hammen, eds., 492–509. New York: Guilford Press, 2009.

Charney, Dennis S., Charles F. Reynolds III, Lydia Lewis, Barry D. Lebowitz, Trey Sunderland, George S. Alexopoulos, et al. "Depression and Bipolar Support Alliance Consensus Statement on the Unmet Needs in Diagnosis and Treatment of Mood Disorders in Late Life." *Archives of General Psychiatry* 60 (2003): 664–672.

Cuijpers, Pim, Annemieke van Straten, and Filip Smit. "Psychological Treatment of Late-Life Depression: A Meta-analysis of Randomized Controlled Trials." *International Journal of Geriatric Psychiatry* 21 (2006): 1139–1149.

Depression in Late Life: Not a Natural Part of Aging. Geriatric Mental Health Foundation, http://www.gmhfonline.org/gmhf/consumer/factsheets/depression_latelife.html.

Malin, Gabrielle J. *Depression and Aging: Make Sure to Seek Treatment.* Mayo Clinic, September 16, 2008, http://www.mayoclinic.com/health/depression-and-aging/MY00259.

Older Adults: Depression and Suicide Facts. National Institute of Mental Health, May 18, 2009, http://www.nimh.nih.gov/health/publications/older-adults-depression-and-suicide-facts-fact-sheet/index.shtml.

Reynolds, Charles F. III, Mary Amanda Dew, Bruce G. Pollock, Benoit H. Mulsant, Ellen Frank, Mark D. Miller, et al. "Maintenance Treatment of Major Depression in Old Age." *New England Journal of Medicine* 354 (2006): 1130–1138.

Steffens, David C., Emeline Otey, George S. Alexopoulous, Meryl A. Butters, Bruce Cuthbert, Mary Ganguli, et al. "Perspective on Depression, Mild Cognitive Impairment, and Cognitive Decline." *Archives of General Psychiatry* 63 (2006): 130–138.

Unützer, Jützer. "Late-Life Depression." *New England Journal of Medicine* 357 (2007): 2269–2276.

OMEGA-3 FATTY ACIDS. Omega-3 fatty acids are an important group of polyunsaturated fats that the body needs to function properly. These fats can be consumed from the **diet** or **dietary supplements**. A growing body of research suggests that omega-3s may help protect the brain against depression.

Two types of omega-3s are eicosapentaenoic acid (EPA) and docosahexaenoic acid (DHA). These fatty acids are found in fish, shellfish, and organ meats. Fatty fish—such as mackerel, lake trout, herring, sardines, albacore tuna, and salmon—are especially rich sources. Another type of omega-3 called alpha-linolenic acid (ALA) is found in foods such as leafy green vegetables, nuts, tofu, and other soy products as well as canola, flaxseed, walnut, and soy oils. ALA can be converted into EPA and DHA within the body. The extent of this conversion is modest, however.

In addition to possible effects on brain health, the benefits of omega-3s for heart health are well established. Human studies have shown that omega-3s can reduce triglyceride (blood fat) levels, and they also may lower blood pressure slightly. Meanwhile, animal and lab studies have demonstrated that omega-3s affect cell functions that are involved in maintaining a normal heart rate and healthy blood flow to the heart.

Omega-3s have been studied in relationship to many other diseases, too. In people with rheumatoid arthritis, omega-3s have been shown to reduce joint pain and decrease the need for medication. Beyond that, any health benefits remain unproven. A series of reports funded by the National Institutes of Health Office of Dietary Supplements found insufficient evidence to draw firm conclusions about the impact of omega-3s on asthma, inflammatory bowel disease, kidney disease, lupus, osteoporosis, diabetes, dementia, multiple sclerosis, or age-related cognitive decline.

Benefits for Depression. Research on the relationship between fatty acids and depression is still preliminary. But some studies that have looked at the occurrence of the disease in different populations have found a relationship between eating more fish and having a lower risk of depression.

Meanwhile, some lab research has shown that people with depression have lower levels of omega-3s in their blood, on average, than those without the disorder. The lower the blood levels of omega-3s, the more severe the depressive symptoms tend to be.

The strongest evidence to date comes from clinical trials in which people with mood disorders were randomly assigned to receive either an omega-3 supplement or a placebo (dummy pill). A recent review article in the *Journal of Clinical Psychiatry* identified 10 such studies that were double-blind, meaning that neither the experimenters nor the participants were aware of who was getting the supplement and who was getting a placebo—a dummy pill that looks like the real thing but does not contain an active ingredient. After pooling the results from a total of 329 participants, the review authors found that omega-3 supplements significantly improved depressive symptoms. Nevertheless, the authors caution that this finding is not definitive, due to limitations in the design of the original studies.

Effects on the Brain. The exact mechanisms by which omega-3s might affect depression are still being explored. However, it is known that omega-3s are abundant in the brain, where they alter the functioning of brain circuits using both **serotonin** and **dopamine**, two brain chemicals that are thought to play roles in depression.

DHA is the major polyunsaturated fatty acid in the brain, and it is critical for brain development and function. Synapses—the gaps between brain cells across which they communicate—are rich in DHA, suggesting that this fatty acid may be involved in the transmission of chemical signals from cell to cell. DHA also is required to produce one member of a family of compounds called resolvins. These compounds help reduce **inflammation** within the brain.

EPA is metabolized inside the body to produce hormone-like substances called eicosanoids. These substances regulate a variety of basic bodily functions, including cell division and growth, muscle activity, blood clotting, hormone secretion, and the movement of calcium into and out of cells. The particular eicosanoids derived from EPA—particularly series-3 prostaglandins—help protect against inflammatory processes that play a part in many diseases. The link between inflammation and depression is not well understood. However, people with depression tend to have elevated levels of substances in their blood that are markers of inflammation.

Omega-6:Omega-3 Ratio. Omega-3s are just one of two major classes of polyunsaturated fatty acids. The other class is called omega-6s. The omega-6 fatty acids are found in many widely consumed foods, including meat; safflower, sunflower, and corn oils; and processed foods made with these oils. Most people in the United States get over 10 times more omega-6 than omega-3 fatty acids in their diet. Among nutrition experts, there is a consensus that Americans should consume more omega-3s and fewer omega-6s to promote good health.

Some scientists have suggested that high intakes of omega-6 fatty acids may contribute to depression. And in fact, higher omega-6 to omega-3 ratios have been observed in people with depression compared to those without the disorder. One possible explanation: In the body, linoleic acid, an omega-6, is converted into another fatty acid called arachidonic acid (AA). Like EPA, AA is metabolized to produce eicosanoids. However, the particular eicosanoids derived from AA promote rather than reduce inflammation.

The science linking all these fatty acids to depression is still speculative. But for overall health, there is general agreement that most Americans would do well to eat more fruits and vegetables and fewer processed foods containing large amounts of omega-6-laden vegetable oils.

Omega-3 Sources. When it comes to **heart disease** prevention, the American Heart Association recommends that people without documented heart disease eat fish at least twice a week as well as include ALA-rich foods in their diets. For people who have already been diagnosed with heart disease, the association recommends consuming about 1 gram of EPA and DHA daily—preferably from fatty fish, but supplements can be considered. For those who need to lower their triglycerides, the association says taking supplements that provide 2 to 4 grams of EPA and DHA daily under a doctor's care may be appropriate. Unfortunately, experts are not yet able to make similarly clear-cut recommendations for preventing or treating depression.

Some studies suggest that EPA may be more beneficial than DHA for depression, but further research is needed to confirm this finding. The optimal dosage of omega-3s for depression has yet to be defined, although several studies have found 1 to 2 grams daily to be effective. Although research results so far are promising, experts advise taking a cautious approach to supplements until more data are in. On the other hand, a varied diet that includes fish and ALA-rich foods is good for health in general—and if it turns out to be good for mood in particular, that is a welcome bonus.

Side Effects and Cautions. In studies of omega-3 supplements for depression and other diseases, side effects have been minor—primarily diarrhea in a minority of users. Some people also report problems with fishy-smelling breath, belching, or abdominal bloating. Prolonged use of fish oil supplements may cause vitamin E deficiency, and overuse of cod liver oil may cause toxic levels of vitamins A and D. In addition, omega-3 supplements may intensify the effects of blood-thinning medications, leading to a risk of excessive bleeding.

As with any dietary supplement, it is wise to talk to a health care provider about taking omega-3s, especially when combining them with medication or substituting them for food. People who have depression or another mental or physical health condition should keep in mind that supplements alone cannot take the place of appropriate treatment.

Bibliography

Consumer FAQ: "Better" Fats (Monounsaturated and Polyunsaturated Fats). American Heart Association, December 2007, http://www.americanheart.org/presenter.jhtml?identifier=3046644.

Fish and Omega-3 Fatty Acids. American Heart Association, http://www.americanheart.org/presenter .jhtml?identifier=4632.

Kiecolt-Glaser, Janice K., Martha A. Belury, Kyle Porter, David Q. Beversdorf, Stanley Lemeshow, and Ronald Glaser. "Depressive Symptoms, Omega-6:Omega-3 Fatty Acids, and Inflammation in Older Adults." *Psychosomatic Medicine* 69 (2007): 217–224.

Lin, Pao-Yen, and Kuan-Pin Su. "A Meta-analytic Review of Double-Blind, Placebo-Controlled Trials of Antidepressant Efficacy of Omega-3 Fatty Acids." *Journal of Clinical Psychiatry* 68 (2007): 1056–1061.

Motivala, Sarosh J., Avishay Sarfatti, Luis Olmos, and Michael R. Irwin. "Inflammatory Markers and Sleep Disturbance in Major Depression." *Psychosomatic Medicine* 67 (2005): 187–194.

Nemets, Hanah, Boris Nemets, Alan Apter, Ziva Bracha, and R. H. Belmaker. "Omega-3 Treatment of Childhood Depression: A Controlled, Double-Blind Pilot Study." *American Journal of Psychiatry* 163 (2006): 1098–1100.

Omega-3 Fatty Acids and Health. National Institutes of Health Office of Dietary Supplements, October 28, 2005, http://dietary-supplements.info.nih.gov/FactSheets/Omega3FattyAcidsandHealth .asp.

Omega-3 Fatty Acids. American Cancer Society, July 12, 2007, http://www.cancer.org/docroot/ETO/ content/ETO_5_3X_Omega-3_Fatty_Acids.asp.

Ross, Brian M., Jennifer Seguin, and Lee E. Sieswerda. "Omega-3 Fatty Acids as Treatments for Mental Illness: Which Disorder and Which Fatty Acid?" *Lipids in Health and Disease* 6 (2007): 21.

P

PANIC DISORDER.   Panic disorder is an anxiety disorder characterized by sudden, unexpected attacks of terror accompanied by symptoms such as a pounding heart, sweating, faintness, and dizziness. Often there is also a sense of imminent danger or impending doom as well as an urge to escape. Such panic attacks strike abruptly in situations that pose little or no actual threat. Yet the feeling of being threatened is very real, and the body and mind react accordingly. Some people with depression who also suffer from anxiety may experience either isolated panic attacks or full-on panic disorder.

For those who do not understand what is happening, panic attacks can be extremely frightening. Some fear that they are having a heart attack or suffering from another life-threatening illness—and, in fact, a medical evaluation is critical to rule out other possible causes for the symptoms. Over time, people begin to fear the attacks themselves. Because they cannot predict when and where the next one will occur, many live in a constant state of dread.

The first panic attacks often occur in late adolescence or early adulthood. However, not everyone who has a panic attack goes on to develop the full-blown disorder, which involves a pattern of recurrent attacks followed by worry over future attacks or avoidance of places or situations in which past attacks have occurred. Some people's lives become quite constrained as they start to avoid day-to-day activities, such as driving, shopping, or even leaving home at all.

Panic disorder affects about six million U.S. adults, two-thirds of whom are women. More than half of people with panic disorder experience depression at some point in the lives. Those with both disorders tend to develop more severe symptoms than those with panic disorder alone. In particular, having both disorders increases the risk of suicidal thoughts and attempts, hospitalization, and extreme avoidance behavior. It also is associated with greater problems getting along at work and in social situations.

Fortunately, with proper treatment, most people can start to feel better and reduce or eliminate panic attacks. Treatment typically involves medication and/or **cognitive-behavioral therapy**. The latter can help people change thinking patterns and behavioral reactions that trigger or worsen panic attacks as well as contribute to depression.

Criteria for Diagnosis.   The symptoms of panic disorder are defined by the ***Diagnostic and Statistical Manual of Mental Disorders, Fourth Edition, Text Revision*** (*DSM-IV-TR*), a diagnostic guidebook published by the American Psychiatric Association and widely used by mental health professionals from many disciplines. The core characteristic of the

Treatment of Panic Disorder

When people have panic disorder and depression simultaneously, both conditions need to be addressed during treatment. Below are some of the main treatment options for panic disorder.

Psychotherapy

Cognitive-behavioral therapy (CBT) helps people identify maladaptive thought and behavior patterns and replace them with more adaptive ones. One CBT technique that may be used is continuous panic monitoring, in which people keep track of their panic attacks in a journal, then look for patterns to help uncover the environmental cues that trigger the attacks. Another CBT technique is exposure therapy, in which people systematically confront the objects or situations that provoke their panic. When a panic attack occurs in the safety of a therapist's office, people learn to control and master the symptoms, making the prospect of a future attack less scary.

Medication

Selective serotonin reuptake inhibitors (SSRIs), a widely prescribed class of **antidepressants**, can help relieve symptoms of anxiety as well as depression. SSRIs are considered a first-choice treatment for panic disorder. If these medications do not provide enough relief, other types of medications that may be prescribed include other antidepressants (such as **serotonin-norepinephrine reuptake inhibitors** and **tricyclic antidepressants**) and benzodiazepines (mild sedatives).

disorder is the presence of repeated, unexpected panic attacks. These attacks are sudden waves of intense fear and apprehension that are accompanied by four or more of the following symptoms: (1) racing or pounding heart, (2) sweating, (3) trembling, (4) shortness of breath, (5) choking sensation, (6) chest pain, (7) nausea or upset stomach, (8) dizziness or faintness, (9) feelings of unreality or detachment from oneself, (10) fear of losing control or going crazy, (11) fear of dying, (12) numbness or tingling sensation, and (13) chills or hot flushes. The symptoms come on abruptly and reach their peak within a matter of minutes.

In the aftermath of panic attacks, people with panic disorder develop persistent concerns about having future attacks or nagging worries about what the attacks might mean. Some make major changes in their lifestyle as a result of such fears. These worries or lifestyle changes last for at least a month.

As the problem progresses, some people develop agoraphobia—anxiety about being in places or situations from which it might be difficult to escape or get help in the event of a panic attack. Agoraphobic fears often center around being in a crowd, standing in line, crossing a bridge, traveling by car, or leaving home alone. The feared situation is avoided or endured only with great distress. In extreme cases, the fear grows so intense that people become housebound. But early treatment may help keep panic disorder from ever reaching this point.

Panic Attacks and Depression. Some people have panic attacks without meeting all the criteria for panic disorder, but even occasional attacks can still be very upsetting. When people with other **anxiety disorders** or major depression have panic attacks, it is generally a sign of more severe disease.

The majority of people who experience a panic attack will eventually have at least one episode of major depression. But the good news is that prompt treatment may derail or delay this process. In a national study including 425 people who had experienced a panic attack, those who received treatment for panic were substantially less likely to develop major depression than those whose panic went untreated.

See also: Comorbidity

Further Information. Anxiety Disorders Association of America, 8730 Georgia Avenue, Suite 600. Silver Spring, MD 20910, (240) 485-1001, www.adaa.org.

Bibliography

American Psychiatric Association. *Diagnostic and Statistical Manual of Mental Disorders.* 4th ed., text rev. Washington, DC: American Psychiatric Association, 2000.

Anxiety Disorders. National Institute of Mental Health, 2007, http://www.nimh.nih.gov/health/publications/anxiety-disorders/summary.shtml.

Goodwin, Renee, and Mark Olfson. "Treatment of Panic Attack and Risk of Major Depressive Disorder in the Community." *American Journal of Psychiatry* 158 (2001): 1146–1148.

Goodwin, Renee, Mark Olfson, Adriana Feder, Milton Fuentes, Daniel J. Pilowsky, and Myrna M. Weissman. "Panic and Suicidal Ideation in Primary Care." *Depression and Anxiety* 14 (2001): 244–246.

Johnson, Michael R., and R. Bruce Lydiard. "Comorbidity of Major Depression and Panic Disorder." *Journal of Clinical Psychology* 54 (1998): 201–210.

Kessler, Ronald C., Paul E. Stang, Hans-Ulrich Wittchen, T. Bedirhan Ustun, Peter P. Roy-Burne, and Ellen E. Walters. "Lifetime Panic-Depression Comorbidity in the National Comorbidity Survey." *Archives of General Psychiatry* 55 (1998): 801–808.

Let's Talk Facts About Panic Disorder. American Psychiatric Association, November 2006, http://healthyminds.org/factsheets/LTF-Panic.pdf.

McLean, Peter D., Sheila Woody, Steven Taylor, and William J. Koch. "Comorbid Panic Disorder and Major Depression: Implications for Cognitive-Behavioral Therapy." *Journal of Consulting and Clinical Psychology* 66 (1998): 240–247.

Panic Attacks and Panic Disorder. Mayo Clinic, March 28, 2008, http://www.mayoclinic.com/health/panic-attacks/DS00338.

Practice Guideline for the Treatment of Patients with Panic Disorder. American Psychiatric Association, May 1998, http://www.psychiatryonline.com/pracGuide/pracGuideTopic_9.aspx.

Vasile, Russell G., Idell Goldenberg, James Reich, Robert M. Goisman, Philip W. Lavori, and Martin B. Keller. "Panic Disorder versus Panic Disorder with Major Depression: Defining and Understanding Differences in Psychiatric Morbidity." *Depression and Anxiety* 5 (1997): 12–20.

When Fear Overwhelms: Panic Disorder. National Institute of Mental Helath, July 30, 2008, http://www.nimh.nih.gov/health/publications/panic-disorder-a-real-illness/summary.shtml.

PARENTAL DEPRESSION. The offspring of parents with **major depression** are at high risk for developing the disorder themselves. As **children** and **adolescents**, they are four to six times more likely to become depressed than other youngsters, and their risk for depression remains elevated even as adults. Yet many children of depressed parents grow up mentally healthy. It is clear that, just as parental depression may confer risk, there are other factors that may enhance resilience. All these factors work together to shape the experience of a particular child.

There are several reasons why having a parent with depression might increase the chance that children will become depressed, too. The genes children inherit undoubtedly play a role. Studies show that **genetic factors** account for about 40 percent to 50 percent of susceptibility to major depression. If genes are like a fuse, **stress** is often the flame that lights it. A parent's depression can cause stress and disruption for the whole family.

The interaction between parent and child may be affected as well. Research has found that mothers with depression tend to be less responsive to their children than nondepressed mothers. They also tend to show greater sadness and irritability, and express fewer positive emotions. These parenting behaviors, in turn, may interfere with healthy attachment.

When conflicts arise between parent and child, depressed mothers tend to withdraw rather than confronting the situation head on. As a result, children may miss out on the chance to learn valuable coping behaviors and interpersonal skills, such as assertiveness and negotiation. Depressed mothers also are prone to having poor self-esteem and taking an unduly negative view of the world, and children may pick up these thinking styles, which feed into depression.

The quality of the relationship between the parents also seems to be important. When one partner in a marriage is depressed, it can put considerable strain on the relationship. Some research has shown that discord between the parents rather than depression itself may be a stronger predictor of problems for the children. On the other hand, a supportive relationship between the parents may help children develop greater resilience.

Protecting the Next Generation. Whether through nature or nurture, depression is often passed down from one generation to the next. Yet it does not inevitably have to be that way. Researchers are currently studying how to improve the odds for children of depressed parents.

One preventive study included 116 families with school-aged children and a parent who had a mood disorder. Two different **prevention programs** were tested: an individualized program that included both parents and children and lasted six to 11 sessions, and a group program that included parents only and lasted two sessions. The programs integrated prior work showing that children who understand their parents' mood disorder and do not feel guilty for it are more likely to do well.

Initial testing of the programs showed promising results. More impressively, two and a half years later, there were still substantial changes in parents' attitudes and behaviors, such as decreased guilt, increased communication with their children, and better understanding of the children's perspective. These changes, in turn, were associated with children's increased understanding of their parents' illness. The children's self-reported symptoms also diminished over time.

As this study shows, **protective factors** can help balance the risk associated with having a depressed parent. For some children, the positives may outweigh the negatives, bringing an end to the legacy of depression.

See also: Attachment Theory; Postpartum Depression; Risk Factors

Bibliography

Beardslee, William R., Tracy R. G. Gladstone, Ellen J. Wright, and Andrew B. Cooper. "A Family-Based Approach to the Prevention of Depressive Symptoms in Children at Risk: Evidence of Parental and Child Change." *Pediatrics* 112 (2003): e119–e131.

Clarke, Gregory N., Mark Hornbrook, Frances Lynch, Michael Polen, John Gale, William Beardslee, et al. "A Randomized Trial of a Group Cognitive Intervention for Preventing Depression in Adolescent Offspring of Depressed Parents." *Archives of General Psychiatry* 58 (2001): 1127–1134.

Critical Issues for Parents with Mental Illness and Their Families. National Mental Health Information Center, http://mentalhealth.samhsa.gov/publications/allpubs/KEN-01–0109/ch4.asp.

Pilowsky, Daniel, Priya Wickramaratne, Yoko Nomura, and Myrna M. Weissman. "Family Discord, Parental Depression, and Psychopathology in Offspring: 20-Year Follow-Up." *Journal of the American Academy of Child and Adolescent Psychiatry* 45 (2006): 452–460.

Sutton, Jonathan M. "Prevention of Depression in Youth: A Qualitative Review and Future Suggestions." *Clinical Psychology Review* 27 (2007): 552–571.

PARKINSON'S DISEASE. Parkinson's disease (PD) is a degenerative disorder of the central **nervous system**. The best-known symptom is trembling of the hands, arms, legs, jaw, or head. However, PD also causes stiffness of the limbs or trunk, slowness of movement, and impaired balance and coordination. Although these movement problems are the hallmarks of PD, other symptoms may occur as well. Up to 60 percent of people with Parkinson's experience some symptoms of depression.

PD is a long-lasting disease that gets progressively worse over time. The average age of onset is 60, and the risk rises with age. Depression often appears early in the disease, sometimes even before other symptoms are noticeable. It is thought to be caused by changes in the brain associated with the disease process. As PD symptoms become more pronounced, people may begin to have trouble walking, talking, or doing everyday tasks. The **stress** of coping with current symptoms and worrying about future ones may make depression worse.

Untreated depression, in turn, may hasten the progression of PD. Research has shown that people with PD who are depressed tend to have more difficulty with daily activities and need medication for movement symptoms sooner than those who are not depressed. On the flip side, treating depression can improve both movement symptoms and overall quality of life.

The Depression Connection. PD occurs when cells in part of the brain called the substantia nigra die or become impaired. Normally, the substantia nigra produces **dopamine**, a brain chemical that is essential for movement and that also influences motivation and the perception of reality. Loss of dopamine is what causes the movement symptoms seen in PD. Low levels of the brain chemical also may contribute to depression. In research on people without PD, dopamine levels seem to fall during depression and rise during **mania** in people who cycle back and forth between the two extremes. Depression also is a side effect of certain medications, such as the blood pressure drug reserpine, that reduce the brain's dopamine supply.

Recent studies have shown that PD also leads to the loss of nerve endings that produce another chemical messenger called **norepinephrine**. This chemical helps control many of the body's involuntary functions, such as heart rate and blood pressure. Loss of norepinephrine could explain some non-movement symptoms of PD, such as orthostatic hypotension, a sudden drop in blood pressure when a person stands up from a lying-down position. The decrease in norepinephrine activity also may play a role in depression.

Serotonin is a third brain chemical that may be affected by PD. This chemical not only influences mood, but also helps regulate sleep, appetite, and sexual drive. In addition, the frontal lobe of the brain, which has an important role in controlling mood, is known to be underactive in PD.

Diagnostic Challenges. Diagnosing depression in someone with PD is not always easy. Some symptoms of depression—such as slowed-down movements, sleep problems, emotional apathy, and lack of energy—are also common symptoms of PD. This makes it easy to either over- or under-diagnose depression, depending on how the overlapping symptoms are interpreted.

When depression does occur, it may not look like a textbook case. Some studies suggest that depressed individuals with PD may be prone to more anxiety and less guilt than depressed people without PD. Also, people with PD whose movement symptoms wax and wane often experience similar fluctuations in their mood. These individuals may look, act, and feel differently depending on the state of their disease at any given time.

Despite these challenges, practice guidelines from the American Academy of Neurology state that standard screening tests can help identify people with PD who are depressed. There is solid evidence that the **Beck Depression Inventory** and **Hamilton Depression**

Rating Scale are probably useful for this purpose. There is also more limited evidence that the **Montgomery-Åsberg Depression Rating Scale** might be useful.

Treatment Considerations. For anyone with PD, it is very important that the disorder be properly treated. Although there is no cure, medications or surgery can sometimes provide dramatic relief from movement symptoms.

Beyond that, **antidepressants** can help ease PD-related depression. Antidepressants work by increasing the brain's supply of dopamine, norepinephrine, and/or serotonin. In people with PD who are depressed, the treatment with the strongest research support is amitriptyline, one of a group of medications called **tricyclic antidepressants**. That does not necessarily mean it is the most effective medication, however—just the best studied one.

Some people also may be helped by **cognitive-behavioral therapy**, a form of **psychotherapy** that teaches people how to change their thoughts and behavior in constructive ways. Having a potentially debilitating disease is a very stressful experience. People with PD may benefit from learning how to better manage stress and deal with social challenges.

See also: Mood Disorder Due to a General Medical Condition; Neurological Disorders; Physical Illness

Further Information. National Institute of Neurological Disorders and Stroke, P.O. Box 5801, Bethesda, MD 20824, (800) 352-9424, www.ninds.nih.gov.

National Parkinson Foundation, 1501 N.W. 9th Avenue/Bob Hope Road, Miami, FL 33136, (800) 327-4545, www.parkinson.org.

Parkinson's Disease Foundation, 1359 Broadway, Suite 1509, New York, NY 10018, (800) 457-6676, www.pdf.org.

Bibliography

Boland, Robert. "Depression in Medical Illness (Secondary Depression)." In *The American Psychiatric Publishing Textbook of Mood Disorders,* by Dan J. Stein, David J. Kupfer and Alan F. Schatzberg, eds., 639–652. Washington, DC: American Psychiatric Publishing, 2006.

Depression. Parkinson's Disease Foundation, http://www.pdf.org/en/depression_pd.

Evaluation and Treatment of Depression, Psychosis and Dementia in Parkinson's Disease. American Academy of Neurology, http://aan.com/professionals/practice/guidelines/Eval_Treatment _PD_Sum.pdf.

Karceski, Steven. "Early Parkinson Disease and Depression." *Neurology* 69 (2007): E2–E3.

Lieberman, A. "Depression in Parkinson's Disease: A Review." *Acta Neurologica Scandinavica* 113 (2006): 1–8.

Menza, Matthew. *Combating Depression in Parkinson's Disease.* Parkinson's Disease Foundation, http://www.pdf.org/en/spring04_Depression.

Parkinson's Disease: Hope Through Research. National Institute of Neurological Disorders and Stroke, September 17, 2008, http://www.ninds.nih.gov/disorders/parkinsons_disease/detail_parkinsons _disease.htm.

Summary: Diagnosis of Depression in Parkinson's Disease. National Institute of Neurological Disorders and Stroke, February 9, 2005, http:/ninds.nih.gov/news_and_events/proceedings/depression _summary.htm.

PARTIAL REMISSION. Partial remission refers to incomplete **recovery** from a mental disorder. In the case of **major depression**, partial remission means that some symptoms hang on after a person starts to get better, even though the full diagnostic criteria for the disorder are no longer met. The term also may be used when all the symptoms of major depression are gone, but the remission period has lasted less than two months.

A year after diagnosis with major depression, about 20 percent of people are in partial remission. These individuals are much more likely to develop another full-blown episode in the future, compared to those who recover completely.

Some people in partial remission feel much better than they did before, but others continue to suffer. Let's say the number of symptoms experienced by a person drops from six to four, falling below the cutoff point required for major depression. Although that sounds like solid improvement, it may be small consolation if the four remaining symptoms are still severe and disabling.

Fortunately, a wide range of treatments are now available to help relieve current suffering and reduce the risk of a future **recurrence**. Although it may take some trial and error, it is usually possible to find a treatment regimen that leads to full remission or at least substantial improvement.

Causes and Risk Factors. One of the strongest predictors of partial remission is having both major depression and **dysthymia** at the same time, a situation sometimes known as **double depression**. Dysthymia is a relatively mild but quite persistent form of depression that lasts for at least two years. During that period, symptoms tend to wax and wane, and at times, they may become intense and numerous enough to qualify as a full-blown episode of major depression superimposed on the dysthymia. Once the symptoms wane again, some signs of major depression may linger, resulting in a partial remission.

Others factors also may increase the risk of an incomplete recovery from major depression. These factors include having a greater number of symptoms at the time of diagnosis, being under high **stress**, and having poor social support. Research in **older adults** has found an association between partial remission and health problems, impaired mobility, dissatisfaction with their current lives, and perceived unhappiness in years past.

Bibliography

American Psychiatric Association. *Diagnostic and Statistical Manual of Mental Disorders.* 4th ed., text rev. Washington, DC: American Psychiatric Association, 2000.

Frances, Allen, Michael B. First, and Harold Alan Pincus. *DSM-IV Guidebook.* Washington, DC: American Psychiatric Press, 1995.

Hybels, Celia F., Dan G. Blazer, and David C. Steffens. "Partial Remission: A Common Outcome in Older Adults Treated for Major Depression." *Geriatrics* 61 (2006): 22–26.

Hybels, Celia F., Dan G. Blazer, and David C. Steffens. "Predictors of Partial Remission in Older Patients Treated for Major Depression: The Role of Comorbid Dysthymia." *American Journal of Geriatric Psychiatry* 13 (2005): 713–721.

Pintor, Luis, Xavier Torres, Victor Navarro, Silvia Matrai, and Cristobal Gastó. "Is the Type of Remission After a Major Depressive Episode an Important Risk Factor to Relapses in a 4-Year Follow Up?" *Journal of Affective Disorders* 82 (2004): 291–296.

Questions and Answers About the NIMH Sequenced Treatment Alternatives to Relieve Depression (STAR*D) Study: All Medication Levels. National Institute of Mental Health, June 26, 2008, http://www.nimh.nih.gov/health/trials/practical/stard/questions-and-answers-about-the-nimh -sequenced-treatment-alternatives-to-relieve-depression-stard-study-all-medication-levels.shtml.

PASTORAL COUNSELOR. Pastoral counselors provide guidance and treatment for mental and emotional disorders in a spiritual context, drawing upon both traditional

psychotherapy and spiritual resources. The ultimate goal is not only successful treatment, but also personal and spiritual growth.

Many people turn to a minster, priest, rabbi, or other member of the clergy when seeking advice on coping with depression and other mental health problems. Although these religious advisors may offer support and suggest resources, most are not equipped to provide actual treatment. Pastoral counselors are the exception. In addition to having in-depth religious or theological training, they are also mental health professionals.

Training and Credentials. The American Association of Pastoral Counselors (AAPC) offers three levels of certification. In addition to education and experience, certification is based on testing and evaluation aimed at selecting counselors who not only are professionally competent, but also possess high personal standards.

According to the association, the typical education for an AAPC-certified pastoral counselor includes a bachelor's degree, a three-year professional degree from a seminary, and a master's degree or above in a mental health field. Education and training vary, however, so interested consumers should ask about the credentials of a pastoral counselor before beginning therapy.

Pastoral Counseling in Action. There are more than 3,000 certified pastoral counselors in the United States. Along with providing treatment for mental disorders, they may offer other services, such as counseling on problems of everyday living, **substance abuse** treatment, and religious retreats. The AAPC is the professional organization representing the field.

Only six states (Arkansas, Kentucky, Maine, New Hampshire, North Carolina, and Tennessee) specifically regulate the pastoral counseling profession. In other states, pastoral counselors may be licensed or certified as a **mental health counselor**, **marriage and family therapist**, **clinical psychologist**, or other mental health professional.

See also: Diagnosis of Depression; Spirituality and Religion; Treatment of Depression

Further Information. American Association of Pastoral Counselors, 9504A Lee Highway, Fairfax, VA 22031-2303, (703) 385-6967, www.aapc.org.

Bibliography

About Pastoral Counseling. American Association of Pastoral Counselors, http://www.aapc.org/about.cfm.

PENN RESILIENCY PROGRAM. The Penn Resiliency Program (PRP)—formerly called the Penn Prevention Program—is a depression prevention curriculum developed at the University of Pennsylvania. It is designed for late-elementary school and middle school students. The program—which teaches cognitive, behavioral, and social problem-solving skills—is based on theories of depression developed by **Aaron T. Beck** (1921–), **Albert Ellis** (1913–2007), and **Martin E. P. Seligman** (1942–). The goal is to ward off depression entirely or keep any current symptoms from getting worse. Overall, results of 13 controlled studies involving more than 2,000 students suggest that the program helps prevent symptoms of depression and anxiety, and these benefits can be long-lasting.

Some strategies used in PRP are similar to those used in **cognitive therapy**, which aims to identify and change unrealistically negative thinking. Such thinking is believed to play a central role in depression. PRP teaches young people to counter unduly negative thinking before they become seriously depressed. Other skills taught in the program include assertiveness, negotiation, decision making, and relaxation.

PRP typically involves twelve 90-minute lessons or eighteen 60-minute lessons. In these lessons, core skills and concepts are introduced through skits, role-playing, short stories, and cartoons. Students then practice the skills in hypothetical examples that mimic real situations they might face. Finally, students put the new skills to use in daily life by doing weekly homework assignments.

In addition to the researchers behind PRP, lessons have been led by graduate students, mental health professionals, teachers, and school counselors. These program leaders receive extensive training and supervision.

Studies looking at the effectiveness of PRP have been conducted not only by the researchers who developed the program, but also by other research teams. Most found that PRP reduced symptoms of depression and anxiety, although some inconsistent findings have been reported. Long-term studies that followed up with students after the program ended have shown that the benefits sometimes last for two years or more.

See also: Adolescents; Prevention of Depression; Prevention Programs; School Issues

Bibliography

Cardemil, Esteban V., Karen J. Reivich, Christopher G. Beevers, Martin E. P. Seligman, and Julie James. "The Prevention of Depressive Symptoms in Low-Income, Minority Children: Two-Year Follow-Up." *Behaviour Research and Therapy* 45 (2007): 313–327.

Evans, Dwight L., and Linda Wasmer Andrews. *If Your Adolescent Has Depression or Bipolar Disorder: An Essential Resource for Parents.* New York: Oxford University Press, 2005.

Gillham, Jane E., Karen J. Reivich, Derek R. Freres, Tara M. Chaplin, Andrew J. Shatté, Barbra Samuels, et al. "School-Based Prevention of Depressive Symptoms: A Randomized Controlled Study of Effectiveness and Specificity of the Penn Resiliency Program." *Journal of Consulting and Clinical Psychology* 75 (2007): 9–19.

Resilience Research in Children. University of Pennsylvania Positive Psychology Center, 2007, http://www.ppc.sas.upenn.edu/prpsum.htm.

Seligman, Martin E. P., with Karen Reivich, Lisa Jaycox, and Jane Gillham. *The Optimistic Child: A Proven Program to Safeguard Children Against Depression and Build Lifelong Resilience.* New York: Houghton Mifflin, 1995.

PERSONALITY FACTORS. Personality refers to the constellation of cognitive traits, emotional patterns, and behavioral styles that make up a person's unique adjustment of life. The nature of an individual's personality colors how that person sees the world and shapes his or her thoughts, feelings, and actions. The interaction between personality and depression has long been a subject of great clinical and research interest. Personality may affect an individual's vulnerability to depression in the face of stressful life events, and it also may influence the course of the illness and the response to treatment.

Much modern research has focused on personality traits—internal characteristics that are relatively stable over time and consistent across many situations. Such traits cannot be observed directly, but they can be inferred from an individual's pattern of beliefs, attitudes, feelings, behaviors, and habits. An example of a trait-based theory is the **five-factor model**, which holds that personality is comprised of five traits: Openness to Experience, Conscientiousness, Extraversion, Agreeableness, and Neuroticism (OCEAN).

An alternative approach conceptualizes personality in terms of personality types—distinct categories into which people can be classified. Although traits are continuous dimensions that people vary on to some degree, types are discrete categories that people either fall into or not on an all-or-none basis. An example of a personality type is the introversion-extraversion dichotomy proposed by Swiss psychologist and psychiatrist Carl Jung (1875–1961).

The distinction between traits and types is of more than just theoretical importance. The two viewpoints have different clinical implications as well. A psychologist who subscribes to personality trait theory sees depression as the result of either gradually getting stronger on a negative trait or weaker on a positive one. Treatment is a gradual process, too, aimed at moderating a trait that has been taken to an unhealthy extreme.

In contrast, a psychologist with a personality type orientation sees depression as arising suddenly when a set of necessary conditions are all met. Treatment may be more difficult, but once a change has finally taken place, it should be more dramatic and complete.

Depressive Personalities. One early theory of personality and depression was formulated by German psychiatrist Emil Kraepelin (1856–1926), who pioneered the modern classification system of mental disorders. As far back as 1921, Kraepelin described something he called "depressive temperament." People with this temperament tended to be gloomy, serious, guilt-ridden, self-reproaching, and low in self-confidence, starting at a young age and lasting throughout their lives. Kraepelin believed that such traits reflected an inherited disposition and laid the foundation for future episodes of full-blown depression.

In the late 1950s, another German psychiatrist, Kurt Schneider (1887–1967), described "depressive psychopathy." Schneider described people with depressive psychopathy as taking pride in their suffering. They tended to be gloomy, pessimistic, serious, unable to relax, quiet, skeptical, duty-bound, self-doubting, and awash in worries. Unlike Kraepelin, though, Schneider placed greater emphasis on the role of life experiences and the environment in molding a depression-prone personality.

Neuroticism and Extraversion. More recently, a number of researchers have tried to identify the core traits that make up personality. Each trait is thought to be a continuum that varies from the high extreme to the low extreme, with most people falling someplace in between. People who are unusually high or low in certain traits are thought to be at risk for psychological problems, including depression.

This viewpoint is grounded in the work of German-born British psychologist Hans Jurgen Eysenck (1916–1997), whose PEN model of personality is comprised of three dimensions: Psychoticism, Extraversion, and Neuroticism. In Eysenck's system, Psychoticism is characterized not only by the risk of having a psychotic episode (a break with reality), but also by aggression and antisocial behavior. Extraversion is typified by positive emotions and sociability, and Neuroticism is typified by negative emotions and emotional instability.

A pair of influential later theories built on Eysenck's work while expanding the number of core traits to five. One is the five-factor (OCEAN) model, proposed by U.S. psychologists Robert R. McCrae (1949–) and Paul T. Costa Jr. The other is the Big Five model, advocated by U.S. psychologist Lewis R. Goldberg (1931–) and colleagues. Like the five-factor model, the Big Five model describes personality in terms of five core traits: Openness to Experience (also called Intellect), Conscientiousness, Extraversion (also called Surgency), Agreeableness, and Neuroticism (also called Emotional Stability). One difference between these two theories is that Big Five proponents see traits strictly as descriptions of behavior, but five-factor proponents also view traits as psychological entities with causal power.

Across all these theories, the traits most often mentioned in relation to depression are Neuroticism and Extraversion. People who are high in Neuroticism (or low in Emotional

Stability) are at increased risk for depression. That comes as no surprise, because Neuroticism is characterized by a propensity for emotional instability and psychological distress. When people who are high in Neuroticism do become depressed, research shows they may be prone to developing other mental disorders at the same time.

Extraversion is characterized not only by sociability, but also by positive emotions. As might be expected, studies have also found that the lower people are in extraversion, the more likely they are to become depressed.

Negative and Positive Affect.　In an effort to refine these two key traits, U.S. psychologists David Watson and Lee Anna Clark introduced a pair of personality dimensions called Negative Affect and Positive Affect. People high in Negative Affect—much like those high in Neuroticism—are prone to depression, anxiety, guilt, hostility, and self-dissatisfaction. They also tend to engage in negative thinking, be low in self-esteem, and feel dissatisfied with life.

People low in Positive Affect—much like those low in Extraversion—are prone to negative moods. They also tend to be unenergetic, withdrawn, and unable to take much pleasure in life. Although depression is a combination of high Negative Affect and low Positive Affect, research suggests that there may be a more specific association with the latter.

Temperament and Character.　An alternative approach to personality traits was proposed by U.S. psychiatrist and geneticist C. Robert Cloninger (1944–). In the mid-1980s, the leading trait theories of the day were rooted in factor analysis, a statistical procedure that boils down large data sets to the smallest number of concepts (factors) required to explain the pattern of relationships in the data. Cloninger took a completely different path, basing his theory on genetic, biological, and pharmacological data.

Using this approach, Cloninger set out to study temperament—the basic foundation of personality, which is grounded in genetics and biology. He identified four main dimensions of temperament: Harm Avoidance (anxious and pessimistic versus outgoing and optimistic), Novelty Seeking (impulsive and quick-tempered versus rigid and slow-tempered), Reward Dependence (warm and approval-seeking versus cold and aloof), and Persistence (persevering and ambitious versus easily discouraged and underachieving).

Although temperament is vitally important, it soon became apparent that it does not capture the full range of personality. In particular, it does not reflect the conscious choices people make about how to use their innate tendencies and abilities. To complete the picture, Cloninger realized that he also needed to study character—a person's characteristic moral, social, and spiritual attitudes. He identified three main dimensions of character: Self-Directedness (reliable and purposeful versus blaming and aimless), Cooperativeness (tolerant and helpful versus prejudiced and revengeful), and Self-Transcendence (self-forgetful and spiritual versus self-conscious and materialistic).

To study his theory, Cloninger developed a test called the Temperament and Character Inventory (TCI). Subsequent research using this test has shown that people with active depression have a different personality profile from both healthy individuals and those with depression that is in remission. One study of 631 adults found that initial TCI scores—particularly high Harm Avoidance and low Self-Directedness—helped account for any changes in depressive symptoms over the following year.

Dependency and Self-Criticism.　Other theorists have described certain personality types that are more or less vulnerable to depression. Interestingly, two very different schools of thought—psychoanalytic and cognitive-behavioral—have independently linked depression to similar personalities.

Psychoanalytic theory focuses on unconscious drives and wishes along with the lasting effects of past events, and cognitive-behavioral theory focuses on current patterns of thought and behavior. Despite this fundamental difference in perspective, leading theorists from each camp have related depression to a tendency to achieve or maintain self-esteem through interpersonal relationships. This tendency leaves an individual open to depression when such relationships fall apart or are lost.

Working from a psychoanalytic framework, U.S. psychologist Sidney J. Blatt categorized people as either high or low in interpersonal dependency. He noted that those with high dependency are overly invested in their relationships and vulnerable to depression in response to interpersonal loss or separation. Coming at the same problem from a cognitive-behavioral angle, U.S. psychiatrist Aaron T. Beck (1921–) categorized people as either high or low in sociotropy—a combination of beliefs, attitudes, and behavioral dispositions that lead a person to place inordinate value on interpersonal relationships and the approval of others. He noted that those high in sociotropy are prone to depression in response to relationship loss or conflict.

A second trait emphasized by Blatt is self-criticism. Those high in self-criticism who fail to meet their own excessively high standards are prone to depression as well. In a similar vein, Beck singled out autonomy—a tendency to overemphasize personal achievement and a sense of power to do what one wants. Those high in autonomy who fail to achieve a personal goal are vulnerable to becoming depressed as well.

No single personality trait holds the key to depression. But the combination of a particular personality and a specific type of **stress** may be enough to trigger or worsen a depressive episode, especially in someone who is genetically prone to the illness.

See also: Attachment Theory; Causes of Depression; Depressive Personality Disorder; Minnesota Multiphasic Personality Inventory; Relationship Issues

Bibliography

Acton, G. Scott. "Five-Factor Model." *Great Ideas in Personality,* July 2001, http://www.personalityresearch .org/bigfive.html.

Acton, G. Scott. "Goldberg." *Great Ideas in Personality,* Janauary 2001, http://www.personalityresearch .org/bigfive/goldberg.html.

Acton, G. Scott. "PEN Model." *Great Ideas in Personality,* January 1999, http://www.personalityresearch .org/pen.html.

Acton, G. Scott. "Watson and Clark." *Great Ideas in Personality,* January 1999, http://www .personalityresearch.org/pen/watson.html.

Clark, Lee Anna, David Watson, and Susan Mineka. "Temperament, Personality, and the Mood and Anxiety Disorders." *Journal of Abnormal Psychology* 103 (1994): 103–116.

Cloninger, C. Robert, Dragan M. Svrakic, and Thomas R. Przybeck. "Can Personality Assessment Predict Future Depression? A Twelve-Month Follow-Up of 631 Subjects." *Journal of Affective Disorders* 92 (2006) 35–44.

Farmer, Richard F., and John R. Seeley. "Temperament and Character Predictors of Depressed Mood Over a 4-Year Interval." *Depression and Anxiety* 26 (2009): 371–381.

Jylhä, Pekka, and Erkki Isometsä. "The Relationship of Neuroticism and Extraversion to Symptoms of Anxiety and Depression in the General Population." *Depression and Anxiety* 23 (2006): 281–289.

Jylhä, Pekka, Tarja Melartin, and Erkki Isometsä. "Relationships of Neuroticism and Extraversion with Axis I and II Comorbidity among Patients with DSM-IV Major Depressive Disorder." *Journal of Affective Disorders* 114 (2009): 110–121.

Luyten, Patrick, Bernard Sabbe, Sidney J. Blatt, Sieglinde Meganck, Bart Jansen, Carmen De Grave, et al. "Dependency and Self-Criticism: Relationship with Major Depressive Disorder, Severity of Depression, and Clinical Presentation." *Depression and Anxiety* 24 (2007): 586–596.

Phillips, Katharine A., John G. Gunderson, Robert M. A. Hirschfeld, and Lauren E. Smith. "A Review of the Depressive Personality." *American Journal of Psychiatry* 147 (1990): 830–837.

Sato, Toru, and Doug McCann. "Sociotropy-Autonomy and Interpersonal Problems." *Depression and Anxiety* 24 (2007): 153–162.

VandenBos, Gary R., ed. "Big Five Personality Model," "Eysenck's Typology" and "Five-Factor Personality Model (FFM)," in *APA Dictionary of Psychology.* Washington, DC: American Psychological Association, 2007.

Yen, Shirley, Meghan E. McDevitt-Murphy, and M. Tracie Shea. "Depression and Personality." In *The American Psychiatric Publishing Textbook of Mood Disorders,* by Dan J. Stein, David J. Kupfer and Alan F. Schatzberg, eds., 673–686. Washington, DC: American Psychiatric Publishing, 2006.

Zohar, Ada H. "The Blatt and Cloninger Models of Personality and Their Relationship with Psychopathology." *Israel Journal of Psychiatry and Related Sciences* 44 (2007): 292–300.

PESSIMISM. Pessimism is the belief that things will go wrong and desired goals will not be reached. A pessimistic attitude, which goes hand in hand with feelings of helplessness and hopelessness, is typical of depression. **Cognitive therapy**, one of the most effective treatments for depression, aims to identify and change unrealistically negative thinking.

In addition to increasing the risk for depression, a long-lasting pattern of pessimistic thinking can have other unwanted consequences. In the early 1960s, outpatients at the Mayo Clinic were given the **Minnesota Multiphasic Personality Inventory** (MMPI), one of the most widely used of all personality tests. Thirty years afterward, 447 of these individuals filled out a questionnaire about their health status. Their earlier MMPI responses were also used to derive an Optimism-Pessimism score for each person. Researchers found that a pessimistic thinking style was associated with worse physical and mental health three decades later.

Beyond the untoward health effects, pessimism can sap a person's motivation, because making an effort to reach a goal is seen as futile. As a result, dyed-in-the-wool pessimists are often underachievers. Studies show that pessimists give up more easily than their optimistic counterparts, and they generally perform less well in school, at work, and on the sports field.

Seligman's View of Pessimism. One important

Pessimism and the Presidency

From Ronald Reagan's "morning in America" to Barack Obama's "yes, we can," Americans love an upbeat message. According to Seligman, that may translate into electing the more optimistic presidential candidate. To test this hypothesis, Seligman and a colleague analyzed the content of 20 nomination acceptance speeches from the Democratic and Republican conventions of 1948 to 1984. In addition to looking for the language of pessimism, the researchers also looked for signs of **rumination**—the tendency to call negative thoughts and feelings to mind often and dwell on the dark side of life.

In nine out of ten elections, the candidate who was higher in pessimistic rumination lost. In Seligman's view, campaign speeches shape public expectations about what a candidate will be like in office. There is a natural tendency to vote for the candidate who gives rise to more hopeful expectations.

theory of pessimism was developed by U.S. psychologist **Martin E. P. Seligman** (1942–), who studied explanatory style—the way people habitually explain negative events to themselves. Seligman focused on three dimensions of explanatory style: permanence (how long the negative event or its cause will last), pervasiveness (how broad its effects are), and personalization (how much people blame themselves).

Pessimists generally believe that a negative event or its cause is permanent, even when there is evidence to the contrary. They tend to think that the negative features of one situation will carry over to other situations as well, undermining whatever they do. And they tend to attribute a negative event to their own flaws, rather than to outside circumstances, other people, or bad luck. Although it is important to take responsibility for one's mistakes, pessimists blame themselves for everything.

In Seligman's view, depression is pessimism taken to an extreme. Studies have shown that people who start out with a pessimistic attitude are more likely to become depressed when faced with a difficult situation. For example, when Seligman and his colleagues studied inmates as they were leaving prison, they found that almost all were depressed to some degree. But those who entered prison as pessimists tended to come out more severely depressed than those who started out with greater optimism.

Beck's View of Depression.   Seligman's views on pessimism and depression closely parallel those of U.S. psychiatrist **Aaron T. Beck** (1921–), who is considered a founding father of cognitive therapy. According to Beck, people with depression often experience streams of negative thoughts that pop up spontaneously. Such thoughts involve viewing themselves, the world, and the future in an unduly negative light. These three types of beliefs roughly correspond to Seligman's concepts of personalization, pervasiveness, and permanence, respectively.

Consider the example of a student who fails a test. A pessimist's first thought might be that he is stupid (negative view of the self; personalization). The pessimist also might believe that his self-perceived stupidity will undercut everything he does in school (negative view of the world; pervasiveness), and it will always be that way (negative view of the future; permanence).

Learning to Be an Optimist.   A pessimistic thinking style tends to be a stable trait that persists over many decades. But Seligman believes that a more optimistic attitude can be learned using techniques similar to those used in cognitive therapy. These techniques include identifying negative interpretations of events, evaluating their accuracy, and when appropriate, coming up with more accurately positive interpretations.

To ferret out errors in thinking, people look for evidence that the cause of the event is able to be changed, specific to the situation and not their own fault. Of course, at times, the facts will not be on their side, and they will have to conclude that their negative interpretation is on the money. At such times, Seligman emphasizes decatastrophizing—countering the tendency to imagine the worst-case consequences of the event.

See also: Learned Helplessness

Bibliography

Acton, G. Scott. "Cognitive Social Theories." *Great Ideas in Personality,* October 2005, http://www.personalityresearch.org/cogsocial.html.

"Learned Helplessness." *Encyclopedia of Childhood and Adolescence,* 1998, http://findarticles.com/p/articles/mi_g2602/is_0003/ai_2602000349.

Seligman, Martin E. P. *Learned Optimism*. New York: Alfred A. Knopf, 1991.

Toshihiko, Maruta, Robert C. Colligan, Michael Malinchoc, and Kenneth P. Offord. "Optimism-Pessimism Assessed in the 1960s and Self-Reported Health Status 30 Years Later." *Mayo Clinic Proceedings* 77 (2002): 748–753.

Zullow, Harold M., Gabriele Oettingen, Christopher Peterson, and Martin E. P. Seligman. "Pessimistic Explanatory Style in the Historical Record: CAVing LBJ, Presidential Candidates, and East Versus West Berlin." *American Psychologist* 43 (1988): 673–682.

PHARMACOTHERAPY. Pharmacotherapy (also called drug therapy) refers to the treatment of a disorder with medication. **Antidepressants** are the standard form of pharmacotherapy for depression. From 1996 to 2005, the percentage of Americans age six and older who took antidepressant medication over the course of a year jumped from six percent to 10 percent. During that same period, among people being treated with antidepressants, use of additional medications increased and use of **psychotherapy** declined, a sign of the growing prominence of drug treatment.

Several factors may have played a role in the recent rise of pharmacotherapy. Since the introduction of second-generation antidepressants in the mid-1980s, a number of antidepressants have been introduced that are as effective as older medications, but that cause fewer serious side effects. Drug companies have aggressively marketed many of these newer medications not only to physicians, but also directly to potential consumers, and updated medical guidelines have advocated their use as first-line treatments. Meanwhile, public awareness of depression and acceptance of drug treatment have grown.

Yet the rise of pharmacotherapy has not been without controversy. Critics argue that antidepressants are significantly riskier than psychotherapy, yet may be no more effective for many people with mild to moderate depression. Physicians and researchers continue to debate whether antidepressants are being overused and their risks are being minimized.

About four out of five people receiving pharmacotherapy for depression are prescribed a single antidepressant. For the rest, another medication is added to the antidepressant to boost its effectiveness or decrease side effects. At times, the add-on medication may be a second antidepressant. At other times, it might be an anti-anxiety or antipsychotic medication, or a prescription sleep aid.

See also: Anticonvulsants; Antipsychotics; Augmentation Therapy; Mood Stabilizers; Treatment of Depression

Further Information. American Society of Health-System Pharmacists, 7272 Wisconsin Avenue, Bethesda MD 20814, (301) 657-3000, www.ashp.org, www.safemedication.com.

Food and Drug Administration, 10903 New Hampshire Avenue, Silver Spring, MD 20993, (888) 463-6332, www.fda.gov.

Institute for Safe Medication Practices, 200 Lakeside Drive, Suite 200, Horsham, PA 19044, (215) 947-7797, www.ismp.org.

Bibliography

Gitlin, Michael J. "Pharmacotherapy and Other Somatic Treatments for Depression." In *Handbook of Depression*. 2nd ed., by Ian H. Gotlib and Constance L. Hammen, eds., 554–585. New York: Guilford Press, 2009.

Lenderts, Susan, and Amir Kalali. "Treatment of Depression: An Update on Antidepressant Monotherapy and Combination Therapy." *Psychiatry* 6 (2009): 15–17.

Olfson, Mark, and Steven C. Marcus. "National Patterns in Antidepressant Medication Treatment." *Archives of General Psychiatry* 66 (2009): 848–856.

PHYSICAL ILLNESS.   Depression often coexists with physical illnesses, such as **cancer, diabetes, heart disease, stroke, human immunodeficiency virus** (HIV) infection, **multiple sclerosis**, and **Parkinson's disease**. In some cases, the other illness is the direct physiological cause of depression. In other cases, the link is psychological rather than physiological. Having a serious illness can be very stressful, and **stress** can trigger or worsen depression in susceptible individuals.

Of course, causation can flow both ways. Depression and the behavior it causes can contribute to physical illness, too. For example, people who are depressed often become sedentary due to lack of energy and loss of motivation. A study of more than 1,000 people with stable coronary heart disease found that physical inactivity was a major contributor to the relationship between heart disease and depression.

At times, depression and physical illness may be linked through a common third factor. For instance, prolonged stress caused by ongoing personal problems can put people at risk for depression. At the same time, it also can decrease cardiovascular health, increase blood glucose (sugar), inhibit wound healing, and heighten pain perception. In addition, when people are under stress, diseases such as psoriasis, rheumatoid arthritis, and inflammatory bowel disease may be more likely to flare up.

Finally, there are also times when it may be pure coincidence that a person develops both depression and another medical illness. But once both conditions are present, they may still affect each other. For example, people with depression may be less likely to take their prescribed medication or make a recommended change in lifestyle.

Studies have shown that people with physical illnesses who are also depressed tend to have more severe symptoms of both conditions. They also may have more trouble adapting to their physical illness and higher medical costs than those without depression. On a more positive note, there is increasing evidence that treating depression often helps improve the outcome of the coexisting physical illness as well.

See also: Comorbidity; Mood Disorder Due to a General Medical Condition

Bibliography

Stress Coping: Stress and Your Health. University of Pittsburgh Medical Center, http://healthylifestyle.upmc.com/StressHealth.htm.

What Illnesses Often Co-exist with Depression? National Institute of Mental Health, January 30, 2009, http://www.nimh.nih.gov/health/publications/depression/what-illnesses-often-co-exist-with-depression.shtml.

Whooley, Mary A., Peter de Jonge, Eric Vittinghoff, Christian Otte, Rudolf Moos, Robert M. Carney, et al. "Depressive Symptoms, Health Behaviors, and Risk of Cardiovascular Events in Patients with Coronary Heart Disease." *JAMA* 300 (2008): 2379–2388.

POLLUTION.   Pollution refers to any substance introduced into the environment that adversely affects the usefulness of a resource or the health of living things. Some such substances act on the **nervous system**. Because depression is a brain disorder, it seems plausible that certain pollutants with neurological effects might contribute to the condition.

Some air pollutants, for example, are known to cause neurological symptoms. A study of emergency department visits in Edmonton, Canada, found that visits for depression tended to rise on days when air pollution levels were high. Although this study showed an association between pollution and depression, it was not designed to tease out whether one factor caused the other. At the very least, though, it indicates that more research is needed on this subject.

Organophosphate Pesticides. One of the best-studied associations between environmental toxins and depression involves organophosphate pesticides. There are about 40 organophosphate pesticides, accounting for approximately half of pesticide use in the United States. These substances kill insects by impairing nervous system activity. More specifically, they inhibit the activity of an enzyme called acetylcholinesterase, which breaks down a chemical messenger in the nervous system called acetylcholine. The net effect is to interfere with the transmission of nerve cell messages.

Studies have shown that acute poisoning with organophosphate pesticides can have long-term consequences, including chronic depression. In one study of farmers and their spouses in Colorado, for example, pesticide exposure at a level high enough to cause poisoning symptoms was associated with a high risk for depressive symptoms.

See also: Environmental Factors

Bibliography

About Air Toxics. Environmental Protection Agency, http://www.epa.gov/air/toxicair/newtoxics.html.

Beseler, Cheryl L., Lorann Stallones, Jane A. Hoppin, Michael C. R. Alavanja, Aaron Blair, Thomas Keefe, et al. "Depression and Pesticide Exposures Among Private Pesticide Applicators Enrolled in the Agricultural Health Study." *Environmental Health Perspectives* 116 (2008): 1713–1719.

Organophosphates. National Institute of Environmental Health Sciences, February 19, 2009, http://tools.niehs.nih.gov/sbrp/research/research4_s3_s5.cfm.

Stallones, Lorann, and Cheryl Besseler. "Pesticide Poisoning and Depressive Symptoms Among Farm Residents." *Annals of Epidemiology* 12 (2002) 389–394.

Szyszkowicz, Mieczyslaw. "Air Pollution and Emergency Department Visits for Depression in Edmonton, Canada." *International Journal of Occupational Medicine and Environmental Health* 20 (2007): 241–245.

POSTPARTUM DEPRESSION. Postpartum depression refers to depression in which the symptoms begin within six months of giving birth. It is more than just a short-lived case of the blues. The symptoms of postpartum depression are long-lasting and wide-ranging. **Women** who develop postpartum depression may have trouble taking care of a newborn or keeping up with other responsibilities at home, work, or school. They may feel guilt about not being the kind of mother they want to be. But like other forms of depression, postpartum depression is an illness, not a personal flaw. The earlier its symptoms are recognized, the earlier treatment can begin, and the sooner women can get back to their usual selves.

From 50 percent to 80 percent of women develop a mild case of "baby blues" soon after giving birth. They may feel happy one minute, then burst into tears the next. Some feel a little down, lose their appetite, find it hard to sleep, or have trouble concentrating. The problems are manageable, though, and they go away on their own within a week or two.

True postpartum depression is a different story. It causes serious distress and disruption for women at a time when society says they should be most happy. Many secretly wonder if they are the only ones to feel this way. Yet the truth is that they are far from alone. About 10 percent to 20 percent of new mothers develop postpartum depression.

Left unrecognized and untreated, the condition affects not only mothers, but also babies. Women with postpartum depression tend to be less involved with their newborns,

Out of the Closet

In the past, postpartum depression was a little-understood condition that often was spoken about in hushed whispers, if at all. Today, however, people have become more aware of this very common—and very treatable—illness. Several celebrities have gone public with their personal experiences, helping raise the condition's profile. Below are personal accounts of postpartum depression as seen through the eyes of two celebrity moms.

Brooke Shields (1965–), U.S. Actress

I was desperate to have a natural and healthy connection with my daughter, but it was feeling so forced. It was as if I were trapped behind a thick glass wall. I had never felt apathy in my life, and when I had least expected it, it crept in and took over. I couldn't shake the feeling of doom and gloom that pervaded each moment. I was afraid of myself and felt threatened by the dangerous thoughts running so calmly through my head. They all felt too real. When would I wake up from this bad dream?

From *Down Came the Rain: My Journey through Postpartum Depression* by Brooke Shields (New York: Hyperion, 2005).

Marie Osmond (1959–), U.S. Singer

The baby was sleeping in the bassinet next to my bed. Looking at his tiny face gave me huge feelings of regret. I starting questioning myself: "What is wrong with you? What are you becoming? Why can't you get through this? Your children depend on you. You have to be strong for them. So many women are less blessed than you are and they don't fall apart!"

From *Behind the Smile: My Journey Out of Postpartum Depression.* Copyright © 2001 by Marie Osmond. By permission of Grand Central Publishing.

which may have repercussions for years to come. Studies suggest that these children may later be prone to learning and behavioral problems as well as trouble interacting with peers. It is one more reason why prompt treatment of postpartum depression is so important.

More Than Baby Blues. The ***Diagnostic and Statistical Manual of Mental Disorders, Fourth Edition, Text Revision*** (*DSM-IV-TR*), a diagnostic guide used by mental health professionals from many disciplines, defines postpartum depression as depression that begins within four weeks of giving birth. However, many experts consider that definition too restrictive. Although postpartum depression usually begins within the first few weeks after delivery, some women do not become depressed until several weeks or months after their baby is born.

Many women with postpartum depression feel sad, empty, irritable, or anxious almost all the time. They may cry frequently or feel as if life isn't worth living. Others are unmotivated and disinterested, even when it comes to caring for their baby. Additional symptoms may include lack of energy, changes in appetite, feelings of worthlessness and trouble sleeping even when the baby is asleep. Some women also are plagued by excessive worries about the baby's health or fears about not being a good mother.

Of course, it is common for new mothers to feel cranky, tired, or worried about doing a good job. But the changes caused by postpartum depression are more drastic, and they hang around for weeks or months, causing serious problems in the woman's daily life.

Postpartum Psychosis. About one-tenth of one percent of new mothers develop a severe disorder called postpartum psychosis. The onset of postpartum psychosis is usually sudden and swift, striking within the first two or three weeks after giving birth. Women with postpartum psychosis have distorted thoughts or perceptions that are seriously out of touch with reality. Some have disturbing thoughts about hurting themselves or harming the baby that intrude uncontrollably into their mind. Other possible symptoms include refusal to eat, frantic energy, ceaseless activity, extreme confusion, incoherent speech, preoccupation with trivial things, and irrational thoughts about being watched or persecuted.

In this state, there is a small but real chance that a woman could hurt herself or her baby. As a result, psychiatric **hospitalization** is usually needed until the woman's symptoms subside. In the hospital, she can receive intensive, specialized care and round-the-clock monitoring.

Causes and Risk Factors. Researchers aren't sure exactly why some women develop postpartum depression and others have only mild baby blues or no blues at all. However, postpartum depression is believed to be linked to the dramatic hormonal shifts that occur during **pregnancy** and right after childbirth. These shifts may lead to chemical changes in the brain that result in depression.

Stress also may be a contributing factor in women who are vulnerable to depression. Giving birth is a major life change, and it can be stressful caring for a new baby, adjusting to new responsibilities, and returning to work after maternity leave. Women who have few family members and friends to rely on or a strained relationship with the baby's father are at increased risk for postpartum depression. Serious problems during pregnancy, premature birth, or a difficult delivery make depression more likely as well.

Postpartum depression is more common in women who have a past history of **major depression**, which involves being in a low mood nearly all the time and/or losing interest or enjoyment in almost everything, or **bipolar disorder**, which involves alternating periods of depression and **mania** (an overly high mood). More than half of women who

---

The Case of Andrea Yates

When *Time* magazine compiled a list of the top 25 crimes of the twentieth century, it came as no surprise that the list included the 2001 case of Andrea Yates, the Texas mother who drowned her four young sons and infant daughter in the family bathtub. As shocking as the crime was, much of the national dialogue about the case centered around Yates's history of severe postpartum depression and psychosis, the missed opportunities for treatment, and the role these factors may have played in the tragedy that ensued.

Yates confessed to the murders. Her lawyers presented an insanity defense, claiming she killed the children while in a delusional state, convinced that Satan was inside her and that she was trying to save the children from hell. At a 2002 trial, the jury rejected this defense and found Yates guilty. She was sentenced to life in prison, but after a successful appeal, she received a second trial in 2006. This time around, the jury found her not guilty by reason of insanity, and she was committed by the court to a state mental hospital.

The Yates case was clearly an extreme aberration. Yet by capturing the nation's attention, it raised public awareness about less extreme, but nonetheless serious, cases of postpartum depression and psychosis. In addition, it stimulated debate about the legal test for criminal insanity. It seemed indisputable that Yates had killed her five children and that she had a history of mental illness. The pivotal question was whether she was so impaired by her illness that she was not criminally responsible for her actions at the time of the killings. The opposite verdicts reached by two different juries in this case illustrate the complexity of the issue.

---

have previously become depressed after the birth of a child will become depressed again when they give birth. Women also are more likely to develop postpartum depression if they have a history of depression during pregnancy or severe premenstrual mood symptoms.

Treatment of Postpartum Depression. When postpartum depression is mild, **psychotherapy** alone may be enough to help women feel better. But for women with more intense symptoms or greater difficulty getting along in daily life, psychotherapy usually is combined with antidepressant medication. Studies show that some **antidepressants** are safe to take while breastfeeding.

Practical help and emotional support at home also can be invaluable. If the depression is severe, experts advise having a relative, friend, or paid helper stay with the mother at all times.

When postpartum psychosis occurs, antidepressants may be prescribed. However, other medications may be used as well, including **antipsychotics**, which help relieve psychotic symptoms, and **mood stabilizers**, which help even out mood swings. Another treatment option is **electroconvulsive therapy**, in which a carefully controlled electrical current is delivered to the brain, producing a brief seizure that is thought to alter some of the electrochemical processes involved in brain functioning.

Women who have had postpartum depression before are at high risk for a repeat episode the next time they give birth. As a result, many treatment providers recommend starting medication and psychotherapy right after delivery. If the risk is very high, psychotherapy might begin during the last two to three months of pregnancy, with medication added in the final weeks before birth, when there is little risk to the fetus. Such measures may help prevent another episode or minimize its impact.

See also: Edinburgh Postnatal Depression Scale; Estrogen; Gamma-Amino-Butyric Acid; Parental Depression; Psychotic Depression

Further Information. American College of Obstetricians and Gynecologists, P.O. Box 96920, Washington, D.C. 20090, (202) 638-5577, www.acog.org.

Postpartum Support International, P.O. Box 60931, Santa Barbara, CA 93160, (800) 944-4773, www.postpartum.net.

Bibliography

American Psychiatric Association. *Diagnostic and Statistical Manual of Mental Disorders.* 4th ed., text rev. Washington, DC: American Psychiatric Association, 2000.

Chua-Eoan, Howard. "The Sad Saga of Andrea Yates, 2001." *Time,* http://www.time.com/time/2007/crimes/index.html.

Cuijpers, Pim, Jessica G. Brännmark, and Annemieke van Straten. "Psychological Treatment of Postpartum Depression: A Meta-Analysis." *Journal of Clinical Psychology* 64 (2008): 103–118.

Factsheet: Postpartum Disorders. Mental Health America, November 8, 2006, http://www.nmha.org/go/information/get-info/depression/postpartum-disorders.

Frances, Allen, Michael B. First, and Harold Alan Pincus. *DSM-IV Guidebook.* Washington, DC: American Psychiatric Press, 1995.

McNamara, Melissa. "Andrea Yates Found Not Guilty: By Reason of Insanity; Will Be Committed to State Mental Hospital." *CBS News* (July 26, 2006).

Moline, Margaret L., David A. Kahn, Ruth W. Ross, Lori L. Altshuler, and Lee S. Cohen. "Postpartum Depression: A Guide for Patients and Families." *Postgraduate Medicine* Special Report (2001): 112–113.

Osmond, Marie with Marcia Wilkie and Judith Moore. *Behind the Smile: My Journey Out of Postpartum Depression.* New York: Warner Books, 2001.

Postpartum Depression and the Baby Blues. American Academy of Family Physicians, February 2008, http://familydoctor.org/online/famdocen/home/women/pregnancy/ppd/gengeng/379.html.

Shields, Brooke. *Down Came the Rain: My Journey Through Postpartum Depression.* New York: Hyperion, 2005.

Understanding Postpartum Depression: Common but Treatable. National Institutes of Health, December 2005, http://newsinhealth.nih.gov/2005/December2005/docs/01features_02.htm.

POST-TRAUMATIC STRESS DISORDER.   Post-traumatic stress disorder (PTSD) is an anxiety disorder that develops after exposure to a traumatic event that evoked intense fear, horror, or helplessness. It is only natural to feel afraid and upset after experiencing or witnessing something very frightening. For people with PTSD, though, these feelings last for weeks, months, or even years. Depression often goes along with the anxiety. In one study, researchers found that over 40 percent of people with PTSD also were suffering from **major depression** months after the traumatic event.

PTSD first gained notoriety as a disorder afflicting military veterans who had been exposed to the trauma of combat. But it can arise after a wide variety of traumatic incidents, including rape and other violent crimes, child abuse, car accidents, plane crashes, terrorist attacks, and natural disasters.

What all these situations have in common is that they involve actual or threatened bodily harm. In some cases, the person with PTSD is the one who suffered or was threatened with injury or death. In other cases, however, the harm may have befallen a loved one, or the person with PTSD may have witnessed something terrifying that happened to a stranger.

PTSD can occur at any age. The symptoms usually begin within the first three months after the traumatic event, although occasionally there is a delay of months or years. About half of people recover completely within three months, but the symptoms continue for over a year in many others. Even once the symptoms start to improve, they may be reactivated by reminders of the trauma. Anniversaries of the incident are often especially difficult.

About 7.7 million U.S. adults have PTSD. The disorder occurs more often in women than in men, and there is evidence that a susceptibility to it runs in families. Fortunately, treatment with appropriate **psychotherapy** and medications often is quite effective.

People who have both PTSD and major depression tend to have more severe symptoms and worse problems getting along in everyday life than those who have just one disorder or the other. They are also more likely to have suicidal thoughts and attempt **suicide** than those with major depression alone. Therefore, for those whose PTSD is accompanied by depression, getting prompt treatment for both disorders is doubly important.

Criteria for Diagnosis.   The symptoms of PTSD are defined by the ***Diagnostic and Statistical Manual of Mental Disorders, Fourth Edition, Text Revision*** (*DSM-IV-TR*), a diagnostic guidebook published by the American Psychiatric Association and widely used by mental health professionals from many disciplines. Symptoms fall into three main categories: (1) reexperiencing the trauma, (2) emotional numbness and avoidance, and (3) a heightened state of arousal. People with PTSD have all three types of symptoms, which persist for more than a month, leading to considerable distress or serious problems getting along in daily life.

Reexperiencing the Trauma.   People with PTSD keep reliving the traumatic event long after it is over. They have one or more of the following symptoms: (a) recurrent,

Treatment of PTSD

When people have PTSD and depression simultaneously, both conditions need to be addressed during treatment. Below are some of the main treatment options for PTSD.

Psychotherapy

Cognitive-behavioral therapy (CBT) helps people identify maladaptive thought and behavior patterns and replace them with more adaptive ones. One offshoot of CBT that may be especially helpful for PTSD is exposure therapy. In exposure therapy, people systematically confront people, places, things, or memories associated with the past trauma that are now safe, but that still evoke intense fear. Through repeated exposures, they learn that the thing they fear no longer poses a real threat.

Medication

Selective serotonin reuptake inhibitors (SSRIs), a widely prescribed class of **antidepressants**, can help relieve symptoms of anxiety as well as depression. SSRIs are considered a first-choice treatment for PTSD. Another class of antidepressants called **serotonin-norepinephrine reuptake inhibitors** show promise for treating PTSD as well. If these medications do not provide enough relief, other types of medication that may be prescribed include **tricyclic antidepressants**, **mood stabilizers**, newer **antipsychotics**, and benzodiazepines (mild sedatives).

Eye Movement Desensitization and Reprocessing

Eye movement desensitization and reprocessing (EMDR) combines elements of exposure therapy with directed shifts in attention. In EMDR, people recall some aspect of a traumatic event while focusing on a back-and-forth stimulus, such as side-to-side eye movements, hand taps, or sounds. Although the theory behind EMDR is still evolving, some research indicates that the treatment may help reduce symptoms of PTSD.

distressing memories of the event that intrude into their thoughts, (b) repeated nightmares about the event, (c) flashbacks in which the person, while awake, acts or feels as if the event is happening again, (d) intense emotional distress when exposed to reminders of the event, and (e) physical reactions to such reminders.

Young children with PTSD may act out aspects of the trauma. Some also develop other problems, such as behaving the way they did when younger, not talking even though they know how, complaining of frequent headaches or stomachaches, and refusing to go places or play with friends.

Emotional Numbness and Avoidance. People with PTSD become less emotionally responsive and begin avoiding things associated with the traumatic event. They have three or more of the following symptoms: (a) efforts to avoid thinking, feeling, or talking about the event, (b) efforts to avoid people, places, or activities that bring back memories of what happened, (c) inability to remember a key part of the trauma, (d) greatly reduced interest or participation in their usual activities, (e) a restricted range of emotions, such as having trouble feeling love for those they are closest to, and (f) a sense of a foreshortened future, such as not expecting to live out a normal life span.

Heightened State of Arousal. People with PTSD live in a constant state of high alert, both physically and psychologically. They have two or more of the following symptoms: (a) trouble falling or staying asleep, (b) **irritability** or angry outbursts, (c) difficulty concentrating, (d) constant vigilance, and (e) being easily startled.

Relationship to Depression. **Environmental factors** help explain why PTSD and major depression so often coexist. On one hand, when people develop depression first, it increases their risk both for experiencing potentially **traumatic events** and for developing PTSD when such experiences occur. On the other hand, when people suffer a trauma first, those who go on to have PTSD are more likely to also become depressed than those who do not develop PTSD. Thus, major depression increases the risk for PTSD, and vice versa.

Yet research indicates that common **genetic factors** may play an even bigger role. The same genes that affect people's likelihood of developing depression in the wake of **stress** and trauma also may affect their chances of developing PTSD. One possibility is that these genes act by influencing a personality trait called neuroticism, characterized by ongoing emotional instability and a tendency toward distress. Neuroticism, which is moderately heritable, has been linked to an increased risk of developing both major depression and PTSD individually.

See also: Anxiety Disorders; Comorbidity

Further Information. National Center for Posttraumatic Stress Disorder, U.S. Department of Veterans Affairs, www.ncptsd.va.gov.

Bibliography

American Psychiatric Association. *Diagnostic and Statistical Manual of Mental Disorders.* 4th ed., text rev. Washington, DC: American Psychiatric Association, 2000.

Anxiety Disorders. National Institute of Mental Health, 2007, http://www.nimh.nih.gov/health/publications/anxiety-disorders/summary.shtml.

Campbell, Duncan G., Bradford L. Felker, Chuan-Fen Liu, Elizabeth M. Yano, JoAnn E. Kirchner, Domin Chan, et al. "Prevalence of Depression-PTSD Comorbidity: Implications for Clinical Practice Guidelines and Primary Care-Based Interventions." *Journal of General Internal Medicine* 22 (2007): 711–718.

Foa, Edna B., and Linda Wasmer Andrews. *If Your Adolescent Has an Anxiety Disorder: An Essential Resource for Parents.* New York: Oxford University Press, 2006.

Koenen, Karestan C., Qiang J. Fu, Karen Ertel, Michael J. Lyons, Seth A. Eisen, William R. True, et al. "Common Genetic Liability to Major Depression and Posttraumatic Stress Disorder in Men." *Journal of Affective Disorders* 105 (2008): 109–115.

Mittal, Dinesh, John C. Fortney, Jeffrey M. Pyne, Mark J. Edlung, and Julie L. Wetherell. "Impact of Comorbid Anxiety Disorders on Health-Related Quality of Life among Patients with Major Depressive Disorder." *Psychiatric Services* 57 (2006): 1731–1737.

Oquendo, Maria A., Jeff M. Friend, Batsheva Halberstam, Beth S. Brodsky, Ainsley K. Burke, Michael F. Grunebaum, et al. "Association of Comorbid Posttraumatic Stress and Major Depression with Greater Risk for Suicidal Behavior." *American Journal of Psychiatry* 160 (2003): 580–582.

Post-traumatic Stress Disorder. National Institute of Mental Health, July 30, 2008, http://www.nimh.nih.gov/health/publications/post-traumatic-stress-disorder-a-real-illness/summary.shtml.

Practice Guideline for the Treatment of Patients with Acute Stress Disorder and Posttraumatic Stress Disorder. American Psychiatric Association, November 2004, http://www.psychiatryonline.com/pracGuide/pracGuideTopic_11.aspx.

Shalev, Arieh Y., Sara Freedman, Tuvia Peri, Dalia Brandes, Tali Sahar, Scott P. Orr, et al. "Prospective Study of Posttraumatic Stress Disorder and Depression Following Trauma." *American Journal of Psychiatry* 155 (1998): 630–637.

Treatment of PTSD. National Center for Posttraumatic Stress Disorder, May 31, 2007, http://www.ncptsd.va.gov/ncmain/ncdocs/fact_shts/fs_treatmentforptsd.html.

PREFRONTAL CORTEX. The prefrontal cortex (PFC) is the forward-most part of each frontal lobe, an area in either half of the brain that lies directly behind the forehead. The PFC is involved in a number of higher mental functions, such as thinking, problem solving, short-term memory, and emotion. **Brain imaging** studies of people with depression have found functional and structural changes in this area that may help explain several symptoms of the disorder.

On a functional level, the dorsolateral (back and side) part of the PFC plays an important role in higher thought, focused attention, and short-term memory. Unusually low activity in this area is associated with slowed-down thoughts and actions, apathy, and problems with attention and memory—all of which are characteristic of depression. Brain imaging studies of people with **major depression** have shown that the dorsolateral PFC tends to be underactive.

The ventromedial (front and middle) part of the PFC connects with other brain structures to form a circuit that regulates the expression and experience of emotions. These other structures include the **hypothalamus**, **hippocampus**, and **amygdala**. Faulty communication within this circuit has been implicated in problems with motivation and mood.

On a structural level, there is evidence that the PFC may shrink in people with major depression. For instance, studies of people with a family history of depression have shown that the ventromedial PFC is up to 40 percent smaller in those who are themselves depressed.

Ventromedial PFC. A closer look at what happens in the ventromedial PFC offers some insight into depression. This area lets people switch from one type of emotion to another, and it is also heavily involved in feelings of reward and pleasure. In addition, dense connections between the ventromedial PFC and deeper structures within the brain make it a likely site for linking the conscious to the unconscious and for ascribing conscious meaning to perceptions.

One line of research has looked at **bipolar disorder**, in which people go back and forth between the two extremes of depression and **mania**, an overly high mood. During the depression phase, the ventromedial PFC tends to be quiet, but during the mania phase, it tends to become overactive. The difference in ventromedial PFC activity may be reflected in people's symptoms. For example, people in the grips of mania find intense meaning in everything they do, but those in the depths of depression find that nothing seems to matter anymore.

See also: Brain Anatomy

Bibliography

Drevets, Wayne C., Joseph L. Price, and Maura L. Furay. "Brain Structural and Functional Abnormalities in Mood Disorders: Implications for Neurocircuitry Models of Depression." *Brain Structure and Function* 213 (2008): 93–118.

Maletic, V., M. Robinson, T. Oakes, S. Iyengar, S. G. Ball, and J. Russell. "Neurobiology of Depression: An Integrated View of Key Findings." *International Journal of Clinical Practice* 61 (2007): 2030–2040.

McEwen, Bruce S. *Stress, Depression and Brain Structure.* Depression and Bipolar Support Alliance, August 30, 2006, http://www.dbsalliance.org/site/PageServer?pagename=about_depression _mcewen.

Parts of the Brain That Slow Down or Speed Up in Depression. Canadian Institute of Neurosciences, Mental Health and Addiction, http://thebrain.mcgill.ca/flash/a/a_08/a_08_cr/a_08_cr_dep/a _08_cr_dep.html.

PREGNANCY.   Pregnancy is often thought to be a time of sublime emotional well-being when **women** are protected from less blissful feelings, such as depression. Yet statistics belie this popular belief. One in five women experiences some depressive symptoms while pregnant, and one in 10 develops full-blown **major depression.**

Several factors influence a woman's risk of depression at this time. Dramatic hormonal shifts occur during pregnancy, and these **hormones** can affect how the brain functions. Also, some women who are already on **antidepressants** stop taking their medication due to concerns about hurting the fetus, and this may cause their symptoms to flare up.

Depending on a woman's situation and attitudes, pregnancy is sometimes very stressful as well, and **stress** can trigger or worsen depression in susceptible individuals. Common sources of stress include mixed or negative feelings about becoming a mother, lifestyle or work changes, lack of social support, relationship problems, and medical concerns.

Yet many women are reluctant to seek help for depression during pregnancy, perhaps because of guilt over the disconnect between what they think they should be feeling and what they actually feel. At the same time, health care providers are often so preoccupied with the pregnancy itself that they miss other problems. In addition, they may write off common symptoms of depression—such as sleep problems, appetite changes, and tiredness—as simply due to being pregnant. All these factors conspire to make depression during pregnancy among the most underdiagnosed and undertreated of all mental health conditions.

Treatment Issues.   The good news is that depression can be treated during pregnancy just as it can at other times. Special care must be taken to protect not only the mother, but also the fetus. On one hand, antidepressants can cross the placenta, so there is always some risk that they might harm the developing fetus. On the other hand, untreated depression poses serious risks as well, because it may lead to poor eating habits, smoking, alcohol or drug use, and suicidal behavior. Untreated major depression also is associated with prolonged or premature labor and low-birth-weight babies.

Unfortunately, definitive data on the safety of antidepressant use during pregnancy are limited, because there are ethical constraints on doing research in pregnant women. Nevertheless, data gleaned from the records of pharmaceutical companies and medical centers provide useful information about several of the most widely prescribed antidepressants.

Conception and Early Pregnancy.   During the first trimester (three months) of pregnancy, some medications can cause serious malformations in the developing fetus. The risk with antidepressants generally seems to be low to modest. To be on the safe side, though, it is a good idea for any woman who is already taking an antidepressant to consult a doctor before trying to conceive. If she has had only one past episode of mild depression and has been feeling well for several months, she might be advised to gradually taper off the medication, perhaps with the help of **psychotherapy**. But if she has had multiple past episodes or more severe symptoms, she might be advised to keep taking medication, choosing one that appears to be relatively safe.

Concerns have been raised about one particular antidepressant, called paroxetine. A possible link has been noted between use of paroxetine during the first trimester of pregnancy and an increased risk of heart birth defects. As a result, this antidepressant is usually not prescribed for women who are pregnant or who might become pregnant.

Later Pregnancy and Childbirth.   Later in pregnancy, the use of **selective serotonin reuptake inhibitors** (SSRIs), a widely prescribed type of antidepressant, has been linked to short-term problems in newborns, including jitteriness, mild respiratory distress, rapid breathing, a weak cry, and poor muscle tone. The newborns are at increased risk for admission to the neonatal intensive care unit.

Some women do fine during pregnancy but develop **postpartum depression** within the first weeks or months after giving birth. Those who have had an episode of postpartum depression in the past are at high risk for another one in the future. In some cases, psychotherapy might begin during the last two to three months of pregnancy, with medication added in the final weeks before giving birth. Such measures help keep postpartum depression from recurring or minimize its impact.

Expert Recommendations. In 2006, the American College of Obstetricians and Gynecologists issued an opinion on antidepressant use during pregnancy. It stated that decisions about using SSRIs and **serotonin-norepinephrine reuptake inhibitors** should be individualized. The potential risks of taking medication during pregnancy should be weighed against the risks of depression, taking each woman's past history and current situation into account.

Another expert consensus guideline published in 2001 reached a similar conclusion. The guideline noted that women who have had only mild symptoms in the past may be able to gradually stop taking medication, ideally before getting pregnant. But for women with more severe depression, the benefits of antidepressants often outweigh the risks.

Further Information. American College of Obstetricians and Gynecologists, 409 12th Street S.W., P.O. Box 96920, Washington, D.C. 20090, (202) 638-5577, www.acog.org.

American Pregnancy Association, 1431 Greenway Drive, Suite 800, Irving , TX 75038, (972) 550-0140, www.americanpregnancy.org.

Centers for Disease Control and Prevention: Birth Defects, Mail-Stop E-86, 1600 Clifton Road, Atlanta, GA 30333, (800) 311-3435, www.cdc.gov/ncbddd/bd.

March of Dimes, 1275 Mamaroneck Avenue, White Plains, NY 10605, (914) 997-4488, www.marchofdimes.com.

National Institute of Child Health and Human Development, P.O. Box 3006, Rockville, MD 20847, (800) 370-2943, www.nichd.nih.gov.

National Women's Health Information Center, (800) 994-9662, www.womenshealth.gov.

Bibliography

American College of Obstetricians and Gynecologists Committee on Obstetric Practice. "ACOG Committee Opinion No. 354: Treatment with Selective Serotonin Reuptake Inhibitors During Pregnancy." *Obstetrics and Gynecology* 108 (2006): 1601–1603.

Dear Healthcare Professional Letter: PAXIL (Paroxetine HCl) and PAXIL CR (Paroxetine HCl) Controlled-Release Tablets. GlaxoSmithKline, September 2005, www.fda.gov/medwatch/safety/2005/Paxil_dearhcp_letter.pdf.

Depression in Women: Understanding the Gender Gap. Mayo Clinic, September 6, 2008, http://www.mayoclinic.com/health/depression/MH00035.

Kahn, David A., Margaret L. Moline, Ruth W. Ross, Lee S. Cohen, and Lori L. Altshuler. "Major Depression During Conception and Pregnancy: A Guide for Patients and Families." *Postgraduate Medicine* (March 2001): 110–111.

Marcus, Sheila M. "Depression During Pregnancy: Rates, Risks and Consequences." *Canadian Journal of Clinical Pharmacology* 16 (2009): e15–e22.

Wise, Dana D., Angela Felker, and Stephen M. Stahl. "Tailoring Treatment of Depression for Women Across the Reproductive Lifecycle: The Importance of Pregnancy, Vasomotor Symptoms, and Other Estrogen-Related Events in Psychopharmacology." *CNS Spectrums* 13 (2008): 647–655, 658–662.

PREMENSTRUAL DYSPHORIC DISORDER. Premenstrual dysphoric disorder (PMDD) is a mood disorder that begins in the week before the onset of a woman's menstrual period and subsides within a few days after her period starts. The hallmark of PMDD is an unpleasant mood characterized by intense depression, anxiety, or **irritability**. Often, the mood symptoms are severe enough to meet the criteria for **major depression** or **generalized anxiety disorder**, but they are shorter-lived. Nevertheless, in some women, they linger for days. In others, there are rapid mood swings interspersed with frequent **crying**.

PMDD is not yet a formally recognized disorder in the *Diagnostic and Statistical Manual of Mental Disorders, Fourth Edition, Text Revision* (*DSM-IV-TR*), a diagnostic guide published by the American Psychiatric Association and used by mental health professionals from many disciplines. At present, women with PMDD may be given the nonspecific diagnosis of "**depressive disorder not otherwise specified.**" However, PMDD has been proposed for inclusion as a distinct entity in the manual's next edition, and it has already been the subject of a large amount of research.

PMDD is actually a severe form of premenstrual syndrome (PMS), a pattern of physical and psychological changes that occur in the days leading up to a woman's menstrual period. The features of PMS vary from woman to woman, and their severity also can vary from month to month. Common psychological manifestations include a blue mood, anxiety, irritability, mood swings, crying spells, poor concentration, and withdrawal from other people. Common physical manifestations include weight gain from fluid retention, abdominal bloating, breast tenderness, acne flare-ups, joint or muscle pain, headaches, fatigue, and constipation or diarrhea.

About three-quarters of women notice some premenstrual changes. In most cases, the changes are subtle and amount to nothing more than a monthly bother. However, about three percent to eight percent of women have full-blown PMDD, with symptoms that are severe enough to put a major strain on their work, school, home, or social life.

Reality or Really Sexist? More than most new diagnoses, PMDD has generated considerable controversy, and not just among doctors and scientists. The debate is as political as it is medical. Some critics charge that the label pathologizes a normal part of female experience. Indeed, one difficulty encountered by researchers trying to study PMS is that many women who believe they have the condition do not meet objective criteria for it. This is perhaps a sign of society's bias toward blaming PMS for ordinary emotional ups and downs in women. Proponents counter that the degree of distress caused by true PMDD takes it well outside of normal territory, and failing to treat it leads to needless suffering for those affected.

A second set of critics concede that a problem exists, but contend that PMDD takes a hormonal disorder and labels it a mental illness. This might open up women to unnecessary **stigma** and discrimination. Proponents note that perturbations in non-sex hormones—such as corticotropin-releasing hormone, cortisol, melatonin, and thyroid hormone—have been linked to a variety of mood disorders, so PMDD is not unique in having a hormonal component. They say the risk of being stigmatized is an argument for changing societal attitudes, not for withholding appropriate care.

Recently, the pendulum of scientific opinion seems to be swinging toward recognizing PMDD as a legitimate entity. But just because a disorder is accepted as real does not mean it is always diagnosed correctly. Formalizing a set of diagnostic criteria for the disorder might help curb overdiagnosis, because it would give doctors a firm basis for deciding who has PMDD and who does not.

Criteria for Diagnosis. According to provisional criteria presented for further study in the *DSM-IV-TR*, women with PMDD experience problems during most menstrual cycles. These problems are more than just the relatively mild, transient changes seen in ordinary PMS. True PMDD symptoms are present most of the time during the week before a woman's menstrual period and are serious enough to interfere with daily life. For instance, a woman might avoid seeing her family and friends or be much less productive at school or work.

Unlike ordinary PMS, which typically causes only a few problems, PMDD causes five or more of the symptoms listed below. At least one of the symptoms must be a depressed, anxious, or irritable mood, or rapid mood swings (the first four items in the following list).

Depressed Mood. Some women feel quite sad, empty, or hopeless. This may show up as frequent thoughts about not being good enough.

Anxious Mood. Other women feel quite anxious, tense, or jittery. It may seem as if they are constantly keyed up or on edge.

Irritable Mood. Still other women feel quite irritable or angry, and their bad mood does not let up quickly. Their constant crankiness may lead to increased conflict with other people.

Rapid Mood Swings. In some cases, women have rapid changes in mood. For instance, they might suddenly become sad or hypersensitive to any hint of rejection. These mood swings may be interspersed with frequent crying spells.

Loss of Interest. PMDD sometimes leads to a loss of interest in usual activities, such as work, school, or hobbies. This may show up as indifference to friends.

Lack of Energy. Another symptom of PMDD is a marked lack of energy. Some women tire more easily than usual or feel unmotivated to do anything.

Trouble Concentrating. Women with PMDD may find it difficult to focus their attention. Some report having trouble remembering things.

Change in Eating Habits. A marked change in appetite is yet another possible symptom. Some women overeat or develop cravings for specific foods.

Change in Sleep Habits. **Sleep disturbances** sometimes occur. They may take the form of either insomnia (having trouble falling or staying asleep) or hypersomnia (oversleeping or being bothered by excessive daytime sleepiness).

Overwhelmed Feeling. Some women with PMDD say they feel overwhelmed. Others report having a disturbing sense of being out of control.

Other Physical Symptoms. PMDD may be associated with additional premenstrual physical changes. Common examples include breast tenderness, headaches, joint or muscle pain, weight gain, or bloating.

A woman who suspects that she might have PMDD may be asked to track which symptoms she has and how severe the symptoms are every day for a few months. On the same calendar or chart, she also marks when she has her menstrual period. Armed with this information, her treatment provider will be better able to assess which symptoms really are related to the woman's menstrual cycle and which are unrelated.

PMDD, Depression, and Anxiety. Women with **mood disorders** or **anxiety disorders** may notice that their symptoms get worse right before their menstrual period. If the symptoms only improve a little but don't go away once their period begins, these women might have major depression, generalized anxiety disorder, or another mood or anxiety condition. PMDD is only diagnosed when premenstrual mood symptoms start to disappear within a few days after menstruation begins and are absent during the first week after the period ends.

In some cases, women may have both PMDD and another disorder at the same time. For instance, this might happen if a woman has both symptoms of major depression that stay fairly constant and another set of symptoms that come and go with her menstrual cycle.

Causes and Risk Factors. Premenstrual symptoms can begin at any time after a girl has her first menstrual period. Some women report that their symptoms got worse in their thirties or after a reproductive event, such as giving birth or having a tubal ligation (getting their "tubes tied"). Genes may play a role as well. Women whose mothers had PMS are more likely to have premenstrual symptoms themselves, compared to women whose mothers were not affected.

A sizable fraction of women with PMDD—estimates range from 30 percent to 76 percent—also develop depression at some point in their lives. A family history of depression is common in PMDD sufferers as well. Yet PMDD seems to be more than just a variant of depression, because a low mood can't account for all the symptoms, and some women with PMDD don't become depressed at all.

Stress may worsen many symptoms of PMDD, but by itself, it does not cause the disorder. Other things that may aggravate specific symptoms, include eating too much salt, which can cause fluid retention, and drinking too much alcohol or caffeine, which can affect mood and energy level.

The Hormonal Connection. PMDD only occurs in women of child-bearing age, so it seems logical to assume that hormonal fluctuations related to the menstrual cycle play a role in causing the disorder. The premenstrual symptoms come and go with these fluctuations, and they also disappear during pregnancy and after menopause.

Cyclic peaks and dips in female **hormones** may affect **serotonin**, a chemical in the brain that influences mood and helps regulate sleep and appetite. Low levels of

Lifestyle Changes That Help

If you have PMDD, your treatment provider may suggest lifestyle changes that help minimize some symptoms and maximize the benefits of treatment.

Modify Your Diet
Limit your intake of salty foods, alcohol, and caffeine. If you are bothered by bloating and an uncomfortable sensation of fullness, try eating more frequent, small meals instead of two or three large ones.

Mind Your Minerals
Consume foods rich in calcium—such as low-fat milk and dairy products, sardines, and kale—which may help reduce both physical and psychological symptoms. Also, eat foods high in magnesium—such as halibut, almonds, soybeans, and spinach—which may help decrease fluid retention, bloating, and breast tenderness. If you are unsure whether you are getting enough of these minerals in your diet, ask your doctor whether you might need a supplement.

Exercise Your Body
Aim for at least 30 minutes of moderate-intensity aerobic exercise—such as brisk walking, cycling, or swimming—on all or most days of the week. Regular exercise helps boost your mood and reduce stress.

Manage Your Stress
Find healthy ways to relax, such as visiting with friends, listening to soothing music, or writing in a journal. Practice deep breathing exercises, which may help relieve headaches, anxiety and insomnia.

serotonin, in turn, may contribute to symptoms such as depression, sleep problems, fatigue, and food cravings.

Treatment of PMDD.   One or more types of medication are often prescribed for PMDD. **Selective serotonin reuptake inhibitors** (SSRIs), a family of antidepressant medications, are the first-line treatment. These medications increase the amount of serotonin available for use in the brain, which helps relieve serotonin-related symptoms. As a treatment for depression, SSRIs are taken daily. But for treating PMDD, they are sometimes taken just during the two weeks preceding menstruation. Three SSRIs have been approved by the Food and Drug Administration (FDA) specifically for treating PMDD: **fluoxetine** (Sarafem), controlled-release Paxil (Paxil CR), and sertraline (Zoloft).

Birth control pills stop ovulation and even out hormonal swings. As a result, they may relieve PMDD symptoms. One type of birth control pill, called drospirenone and ethinyl estradiol (Yaz), has been approved by the FDA specifically for this use.

Diuretics—drugs that help the body shed excess fluid through urine—may decrease weight gain and bloating due to fluid retention. Nonsteroidal anti-inflammatory drugs—medications that relieve pain and reduce inflammation—may ease cramping and breast discomfort.

Psychotherapy may help women gain better control over the psychological symptoms of PMDD. Classes that educate women about how to manage stress and cope with other symptoms may be helpful as well.

See also: Circadian Rhythms; Dysphoria; Estrogen

Bibliography

American Psychiatric Association. *Diagnostic and Statistical Manual of Mental Disorders.* 4th ed., text rev. Washington, DC: American Psychiatric Association, 2000.

Bhatia, Subhash C., and Shashi K. Bhatia. "Diagnosis and Treatment of Premenstrual Dysphoric Disorder." *American Family Physician* 66 (2002): 1253–1254.

Chen, Ingfei. "A Clash of Science and Politics Over PMS." *New York Times* (December 19, 2008).

Daw, Jennifer. "Is PMDD Real?" *Monitor on Psychology* (October 2002).

Moline, Margaret L., David A. Kahn, Ruth W. Ross, Lee S. Cohen, and Lori L. Altshuler. "Premenstrual Dysphoric Disorder: A Guide for Patients and Families." *Postgraduate Medicine* Special Report (2001): 108–109.

PMS and PMDD. Cleveland Clinic, http://www.clevelandclinic.org/health/health-info/docs/ 2400/2447.asp?index=9132.

Premenstrual Dysphoric Disorder (PMDD). American Academy of Family Physicians, January 2008, http://familydoctor.org/online/famdocen/home/women/mental/752.html.

Premenstrual Syndrome. Mayo Clinic, December 7, 2007, http://www.mayoclinic.com/health/ premenstrual-syndrome/DS00134.

Premenstrual Syndrome. National Women's Health Information Center, January 2007, http:// womenshealth.gov/faq/pms.htm.

Yaz Home Page. Bayer HealthCare Pharmaceuticals, http://www.yaz-us.com/home.jsp.

PREVENTION OF DEPRESSION.   In the health care world, the goal of prevention is to keep a disorder from starting, worsening, or recurring. When it comes to depression, there is no surefire way to prevent it. But taking steps to decrease **stress**, enhance problem solving, and increase **social support** may reduce a person's risk of becoming depressed in the first place. Getting appropriate treatment at the earliest sign of trouble may help keep symptoms from becoming more severe, and sticking with **maintenance treatment** even after the depression has lifted may help ward off a **recurrence**.

Scientists have defined three levels of preventive care. Primary prevention aims to prevent the initial onset of an illness in people who do not yet have it. Secondary prevention aims to stop or reduce existing symptoms and keep more severe ones from developing in people who show early signs of the illness. Tertiary prevention aims to prevent a recurrence of the illness in people who have recovered from a previous episode.

Depression strikes individuals of both sexes, all ages, and every **ethnicity**. Nevertheless, some people have a higher risk than others. **Risk factors** for depression include a family history of the disorder, female gender, stressful life events, childhood trauma, **physical illness**, **substance abuse**, low **socioeconomic status**, poor self-esteem, and a pessimistic mindset. The more risk factors an individual has, the greater the potential benefit of preventive measures.

Prevention of Late-Life Depression. Some risk factors—such as heredity and gender—cannot be changed, but others are modifiable. Research in **older adults** shows how knowledge of risk factors can be translated into protective measures that make a real difference. Following are examples of risk factors and preventive steps for late-life depression:

Risk factor: Chronic medical conditions.

Preventive step: Patient education programs teach people with conditions such as arthritis and diabetes how to live better with their illness. Such programs have been shown to reduce depressive symptoms in participants.

Risk factor: Low to medium levels of physical activity.

Preventive step: Regular, consistent **exercise** has been shown to decrease depressive symptoms and improve physical and psychological health.

Risk factor: Fewer than three close friends or relatives.

Preventive step: Social activities—for instance, volunteering, participating in community organizations, and attending religious services—have been shown to reduce depression risk, especially in older women.

Risk factor: Recent death of a spouse.

Preventive step: **Support groups** for the bereaved allow members to share emotional support as well as practical advice on coping with single life. Such programs may improve psychological adjustment and social well-being.

See also: Prevention Programs; Protective Factors

Bibliography

Ahern, Melissa M., and Michael Hendryx. "Community Participation and the Emergence of Late-Life Depressive Symptoms: Differences Between Women and Men." *Journal of Women's Health* 17 (2008): 1463–1470.

Clarke, Gregory N., Wesley Hawkins, Mary Murphy, Lisa B. Sheeber, Peter M. Lewinsohn, and John R. Seeley. "Targeted Prevention of Unipolar Depressive Disorder in an At-Risk Sample of High School Adolescents: A Randomized Trial of a Group Cognitive Intervention." *Journal of the American Academy of Child and Adolescent Psychiatry* 34 (1995): 312–321.

Depression (Major Depression): Prevention. Mayo Clinic, February 14, 2008, http://www.mayoclinic.com/health/depression/DS00175/DSECTION=prevention.

Depression and Anxiety Prevention for Older Adults. Older Americans Substance Abuse and Mental Health Technical Assistance Center, http://www.samhsa.gov/OlderAdultsTAC/docs/ Depression_Booklet.pdf.

Muñoz, Ricardo F., Huynh-Nhu Le, Gregory N. Clarke, Alinne Z. Barrera, and Leandro D. Torres. "Preventing First Onset and Recurrence of Major Depressive Episodes." In *Handbook of Depression.* 2nd ed., by Ian H. Gotlib and Constance L. Hammen, eds., 533–553. New York: Guilford Press, 2009.

Schoevers, Robert A., Filip Smit, Dorly J. H. Deeg, Pim Cuijpers, Jack Dekker, Willem van Tilburg, et al. "Prevention of Late-Life Depression in Primary Care: Do We Know Where to Begin?" *American Journal of Psychiatry* 163 (2006): 1611–1621.

Spence, Susan H., Jeanie K. Sheffield, and Caroline L. Donovan. "Preventing Adolescent Depression: An Evaluation of the Problem Solving for Life Program." *Journal of Consulting and Clinical Psychology* 71 (2003): 3–13.

PREVENTION PROGRAMS.   Prevention programs are intended to reduce the risk of a disorder for both individual participants and target populations. Efforts can be aimed at preventing the initial onset of the disorder, the development of more severe symptoms, or the occurrence of future episodes. The discussion below focuses on the former— interventions designed to keep depression from ever starting in the first place.

Such interventions can be divided into three types, depending on how participants are chosen. Universal programs target the general public, regardless of risk. Selective programs target high-risk individuals or groups, and indicated programs target individuals with early symptoms who do not yet meet diagnostic criteria for the disorder. Research suggests that selective or indicated programs may be more effective than universal ones.

Because depression often starts in adolescence or early adulthood, most prevention programs are school-based initiatives aimed at young people. In general, research on these programs has shown small positive effects in the short term. Many studies have found that the benefits tend to fade over time, although some have shown more sustained effects. Periodic phone check-ins or follow-up meetings may help keep the benefits going for longer, much as booster shots help keep some vaccines working.

Typically, depression prevention programs consist of eight to 18 group meetings held at school. Most have used strategies adapted from **cognitive-behavioral therapy**, a proven treatment for depression that teaches people how to identify and change maladaptive thoughts and behaviors. Specific training in problem solving, social skills, and **stress management** may be included. Some programs have concurrent meetings for parents that aim to foster close family bonds and strengthen parenting skills.

Sampler of Programs.   Following are brief descriptions of three depression prevention programs for **children** and **adolescents**. Results so far have been encouraging, but more research and refinement are needed.

Penn Resiliency Program.   The **Penn Resiliency Program** is a depression-prevention curriculum designed for late-elementary school and middle school students. The program involves twelve 90-minute lessons or eighteen 60-minute lessons. In these lessons, core skills are first presented through skits, role-playing, short stories, and cartoons. They are then practiced in hypothetical scenarios and homework assignments. The skills taught include assertiveness, negotiation, decision-making, relaxation, and strategies for countering unduly negative thoughts. Overall, results of thirteen controlled studies suggest that the program helps prevent symptoms of depression and anxiety, and these benefits can be long-lasting.

Coping with Stress. The Coping with Stress (CWS) course is an offshoot of the Adolescent Coping with Depression program, a group treatment for adolescents with depression. The CWS course, aimed at preventing depression in at-risk high school students, consists of 15 hourlong meetings. Like its predecessor, it rests on a firm foundation of cognitive-behavioral principles. The first few sessions provide an overview of depression and its relationship to **stress**. Subsequent sessions are devoted to learning how to change unrealistically negative thoughts, which are thought to underlie depression. Research has shown that the course can reduce the risk for full-blown depression in adolescents who were already showing early signs of depressive symptoms.

Problem Solving for Life. The Problem Solving for Life course is a universal prevention program targeting eighth graders. It consists of eight 45- to 50-minute sessions conducted weekly during school. The focus is on problem solving and restructuring of counterproductive thoughts. A study involving 1,500 students at 16 Australian schools found decreases in depressive symptoms and increases in problem-solving skills in students at high risk for depression. Similar but smaller effects were seen in low-risk students. When researchers checked in a year later, though, these initial gains had been lost.

See also: Group Therapy; Prevention of Depression; Protective Factors

Bibliography

Cardemil, Esteban V., Karen J. Reivich, Christopher G. Beevers, Martin E. P. Seligman, and Julie James. "The Prevention of Depressive Symptoms in Low-Income, Minority Children: Two-Year Follow-Up." *Behaviour Research and Therapy* 45 (2007): 313–327.

Clarke, Gregory N., Wesley Hawkins, Mary Murphy, Lisa B. Sheeber, Peter M. Lewinsohn, and John R. Seeley. "Targeted Prevention of Unipolar Depressive Disorder in an At-Risk Sample of High School Adolescents: A Randomized Trial of a Group Cognitive Intervention." *Journal of the American Academy of Child and Adolescent Psychiatry* 34 (1995): 312–321.

Clarke, Gregory, and Peter M. Lewinsohn. *The Adolescent Coping with Stress Class: Leader Manual.* Portland, OR: Kaiser Permanente Center for Healthy Research, 1995.

Garber, Judy. "Prevention of Depression: Are We There Yet?" *Clinical Psychology Science and Practice* 15 (2008): 336–341.

Horowitz, Jason L., and Judy Garber. "The Prevention of Depressive Symptoms in Children and Adolescents: A Meta-analytic Review." *Journal of Consulting and Clinical Psychology* 74 (2006): 401–418.

Merry, Sally N., Heather H. McDowell, Sarah E. Hetrick, Julliet J. Bir, and N. Muller. "Psychological and/or Educational Interventions for the Prevention of Depression in Children and Adolescents (Review)." *Cochrane Database of Systematic Reviews* 2 (2004): art. no. CD003380.

Muñoz, Ricardo F., Huynh-Nhu Le, Gregory N. Clarke, Alinne Z. Barrera, and Leandro D. Torres. "Preventing First Onset and Recurrence of Major Depressive Episodes." In *Handbook of Depression.* 2nd ed., by Ian H. Gotlib and Constance L. Hammen, eds., 533–553. New York: Guilford Press, 2009.

Resilience Research in Children. University of Pennsylvania Positive Psychology Center, 2007, http://www.ppc.sas.upenn.edu/prpsum.htm.

Spence, Susan H., Jeanie K. Sheffield, and Caroline L. Donovan. "Preventing Adolescent Depression: An Evaluation of the Problem Solving for Life Program." *Journal of Consulting and Clinical Psychology* 71 (2003): 3–13.

Sutton, Jonathan M. "Prevention of Depression in Youth: A Qualitative Review and Future Suggestions." *Clinical Psychology Review* 27 (2007): 552–571.

PROBLEM-SOLVING TREATMENT. Problem-solving treatment (PST) is an approach to treating depression in which patients identify and address life problems that are contributing to their symptoms. The treatment program is designed to be used by specially trained doctors and nurses in a primary care medical setting. Research suggests that PST is as effective as **antidepressants** when prescribed by primary care doctors.

Ideally, every person with depression would have access to treatment by a mental health specialist. In reality, many depressed people wind up in the office of a primary care doctor with complaints such as lack of energy and unexplained aches and pains. PST is designed to give the medical staff an effective way of treating depression that is relatively brief and appealing to patients who prefer not to take medication.

The premise behind PST is that symptoms of depression often are caused or worsened by problems in everyday life. Most people with depression intuitively recognize this connection, so they may readily accept PST as a sensible coping strategy. PST gives patients a step-by-step framework for resolving practical problems, with the assumption that their symptoms will improve as their problems decrease.

The Process at a Glance. PST has three main steps. First, the health care provider helps the patient link depressive symptoms to day-to-day problems. Second, these problems are discussed and clarified. Third, a plan is developed to solve the problems in a structured way. The latter step involves generating a number of possible solutions for each problem, choosing the best solution, acting on that choice, and evaluating how well it worked.

The PST program typically requires four to six one-on-one sessions. The first two sessions are usually an hour long, and subsequent sessions last 30 minutes, for a total treatment time of three to four hours. Initially, sessions generally are scheduled a week apart. Later sessions may be separated by longer intervals.

PST can be carried out by trained health care providers from various disciplines, including primary care doctors, nurses, and mental health professionals. The treatment is a scaled-down version of **cognitive-behavioral therapy** (CBT), a form of **psychotherapy** that focuses on changing self-defeating thoughts and behaviors, so it may be mastered more quickly by providers with a background in CBT.

Benefits for Depression. Research has found that problem solving can be an effective treatment for depression in primary care. In a study conducted at nine sites across Europe, 452 people with depression or an adjustment disorder were randomly assigned to one of three groups: PST, a patient education course on depression, or neither program. The results showed that both PST and the course reduced the severity and duration of depression. People in both these groups also reported

Variations on the Theme

Besides the treatment described in this article, other problem-solving strategies also have been used to treat depression.

Social Problem-Solving Therapy
This treatment, developed in the 1980s, focuses not only on solving problems, but also on changing attitudes that may interfere with putting solutions into action. The treatment usually is presented in 10 to 12 group sessions.

Self-Examination Therapy
This treatment involves identifying major life goals, putting energy only into problems related to those goals, and accepting situations that cannot be changed. Problem-solving skills are the core element. The treatment typically is presented in a guided self-help format.

improved mental and social functioning. Judging by how many people completed the two programs, though, people generally preferred PST over the course.

PST is most likely to benefit people with mild to moderate depression. Those with severe symptoms generally need more intensive treatment than PST alone provides. But even those with severe depression may benefit from learning specific problem-solving skills, which are sometimes incorporated into CBT and other forms of psychotherapy.

One disadvantage of PST is the amount of time it takes. Although considered a brief treatment, PST is still time-consuming compared to the standard doctor's office visit. Another drawback is the lack of trained doctors and nurses. More health care providers might seek training in the future, however, if the benefits of PST continue to be borne out by research.

See also: Treatment of Depression

Bibliography

Cuijpers, Pim, Annemieke van Straten, and Lisanne Warmerdam. "Problem Solving Therapies for Depression: A Meta-analysis." *European Psychiatry* 22 (2007): 9–15.

Dowrick, Christopher, Graham Dunn, Jose Luis Ayuso-Mateos, Odd Steffen Dalgard, Helen Page, Ville Lehtinen, et al. "Problem Solving Treatment and Group Psychoeducation for Depression: Multicentre Randomised Controlled Trial." *BMJ* 321 (2000): 1450–1454.

Mynors-Wallis, Laurence M., Dennis H. Gath, Ann Day, and Frances Baker. "Randomised Controlled Trial of Problem Solving Treatment, Antidepressant Medication, and Combined Treatment for Depression in Primary Care." *BMJ* 320 (2000): 26–30.

Mynors-Wallis, Laurence. *Problem-Solving Treatment for Anxiety and Depression.* New York: Oxford University Press, 2005.

PROTECTIVE FACTORS. Protective factors are personal traits or environmental characteristics that decrease the likelihood of developing a disorder. Researchers have identified a number of psychological, social, and environmental factors that reduce vulnerability to depression. By emphasizing these factors, individuals may be able to prevent depression, decrease symptom severity, or ward off future episodes.

Stress is the trigger for many bouts of depression, especially in the initial stages. By practicing **stress management** strategies and **relaxation techniques**, people may be able to stop some mood symptoms before they start. Other steps that help keep stress and depression at bay include seeking **social support**, getting regular **exercise**, and making time for enjoyable leisure activities.

For many people, **spirituality and religion** offer a pathway to inner peace. Studies have found an association between higher levels of spiritual or religious involvement and lower levels of depressive symptoms.

Optimism and a sense of humor are powerful antidotes to the gloominess and negative thinking that characterize depression. When times are tough, research shows that these qualities can help people bounce back.

See also: Cognitive Factors; Prevention of Depression; Prevention Programs; Risk Factors

Bibliography

Chang, Edward C., and Lawrence J. Sanna. "Optimism, Pessimism, and Positive and Negative Affectivity in Middle-Aged Adults: A Test of a Cognitive Affective Model of Psychological Adjustment." *Psychology and Aging* 16 (2001): 524–531.

Gotlib, Ian H., and Constance L. Hammen, eds. *Handbook of Depression.* 2nd ed. New York: Guilford Press, 2009.

Nezu, Arthur M., Christine M. Nezu, and Sonia E. Blissett. "Sense of Humor as a Moderator of the Relation Between Stressful Events and Psychological Distress: A Prospective Analysis." *Journal of Personality and Social Psychology* 54 (1988): 520–525.

Southwick, Steven M., Meena Vythilingam, and Dennis S. Charney. "The Psychobiology of Depression and Resilience to Stress: Implications for Prevention and Treatment." *Annual Review of Clinical Psychology* 1 (2005): 255–291.

Stein, Dan J., David J. Kupfer, and Alan F. Schatzberg, eds. *The American Psychiatric Publishing Textbook of Mood Disorders.* Washington, DC: American Psychiatric Publishing, 2006.

PSYCHIATRIC NURSE.   A psychiatric nurse is a registered nurse (RN) who specializes in the assessment and care of individuals with mental, emotional, and behavioral disorders. There are two levels of psychiatric nursing. At the basic level, registered nurses assess mental health needs as well as develop and carry out a plan of nursing care. Some may provide **psychotherapy** or help patients manage their medication, but only under the supervision of a physician.

At the advanced level, advanced practice registered nurses (APRN) who specialize in psychiatric-mental health nursing can work as independent professionals. In addition to all the functions performed at the basic level, they can provide psychotherapy without supervision. In most states, they also can prescribe medication. As a result, **pharmacotherapy** is often an important part of the treatment provided by advanced practice psychiatric nurses for patients with depression and other mental disorders.

Training and Credentials.   Basic-level psychiatric nurses are registered nurses. They have completed a two-year program leading to an associate's degree in nursing, a three-year hospital program leading to a diploma in nursing, or a four-year college or university program leading to a bachelor's degree.

Advanced practice psychiatric nurses are registered nurses who hold at least a master's degree and have met advanced educational and clinical requirements. "Advanced practice registered nurse" is actually an umbrella term. The category includes nurse practitioners (NP) and clinical nurse specialists (CNS). In general, nurse practitioners tend to focus on medical diagnosis, including the diagnosis of physical disorders with psychiatric symptoms, and medication treatment. Clinical nurse specialists tend to focus on psychotherapy or fill managerial or educational jobs. But there is a lot of overlap between the roles, and the way each is defined varies from state to state. Some states do not differentiate between the two roles and use the same advanced practice licensure for all master's-level psychiatric nurses.

Some advanced practice psychiatric nurses subspecialize in areas such as child-adolescent mental health nursing or gero-psychiatric nursing. Others take on consultation-liaison roles, working with patients who have both physical and psychiatric problems, or with the patients' caregivers.

Psychiatric Nursing in Action.   Psychiatric nurses work in hospitals, mental health clinics, home health care agencies, and community health centers. Some advanced practice psychiatric nurses have private psychotherapy practices. The American Nurses Association is the leading professional organization representing registered nurses in the United States. The American Psychiatric Nurses Association, with nearly 5,000 members, is the national professional organization for those who specialize in psychiatric-mental health nursing.

All states require licensure for nurses. In addition to graduating from an approved nursing program, applicants for a license must pass a national licensing exam. The National

Council of State Boards of Nursing is the organization for state boards that regulate the profession.

See also: Diagnosis of Depression; Treatment of Depression

Further Information. American Nurses Association, 8515 Georgia Avenue, Suite 400, Silver Spring, MD 20910, (800) 274-4262, www.nursingworld.org.

American Psychiatric Nurses Association, 1555 Wilson Boulevard, Suite 602, Arlington, VA 22209, (866) 243-2443, www.apna.org.

National Council of State Boards of Nursing, 111 E. Wacker Drive, Suite 2900, Chicago, Illinois 60601, (312) 525-3600, www.ncsbn.org.

Bibliography

About Psychiatric-Mental Health Nurses (PMHNs). American Psychiatric Nurses Association, http://www.apna.org/i4a/pages/index.cfm?pageid=3292.

Bureau of Labor Statistics. "Registered Nurses," in Occupational Outlook Handbook, 2006–07 Edition. Washington, DC: U.S. Department of Labor, 2005.

PSYCHIATRIST. Psychiatrists are medical doctors who specialize in the diagnosis and treatment of mental, emotional, and behavioral disorders. Due to their medical background, psychiatrists are uniquely qualified to assess both mental and physical aspects of depression. As part of the diagnostic process, they can perform or order medical laboratory tests and **brain imaging**. Although no lab tests or brain scans directly diagnose depression, such testing can be helpful in ruling out other possible causes for symptoms.

Of all health care professionals, psychiatrists have the most extensive training in the use of medication to treat depression and other mental disorders. As a result, **pharmacotherapy**, or drug therapy, is a prominent feature of psychiatric treatment. In fact, many psychiatrists focus primarily or exclusively on prescribing and monitoring medication, relying on mental health professionals from other fields to provide **psychotherapy**, or "talk therapy," for their patients who need it. Other psychiatrists, however, conduct psychotherapy themselves in addition to prescribing medication.

Debate over Psychopharmacology. The term "psychopharmacologist" often is applied to psychiatrists whose practices are limited to medication treatment. This is not a formally recognized subspecialty of psychiatry, so it is unclear whether psychiatrists who call themselves psychopharmacologists actually have a higher level of prescribing expertise than other psychiatrists. Nevertheless, it is an increasingly common term among both doctors and patients.

The rise of the psychopharmacologist role can be traced to the modern managed care system, which puts a premium on keeping health care costs down. Because psychiatrists' time is expensive, managed care companies often prefer that psychotherapy be provided by other mental health professionals whose time is less costly. Psychiatrist visits are kept to the minimum needed to prescribe and check medications. Critics have noted that this type of system limits the input of psychiatrists and relegates them to a supporting role, perhaps squandering some of their mental health expertise.

Proponents argue that the psychopharmacologist role is simply an efficient way of using psychiatrists' time and encouraging a team approach among mental health professionals. The ongoing debate is relevant to people with depression, because medication, either alone or combined with psychotherapy, often plays a role in their treatment.

Other Psychiatric Treatments. The vast majority of people with depression can be helped with medication, psychotherapy, or a combination of both. But for a select group of people with severe symptoms or uncontrollable suicidal thoughts, psychiatrists may turn to other medical options. For example, **electroconvulsive therapy** (ECT) involves passing a carefully controlled electrical current through the patient's brain, which induces a brief seizure. ECT is thought to alter some of the electrochemical processes involved in brain functioning. It has been shown to produce substantial improvement in most people with severe depression, even those who are not helped by other treatments.

Psychiatric **hospitalization** is another option that may be used for severe symptoms or suicidal urges. Psychiatrists admit patients to the hospital when it is deemed that they would benefit from intensive, specialized care and close, round-the-clock monitoring. The hospitalization is usually short-term, similar to hospital care for other medical illnesses.

Training and Credentials. Like other medical doctors, psychiatrists have an MD or DO degree. After completing medical school, they spend their first year of residency training taking care of patients with all kinds of medical conditions. Psychiatrists-in-training then spend at least three more years in a psychiatric residency, where they learn about diagnosing and treating mental disorders.

Upon finishing their residency, most psychiatrists take an exam given by the American Board of Psychiatry and Neurology to become board certified in their specialty. Some psychiatrists also continue their training beyond the initial four years so that they can subspecialize in an area such as child and adolescent psychiatry or geriatric psychiatry.

Psychiatry in Action. Of the approximately 42,000 U.S. psychiatrists, about half have private practices. Other settings in which psychiatrists work include general and psychiatric hospitals, university medical centers, community agencies, nursing homes, rehabilitation programs, schools, and prisons. The American Psychiatric Association, with over 35,000 members, is the leading professional society for psychiatrists in the United States.

All states require licensure for medical doctors, including psychiatrists. Applicants for a medical license must submit proof of prior education and training, provide details about their work history, and pass a rigorous exam. The licensing and

Subspecialties in Psychiatry

The American Board of Psychiatry and Neurology recognizes four subspecialties within psychiatry.

Addiction Psychiatry
This field focuses on the evaluation and treatment of individuals with alcohol and drug abuse problems, including those who have both substance-related problems and other psychiatric disorders.

Child and Adolescent Psychiatry
This field focuses on the diagnosis and treatment of mental, emotional, behavioral and developmental disorders in children and teenagers.

Forensic Psychiatry
This field focuses on the evaluation and treatment of individuals who are involved with the legal system or spending time in prisons or jails.

Geriatric Psychiatry
This field focuses on the diagnosis and treatment of mental and emotional disorders in elderly individuals, including those who have both psychiatric problems and physical illnesses.

regulation of psychiatrists and other medical doctors is handled by each state's medical board.

See also: Diagnosis of Depression; Treatment of Depression

Further Information.   American Board of Psychiatry and Neurology, 2150 E. Lake Cook Road, Suite 900, Buffalo Grove, IL 60089, (847) 945-7900, www.abpn.com.

American Medical Association, 515 North State Street, Chicago, IL 60654, (800) 621-8335, www.ama-assn.org.

American Psychiatric Association, 1000 Wilson Boulevard, Suite 1825, Arlington, VA 22209,(888) 357-7924, www.psych.org, www.healthyminds.org.

Federation of State Medical Boards, P.O. Box 619850, Dallas, TX 75261, (817) 868-4000, www.fsmb.org.

Bibliography

ABPN Specialties and Subspecialties Descriptions. American Board of Psychiatry and Neurology, http://www.abpn.com/spec_subspec_description.htm.

Bureau of Labor Statistics. "Physicians and Surgeons," in *Occupational Outlook Handbook, 2006–07 Edition.* Washington, DC: U.S. Department of Labor, 2005.

Kontos, Nicholar, John Querques, and Oliver Freudenreich. "The Problem of the Psychopharmacologist." *Academic Psychiatry* 30 (2006): 218–226.

What Is a Psychiatrist? American Psychiatric Association, http://www.healthyminds.org/whatisapsychiatrist.cfm.

PSYCHODYNAMIC THERAPY.   Psychodynamic therapy is a form of **psychotherapy** that emphasizes the role of past events in molding current experiences as well as the importance of unconscious influences on behavior. Traditionally, this type of psychotherapy is conducted over a period of several months or even a few years, although shorter-term variants have been introduced.

Other therapies for treating depression often focus on immediate symptom relief. Psychodynamic therapy has a more ambitious goal. It aims to change the deep-rooted psychological conflicts that make people vulnerable to becoming depressed in the first place.

The subject matter of psychodynamic therapy is often much broader than that of other therapies. It encompasses past and current problems in interpersonal relationships as well as psychological conflicts related to shame or guilt. It also extends to repressed material—in other words, painful memories and unacceptable impulses that have been pushed out of conscious awareness as a way of defending against anxiety.

Historical Roots.   Psychodynamic therapy evolved out of the work of **Sigmund Freud** (1856–1939), the Austrian neurologist and psychiatrist who developed psychoanalysis, the first major school of psychotherapy. Freud believed that unconscious drives and wishes exert a large influence over people's lives, and in order to change, people need to understand these unconscious influences. Making the unconscious conscious is still a core concept in psychodynamic therapy.

Freud also talked about the central role of childhood experiences in shaping later behavior. Some Freudian concepts have fallen out of favor. For instance, therapists today may downplay Freud's theory of psychosexual development, which stated that the step-by-step growth of sexuality in infancy, childhood, and adolescence has a far-reaching impact on adult personality. But modern psychodynamic theory still emphasizes that childhood events affect

Psychoanalysis in the Twenty-First Century

Psychoanalysis, the form of psychotherapy originated by Freud, is still practiced today as a long-term, in-depth treatment for psychiatric disorders as well as a method of promoting personal growth. In psychoanalysis, a person explores memories and feelings from the past as a means to understanding current feelings and behavior. Specific therapeutic techniques include dream analysis, which involves interpreting dream content to reveal underlying meanings, and free association, which involves freely expressing whatever comes to mind without censoring the material first as a way of accessing unconscious thoughts and feelings.

In formal psychoanalysis, clients lie on a couch with the therapist sitting unseen behind them. The process is intensive, often requiring several sessions a week for many years. Not surprisingly, the cost and time commitment are deterrents for most people. In addition, research evidence is lacking to support the effectiveness of psychoanalysis as a treatment for depression. For those with the will and the means, however, psychoanalysis can be one route to greater self-understanding.

how people act and feel as adults, often for reasons they don't understand until they explore these issues in therapy.

Although psychodynamic therapy is similar to Freudian psychoanalysis, there are critical differences. Of the two, psychodynamic therapy is less time-consuming and more results-oriented.

The Process at a Glance. Although several different forms of psychodynamic therapy are currently practiced, all emphasize past experiences as well as unconscious feelings and drives. The goal is to increase insight into these forces and resolve psychological conflicts that underlie mental disorders. It is assumed that this new understanding, in turn, will lead to better functioning. However, behavior change is the secondary effect of therapy, not the primary focus.

The psychodynamic therapist generally takes the role of a caring but neutral listener rather than an openly supportive ally. This fosters the development of transference, in which the patient directs toward the therapist unconscious wishes and feelings that originally were directed toward another important person in the patient's life, such as a parent.

Psychodynamic therapy typically occurs in one or two sessions per week. Traditionally, the duration of treatment is left open-ended. But unlike Freudian psychoanalysis, which can last for several years, most psychodynamic therapy is completed in two years or less.

Initial Phase. Psychodynamic therapy is divided into three phases. In the initial phase, the patient and therapist lay the groundwork for the therapeutic process and their relationship. Among other things, the patient talks about the stressful events, perceptions, and feelings that accompanied the start of depression. As the story unfolds, the therapist helps the patient identify the unique dynamics underlying his or her symptoms.

For example, some people are extremely sensitive to any real or imagined loss or rejection, stemming from the experience of loss or rejection early in life. As adults, these people may suffer from low self-esteem or fly into a rage at any perceived slight.

Intermediate Phase. During the intermediate phase, the dynamics uncovered in the initial phase are explored from various perspectives. The patient examines how internal conflicts are experienced in feelings, perceptions, and fantasies, as well as how they are manifested in past and present relationships. The goal is greater understanding of and control over the psychological conflicts that make the patient vulnerable to becoming depressed.

For instance, people who are hypersensitive to any slight can come to understand how old losses or rejections are still affecting them today. As a result, their self-esteem is improved, as is their ability to handle disappointments and criticism effectively.

Termination Phase. Termination, or the conclusion of treatment, offers a final opportunity to work through the dynamics of depression. For many patients, there is a real sense of loss at ending the relationship with the therapist. By coping with any feelings of rejection or anger that arise, they further develop their ability to handle loss in real-world relationships.

Brief Psychodynamic Therapy. Recently, shorter-term variants of psychodynamic therapy have been introduced. These therapies generally require 12 to 20 weekly sessions. To accommodate the tighter timeframe, the goals of therapy are pared down. Treatment might focus on understanding the origin of just the most troublesome symptoms or resolving just a single psychological conflict.

To move the process along at a faster clip, therapists using brief psychodynamic therapy may take a more active role than those practicing longer-term therapy. For example, they may rely more heavily on confrontation, a technique in which therapists make statements or ask questions that lead a patient to face the reality of a situation.

Benefits for Depression. Psychodynamic therapy is a widely used treatment for depression. Yet its effectiveness has not been rigorously documented in controlled studies. One problem with existing studies on psychodynamic therapy for depression is that many included patients did not meet established diagnostic criteria. Another problem is that the methods used in psychodynamic therapy often have been poorly defined.

Existing studies on brief psychodynamic therapy indicate that it is more effective than a control condition in which people are simply put on a waiting list. However, the benefits appear to be less pronounced than for either **cognitive-behavioral therapy**, which helps people change habitual patterns of thinking and behaving that are associated with their depression, or **interpersonal therapy**, which helps people address interpersonal triggers for their mental, emotional, and behavioral symptoms.

More research is needed on both longer-term and brief psychodynamic therapy. Although the psychodynamic approach is popular, its effectiveness remains unclear. In addition, some people with depression may be unable to participate in this type of therapy until their worst symptoms have been controlled by other treatments.

One area in which psychodynamic therapy may have particular promise is in treating depression that occurs along with a personality disorder. This type of disorder involves a pervasive pattern of perceiving, relating to, and thinking about the self and the outside world that interferes with long-term functioning. Personality disorders are notoriously resistant to change, but psychodynamic therapy, with its emphasis on making fundamental changes in personality, seems well suited to the challenge.

See also: Treatment of Depression

Further Information. American Psychoanalytic Association, 309 East 49th Street, New York, NY 10017, (212) 752-0450, apsa.org.

Bibliography

About Psychoanalysis. American Psychoanalytic Association, 2006, http://apsa.org/AboutPsychoanalysis/ tabid/202/Default.aspx.

American Psychiatric Association Work Group on Major Depressive Disorder. *Practice Guideline for the Treatment of Patients with Major Depressive Disorder.* 2nd ed. Washington, DC: American Psychiatric Publishing, 2000.

Busch, Frederic N., Marie Rudden, and Theodore Shapiro. *Psychodynamic Treatment of Depression.* Washington, DC: American Psychiatric Publishing, 2004.

Levenson, Hanna, Stephen F. Butler, Theodore A. Powers, and Bernard D. Beitman. *Concise Guide to Brief Dynamic and Interpersonal Therapy.* 2nd ed. Washington, DC: American Psychiatric Publishing, 2002.

Markowitz, John C., Martin Svartberg, and Holly A. Swartz. "Is IPT Time-Limited Psychodynamic Psychotherapy?" *Journal of Psychotherapy Practice and Research* 7 (1998): 185–195.

Psychotherapy: An Overview of the Types of Therapy. Mayo Clinic, September 1, 2006, http://www.mayoclinic.com/health/psychotherapy/MH00009.

U.S. Department of Health and Human Services. *Mental Health: A Report of the Surgeon General.* Rockville, MD: U.S. Department of Health and Human Services, 1999.

PSYCHOEDUCATION.   Psychoeducation refers to information about an illness and its treatment that is provided to someone living with the condition, either as a patient or as a family member. The goal is to help that person understand what is happening so he or she can cope better with symptoms, make informed treatment decisions, choose the best **self-help** strategies, and minimize the risk of future problems.

Psychoeducation may be provided as a component of **psychotherapy**, or it may be offered separately. It can take several forms, such as discussing concerns with a health care provider, participating in a class, reading print or online materials, listening to audio recordings, or viewing video presentations.

It seems logical that the more people know about depression, the better they will be able to deal with it. Research supports this view. In one study conducted at nine sites across Europe, 452 adults with depression or an adjustment disorder were randomly assigned to eight group sessions of psychoeducation, six individual sessions of **problem-solving therapy**, or a control group. The study showed that both the psychoeducation course and the problem-solving therapy reduced the severity and duration of depression.

Psychoeducation also can help family members learn how to support the depressed person more effectively and solve problems that interfere with recovery. Plus, by becoming more informed, family members can discover how to take care of their own needs and reduce stress for the whole family.

On the downside, an in-depth program of psychoeducation might make some people with depression feel anxious or overwhelmed. Others might have problems with concentration or memory, which could limit how much information they absorb and retain. In addition, different people have different learning styles, and although some may prefer material presented in a lecture format, others may be more comfortable reading a book or perusing a Web site. For the best results, it may be important to match the type, amount, and format of the information to the individual's preferences, abilities, and needs.

Bibliography

Dowrick, Christopher, Graham Dunn, Jose Luis Ayuso-Mateos, Odd Steffen Dalgard, Helen Page, Ville Lehtinen, et al. "Problem Solving Treatment and Group Psychoeducation for Depression: Multicentre Randomised Controlled Trial." *BMJ* 321 (2000): 1450–1454.

Family Psychoeducation: Information for Consumers. National Mental Health Information Center, http://mentalhealth.samhsa.gov/cmhs/communitysupport/toolkits/family/InfoConsumer.asp.

Family Psychoeducation: Information for Families and Other Supporters. National Mental Health Information Center, http://mentalhealth.samhsa.gov/cmhs/communitysupport/toolkits/family/InfFamily.asp.

PSYCHOTHERAPY. Psychotherapy involves the use of "talk therapy" and other psychological techniques to treat mental disorders. The focus is on changing detrimental behaviors, thoughts, moods, emotions, and perceptions that may be contributing to a person's problems. Psychotherapy is one of the two main treatment options for depression; the other is medication.

Several types of psychotherapy can be beneficial for people with depression. The two with the strongest research support are **cognitive-behavioral therapy** (CBT) and **interpersonal therapy** (IPT). In CBT, individuals work to change habitual patterns of thinking and behaving that are associated with their depression. In IPT, individuals work to address interpersonal triggers for their mental, emotional, and behavioral symptoms. Research has shown that both CBT and IPT can be effective as short-term (12- to 20-week) therapies for depression.

For mild to moderate depression, psychotherapy alone is sometimes sufficient. For more severe depression, psychotherapy may not be enough by itself, so it is often combined with **antidepressants**.

The Therapeutic Partnership. Psychotherapy relies heavily on verbal interaction between a patient and a therapist. Although the therapist serves as a guide, the patient plays an active and central role in the treatment process. The best results are achieved when both parties tackle the process with vigor, concentration, and commitment. Therapy sessions typically last 45 to 50 minutes. Homework activities also may be assigned between sessions.

The relationship between patient and therapist is unique. Although it is not a friendship, it is most effective when built upon trust and rapport. Confidentiality is another key element, which is emphasized in the ethical codes published by the American Psychiatric Association, American Psychological Association, and other professional organizations.

Both parties have responsibilities. To get the most out of psychotherapy, the patient must be honest and forthright, even when it involves talking about topics that may be embarrassing or uncomfortable. The patient also should be actively engaged in the process, open to new insights, and willing to take steps for change. Meanwhile, the therapist must be willing to listen carefully and respectfully. The therapist also should guide the patient in recognizing and modifying unhealthy patterns.

Approaches to Psychotherapy. By some estimates, there are currently over 400 different therapeutic approaches. However, most boil down to one of three basic orientations.

Action-Oriented Therapies. These approaches focus on current patterns of thought and behavior rather than past experiences. A classic example is **behavioral therapy**, which systematically uses the principles of learning to decrease undesirable behaviors and increase desirable ones. The primary goal is to help patients make positive changes, whether or not they understand how their problems started. CBT, an outgrowth of behavioral therapy, falls solidly into this category. IPT, with its stress on changing interpersonal behaviors and learning new social and communication skills, also may be considered an action-oriented therapy.

Insight-Oriented Therapies. These approaches focus on self-understanding, based on the assumption that greater insight will lead to better functioning. The best-known example is **psychodynamic therapy**, which emphasizes the role of past events in shaping current experiences as well as the importance of unconscious influences on behavior. Although psychodynamic therapy is frequently used for depression, its effectiveness has not been as

Types of Psychotherapists

Mental health professionals from several disciplines provide psychotherapy. Each field has its own licensure requirements, which vary from state to state. In addition, the disciplines differ in training, credentials, and typical treatment approach.

	Training and Credentials	Typical Treatment Approach	Can Prescribe Medication?
Psychiatrist	Medical school plus at least four years of residency training. Many are board certified by the American Board of Psychiatry and Neurology.	Prescribing and monitoring medication. Some provide psychotherapy as well. Others work closely with therapists from other fields.	Yes
Clinical Psychologist	Doctoral degree including a clinical internship plus at least one year of postdoctoral experience. Some supervised are board certified by the American Board of Professional Psychology.	Providing psychotherapy and doing psychological testing. Some also provide other psychologically based treatments, such as cognitive rehabilitation and biofeedback.	In New Mexico and Louisiana only, with advanced training.
Psychiatric Nurse	Licensure as a registered nurse plus additional training in mental health care. Advanced practice registered nurses have a master's degree or above in psychiatric-mental health nursing.	Providing psychotherapy and helping manage medication. Some are supervised by medical doctors, but those with advanced practice credentials may work independently.	In many states, with advanced training.
Clinical Social Worker	Master's degree or above, usually plus two years of supervised clinical experience.	Providing psychotherapy and helping people overcome social and health problems. Some provide assistance in getting help from government agencies.	No
Marriage and Family Therapist	Typically master's degree or above plus post-degree experience. A few states do not require licensure or certification, however.	Providing individual, couples, and family therapy. The focus is on mental health problems in the context of close relationships.	No
Mental Health Counselor	Typically master's degree or above plus post-degree experience. California does not require licensure or certification, however.	Providing psychotherapy and advising people on how to cope with problems of everyday living. Therapy often takes a problem-solving approach.	No
Pastoral Counselor	Training as a mental health professional plus in-depth religious or theological training. Requirements for licensure or certification vary.	Providing psychotherapy in a spiritual context. Both spiritual resources and psychological techniques are utilized for healing and growth.	No

well established as that of CBT and IPT. In some cases, psychodynamic therapy may not be feasible until the worst symptoms of depression are under control with other treatments.

Growth-Oriented Therapies. These approaches often are grouped together under the label humanistic therapy. They are concerned with fostering personal growth through direct experience. The primary focus is on current feelings, rather than thoughts and behaviors, as well as the potential for future development. Other common themes include taking responsibility for oneself and putting trust in spontaneous feelings and natural processes. **Emotion-focused therapy** is one growth-oriented approach that has been adapted to the treatment of depression.

Group, Couples, and Family Therapy. Any of these approaches can be used in individual therapy, in which a patient works one-on-one with a therapist. However, the approaches also are sometimes used in situations where more than one person meets with the therapist at the same time. **Group therapy** involves bringing together several patients with similar diagnoses or issues for therapy sessions. The interaction among group members adds an extra dimension to each person's therapy, providing support and perhaps modifying behavior. The therapist can use the interaction to help group members explore shared problems.

Couples therapy and **family therapy** are a little different, in that the "patient" is the relationship rather than an individual. Partners or family members may meet with the therapist either separately or at the same time, but the focus remains on how they relate to one another. The assumption is that destructive relationship patterns can contribute to a host of mental, emotional, and behavioral problems, including depression. One person's depression, in turn, can take a heavy toll on a marriage or family. The aim of couples and family therapy is to correct faulty patterns of interaction, improving the relationship as a whole and helping the individuals in it function better.

Risks and Benefits. One downside to medication is the risk of harmful side effects. Psychotherapy is relatively safe by comparison. Nevertheless, it may involve confronting unpleasant situations or disturbing thoughts and feelings. Occasionally, the process may give rise to considerable distress, which is one reason it is crucial that psychotherapy be carried out by a qualified mental health professional.

Appropriate psychotherapy can help people with depression pinpoint and address factors that may be contributing to their symptoms. Psychotherapy also can help depressed individuals regain a sense of control over their lives and return to activities that were once sources of pleasure and meaning. As the depression starts to lift, people gradually become able to experience enjoyment and fulfillment in their lives again.

In addition, research suggests that appropriate psychotherapy may reduce the risk of future episodes of depression or decrease their severity. Through psychotherapy, people with depression can learn lifelong skills that help them cope more effectively with future problems and avoid unnecessary suffering.

See also: Cognitive Behavioral Analysis System of Psychotherapy; Cognitive Therapy; Dialectical Behavior Therapy; Treatment of Depression

Bibliography

American Psychiatric Association Work Group on Major Depressive Disorder. *Practice Guideline for the Treatment of Patients with Major Depressive Disorder.* 2nd ed. Washington, DC: American Psychiatric Publishing, 2000.

Bureau of Labor Statistics. *Occupational Outlook Handbook, 2006–07 Edition.* Washington, DC: U.S. Department of Labor, 2005.

Depression. National Institute of Mental Health, 2000, http://www.nimh.nih.gov/health/publications/depression/summary.shtml.

Harvard Medical School. *Understanding Depression.* Boston: Harvard Health Publications, 2003.

How Psychotherapy Helps People Recover from Depression. American Psychological Association, 2004, http://apahelpcenter.org/articles/article.php?id=49.

Psychotherapy. American Psychiatric Association, http://healthyminds.org/psychotherapy.cfm.

Types of Mental Health Providers. Mayo Clinic, 2007, http://www.mayoclinic.com/health/mental-health/MH00074.

U.S. Department of Health and Human Services. *Mental Health: A Report of the Surgeon General.* Rockville, MD: U.S. Department of Health and Human Services, 1999.

PSYCHOTIC DEPRESSION.   Psychotic depression is a severe form of depression in which people not only have the usual symptoms, but also develop distorted beliefs or perceptions that are seriously out of touch with reality. These distortions can take the form of delusions and/or hallucinations. Delusions are false personal beliefs that have no basis in reality, but that remain unchanged even in the face of strong evidence to the contrary. Hallucinations are false sensory impressions in which the person sees, hears, tastes, smells, or feels something that is not really there.

Most often, the delusions or hallucinations are mood-congruent—in other words, they center on typical themes of depression, such as low self-esteem, guilt, death, and meaninglessness. For example, people might have delusional beliefs that they are being punished by becoming ill, that they are responsible for the illness of a loved one, that their body is rotting away, or that the world is headed for immediate destruction. Hallucinations might involve hearing voices that berate the person for shortcomings or sins.

Less commonly, the delusions or hallucinations are mood-incongruent—in other words, they don't involve typical depressive themes. For example, people might have delusional beliefs that they are being followed or that others can hear their thoughts, insert thoughts into their brain, or control their actions. Hallucinations might involve hearing voices that warn the person about being watched or seeing things that don't actually exist. People with mood-incongruent symptoms are more likely to have depression that is difficult, but certainly not impossible, to treat.

Causes and Risk Factors.   Studies have found that psychotic symptoms occur in 14 percent to 19 percent of people with **major depression**, a form of depression that involves being in a low mood nearly all the time and/or losing interest or enjoyment in almost everything. In major depression, these feelings last for at least two weeks, are associated with several other symptoms, and lead to serious problems getting along in everyday life. More than half of people who have recovered from an episode of major depression go on to have another episode later. The presence of psychotic features may further increase the risk of a repeat episode.

People who develop psychotic symptoms during a bout of depression also are more likely to have **bipolar disorder**, in which periods of depression alternate with periods of **mania**, an overly high mood. Although the psychotic symptoms are often temporary, people who develop them should seek treatment immediately to minimize any complications and avoid putting themselves or other people in danger.

Treatment of Psychotic Depression.   For people with psychotic depression, the initial treatment is sometimes **electroconvulsive therapy** (ECT). This treatment involves passing a carefully controlled electrical current through the person's brain, which induces a brief seizure that is thought to alter some of the electrochemical processes involved in brain functioning. Modern ECT is painless and relatively safe, and it can bring a quicker end to psychotic symptoms than other depression treatments.

Medication is almost invariably prescribed as well. It may be an alternative to ECT, an additional treatment if ECT is not fully effective, or a follow-up treatment to keep symptoms from returning. The initial choice usually is an antidepressant, a medication specifically designed for treating depressive symptoms. By reducing the severity of depression, **antidepressants** may relieve psychotic symptoms or prevent a **recurrence**.

If the antidepressant alone isn't enough, the doctor may prescribe an antipsychotic medication. **Antipsychotics** are specifically designed to relieve or prevent psychotic symptoms. Some newer antipsychotics also help even out the mood swings of people with bipolar disorder.

As the most severe symptoms begin to subside, **psychotherapy** also may be helpful. Psychotic depression is a severe mental disorder that needs immediate attention. But with proper treatment, most people begin to feel better and get back to their normal lives, often in a matter of weeks.

Bibliography

American Psychiatric Association. *Diagnostic and Statistical Manual of Mental Disorders.* 4th ed., text rev. Washington, DC: American Psychiatric Association, 2000.

Goes, Fernando S., Bradley Sadler, Jennifer Toolan, Rachel D. Zamoiski, Francis M. Mondimore, Dean F. MacKinnon, et al. "Psychotic Features in Bipolar and Unipolar Depression." *Bipolar Disorders* 9 (2007): 901–906.

Ohayon, Maurice M., and Alan F. Schatzberg. "Prevalence of Depressive Episodes with Psychotic Features in the General Population." *American Journal of Psychiatry* 159 (2002): 1855–1861.

The Stanford Algorithm Project: Treatment of Psychotic Major Depression. Stanford University School of Medicine, January 20, 2003, http://psychoticdepressionalgorithm.stanford.edu.

Wijkstra, J., J. Lijmer, F. Balk, J. Geddes, and W. A. Nolen. "Pharmacological Treatment for Psychotic Depression." *Cochrane Database of Systematic Reviews* 4 (2005): art. no. CD004044.

R

RANDOMIZED CONTROLLED CLINICAL TRIAL. A randomized controlled clinical trial is the gold standard in research on medical and psychological treatments. A "**clinical trial**" is a research study designed to answer specific questions about the safety and/or effectiveness of a drug or therapy. Each trial includes one or more treatment groups. "Controlled" means that the study also includes a non-treatment group for comparison's sake. "Randomized" means that participants are assigned randomly—in other words, by chance—to a particular treatment or control group.

At times, the control group receives a placebo—a sugar pill, nonspecific therapy, or other sham treatment that resembles the real thing but has no therapeutic value. At other times, the control group receives standard care for a condition without the addition of the treatment under investigation. And in still other cases, participants in the control group are assigned to a wait-list control, which means they are put on a waiting list during the study period but receive the investigational treatment once the study is over.

Some randomized controlled clinical trials are double-blind. This means that neither participating individuals nor study staff knows which participants are getting the real treatment and which are receiving a placebo. The double-blind technique is intended to keep people's expectations from consciously or subconsciously affecting the results of a study.

A randomized controlled study design lets researchers determine which changes in the treatment group over time are due to the treatment itself. For example, in research on an antidepressant, 60 percent of patients in the antidepressant group might get better over the course of the study, compared to 25 percent of those in the placebo group. In this example, it appears that 35 percent of improvement is due to the direct effects of the antidepressant.

Further Information. National Library of Medicine, 8600 Rockville Pike, Bethesda, MD 20894, (888) 346-3656, www.clinicaltrials.gov, www.pubmed.gov.

Bibliography

Glossary of Clinical Trials Terms. National Library of Medicine, March 18, 2008, http://clinicaltrials.gov/ct2/info/glossary.

Understanding Clinical Trials. National Library of Medicine, September 20, 2007, http://clinicaltrials.gov/ct2/info/understand.

RAPID CYCLING. Rapid cycling is a pattern seen in some people with **bipolar disorder**, a condition characterized by moods that shift back and forth from overly high to overly low. In rapid cycling, a person has four or more mood episodes in a single year. For some, moods quickly go from high to low and back again over the course of just a few days or even hours. When there are at least four mood episodes a month, it is called ultra-rapid cycling. And when there are several mood switches a day, the term ultradian cycling is used.

By any name, it is an emotional rollercoaster that can leave a person feeling overwhelmed and out of control. Although the term "cycling" might sound as if the mood episodes recur in a regular pattern, that is not actually the case. Often the timing and order of the episodes seem random, and the unpredictability just makes them all the harder to handle.

People with rapid cycling may not respond as well to treatment as those with other forms of bipolar disorder. That does not mean the situation is hopeless, however. To the contrary, proper treatment can help reduce the severity and duration of mood episodes. And getting help promptly may be especially important for people with rapid cycling, because the longer someone with this pattern goes without being treated, the more resistant to treatment the person's symptoms may become.

Forms of Bipolar Disorder. Rapid cycling arises in about 5 to 15 percent of people with **bipolar I** disorder. In this classic form of bipolar disorder, the high mood takes the form of full-blown **mania**, in which elation is exaggerated to the point where it can lead to wildly irrational thinking, dangerous risk taking, or nonstop activity and sleeplessness. In many people with rapid cycling, mania also causes extreme **irritability** or angry outbursts. Often, but not always, there has been a prior episode of **major depression**.

Rapid cycling also arises in some people with **bipolar II** disorder. In this form of the illness, major depression alternates with hypomania, a milder version of the overly high mood.

Technically speaking, a mood episode must last at least two weeks to qualify as major depression, one week for mania (unless it is severe enough to require hospitalization), and four days for hypomania. Many people with ultra-rapid or ultradian cycling do not meet these time requirements, even though they have all the requisite symptoms. In this case, the diagnosis may be **bipolar disorder not otherwise specified**, a catchall category for situations in which bipolar disorder is serious enough to need treatment, but does not meet all the criteria for bipolar I or II.

Course of the Illness. Some people with bipolar disorder develop rapid cycling right from the start. For most, though, it comes on gradually. When bipolar disorder is not adequately treated, mood episodes tend to get shorter and more frequent with time. Eventually, the mood swings may occur frequently enough to qualify as rapid. With treatment, most people return to a pattern of longer, less frequent episodes—or, in the best case, a stable mood. Only a small fraction continue to struggle with rapid cycling indefinitely.

Over the course of a year, people with rapid cycling tend to spend considerably more time than those with non-rapid cycling in a state of mania or hypomania. They also are apt to spend somewhat more time depressed, although the difference is not as great.

Causes and Risk Factors. Those whose bipolar disorder begins early, while they are still children or young adolescents, are at especially high risk for rapid cycling. Research indicates that well over half of young people with bipolar disorder may have the rapid mood shifts. Studies also have shown that physical and sexual abuse in childhood are associated with both early bipolar disorder and rapid cycling, as well as with more severe symptoms in adulthood.

Although bipolar disorder in its classic form is about equally common between the two sexes, women are more likely to develop rapid cycling than men. The reason for this gender difference is still unclear. The quick shifts in mood do not seem to be linked to any particular phase of the menstrual cycle or to being either pre- or post-menopausal.

Some people with rapid cycling have thyroid gland problems, and it has been suggested that one cause of frequent mood swings might be inadequate amounts of thyroid hormone in the brain. Even in rapid cyclers with normal levels of thyroid hormone in their blood, treatment with thyroid hormone pills may lead to more stable moods.

The Kindling Effect. One possible explanation for why mood shifts tend to become more rapid over time is known as the **kindling effect**. According to the kindling theory, the first bouts of depression or mania are triggered by stressful real-life events, such as the death of a loved one or an upcoming move.

These early episodes may spark long-lasting changes in the brain that make it increasingly sensitive to future **stress**. As time goes on, less and less may be needed to set off the next episode. Eventually the person may start having episodes without any obvious trigger at all.

Antidepressant Backfire. One area of longstanding debate is the role that certain **antidepressants** may play in rapid cycling. For people with major depression alone, these medications can be a godsend. But in people who are prone to mania, antidepressants may trigger a sudden switch to a manic state or prolong a rapid cycling pattern once it has started. Some studies have found that women are more sensitive to this effect than men.

The type of antidepressants most strongly implicated are **tricyclic antidepressants** (TCAs). There is evidence that a more widely prescribed type, **selective serotonin reuptake inhibitors**, may be less likely than TCAs to speed up mood shifts. When an antidepressant does bring on or worsen rapid cycling, the problem often subsides once the medication is stopped. But a word of caution: People currently taking an antidepressant should not stop taking it or change the dose without first talking to their doctor. Otherwise, they could do more harm than good.

See also: Hypothyroidism

Bibliography

American Psychiatric Association. *Diagnostic and Statistical Manual of Mental Disorders.* 4th ed., text rev. Washington, DC: American Psychiatric Association, 2000.

Bauer, M., S. Beaulieu, D. L. Dunner, B. Lafer, and R. Kupka. "Rapid Cycling Bipolar Disorder: Diagnostic Concepts." *Bipolar Disorders* 10 (2008): 153–162.

Bipolar Disorder. National Institute of Mental Health, April 3, 2008, http://www.nimh.nih.gov/health/publications/bipolar-disorder/complete-publication.shtml.

Evans, Dwight L., and Linda Wasmer Andrews. *If Your Adolescent Has Depression or Bipolar Disorder: An Essential Resource for Parents.* New York: Oxford University Press, 2005.

Kupka, Ralph W., David A. Luckenbaugh, Robert M. Post, Trisha Suppes, Lori L. Altshuler, Paul E. Keck Jr., et al. "Comparison of Rapid-Cycling and Non-Rapid-Cycling Bipolar Disorder Based on Prospective Mood Ratings in 539 Outpatients." *American Journal of Psychiatry* 162 (2005): 1273–1280.

Rapid Cycling and Its Treatment. Depression and Bipolar Support Alliance, May 4, 2006, http://www.dbsalliance.org/site/PageServer?pagename=about_publicationp_rapidcycling.

REACTIVE DEPRESSION. Reactive depression is a term sometimes used to describe a depressed mood that is apparently triggered by a distressing situation. The classic example is an **adjustment disorder with depressed mood**, which is a psychological response to a stressful event that is out of proportion to the situation or causes significant problems in daily life. When an adjustment disorder is accompanied by a depressed mood, it leads to symptoms such as a feeling down, **crying** frequently, or having a sense of hopelessness.

Other forms of depression, including **major depression** and **dysthymia**, may be triggered by **stress** as well. In major depression, the person is in a low mood nearly all the time and/or loses interest or enjoyment in almost everything, and these feelings last for at least two weeks. In dysthymia, the person experiences a down mood that is relatively mild but quite long-lasting, occurring more days than not for at least two years.

Outside Influences. A concept that is closely related to reactive depression is exogenous depression, which refers to a depressed mood that is thought to be caused by external, **environmental factors**. At one time, it was common to classify depression as either exogenous or endogenous (resulting from internal, biological, or **genetic factors**). This classification was believed to have important implications for treatment, with psychotherapy indicated for the exogenous form of depression and medication for the endogenous kind.

Today, however, this dichotomy has largely been abandoned. The expected differences in treatment response were not borne out by research, and other clear-cut distinctions in symptoms and outcome were generally lacking as well. As a result, diagnostic schemes based on presumed causation were replaced by ones based on actual symptoms.

Most experts now believe that depression results from the complex interplay of both internal and external forces. A person might inherit a genetic tendency to become depressed, for example, but that tendency may not be activated until a stressful situation comes along. Likewise, a person's depressed mood might be brought on by a stressful event, but it may still be accompanied by changes in how the brain functions.

In the modern view, depression is usually not seen as purely reactive (exogenous) or nonreactive (endogenous). Nevertheless, many episodes of depression do seem to be precipitated by a stressful situation, and learning to better manage the situation and cope with future stress is often helpful. In that sense, the concept of reactive depression remains as valid today as it ever was.

See also: Diagnostic and Statistical Manual of Mental Disorders, Fourth Edition, Text Revision

Bibliography

Kessing, Lars Vedel. "Endogenous, Reactive and Neurotic Depression: Diagnostic Stability and Long-Term Outcome." *Psychopathology* 37 (2004): 124–130.

Schwartz, Arthur, and Ruth M. Schwartz. *Depression Theories and Treatments: Psychological, Biological, and Social Perspectives.* New York: Columbia University Press, 1993.

RECEPTORS.   Receptors are specialized sites on cells that receive and react with chemical messages. Many **neurotransmitters** and **hormones**—chemical messengers of the **nervous system** and **endocrine system**, respectively—exert their effects by binding to receptors. As a result, receptors play a critical role in communication between brain cells. A malfunction at this point may contribute to mental and neurological disorders, including depression.

Perhaps the best-studied receptors in relation to depression are the 5-hydroxytryptamine (5-HT) receptors, which bind to the neurotransmitter **serotonin**. This neurotransmitter has many functions, including helping regulate mood, sleep, appetite, and sexual drive.

Seven different families of 5-HT receptors have been found, and subtypes within each have been identified.

5HT1B Serotonin Receptors. Scientists are just starting to learn which of the 5-HT subtypes affect depression and how. 5-HT1B receptors are among the ones that have been singled out for study. For these receptors to become functional, they must move from the interior of brain cells to the membrane on the cells' surface. A protein called P11 is required for this movement to occur.

The less P11 is present, the fewer receptors there are to detect and react with serotonin, and low serotonin activity is thought to play a major role in depression. Theoretically, then, it stands to reason that depression might be related to having low P11 and thus too few 5-HT1B receptors.

Turn-Ons and Turn-Offs

Some 5-HT receptors excite activity in a receiving cell, and others inhibit it. This explains how one brain chemical—serotonin—can have a variety of effects. Below is a closer look at how two opposing types of 5-HT receptors operate.

5-HT1 Receptors

When serotonin binds with a 5-HT1 receptor, it changes the receptor's configuration. This activates a type of protein found in the cell membrane, called a G protein. The G protein opens an ion channel, a gate in the cell membrane through which electrically charged atoms, called ions, can pass. The ion channel allows potassium ions to leave the cell. Because the potassium ions are positively charged, their exit makes the charge inside the cell more negative. This, in turn, makes it harder to trigger an electrical impulse. Thus, the overall effect is to inhibit activity within the cell.

5-HT2 Receptors

When serotonin binds with a 5-HT2 receptor, it also activates a G protein. In this case, though, the G protein closes an ion channel, holding potassium ions in the cell. As the positively charged potassium ions build up, it is easier to trigger an electrical impulse. Thus, the overall effect is to excite activity within the cell.

A growing body of evidence supports this idea. When scientists inactivated the P11 gene in mice, the animals behaved in a depressed manner, but when the gene was over-expressed, the animals acted as if they had been given an antidepressant. Also, when scientists examined human brain tissue after death, they found lower levels of P11 in people who had been depressed, compared to those who had not.

Other Types of Receptors. Receptors other than those for serotonin may be important in depression as well. The neurotransmitter **glutamate** acts on receptors for N-methyl-d-aspartate (NMDA) and alpha-amino-3-hydroxy-5-methylisoxazole-4-propionic acid (AMPA). Stimulation of these receptors is helpful up to a point, but overstimulation may be harmful. **Antidepressants** in general are thought to work partly by helping brain cells keep their sensitivity to glutamate in check.

Beyond that, specific antidepressants may have their own particular effects on receptors. For instance, **noradrenergic and specific serotonergic antidepressants** (NaSSAs) prevent a couple of other neurotransmitters—**norepinephrine** and epinephrine—from binding with alpha-2 receptors. Normally, one job of these receptors is to receive chemical messages telling the cell when it is time to stop releasing serotonin and more norepinephrine. But NaSSAs keep the message from going through, so the cell keeps pumping out norepinephrine and serotonin, giving mood a lift.

See also: Second Messengers

Bibliography

Brain Basics: Know Your Brain. National Institute of Neurological Disorders and Stroke, May 1, 2007, http://www.ninds.nih.gov/disorders/brain_basics/know_your_brain.htm.

Combined Reuptake Inhibitors and Receptor Blockers. Mayo Clinic, December 10, 2008, http://www.mayoclinic.com/health/mental-health/MH00070.

Glennon, Richard A., Malgorzata Dukat, and Richard B. Westkaemper. "Serotonin Receptor Subtypes and Ligands." *Neuropsychopharmacology: The Fourth Generation of Progress.* American College of Neuropsychopharmacology, http://www.acnp.org/g4/GN401000039/Ch039.html.

Serotonin and Other Molecules Involved in Depression: Intermediate. Canadian Institute of Neurosciences, Mental Health and Addiction, http://thebrain.mcgill.ca/flash/i/i_08/i_08_m/i_08_m_dep/i_08_m_dep_isrs.html.

Society for Neuroscience. *Brain Facts: A Primer on the Brain and Nervous System.* 6th ed. Washington, DC: Society for Neuroscience, 2008.

"Toward a New Approach to Depression: An Interview with Paul Greengard, Ph.D." *Advances in Brain Research.* Dana Foundation, 2007, http://www.dana.org/news/publications/detail.aspx?id=6462.

Tricyclic Antidepressants. Mayo Clinic, December 10, 2008, http://www.mayoclinic.com/health/mental-health/MH00069.

RECOVERY.   Recovery from a mental disorder refers to substantial improvement that allows a person to live, work, learn, and participate fully in the community. For those with depression, the term usually implies that symptoms have gone away or are greatly reduced. In practical terms, recovery is sometimes defined as six months of sustained remission—the resolution of symptoms to a level similar to that of healthy individuals.

Not everyone has the same goals for recovery, however. If you are being treated for depression, your mental health care provider can help you define exactly what recovery means to you. Then you should revisit your goals periodically, because your personal definition of a full and rewarding life is apt to change over time.

See also: Partial Remission

Bibliography

American Psychiatric Association. *Diagnostic and Statistical Manual of Mental Disorders.* 4th ed., text rev. Washington, DC: American Psychiatric Association, 2000.

Myths and Facts About Mental Health. Substance Abuse and Mental Health Services Administration, http://allmentalhealth.samhsa.gov/myths_facts.html.

Recovery. National Alliance on Mental Illness, http://www.nami.org/Content/NavigationMenu/Find_Support/Consumer_Support/Recovery.htm.

Recovery Steps. Depression and Bipolar Support Alliance, December 29, 2006, http://www.dbsalliance.org/site/PageServer?pagename=recoverysteps.

U.S. Department of Health and Human Services. *Mental Health: A Report of the Surgeon General.* Rockville, MD: U.S. Department of Health and Human Services, 1999.

RECURRENCE.   A recurrence is a new episode of an illness after a period of wellness. In theory, it is slightly different from a relapse, which is the return of symptoms from a prior episode that never fully resolved, even though the person got quite a bit better for a while. In practice, it can be very difficult to tell one from the other. Both relapse and recurrence are common after short-term treatment for depression.

To ward off these problems, long-term treatment frequently is needed. Treatment aimed at preventing a recurrence is called maintenance therapy, and treatment aimed at preventing a relapse is called continuation therapy. Both terms refer to treatment that continues even after the person is feeling better.

See also: Continuation Treatment; Maintenance Treatment; Recurrent Depression

Bibliography

Kupfer, David J. "Acute Continuation and Maintenance Treatment of Mood Disorders." *Depression* 3 (1995): 137–138.

U.S. Department of Health and Human Services. *Mental Health: A Report of the Surgeon General.* Rockville, MD: U.S. Department of Health and Human Services, 1999.

RECURRENT BRIEF DEPRESSION. Recurrent brief depression (RBD) is a term that is sometimes used for a mood disorder that causes the same number and severity of symptoms as **major depression**, but in shorter episodes that recur at least monthly for 12 straight months. Although these episodes last less than two weeks, they can add up to considerable distress over the course of a year. In one long-term study, people with RBD averaged 43 days of depression annually, compared to 75 days in those with major depression.

RBD is not yet a formally recognized disorder in the ***Diagnostic and Statistical Manual of Mental Disorders, Fourth Edition, Text Revision*** (*DSM-IV-TR*), a diagnostic guide published by the American Psychiatric Association and used by mental health professionals from many disciplines. At present, individuals with RBD may be given the nonspecific diagnosis of "**depressive disorder not otherwise specified**." RBD is being considered for possible inclusion as a distinct entity in the manual's next edition, however.

Historical Roots. Although scientific research on RBD is still at a fairly early stage, the condition has been described clinically since at least the mid-nineteenth century. In 1852, Eduard Pohl used the term "periodic melancholia" for episodes of depression that lasted from hours to days.

More than a century later, in 1975, U.S. psychiatrist Robert L. Spitzer and his colleagues described a condition called "intermittent depressive disorder," characterized by a pattern in which periods of depression lasting from hours to several days alternated with periods of normal mood lasting from hours to weeks. Intermittent depressive disorder was included in their Research Diagnostic Criteria, a system of symptom-based diagnostic criteria for mental disorders that helped pave the way for the third edition of the *DSM* (*DSM-III*). The disorder did not find its way into the *DSM-III*, however, and it failed to gain a foothold among mental health professionals.

The term RBD was introduced in 1985 by Swiss researcher Jules Angst (1926–), a psychiatry professor at the University of Zurich. His concept of RBD is the one in use today. It is included in the *The International Classification of Diseases, Tenth Edition* (*ICD-10*), a system for categorizing diseases devised by the World Health Organization. Angst's definition of RBD was based on results of his Zurich Study, a long-running study of young adults in Zurich, Switzerland, launched in 1978. This study found that 12.5 percent of people developed pure RBD—that is, RBD in the absence of any other mood disorder—at some point in their lives. But unlike major depression, which occurs more often in women than men, RBD was about equally common in both sexes.

Criteria for Diagnosis. Like people with major depression, those with RBD have one or both of two core symptoms: (1) a low mood nearly all the time, and (2) loss of interest or enjoyment in almost everything. At the same time, they may experience associated problems: (3) weight gain or weight loss, (4) trouble sleeping or oversleeping, (5) restless activity or slowed-down movements, (6) constant tiredness or lack of energy, (7) feelings of worthlessness or inappropriate guilt, (8) difficulty concentrating or making decisions, and (9) recurring thoughts of death or **suicide**.

To meet the criteria for either RBD or major depression, people must have at least five of the nine symptoms listed above, and the intensity of these symptoms can range from mild to severe. The difference is that the symptoms must last at least two weeks to be considered major depression, but they last only 2 to 13 days in those with RBD. In fact, the typical RBD episode is just 2 to 4 days long. Yet these short episodes are still disruptive, in part because they return at least once a month for a year. Each time the symptoms recur, they cause some distress or interfere somewhat with daily life. In certain cases, people may function nearly normally, but that is accomplished only through greatly increased effort.

In women, the monthly bouts of depression are not associated strictly with their menstrual cycles. Women whose low moods and other symptoms regularly appear right before their menstrual periods might have **premenstrual dysphoric disorder** instead.

Treatment of RBD. Left untreated, RBD can breed repeated turmoil at home, work, or school. It also is associated with an increased risk of suicide. As with other types of depression, mental health professionals may recommend **psychotherapy** or **antidepressants**. But due to a dearth of well-designed studies, it is still unclear which treatment approach is most likely to be effective.

RBD often occurs along with other mental, emotional, and behavioral disorders, such as **anxiety disorders** and **substance abuse**. In one study, for instance, 40 percent of people being treated for anxiety had a recurrent problem with brief depression. In such people, treating the coexisting condition may help the depression as well.

Bibliography

American Psychiatric Association. *Diagnostic and Statistical Manual of Mental Disorders.* 4th ed., text rev. Washington, DC: American Psychiatric Association, 2000.

Angst, J., and A. Dobler-Mikola. "The Zurich Study: A Prospective Epidemiological Study of Depressive, Neurotic and Psychosomatic Syndromes. IV. Recurrent and Nonrecurrent Brief Depression." *European Archives of Psychiatry and Neurological Sciences* 234 (1985): 408–416.

Bauer, Michael, Peter C. Whybrow, Jules Angst, Marcio Versiani, Hans-Jürgen Möller, and the WFSBP Task Force on Treatment Guidelines for Unipolar Depressive Disorders. "World Federation of Societies of Biological Psychiatry (WFSBP) Guidelines for Biological Treatment of Unipolar Depressive Disorders, Part 2: Maintenance Treatment of Major Depressive Disorder and Treatment of Chronic Depressive Disorders and Subthreshold Depressions." *Biological Psychiatry* 3 (2002): 69–86.

Pezawas, Lukas, Jules Angst, Alex Gamma, Vladeta Ajdacic, Dominique Eich, and Wulf Rössler. "Recurrent Brief Depression—Past and Future." *Progress in Neuro-psychopharmacology and Biological Psychiatry* 27 (2003): 75–83.

Williams, W. Robert, Jonathan P. Richards, Jamal R. M. Ameen, and Julie Davies. "Recurrent Brief Depression and Personality Traits in Allergy, Anxiety and Premenstrual Syndrome Patients: A General Practice Survey." *Medical Science Monitor* 13 (2007): CR118-CR124.

RECURRENT DEPRESSION. Recurrent depression is characterized by the occurrence of more than one episode of **major depression** over the course of a person's lifetime. About 60 percent of people who have recovered from a first episode of major depression go on to have a **recurrence**—in other words, a repeat bout of the illness. The risk just goes up with subsequent episodes. After three bouts of major depression, the odds of a fourth rise to 90 percent.

Repeat episodes follow four main patterns. In the first, there is full **recovery** between bouts of major depression. In the second, there is only partial recovery between episodes, with some symptoms hanging on after the person gets better. In the third, there is full between-episode recovery from major depression, but the person also has **dysthymia**, another form of depression that is relatively mild but quite long-lasting. As a result, the person continues to have problems caused by dysthymia even after the major depression goes away. In the fourth, there is only partial between-episode recovery from major depression, and dysthymia is present at the same time.

Course of Recurrent Depression

The ***Diagnostic and Statistical Manual of Mental Disorders, Fourth Edition, Text Revision*** (*DSM-IV-TR*) uses "longitudinal course specifiers" to describe the different patterns of recurrent depression.

DSM-IV-TR Specifier (and Coexisting Diagnosis)	**Full Recovery Between Episodes**	**Dysthymia at the Same Time**
With Full Interepisode Recovery (No Dysthymia)	X	
Without Full Interepisode Recovery (No Dysthymia)		
With Full Interepisode Recovery (with Dysthymia)	X	X
Without Full Interepisode Recovery (with Dysthymia)		X

The distinction between recurrent and nonrecurrent depression seems to be an important one. From a genetic point of view, people who have recurrent depression are more likely to come from families with a history of major depression than those who just have a single episode. From a clinical point of view, because people who have had one recurrence are at such high risk for another, it is crucial that they stay on **maintenance therapy**—treatment that is continued long-term, even during well periods.

The more bouts of depression people experience, the more distress and disruption they suffer over the course of their lives. Later episodes tend to become more frequent and severe, especially if people do not get proper treatment. Nevertheless, there is good reason for optimism, as experts constantly learn more about how to prevent and treat recurrences.

See also: Double Depression; Kindling Hypothesis; Partial Remission; Recurrent Brief Depression

Bibliography

American Psychiatric Association. *Diagnostic and Statistical Manual of Mental Disorders.* 4th ed., text rev. Washington, DC: American Psychiatric Association, 2000.

Greden, John F. "The Burden of Recurrent Depression: Causes, Consequences, and Future Prospects." *Journal of Clinical Psychiatry* 62 (2001): 5–9.

Hollon, Steven D., Richard C. Shelton, Stephen Wisniewski, Diane Warden, Melanie M. Biggs, Edward S. Friedman, et al. "Presenting Characteristics of Depressed Outpatients as a Function of Recurrence: Preliminary Findings From the STAR*D Clinical Trial." *Journal of Psychiatric Research* 40 (2006): 59–69.

Klein, Daniel N., Stewart A. Shankman, and Brian R. McFarland. "Classification of Mood Disorders." In *The American Psychiatric Publishing Textbook of Mood Disorders,* by Dan J. Stein, David J. Kupfer, and Alan F. Schatzberg, eds., 17–32. Washington, DC: American Psychiatric Publishing, 2006.

RELATIONSHIP ISSUES.   Relationship factors play an important role in the cause, course, and consequences of depression. On one hand, interpersonal loss or conflict is a major source of **stress**, which may trigger or worsen an episode of depression in someone who is vulnerable to the illness. On the other hand, withdrawn, apathetic, depressed behavior can lead to interpersonal rejection or conflict, creating or worsening relationship problems.

This interaction explains why depression is often described as a family illness. Literally speaking, a genetic predisposition to depression may be passed down through families. But beyond that, when one person becomes depressed, the ripple effects are felt by others who are close to that individual. Family members and friends may feel put off or shut out, or they may blame themselves for a loved one's deep unhappiness.

Not all relationships are affected the same way, though. Some relationships are adaptable and sturdy enough to weather even tough challenges, but others are more fragile. The ability to adapt may be influenced by factors such as major life changes, economic resources, the mental health of significant others, and the availability of outside support.

When family and friends are overwhelmed by too many problems or have their own mental or physical health issues to contend with, they may not be able to provide support to the depressed individual. As a result, that person's symptoms may get worse or take longer to improve.

In contrast, when family and friends are able to respond effectively to a loved one's depression, they can have a powerfully uplifting effect. Consequently, the depressed person's symptoms may be milder or quicker to resolve. Family and friends also may encourage a loved one to seek professional help, stick to a treatment plan, and make recommended lifestyle changes.

How Depression Affects Couples.   Research has shown that up to 40 percent of adults living with a depressed person have experienced depression at some point themselves. To an extent, this may be because people who are prone to depression tend to be attracted to each other and end up getting married. But once two depression-prone individuals are living under the same roof, they also may feed each other's illness. The stress of living with one person's depressive symptoms may make the other person's worse.

That is not always the case, however. One factor that may help determine whether being married is a help or a hindrance is the nature of the relationship before depression struck. Couples with good communication, shared values, and a strong commitment to each other are often able to sustain solid, supportive relationships in spite of one person's depression.

Potential Pitfalls.   Recognizing that the problem is depression can make a big difference. Otherwise, the well partner may not understand why the other person is being so negative, withdrawn, disinterested, or irritable. When the well partner becomes upset by

When a Loved One Is Depressed

Depression touches not only the person who is ill, but also everyone who lives with or cares about that individual. In fact, family members and friends may recognize that there is a serious problem before the person who is depressed does. Even when the depressed individual realizes that something is terribly wrong, he or she may lack the energy or motivation to do anything about it. Often, it is up to concerned family and friends to open a dialogue and urge the depressed person to seek professional help. Following are some tips for offering support.

Encourage Getting Treatment

Talk to the depressed person about what you have seen and why you are concerned. If the person is having trouble taking the first step toward getting help, provide a number he or she can call. Your family doctor, health insurance provider, or employee assistance program may be a good starting point. The Substance Abuse and Mental Health Services Administration also offers free treatment referrals at (800) 662–4357, mentalhealth.samhsa.gov/databases.

If the other person's depression is life-threatening or debilitating, you might need to make the first move yourself. Contact a doctor or hospital right away.

Learn More about Depression

The more you know, the better equipped you will be to provide support. Educating yourself helps you understand why a loved has become so withdrawn, pessimistic, or disinterested in the relationship. The problem is the illness, not you.

Lend a Sympathetic Ear

Let your loved one know that you are there to listen. It can be hard for someone with depression to muster up the energy and desire to talk. When it happens, pay close attention, and avoid judging or dismissing what the other person has to say.

Take Good Care of Yourself

Living with or caring for someone who is depressed can be demanding and stressful. Nurture your own mental health by eating well, exercising regularly, getting enough sleep, and making time to do things that are fun and relaxing.

Be Realistic about Recovery

Don't expect your loved one to get better overnight. If you are looking for a quick return to normal, you are apt to be disappointed, and your relationship may suffer. Keep in mind that **recovery** is a gradual process that can take months.

this seemingly thoughtless behavior, the depressed partner may just withdraw further and sink deeper into depression.

Even when the well partner is understanding, the partner with depression may have trouble accepting support if he or she feels unworthy of love. In addition, people with depression often are apathetic, hopeless, guilty, anxious, or drained of energy. They may find it hard to concentrate on anything, including another person's needs. At the same time, they may be worried about imposing their pain on someone else or concerned that they will sound "crazy" if they talk frankly about how they feel.

Dependency and Reassurance-Seeking. Depression can cause relationship turmoil. By the same token, relationship problems may contribute to depression. U.S. psychologist Sidney J. Blatt noted that some people are high in dependency—in other words, they are overly invested in their relationships and place inordinate value on the approval of others. Such individuals may be vulnerable to depression in response to interpersonal loss or separation.

In a similar vein, U.S. psychologist James C. Coyne observed that when a depressed person feels unlovable and worthless, he or she may attempt to ease these feelings by seeking reassurance from a significant other. But even if the other person responds, the person with depression may find it hard to believe positive feedback is genuine. This nagging doubt pushes the depressed individual to keep seeking reassurance again and again. Eventually, the significant other grows frustrated and annoyed, which only heightens the depressed person's insecurity. It is a vicious cycle that leaves the depressed person feeling more rejected and dejected than ever.

Besides overtly asking for reassurance, some people with depression may subconsciously seek out negative reactions from others, which only confirm and strengthen their low opinion of themselves. Researchers have found that depressed students seek more negative feedback and are more rejected by others than nondepressed students.

Healing Troubled Relationships. Because relationship problems are so common, most forms of **psychotherapy** used to treat depression address this area to some extent. One type of therapy, called **interpersonal therapy**, is specifically designed to identify and correct the interpersonal triggers for depression.

Therapy is often done in individual sessions between a patient and therapist. But when relationship issues are a major focus, it sometimes helps to include significant others in the process as well. **Family therapy** brings together members of a family for sessions, with the goal of improving relationships between individual members and changing dysfunctional behavior patterns of the family unit as a whole. **Couples therapy** involves having the same therapist treat both partners in a committed relationship at the same time, with the goal of resolving problems and improving support between them.

See also: Attachment Theory; Personality Factors; Social Support

Bibliography

DePaulo, J. Raymond Jr. *Understanding Depression: What We Know and What You Can Do About It.* New York: John Wiley and Sons, 2002.

Depression: Supporting a Family Member or Friend with Depression. Mayo Clinic, May 30, 2008, http://www.mayoclinic.com/health/depression/MH00016.

Helping a Friend or Family Member with Depression or Bipolar Disorder. Depression and Bipolar Support Alliance, November 11, 2006, http://www.dbsalliance.org/site/PageServer?pagename=about_publications_helping.

Joiner, Thomas E. Jr., and Katherine A. Timmons. "Depression in Its Interpersonal Context." In *Handbook of Depression.* 2nd ed., by Ian H. Gotlib and Constance L. Hammen, eds., 322–339. New York: Guilford Press, 2009.

Luyten, Patrick, Bernard Sabbe, Sidney J. Blatt, Sieglinde Meganck, Bart Jansen, Carmen De Grave, et al. "Dependency and Self-Criticism: Relationship with Major Depressive Disorder, Severity of Depression, and Clinical Presentation." *Depression and Anxiety* 24 (2007): 586–596.

Schmidt, Norman B., Kristen L. Schmidt, and Jeffery E. Young. "Schematic and Interpersonal Conceptualizations of Depression: An Integration." In *The Interactional Nature of Depression: Advances in Interpersonal Approaches,* by Thomas Joiner and James C. Coyne, eds., 127–148. Washington, DC: American Psychological Association, 1999.

Starr, Lisa R., and Joanne Davila. "Excessive Reassurance Seeking, Depression, and Interpersonal Rejection: A Meta-analytic Review." *Journal of Abnormal Psychology* 117 (2008): 762–775.

Whisman, Mark A., Lisa A. Uebelacker, and Lauren M. Weinstock. "Psychopathology and Marital Satisfaction: The Importance of Evaluating Both Partners." *Journal of Consulting and Clinical Psychology* 72 (2004): 830–838.

Williams, David R., and Harold W. Neighbors. "Social Perspectives on Mood Disorders." Nunes, Edward, Eric Rubin, Kenneth Carpenter, and Deborah Hasin. "Mood Disorders and Substance Use." In *The American Psychiatric Publishing Textbook of Mood Disorders,* by Dan J. Stein, David J. Kupfer, and Alan F. Schatzberg, eds., 145–158. Washington, DC: American Psychiatric Publishing, 2006.

RELAXATION TECHNIQUES. Relaxation techniques are a group of methods for reducing tension, inducing calmness, and counteracting **stress**. Some people also use these techniques to help manage depression in everyday life. Although large, long-term studies are still needed, several small studies indicate that learning to relax helps ease symptoms of depression. When combined with antidepressant medication, it may lead to greater improvement than medication alone.

On a psychological level, most relaxation techniques involve increasing body awareness or refocusing attention to calm the mind. On a physiological level, these techniques activate the relaxation response—the body's natural mechanism for reversing the physical changes brought on by stress.

In the right amount at the right time, stress has a protective function, gearing up the mind and body to respond to a crisis or challenge. But when stress is excessive or prolonged, it can exact a harsh toll on mental and physical health. Among other adverse effects, it may trigger or worsen depression.

The Relaxation Response. Scientifically speaking, stress is the body's automatic, protective reaction to a perceived threat or challenge—in short, any situation that requires a sudden behavioral adjustment. In response to this type of situation, the mind and body swing into a state of heightened alertness and arousal. Metabolism, heart rate, breathing rate, and muscle tension all increase.

In the late 1960s, U.S. cardiologist Herbert Benson (1935–) described a counterbalancing mechanism that reverses those changes in the body, which he dubbed the relaxation response. Metabolism, heart rate, breathing rate, and muscle tension decrease in this physical state of deep rest. Research shows that regular practice of techniques that elicit the relaxation response can lead to lasting physical and mental changes, including fewer aches and pains, more energy, improved concentration, and enhanced coping.

Techniques for Relaxing. Relaxation techniques involve more than simply pursuing a hobby, playing a game, or unwinding with friends. Although these activities can be fun and restful, the goal of a formal relaxation technique is to bring on the physiological relaxation response at will. Several methods can be used for this purpose. Whatever method a person prefers, the key is to practice it often. Many experts recommend practicing a relaxation technique for at least 10 to 20 minutes daily.

Mantra Meditation. **Meditation** involves focusing the mind intently on a particular thing or activity while becoming relatively oblivious to everything else. In mantra meditation, the focus is on a mantra—a special word, phrase, or sound that is repeated, either silently or aloud, to keep distracting thoughts from entering the mind. The goal is to achieve a state of pure, relaxed awareness. Transcendental Meditation, derived from Hindu traditions, is one popular form of mantra meditation.

Mindfulness Meditation. Mindfulness meditation, rooted in Buddhist practices, involves fully focusing on whatever is being experienced from moment to moment, without reacting to or judging that experience. Often, the point of focus during meditation is the flow of breath in and out of the body. Mindfulness is a core feature of **mindfulness-based cognitive therapy**, a treatment approach designed to help people who have recovered from depression avoid a recurrence. The approach teaches people to be more aware of changes in feelings and thoughts, so they can react to those changes promptly and effectively. At the same time, a mindful attitude helps people accept distressing moods or thoughts without becoming unduly alarmed.

Progressive Muscle Relaxation. Progressive muscle relaxation, developed by U.S. physician Edmund Jacobson (1888–1983) in the 1920s, involves systematically tensing and relaxing all the major muscle groups of the body in turn. As people do this, they grow more aware of the feelings associated with tension and relaxation, which helps them become attuned to muscle tension at other times. Studies have shown that progressive muscle relaxation can help reduce symptoms of depression in people with various medical conditions, including chronic lung disease and cancer.

Imagery. Imagery uses the power of imagination to bring about changes in thoughts, feelings, and physical responses. Another common name for the approach is visualization. But although visualization implies seeing something with the mind's eye, imagery can bring to bear any of the senses, including hearing, sight, taste, and touch. For instance, someone might imagine relaxing on the beach while watching a beautiful sunset, listening to the soothing sound of waves, smelling the salty sea air, and feeling the warmth of the sun. Guided imagery is a variation, in which another person or a voice on a recording leads the imagery process.

Yoga. **Yoga** is a mind-body practice, rooted in the ancient traditions of India, which combines physical postures, breathing techniques, and meditation. Studies

Toe-to-Head Relaxation

Below is a step-by-step look at progressive muscle relaxation. Before trying this approach, check with a doctor if you have an acute injury or chronic pain. If tensing a muscle causes pain or cramping, stop immediately.

First, find a quiet spot away from distractions. Assume a comfortable position lying or sitting down. Close your eyes, if you wish.

Second, take some slow, deep breaths to relax. Focus on your breath going in and out until your body feels loose and your mind is calm.

Third, bring your focus to your right foot and lower leg. Tense the muscles there, flexing your ankle and pulling your toes toward you. Hold for about five seconds, and notice how the tension feels. Then release, letting your foot fall back into its natural position and your leg go limp. Take several seconds to notice how the relaxation feels. Repeat a few times.

Fourth, alternately tense and relax other parts of your body in turn: right upper leg (tightening your right thigh and buttock muscles), left foot and lower leg, left upper leg, abdomen (squeezing your abdominal muscles tight), right hand and arm (making a fist and tightening your arm muscles), left hand and arm, chest (expanding your chest wider), shoulders (shrugging up toward your ears), neck (bending your chin toward your chest), jaw (biting down lightly and pulling back the corners of your mouth), and forehead (wrinkling the brow and squeezing the eyes shut). After tensing and relaxing a body part, repeat the process a few times before moving on to the next area.

Fifth, continue lying quietly for a few more minutes. Enjoy the feeling of relaxation throughout your body.

indicate that yoga may help counteract stress, improve mood, and promote a sense of well-being. Research also suggests that yoga may help people manage conditions such as depression, anxiety, and sleep problems.

Tai Chi.   Tai chi originated in ancient China as a martial art and means of self-defense. Over time, it evolved into a type of moving meditation, combining slow, flowing movements with a calm, alert state of mind. Studies suggest that tai chi may help relieve stress, reduce depression and anxiety, improve balance and coordination, increase flexibility and strength, enhance sleep quality, and promote overall well-being. Because the movements are so gentle, it is one form of exercise that can be done by people of all ages and fitness levels.

See also: Stress Management

Further Information.   Benson-Henry Institute for Mind Body Medicine, 151 Merrimac Street, Boston, MA 02114, (617) 643-6090, www.mbmi.org.

Bibliography

Andrews, Linda Wasmer. *Stress Control for Peace of Mind.* New York: Main Street, 2005.

Benson, Herbert. *The Relaxation Response.* New York: Morrow, 1975.

Elicit the Relaxation Response. Benson-Henry Institute for Mind Body Medicine, http://www.mbmi .org/basics/whatis_rresponse_elicitation.asp.

Ernst, Edzard, Julia I. Rand, and Clare Stevinson. "Complementary Therapies for Depression: An Overview." *Archives of General Psychiatry* 55 (1998): 1026–1032.

Jorm, Anthony F., Helen Christensen, Kathleen M. Griffiths, and Bryan Rodgers. "Effectiveness of Complementary and Self-Help Treatments for Depression." *Medical Journal of Australia* 176 (2002): S84-S96.

Meditation: An Introduction. National Center for Complementary and Alternative Medicine, February 2009, http://nccam.nih.gov/health/meditation/overview.htm.

Meditation: Take a Stress-Reduction Break Wherever You Are. Mayo Clinic, April 21, 2009, http://www.mayoclinic.com/health/meditation/HQ01070.

Progressive Muscle Relaxation. National Jewish Health, 2009, http://www.nationaljewish.org/ healthinfo/lifestyle/relax/muscle-relaxation.aspx.

Relaxation Techniques: Learn Ways to Calm Your Stress. Mayo Clinic, May 7, 2007, http://www .mayoclinic.com/health/relaxation-technique/SR00007.

Segal, Zindel V., J. Mark G. Williams, and John D. Teasdale. *Mindfulness-Based Cognitive Therapy for Depression: A New Approach to Preventing Relapse.* New York: Guilford Press, 2002.

Tai Chi: Improved Stress Reduction, Balance, Agility for All. Mayo Clinic, November 15, 2007, http://www.mayoclinic.com/health/tai-chi/SA00087.

The Relaxation Response. Benson-Henry Institute for Mind Body Medicine, http://www.mbmi .org/basics/whatis_rresponse_TRR.asp.

The Stress Response. Benson-Henry Institute for Mind Body Medicine, http://www.mbmi.org/ basics/whatis_stress_response.asp.

Yoga for Health: An Introduction. National Center for Complementary and Alternative Medicine, May 2008, http://nccam.nih.gov/health/yoga/introduction.htm.

REUPTAKE.   Reuptake is the process by which chemical messengers in the brain, called **neurotransmitters**, are absorbed back into the cells that originally released them. Many **antidepressants** work by blocking the reuptake of **serotonin**, **norepinephrine**, and/or **dopamine**—neurotransmitters thought to be involved in depression. This leaves more of the neurotransmitter available for use by the brain, which may enhance the sending of nerve impulses.

Reuptake is carried out by protein complexes called transporters. To transmit a message from one brain cell to another, the sending cell releases a neurotransmitter into the tiny gap between the two cells, called the synapse. Once the message has been delivered, the **transporter** carries the neurotransmitter back into the sending cell, where it can be reabsorbed and reused.

See also: Axelrod, Julius; Serotonin Transporter Gene

Bibliography

Norepinephrine and Dopamine Reuptake Inhibitors (NDRIs). Mayo Clinic, December 10, 2008, http://www.mayoclinic.com/health/antidepressants/MH00068.

Selective Serotonin Reuptake Inhibitors (SSRIs). Mayo Clinic, December 10, 2008, http://www.mayoclinic.com/health/ssris/MH00066.

Serotonin and Norepinephrine Reuptake Inhibitors (SNRIs). Mayo Clinic, December 10, 2008, http://www.mayoclinic.com/health/antidepressants/MH00067.

REYNOLDS ADOLESCENT DEPRESSION SCALE. The Reynolds Adolescent Depression Scale (RADS) is a self-report questionnaire designed to assess symptoms of depression in **adolescents**. The RADS was introduced by U.S. psychologist William M. Reynolds in 1987. In 2002, a second edition (RADS-2) was published. In this edition, the age span for test takers was expanded to cover ages 11 through 20.

The RADS-2, which takes about 10 minutes to complete, consists of 30 items. Most of the items are symptoms of **major depression** or **dysthymia**, but some reflect opposite feelings (for example, "I feel happy"). For each item, adolescents are asked to rate how often they feel that way on a four-point scale, ranging from "almost never" to "most of the time."

The RADS-2 can be used as a screening tool in schools and other settings. Adolescents who are identified as likely to be depressed on the RADS-2 can then be given a full diagnostic evaluation. It also can be used in clinical settings, where the test is repeated over the course of treatment to see how symptoms are changing. A version of the test for younger children, the Reynolds Child Depression Scale, is available as well.

Pros and Cons of the RADS-2. The reliability of the RADS-2—that is, the extent to which the results obtained are consistent and repeatable—has been well documented. Research has shown that the test has good internal consistency, the degree to which all the items are measuring the same thing. There is also a strong correlation between test scores when the same person retakes the test within two weeks.

Scores on the RADS-2 are highly correlated with those on other depression rating scales, one way of establishing that the test actually is measuring what it purports to measure. With the introduction of the RADS-2, the recommended minimum score for identifying depression was lowered from 77 to 61. Using this new cutoff score, the test appears to perform well in terms of both sensitivity, the likelihood of a positive result for someone who really is depressed, and specificity, the likelihood of a negative result for someone who does not have depression.

The RADS-2 has been used successfully in various groups of adolescents, including those with cognitive disabilities, emotional disorders, and behavioral problems. As a scale designed specifically for assessing depression at this age, it meets a definite need. And thanks to extensive testing in both the general student population and adolescents in treatment, the RADS-2 seems to fulfill that need admirably.

See also: Diagnosis of Depression; Screening Tests

Bibliography

Brotman, Laurie Miller, Dimitra Kamboukos, and Rachelle Theise. "Symptom-Specific Measures for Disorders Usually First Diagnosed in Infancy, Childhood, or Adolescence." In *Handbook of Psychiatric Measures,* 2nd ed., by A. John Rush Jr., Michael B. First, and Deborah Blacker, eds., 309–342. Washington, DC: American Psychiatric Publishing, 2008.

Reynolds Adolescent Depression Scale, 2nd Ed. (RADS-2). Psychological Assessment Resources, http://www3.parinc.com/products/product.aspx?Productid=RADS-2.

RISK FACTORS.   Risk factors are personal traits or environmental characteristics that increase the likelihood of developing a disorder, such as depression. Some risk factors—such as family history and gender—cannot be changed, but others are modifiable. Identifying the latter is a critical first step in the **prevention of depression**.

Although depression strikes people of both sexes, all ages, and every background, certain factors increase the risk for a particular individual. By learning about these factors and taking preemptive action, some people may be able to ward off depression, minimize its effects, or prevent a recurrence.

Increasing the Risk.   A wide range of genetic, biological, psychological, social, and environmental factors may affect a particular individual's mental health. Below are some of the more important risk factors for depression, based on research to date.

Family History.   Depression is two to four times more common in people who have a close relative with a mood disorder, compared to those with no such family history. The risk of depression is also increased in those with a family history of **suicide**.

Gender and Childbirth.   **Women** are twice as likely as men to become depressed, regardless of ethnic group or economic status. Those who have recently given birth are uniquely at risk for **postpartum depression**.

Stressful Life Events.   Stressful life events—such as the death of a loved one, divorce, or job loss—are associated with an increased risk of depression. Sources of lasting **stress**—such as long-term relationship conflicts, work pressures, or financial problems—may trigger or worsen depression as well.

Early Childhood Trauma.   **Traumatic events** experienced early in life can have effects even decades later. Child physical or sexual abuse, child neglect, or the early death of a parent are linked to depression in adulthood.

Social Isolation.   Loneliness and lack of **social support** are strong predictors of depression. People who live alone have higher rates of depression than those with housemates. Also, widowed, divorced, or separated individuals are more likely to be depressed than those who are currently married.

Serious Medical Illness.   Depression often occurs side by side with a **physical illness**, such as **cancer**, **heart disease**, or **Alzheimer's disease**. In some cases, the other illness is a direct cause of depression. In other cases, the risk is mediated by the stress of living with illness, pain, or disability.

Drug or Alcohol Abuse.   **Substance abuse** or addiction often coexists with depression. **Alcohol** and certain drugs may cause depressive symptoms directly. Additionally, in people with a genetic tendency to depression, certain substances may trigger changes in critical brain chemicals or signaling pathways.

See also: Environmental Factors; Genetic Factors; Protective Factors

Bibliography

Depression (Major Depression): Risk Factors. Mayo Clinic, February 14, 2008, http://www
.mayoclinic.com/health/depression/DS00175/DSECTION=risk-factors.
Gotlib, Ian H., and Constance L. Hammen, eds. *Handbook of Depression.* 2nd ed. New York:
Guilford Press, 2009.
Stein, Dan J., David J. Kupfer, and Alan F. Schatzberg, eds. *The American Psychiatric Publishing
Textbook of Mood Disorders.* Washington, DC: American Psychiatric Publishing, 2006.
Understanding Depression: Signs, Symptoms, Causes and Help. Helpguide, http://www.helpguide.org/
mental/depression_signs_types_diagnosis_treatment.htm.

RUMINATION.   Rumination refers to repetitive, passive thinking about negative feelings, distressing symptoms, and the dark side of life. It is a common response to negative
moods and a prominent feature of **major depression**. Studies have shown that people who
ruminate when they are sad or blue are prone to higher levels of depression over time than
people who don't ruminate, even when initial levels of depression are taken into account.

Rumination is closely related to the irrationally negative thoughts that are characteristic
of depression. The need to identify and change such self-defeating thoughts is the basic
premise of **cognitive therapy**. These thoughts tend to be brief, shorthand appraisals of a
situation, and they often focus on loss, failure, and hopelessness. They may be a starting
point for full-fledged rumination, which is a longer chain of repeated, negative thinking.

Many people with depression have deep-seated beliefs that underlie their rumination.
For instance, some believe that they should focus inwardly on their feelings and their
situation when they become depressed. Their intention is usually to gain self-insight, an
admirable goal. But if their thoughts turn to endless rumination about problems and not
solutions, their thinking can have the opposite effect. Studies have shown that such rumination actually helps maintain depressive symptoms and impairs problem-solving abilities.

Direct evidence for the harmful effects of rumination come from experimental studies
involving people who naturally lean toward **dysphoria**, an unpleasant mood characterized
by sadness, irritability, or anxiety. Rumination was induced by asking them to focus on
their feelings, physical symptoms, and personal characteristics. The participants' moods,
thoughts, and/or behavior, which were assessed before and after the rumination period,
tended to turn in a more depressed direction afterward.

Nolen-Hoeksema's Theory of Rumination.   Different psychologists have looked at
rumination in slightly different ways. One influential view has been proposed by U.S. psychologist Susan Nolen-Hoeksema (1959–), who has theorized that people who are
depressed tend to ruminate on the nature, causes, and consequences of their symptoms.
Getting stuck in this style of thinking only worsens and prolongs the symptoms, increasing the odds that a down mood will turn into full-blown depression and that an episode of
depression will evolve into a chronic condition.

Nolen-Hoeksema has described various ways that rumination may prolong depression.
First, rumination makes it more likely that people will use irrationally negative thoughts
and memories to understand their current situation. Second, rumination tends toward
pessimistic and fatalistic thinking, which gets in the way of effective problem solving.
Third, people who constantly ruminate often alienate those around them with their negative attitude, and the loss of social support just feeds their depression.

Nolen-Hoeksema has found strong evidence for a link between rumination and depression in her research. In one study, rumination and depression were assessed in 137 college

students just before an earthquake struck the San Francisco Bay area in 1987. The students' depression was reassessed 10 days and seven weeks later. Those who had been ruminators before the earthquake had higher levels of depression afterward, even once researchers statistically controlled for their prior level of depression and the amount of earthquake-related harm or hardship they had suffered.

In more recent research, Nolen-Hoeksema and her colleagues have explored the relationship between rumination and other conditions that frequently occur along with depression. The results suggest that rumination may contribute not only to depression, but also to **eating disorders**, **substance abuse**, and **anxiety disorders**.

The Gender Gap. **Women** are twice as likely as men to become depressed. Research has shown that women are also more prone to rumination, and Nolen-Hoeksema has argued that this tendency may play a big role in their increased risk for depression. Of course, this begs of the question of why women are more likely to ruminate.

Several possible explanations have been proposed. Women may be at higher risk than men for certain chronically stressful situations (low income, single parenthood) and traumatic events (rape, domestic violence). Such experiences may shatter their sense of security and trust, which in turn could fuel rumination. Women also may be more likely to believe that negative feelings are impossible to control because they weren't taught to respond to such feelings with active problem solving as children. In addition, women may feel more responsible for maintaining harmony in their relationships, which encourages them to pay extra attention to how the relationship is going and their feelings about it.

Brooding versus Reflection. Theorists such as Nolen-Hoeksema have mainly focused on the harmful side of rumination. But looking inward can have a helpful side, too, when it leads to active problem-solving. Research has shown that this type of purposeful reflection sometimes increases negative feelings in the short term. In the long run, however, it is associated with less depression.

Rumination, in contrast, is a passive process. People brood about their problems without ever taking action to solve them. Two factors that may contribute to passive brooding are a history of long-lasting **stress** and a low sense of personal effectiveness. Once people have fallen into a pattern of thinking about what's wrong with their lives but not how to make things better, it becomes easier to repeat this pattern over and over.

Cognitive therapy can help people break out of this self-destructive pattern. In cognitive therapy, people identify and challenge maladaptive thoughts and learn to embrace more adaptive thinking. But Nolen-Hoeksema has argued that any form of **psychotherapy** that provides an explanation for depression and a set of effective steps for overcoming problems may interrupt rumination and thereby help people feel better.

See also: Chronic Depression; Cognitive Factors

Bibliography

Law, Bridget Murray. "Probing the Depression-Rumination Cycle." *Monitor on Psychology* (November 2005).

Lyubomirsky, Sonja, and Susan Nolen-Hoeksema. "Effects of Self-Focused Rumination on Negative Thinking and Interpersonal Problem Solving." *Journal of Personality and Social Psychology* 69 (1995): 176–190.

Lyubomirsky, Sonja, Nicole D. Caldwell, and Susan Nolen-Hoeksema. "Effects of Ruminative and Distracting Responses to Depressed Mood on Retrieval of Autobiographical Memories." *Journal of Personality and Social Psychology* 75 (1998): 166–177.

Nolen-Hoeksema, Susan, and Jannay Morrow. "A Prospective Study of Depression and Posttraumatic Stress Symptoms After a Natural Disaster: The 1989 Loma Prieta Earthquake." *Journal of Personality and Social Psychology* 61 (1991): 115–121.

Nolen-Hoeksema, Susan, Eric Stice, Emily Wade, and Cara Bohon. "Reciprocal Relations Between Rumination and Bulimic, Substance Abuse, and Depressive Symptoms in Female Adolescents." *Journal of Abnormal Psychology* 116 (2007): 198–207.

Nolen-Hoeksema, Susan. "The Role of Rumination in Depressive Disorders and Mixed Anxiety/Depressive Symptoms." *Journal of Abnormal Psychology* 109 (2000): 504–511.

Papageorgiou, Costas, and Adrian Wells, eds. *Depressive Rumination: Nature, Theory and Treatment.* Hoboken, NJ: John Wiley and Sons, 2004.

S

S-ADENOSYL-L-METHIONINE.   S-adenosyl-L-methionine (SAMe) is a compound that occurs naturally in the body, where it helps form chemical messengers in the brain and maintain levels of an antioxidant that protects cells from damage. SAMe is produced in the body from methionine, a sulfur-containing amino acid, and adenosine triphosphate, an energy-producing compound. It also is sold in pill form. As one of the most popular **dietary supplements**, SAMe has been studied extensively as a possible treatment for depression, osteoarthritis, liver disease, and other conditions.

The evidence for a link to depression comes from several sources. One area where SAMe is concentrated inside the body is the brain. There it plays a role in the synthesis of various chemicals, including **serotonin** and **dopamine**, both of which influence mood. Research has shown that people with severe depression have lower levels of SAMe in their cerebrospinal fluid, on average, than those without depression. In addition, the process by which the body makes SAMe requires **folate** and **vitamin B12**, and deficiencies in these vitamins have been associated with depression as well.

Benefits for Depression.   Two separate assessments of the research evidence to date have concluded that SAMe has some benefits for adults with depression. In one, researchers from the federal Agency for Healthcare Research and Quality analyzed the pooled results from 28 previously published studies. The researchers found that treatment with SAMe led to a greater decrease in symptoms of depression after three weeks compared to a placebo (dummy pill). The degree of improvement was similar to that seen with antidepressant medication.

In a systematic review of the published literature, Yale researchers also concluded that SAMe appears to have a role in the management of adult depression. However, the researchers noted that the studies were all short term, so questions remain about the long-term effects of SAMe.

SAMe Supplements.   The best dosage for SAMe supplements has yet to be determined. In studies of people with depression, the most common dose has been 800 mg to 1,600 mg daily for up to six weeks. Because SAMe won't work without adequate folate and vitamin B12, it is important to get enough of these vitamins from foods or supplements.

Side Effects and Cautions.   One major advantage of SAMe is that people taking it report fewer side effects than those taking traditional **antidepressants**. But some side effects may still occur, especially at high doses, including nausea, diarrhea, insomnia, headaches, and restlessness. To reduce the chance of an upset stomach, it may help to buy enteric-coated pills and take them on an empty stomach. To decrease the chance of sleep problems, it may help to take SAMe early in the day.

SAMe also may increase the side effects of other antidepressant or anti-anxiety medicines. As with any dietary supplement, it is wise to talk to a health care provider before taking SAMe, especially when combining it with medication. Depression can get worse if not adequately treated, so anyone who develops symptoms that cause serious distress or interfere with the ability to get along in daily life should seek professional help rather than relying on self-care alone.

Bibliography

Agency for Healthcare Research and Quality. *S-Adenosyl-L-Methionine for Treatment of Depression, Osteoarthritis, and Liver Disease: Summary.* Evidence Report/Technology Assessment no. 64. Rockville, MD: Agency for Healthcare Research and Quality, 2002.

Chiaie, Roberto Delle, Paolo Pancheri, and Pierluigi Scapicchio. "Efficacy and Tolerability of Oral and Intramuscular S-Adenosyl-L-Methionine 1, 4-Butanedisulfonate (SAMe) in the Treatment of Major Depression: Comparison with Imipramine in 2 Multicenter Studies." *American Journal of Clinical Nutrition* 76 suppl. (2002): 1172S–1176S.

Natural Standard Research Collaboration. *SAMe.* Mayo Clinic, December 1, 2005, http://www.mayoclinic.com/health/Same/NS_patient-same.

Williams, Anna-Leila, Christine Girard, Danny Jui, Alyse Sabina, and David L. Katz. "S-Adenosyl-methionine (SAMe) as Treatment for Depression: A Systematic Review." *Clinical and Investigative Medicine* 28 (2005): 132–139.

SADNESS. Sadness refers to an emotional state of unhappiness. A certain amount of sadness is an inevitable part of life. In many cases, it is a perfectly normal and appropriate response to an unpleasant situation. It is only when the sadness lasts for most of the day, almost every day, over a period of weeks, months, or even years that it is considered abnormal. When long-lasting sadness is combined with other symptoms and is intense enough to interfere with everyday activities, it is one of the hallmarks of **major depression**.

Philosophers have long regarded sadness as one of a small number of fundamental emotions. French philosopher René Descartes (1596–1650) considered sadness to be among the six primary passions (sadness, love, hatred, desire, joy, admiration) from which all other emotions spring. Dutch philosopher Benedict de Spinoza (1632–1677) included sorrow on his short list of three primary emotions (sorrow, joy, desire).

More recently, several psychologists have developed scientific theories of **emotion** and sadness figures prominently on most of their lists of core emotions as well. Starting in the early 1960s, U.S. psychologist Robert Plutchik (1927–2006) proposed an evolutionary theory that views emotions as serving an adaptive role in helping ensure survival. Plutchik included sadness among eight primary emotions (sadness, fear, anger, joy, acceptance, disgust, anticipation, surprise) from which all others are derived. Around the same time, U.S. psychologist Silvin Tomkins theorized that emotions are the primary motivational force driving human behavior. He included distress, which can be described subjectively as sadness, on his list of eight basic emotions (distress, interest, joy, surprise, disgust, anger, shame, fear).

Role of Normal Sadness. Sadness is often thought of as a negative emotion because it isn't pleasant to experience. But sadness also may serve a positive purpose by helping people respond effectively to distressing situations. Plutchik has noted that sadness is often brought on by the loss of someone or something important. This loss may lead to **crying**, a sad facial expression, and other distress signals. Such signals, in turn, typically elicit sympathetic feelings on the part of other people, who may then offer their help and support.

In Plutchik's view, depression can be considered an extreme, persistent distress signal that constantly seeks to elicit helpful behavior from others. In that sense, even depression can be seen as having a positive side. The problem with depression is that it involves living in a state of unremitting distress, which inevitably takes its toll on a person's mental and physical well-being. In addition, when distress signals are continual, they may be self-defeating, driving away others rather than attracting help.

Bibliography

American Psychiatric Association. *Diagnostic and Statistical Manual of Mental Disorders.* 4th ed., text rev. Washington, DC: American Psychiatric Association, 2000.

Plutchik, Robert. *Emotions and Life: Perspectives From Psychology, Biology, and Evolution.* Washington, DC: American Psychological Association, 2003.

SCHIZOAFFECTIVE DISORDER. Schizoaffective disorder is a condition that combines features of schizophrenia with those of a mood disorder. Schizophrenia is a severe mental disorder that produces symptoms such as distorted thoughts and perceptions. **Mood disorders** are characterized by a mood that is excessively low (depression) or excessively high (**mania**).

Although the term "schizoaffective disorder" has been in use since 1933, experts are still debating whether it is really a distinct condition. Some argue that it is simply a subtype of schizophrenia, **major depression**, or **bipolar disorder**. Others hold that the illness is different enough to warrant its own diagnosis.

By any name, schizoaffective disorder is a serious condition. Without treatment, people with the disorder may have trouble going to school, holding down a job, and connecting with others. They may rely heavily on family help or community services to get along. They also have an increased risk of **suicide** and **substance abuse**. With proper treatment, however, most can lead richer, more independent lives. In general, the outlook is better than for people with schizophrenia alone.

Criteria for Diagnosis. The symptoms of schizoaffective disorder are defined by the ***Diagnostic and Statistical Manual of Mental Disorders, Fourth Edition, Text Revision*** (*DSM-IV-TR*), a diagnostic guidebook published by the American Psychiatric Association and widely used by mental health professionals from many disciplines. According to the *DSM-IV-TR*, people with schizoaffective disorder have periods of illness during which they experience both psychotic symptoms and mood symptoms at the same time. However, unlike people with **psychotic depression** or severe bipolar disorder, they also go through phases when they have psychotic symptoms alone without any mood disturbance.

Psychotic Symptoms. During the phase when both psychotic and mood symptoms are present, people experience one or more of the following: (1) delusions, which are false personal beliefs with no basis in reality that remain unchanged even in the face of strong evidence to the contrary; (2) hallucinations, which are false sensory impressions that lead the person to see, hear, taste, smell, or feel something that is not really there; (3) disorganized speech; (4) bizarre behavior; or (5) negative symptoms, which include an extreme lack of emotional expression, greatly reduced speech, or a pervasive lack of motivation.

Only one symptom is required if the delusions are bizarre or if the hallucinations consist of either a voice keeping up a running commentary or multiple voices conversing.

Otherwise, at least two symptoms are required. The symptoms are present much of the time for a minimum of one month unless they are cut short by treatment.

Mood symptoms occur along with the psychotic ones for a substantial part of the total illness. But for at least two weeks, the mood symptoms are absent, yet the person still experiences delusions or hallucinations.

Mood Symptoms. Schizoaffective disorder is categorized as either "depressive type" or "bipolar type," depending on the kind of mood symptoms that are experienced. In the depressive type, people have an episode of major depression, during which they are in a low mood nearly all the time for weeks or months. This depressed mood is associated with several other symptoms and is serious enough to cause significant problems in daily life.

In the bipolar type, people experience mania, sometimes alternating with depression. During a bout of mania, elation is exaggerated to the point where it can lead to wildly irrational thinking, dangerous risk taking, or out-of-control bouts of nonstop activity and sleeplessness.

Pattern of Symptoms. The order in which the psychotic and mood symptoms appear and the length of time they last vary from person to person. But the following example illustrates a typical pattern: A person's illness starts with hearing voices and having irrational thoughts about being followed. After a month, the person falls into a deep depression. The psychotic symptoms and mood symptoms continue together for four months. Then the person recovers from the depression, but the hallucinations and delusions hang on for another month.

In this example, the total period of illness is six months. The psychotic symptoms alone are present for two months, and both psychotic and mood symptoms are present the rest of the time. If the depression had been briefer—say, lasting just a few weeks of the six-month period—the person would have been diagnosed with schizophrenia. To qualify as schizoaffective disorder, the mood disturbance must be a big part of the illness.

Causes and Risk Factors. Schizoaffective disorder can begin at any age from adolescence to late life. It most often starts in early adulthood, however. The disorder is more common in women than in men, a difference that is largely accounted for by a higher rate of the depressive type among women.

Genes seem to be an important risk factor. One massive, long-term study examined data on everyone born in Denmark after 1952 along with their parents and siblings. The researchers found an increased risk of schizoaffective disorder among those whose parents and siblings had either schizophrenia or bipolar disorder. The association with these two conditions was about equally powerful, indicating a strong genetic link to each.

Environmental factors also may play a role. Some experts have speculated that prenatal exposure to toxins or viruses might be a contributing factor. Others have implicated complications during childbirth. Any of these factors could lead to abnormalities in brain development.

Whether set in motion by genes, the environment, or both, schizoaffective disorder is thought to involve changes in brain chemistry. In particular, there may be abnormalities in **serotonin** and **dopamine**, two chemicals that relay messages within the brain and help regulate mood.

Treatment of Schizoaffective Disorder. Schizoaffective disorder is more complicated to treat than a mood disorder alone, and the prognosis is generally not as good. As a result, long-term treatment is critical. Most people respond best to medications combined with **psychotherapy**. But the exact combination that is most effective for a given person depends on the type and severity of the symptoms.

Antipsychotics are medications specifically designed to relieve or prevent psychotic symptoms, including hallucinations and delusions. They are part of the treatment regimen for most people with schizoaffective disorder. In addition, those with the depressive type may take **antidepressants**, which help relieve depression, and those with the bipolar type may take **mood stabilizers**, which help even out mood swings.

Psychotherapy and counseling can help people with schizoaffective disorder better understand their condition and feel more hopeful. Treatment sessions typically focus on solving problems, making plans, improving relationships, and learning specific new behaviors that can be applied at home, work, or school.

Isolation and loneliness are issues for many people with schizoaffective disorder. **Group therapy** lets people discuss their problems with others under the guidance of a therapist. The group setting also provides an opportunity to practice social skills and offers a reality check for people who are experiencing delusions or hallucinations.

Bibliography

American Psychiatric Association. *Diagnostic and Statistical Manual of Mental Disorders.* 4th ed., text rev. Washington, DC: American Psychiatric Association, 2000.

Cheniaux, Elie, J. Landeira-Fernandez, Leonardo Lessa Telles, José Luiz M. Lessa, Allan Dias, Teresa Duncan, et al. "Does Schizoaffective Disorder Really Exist: A Systematic Review of the Studies That Compared Schizoaffective Disorder with Schizophrenia or Mood Disorders." *Journal of Affective Disorders* 106 (2008): 209–217.

Klein, Daniel N., Stewart A. Shankman, and Brian R. McFarland. "Classification of Mood Diorders." In *The American Psychiatric Publishing Textbook of Mood Disorders,* by Dan J. Stein, David J. Kupfer, and Alan F. Schatzberg, eds., 17–32. Washington, DC: American Psychiatric Publishing, 2006.

Lake, Charles Ray, and Nathaniel Hurwitz. "Schizoaffective Disorder Merges Schizophrenia and Bipolar Disorders as One Disease: There Is No Schizoaffective Disorder." *Current Opinion in Psychiatry* 20 (2007): 365–379.

Laursen, Thomas Munk, Rodrigo Labouriau, Rasmus W. Licht, Aksel Bertelsen, Trine Munk-Olsen, and Preben Bo Mortensen. "Family History of Psychiatric Illness as a Risk Factor for Schizoaffective Disorder: A Danish Register-Based Cohort Study." *Archives of General Psychiatry* 62 (2005): 841–848.

Schizoaffective Disorder. Mayo Clinic, December 22, 2006, http://www.mayoclinic.com/health/schizoaffective-disorder/DS00866.

SCHOOL ISSUES.   One hallmark of **clinical depression** is having symptoms that are serious enough to interfere with life in everyday settings, including school. For **children** and **adolescents**, school is a place not only to learn about academic matters, but also to spend time with friends and get involved in extracurricular activities. Untreated depression can get in the way of this vital academic, social, and personal growth.

Depression is often associated with academic problems or a drop in grades. Young people who are depressed may find it very difficult to pay attention, think clearly, solve problems, and recall information. They also may lack the energy and motivation to do their best on schoolwork or even show up for class. In addition, depressed students often withdraw from classmates and lose all interest in after-school activities, such as sports, music, or drama.

Lessons in Defeat.   The relationship between depression and school problems is a two-way street. Research shows that early academic problems may contribute to later depression. For example, a study of Baltimore schoolchildren found that black first-graders—especially girls—who were already doing poorly in school were at risk of being depressed by junior high.

One way young people find meaning and direction in life is by pursuing academic goals. Failure to reach these goals may give rise to feelings of discouragement and despair. It also may lead to negative social experiences, such as teasing and rejection by classmates, which further increase school-related **stress**. In addition, academic failure may instill long-lasting beliefs about lack of personal competence and control. These factors set the stage for hopelessness, **pessimism**, and depression.

Schools That Make the Grade. School has a pervasive influence on the lives of young people. Although this influence is sometimes negative, especially if a student is having trouble, it can also be very positive and even preventive. Structured, supportive school environments promote beliefs about personal mastery that may help protect against depression. When students are struggling academically, early help with learning problems may lower the risk of developing depression in the future.

Some schools have gone a step further by offering programs that are explicitly designed to promote **mental health** and help prevent depression. The **Penn Resiliency Program** is one such program for late elementary-school and middle-school students. Based partly on the principles of **cognitive therapy**, it aims to teach students the skills they need to avoid unduly negative thinking before they become seriously depressed. The goal is to ward off depression completely or keep any current symptoms from getting worse. Overall, results of 13 controlled studies involving more than 2,000 students suggest that the program helps prevent symptoms of depression and anxiety, and these benefits can be long-lasting.

As such results attest, good schools can help teach students the skills they need to cope effectively with challenges and stress. A supportive school environment that offers every student a chance for success also can foster optimism and self-confidence. In students who are prone to depression, such factors may reduce mood symptoms and promote better overall mental health.

See also: Individuals with Disabilities Education Act; Learning Disorders; Prevention Programs

Further Information. IDEA Partnership, 1800 Diagonal Road, Suite 320, Alexandria, VA 22314, (877) 433-2463, www.ideapartnership.org.

National Association of School Psychologists, 4340 E. West Highway, Suite 402, Bethesda, MD 20814, (301) 657-0270, www.nasponline.org.

Bibliography

American Psychiatric Association. *Diagnostic and Statistical Manual of Mental Disorders.* 4th ed., text rev. Washington, DC: American Psychiatric Association, 2000.

Evans, Dwight L., and Linda Wasmer Andrews. *If Your Adolescent Has Depression or Bipolar Disorder: An Essential Resource for Parents.* New York: Oxford University Press, 2005.

Fröjd, Sari A., Eeva S. Nissinen, Mirjami U. I. Pelkonen, Mauri J. Marttunen, Anna-Maija Koivisto, and Riittakerttu Kaltiala-Heino. "Depression and School Performance in Middle Adolescent Boys and Girls." *Journal of Adolescence* 31 (2008): 485–498.

Gillham, Jane E., Karen J. Reivich, Derek R. Freres, Tara M. Chaplin, Andrew J. Shatté, Barbra Samuels, et al. "School-Based Prevention of Depressive Symptoms: A Randomized Controlled Study of Effectiveness and Specificity of the Penn Resiliency Program." *Journal of Consulting and Clinical Psychology* 75 (2007): 9–19.

Herman, Keith C., Sharon F. Lambert, Wendy M. Reinke, and Nicholas S. Ialongo. "Low Academic Competence in First Grade as a Risk Factor for Depressive Cognitions and Symptoms in Middle School." *Journal of Counseling Psychology* 55 (2008): 400–410.

Maughan, Barbara, Richard Rowe, Rolf Leober, and Magda Stouthamer-Loeber. "Reading Problems and Depressed Mood." *Journal of Abnormal Child Psychology* 31 (2003): 219–229.

Resilience Research in Children. University of Pennsylvania Positive Psychology Center, 2007, http://www.ppc.sas.upenn.edu/prpsum.htm.

Sideridis, Georgios D. "Goal Orientation, Academic Achievement, and Depression: Evidence in Favor of a Revised Goal Theory Framework." *Journal of Educational Psychology* 97 (2005): 366–375.

SCREENING TESTS. Screening tests for depression are used to identify individuals who may need treatment or monitoring for the disorder. Such tests in themselves are not sufficient for diagnosing depression. However, they may help detect any depressive symptoms and indicate whether further evaluation by a medical or mental health professional is needed.

The best depression screening tests are designed to have high sensitivity—the likelihood that a person with depression will be identified as such by the test. Examples of popular screening tests include the **Beck Depression Inventory**, **Center for Epidemiologic Studies Depression Scale**, **Inventory of Depressive Symptomatology**, **Zung Self-Rating Depression Scale**, and **Hospital Anxiety and Depression Scale**. For specific age groups, the **Children's Depression Inventory**, **Reynolds Adolescent Depression Scale**, or **Geriatric Depression Scale** may be used.

> **Two Little Questions**
>
> The U.S. Preventive Services Task Force recommends that physicians screen medical patients for depression by asking two simple questions: "Over the past two weeks, have you felt down, depressed, or hopeless?" and "Over the past two weeks, have you felt little interest or pleasure in doing things?" According to the task force, this simple method may work as well as longer screening tests.

See also: National Depression Screening Day

Further Information. Mental Health America, 2000 N. Beauregard Street, 6th Floor Alexandria, VA 22311, (800) 969-6642, www.depression-screening.org.

Screening for Mental Health, One Washington Street, Suite 304, Wellesley Hills, MA 02481, (781) 239-0071, mentalhealthscreening.org.

TeenScreen, National Center for Mental Health Checkups at Columbia University, 1775 Broadway, Suite 610, New York, NY 10019, (212) 265-4453, www.teenscreen.org.

Bibliography

Rush, A. John Jr., Michael B. First, and Deborah Blacker, eds. *Handbook of Psychiatric Measures,* 2nd ed. Washington, DC: American Psychiatric Publishing, 2008.

U.S. Preventive Services Task Force. *Screening for Depression: Recommendations and Rationale.* Agency for Healthcare Research and Quality, May 2002, http://www.ahrq.gov/Clinic/3rduspstf/depression/depressrr.htm.

Whooley, Mary A., Andrew L. Avins, Jeanne Miranda, and Warren S. Browner. "Case-Finding Instruments for Depression: Two Questions Are as Good as Many." *Journal of General Internal Medicine* 12 (1997): 439–445.

SEASONAL AFFECTIVE DISORDER.   Seasonal affective disorder (SAD) is a form of **major depression** in which the symptoms start and stop around the same time each year for at least two years running. Typically, the symptoms begin in fall or winter and subside in spring.

Major depression itself involves being in a low mood nearly all the time and/or losing interest or enjoyment in almost everything. These feelings last for at least two weeks, lead to problems getting along in everyday life, and are associated with several other symptoms. In SAD, those symptoms often include lack of energy, oversleeping, overeating, weight gain, and a craving for carbohydrates (sweet or starchy foods).

Of course, many people get a mild case of the winter doldrums. They may feel a little blue, pack on a few pounds, or have trouble waking up in the morning. But for those with SAD, the symptoms are bad enough to interfere with daily life at home, work, or school. Such individuals may feel constantly down and tired, and they may withdraw from others and lose interest in activities they once enjoyed. Fortunately, treatment can help lift their mood and get them back on track without having to wait for spring.

Dark Days of Winter.   The timing of SAD seems to be related to winter's long, dark nights. Just as the seasonal change in sunlight affects the behavior of animals, so it may lead to SAD in certain people. The strongest evidence implicates seasonal changes in **circadian rhythms**, the body's internal system for regulating physiological and behavioral cycles that repeat daily, such as the sleep-wake cycle. People with SAD may have abnormalities in how the body manages circadian rhythms or matches them to the 24-hour day.

Melatonin is a hormone produced by the pineal gland in the brain that has a mild drowsiness-inducing effect. The secretion of this hormone follows a daily rhythm that is synchronized to the cycle of darkness and light. Melatonin production switches off in response to sunlight, then switches back on once darkness falls, helping people feel drowsy. Some research indicates that people with SAD may experience changes in the daily timing of melatonin secretion, compared to those without the disorder.

Lack of **serotonin** also may contribute to SAD. Serotonin is a brain chemical that influences mood and helps regulate sleep, appetite, and sexual drive. Reduced sunlight may cause a drop in serotonin metabolism, and low levels of serotonin have been implicated in depression.

The SAD-Ness of Emily Dickinson

There's a certain Slant of light,
  Winter Afternoons—
  That oppresses, like the Heft
  Of Cathedral Tunes—

The above stanza by U.S. poet Emily Dickinson (1830–1886) comes from one of her most beloved poems. It is also one of the best examples of why some scholars think Dickinson may have suffered from SAD. And in fact, a modern analysis of her work has found a seasonal pattern characterized by less creative output during the fall and winter over a critical four-year period. The term "seasonal affective disorder" would not be coined for more than a century after this poem was written, but Dickinson still found the words she needed to convey the dark, heavy mood of a wintry afternoon.

Discovery of SAD. People have long noted a tendency for moods to follow the seasons. In ancient Greece, Hippocrates (ca. 460 BC–ca. 375 BC) wrote that the change of seasons could cause disease, and Aretaeus of Cappadocia (ca. AD 150–ca. AD 200) advocated treating a gloomy mood with sunlight. In the mid-nineteenth century, German psychiatrist Wilhelm Griesinger (1817–1868) described a seasonal mood disorder characterized by melancholy in fall or winter and mania in spring.

But it was not until the early 1980s that U.S. psychiatrist Norman E. Rosenthal and his colleagues at the National Institute of Mental Health described the syndrome known as SAD. They also pioneered the systematic use of **light therapy**—daily exposure to very bright light from an artificial source—to treat the disorder.

Rosenthal was initially intrigued after hearing about two individuals who seemed to be struggling with a special, seasonal type of depression. He had noticed similar, if less pronounced, changes in his own mood during the winter months. The first, small study of light therapy for SAD, published in 1984, found positive effects, and a **Seasonal Pattern Assessment Questionnaire** was introduced three years later. In the intervening years, hundreds of studies from around the world have greatly expanded the understanding of SAD and its treatment.

Criteria for Diagnosis. The ***Diagnostic and Statistical Manual of Mental Disorders, Fourth Edition, Text Revision*** (*DSM-IV-TR*), a diagnostic guide used by mental health professionals from many disciplines, does not give SAD its own diagnostic category. Instead, the disorder is designated by a "seasonal pattern" modifier, which can be applied to episodes of major depression. These episodes can occur either in people with depression alone or in those with bipolar disorder.

Timing is everything when it comes to SAD. The episodes of depression must have come and gone around the same time each year for the past two years, without any nonseasonal episodes in between. In addition, for SAD to be diagnosed, the number of seasonal episodes must outnumber any nonseasonal ones over the course of a person's lifetime.

SAD does not apply to situations where depression seems to be linked to a seasonal source of social **stress**, such as being out of work every winter. Instead, the term is reserved for depression that appears to be tied to the season itself. In most

---

Off to a Bright Future

In his book *Winter Blues: Everything You Need to Know to Beat Seasonal Affective Disorder* (rev. ed., 2006), Rosenthal recalls the excitement surrounding the first controlled study of light therapy for SAD:

> Nine patients responded to bright light, and the dim light proved ineffective. I began to use the lights myself and was sure that they made me feel better. Some of my colleagues requested them, too. After a few weeks I had to put a big sign in front of the dwindling stack of light boxes, asking anyone who wanted to borrow a fixture to discuss it with me first so that we would have enough for the study. A local psychiatrist, whom I had initially polled about the existence of people with SAD, and who had told me that he did not know of any, called to say that he had realized that he himself had the syndrome and asked about how he might use the lights himself.

From *Winter Blues: Everything You Need to Know to Beat Seasonal Affective Disorder* (rev. ed.) by Norman E. Rosenthal, MD. 2006. Copyright Guilford Press. Reprinted with permission of The Guilford Press.

---

cases, the depressive episodes begin in fall or winter and end in spring. Occasionally, people have seasonal summer depression, but this is much less common.

Like other people with major depression, those with SAD experience a low mood nearly all the time and/or a loss of interest or enjoyment in almost everything. In addition, they develop several other associated symptoms. Theoretically, any of the symptoms that characterize major depression can occur. However, certain symptoms are especially typical of SAD. In fact, some researchers contend that the definition of SAD should include people who develop these symptoms like clockwork every winter even if they don't meet the full diagnostic criteria for major depression.

Lack of Energy. Nearly everyone with SAD experiences a sharp drop-off in energy level. Even the smallest tasks may start to feel like major chores. This symptom is often the most prominent feature of the disorder, even more than the sadness and disinterest that are the classic hallmarks of a depressed mood.

Sleeping Too Much. People with SAD often oversleep in the morning, which may lead to being late at work or not getting the children to school on time. Despite sleeping more hours, they may not feel refreshed upon awakening.

Eating Too Much. Overeating is also common among people with SAD, who frequently report an increase in appetite.

Craving Carbohydrates. People with SAD often change not only the amount they eat, but also the types of foods they choose. Many crave high-carbohydrate foods, such as bread, pasta, potatoes, and sweets.

Weight Gain. Not surprisingly, the change in eating habits coupled with inactivity often leads to unwanted weight gain.

Causes and Risk Factors. Using *DSM-IV-TR* criteria to diagnose SAD, studies have found a lifetime prevalence of about one percent to two percent in North America. As a general rule, the farther away from the equator people live, the more likely they may be to develop the disorder. This seems logical, given the greater change in seasonal sunlight at higher latitudes. Nevertheless, a small fraction of people in the southern United States still develop SAD.

Women with SAD outnumber men. But it is unclear whether women have an increased risk of SAD over and above their higher rate of depression in general. Age is another predictor of a seasonal pattern in depression. The prevalence of SAD tends to increase from the teen years through the mid-fifties, then decline after that.

Treatment of SAD. Light therapy has proved to be an effective treatment for SAD. It involves sitting in front of a light box—a small, portable device containing fluorescent bulbs or tubes. The light emitted is much brighter than ordinary indoor lighting—typically 10,000 lux, compared to less than 400 lux in an average living room with the lights on in the evening. Light therapy sessions usually last for 30 minutes or longer a day. For the best results, sessions generally are scheduled in the morning soon after waking up. Doing light therapy at night should be avoided, because it may interfere with sleep.

Many people find that their mood begins to lift within a week after starting light therapy, although some people need up to a month to feel the full benefit. Continuing light therapy throughout the winter is important to help ensure that the symptoms don't return.

Antidepressants also may be prescribed. In 2006, bupropion extended-release tablets (Wellbutrin XL) became the first antidepressant approved by the Food and Drug Administration specifically for the prevention of depression in people with a history of SAD. However, other antidepressants may help prevent or treat SAD as well, especially **selective**

serotonin reuptake inhibitors, which increase the amount of serotonin available for use by the brain.

Psychotherapy may provide additional relief. One type that appears to be beneficial is **cognitive-behavioral therapy** (CBT), which helps people change self-defeating thoughts and maladaptive behaviors. When CBT is geared to SAD, it may include challenging negative thoughts about winter and suggesting ways to schedule pleasant activities into winter days.

In a six-week study, adults with SAD were randomly assigned to get one of four treatments: CBT in a group setting twice a week, light therapy for 90 minutes every day, both treatments combined, or a control condition. After six weeks, CBT alone, light therapy alone, and the combination of both led to comparable improvements in symptoms of depression relative to the control.

On the Horizon. Two experimental treatments for SAD, **dawn simulation** and **negative ion therapy**, have shown promise in early studies as well. In dawn simulation, a timer gradually turns on a lamp in the person's bedroom early in the morning, before the natural winter dawn. The lamp, which simulates dawn in springtime, emits light that is much less bright than what is used for standard light therapy.

Negative ion therapy uses a small electronic device to produce charged air particles. These particles are created naturally by environmental forces such thunderstorms and roaring surf, and natural concentrations tend to be higher in summertime. In this treatment, people with SAD are exposed to high levels of artificially created charged particles in an effort to mimic summer conditions.

One advantage to dawn simulation and negative ion therapy is that both treatments can be administered while the person sleeps, requiring no special effort. But although preliminary results have been encouraging, more research is needed to establish their effectiveness.

See also: Norepinephrine-Dopamine Reuptake Inhibitors

Bibliography

American Psychiatric Association. *Diagnostic and Statistical Manual of Mental Disorders.* 4th ed., text rev. Washington, DC: American Psychiatric Association, 2000.

DeAngelis, Tori. "Promising New Treatments for SAD." *Monitor on Psychology* (February 2006).

Eagles, John M. "Light Therapy and the Management of Winter Depression." *Advances in Psychiatric Treatment* 10 (2004): 233–240.

FDA Approves the First Drug for Seasonal Depression. Food and Drug Administration, June 12, 2006, http://www.fda.gov/bbs/topics/NEWS/2006/NEW01388.html.

Lam, Raymond W., and Anthony J. Levitt, eds. *Canadian Consensus Guidelines for the Treatment of Seasonal Affective Disorder.* Clinical & Academic Publishing, 1999.

Let's Talk Facts About Seasonal Affective Disorder. American Psychiatric Association, 2006, http://healthyminds.org/factsheets/LTF-SAD.pdf.

Lewy, Alfred J., Bryan J. Lefler, Jonathan S. Emens, and Vance K. Bauer. "The Circadian Basis of Winter Depression." *Proceedings of the National Academy of Sciences of the USA* 103 (2006): 7414–7419.

McDermott, John F. "Emily Dickinson Revisited: A Study of Periodicity in Her Work." *American Journal of Psychiatry* 158 (2001): 686–690.

Questions and Answers About Seasonal Affective Disorder and Light Therapy, Society for Light Treatment and Biological Rhythms, May 2000, http://www.websciences.org/sltbr.

Rohan, Kelly J., Kathryn A. Roecklein, Kathryn Tierney Lindsey, Leigh G. Johnson, Robert D. Lippy, Timothy J. Lacy, et al. "A Randomized Controlled Trial of Cognitive-Behavioral Therapy, Light Therapy, and Their Combination for Seasonal Affective Disorder." *Journal of Consulting and Clinical Psychology* 75 (2007): 489–500.

Rosenthal, N. E., D. A. Sack, J. C. Gillin, A. J. Lewy, F. K. Goodwin, Y. Davenport, P. S. Mueller et al. "Seasonal Affective Disorder: A Description of the Syndrome and Preliminary Findings with Light Therapy." *Archives of General Psychiatry* 41 (1984): 72–80.

Rosenthal, N. E., M. Genhart, F. M. Jacobsen, R. G. Skwerer, and T. A. Wehr. "Disturbances of Appetite and Weight Regulation in Seasonal Affective Disorder." *Annals of the New York Academy of Sciences* 499 (1987): 216–230.

Rosenthal, Norman E. *Winter Blues: Everything You Need to Know to Beat Seasonal Affective Disorder.* Rev. ed. New York: Guilford Press, 2006.

Seasonal Affective Disorder. Mayo Clinic, September 24, 2007, http://www.mayoclinic.com/print/seasonal-affective-disorder/DS00195.

Seasonal Affective Disorder: Treatment with Light Therapy. Mayo Clinic, June 5, 2008, http://www.mayoclinic.com/health/seasonal-affective-disorder/MH00023.

Srinivasan, Venkataramanujan, Marcel Smits, Warren Spence, Alan D. Lowe, Leonid Kayumov, Seithikurippu R. Pandi-Perumal, et al. "Melatonin in Mood Disorders." *World Journal of Biological Psychiatry* 7 (2006): 138–151.

Terman, Michael, and Jiuan Su Terman. "Controlled Trial of Naturalisitic Dawn Simulation and Negative Air Ionization for Seasonal Affective Disorder." *American Journal of Psychiatry* 163 (2006): 2126–2133.

Wehr, Thomas A., Wallace C. Duncan Jr., Leo Sher, Daniel Aeschbach, Paul J. Schwartz, Erick H. Turner, et al. "A Circadian Signal of Change of Season in Patients with Seasonal Affective Disorder." *Archives of General Psychiatry* 58 (2001): 1108–1114.

SEASONAL PATTERN ASSESSMENT QUESTIONNAIRE. The Seasonal Pattern Assessment Questionnaire (SPAQ) is a self-report test that assesses the size of any seasonal change in sleep, social activity, mood, weight, appetite, and energy level. Introduced by U.S. psychiatrist Norman E. Rosenthal and his colleagues in 1987, the SPAQ is designed to look for **seasonal affective disorder** (SAD), a form of depression in which symptoms start and stop at about the same time each year. It is the most commonly used test in SAD research, and it is also widely used in clinical practice.

The SPAQ asks people to rate seasonal changes on a scale from "no change" to "extremely marked change." People also are asked to rate the impairment caused by seasonal changes, from no problem to disabling. In other questionnaire items, people report the months during which certain feelings or behaviors are most prominent, the amount their weight fluctuates over the course of a year, the number of hours they sleep nightly during each season, and any seasonal change in food preferences.

Pros and Cons of the SPAQ. Most common tests for measuring depression are ill-suited to assessing SAD. They neither evaluate the symptoms most characteristic of the disorder nor look for a seasonal pattern. The SPAQ fills a void left by these other tests. As a screening tool for SAD, it has a high degree of face validity—the extent to which it appears on the surface to be appropriate for assessing the disorder.

However, studies of the SPAQ have yielded mixed results. It has been reported to have low sensitivity—the likelihood of a positive result on the test for someone who actually has SAD. In some but not all research, it also has fallen short on specificity—the likelihood of a negative result on the test for someone who actually does not have the disorder. In addition, the SPAQ is designed to be a retrospective test, in which people report on their feelings and behaviors in the past. Another criticism is that people's answers tend to differ depending on which time of year the test is taken.

A newer test for assessing SAD, called the Seasonal Health Questionnaire, has been reported to have better sensitivity and specificity than the SPAQ. But more research is still needed to confirm these initial findings. For now, the SPAQ remains by far the best-studied and most popular test for measuring SAD. Although it has limitations, it may be useful as a screening tool for identifying people in need of further evaluation and as a clinical tool for finding out more about seasonal symptoms in individuals who have already been diagnosed with depression.

See also: Diagnosis of Depression

Bibliography

Kasper, S., T. A. Wehr, J. J. Bartko, P. A. Gaist, and N. E. Rosenthal. "Epidemiological Findings of Seasonal Changes in Mood and Behavior: A Telephone Survey of Montgomery County, Maryland." *Archives of General Psychiatry* 46 (1989): 823–833.

Lam, Raymond W. and Anthony J. Levitt, eds. *Canadian Consensus Guidelines for the Treatment of Seasonal Affective Disorder.* Clinical & Academic Publishing, 1999.

Lund, Eiliv, and Vidje Hansen. "Responses to the Seasonal Pattern Assessment Questionnaire in Different Seasons." *American Journal of Psychiatry* 158 (2001): 316–318.

Lurie, Stephen J., Barbara Gawinski, Deborah Pierce, and Sally J. Rousseau. "Seasonal Affective Disorder." *American Family Physician* 74 (2006): 1521–1524.

Mersch, Peter Paul A., Nanette C. Vastenburg, Ybe Meesters, Antoinette L. Bouhuys, Domien G. M. Beersma, Rutger H. van den Hoofdakker et al. "The Reliability and Validity of the Seasonal Pattern Assessment Questionnaire: A Comparison Between Patient Groups." *Journal of Affective Disorders* 80 (2004): 209–219.

Raheja, Sunil K., Elizabeth A. King, and Christopher Thompson. "The Seasonal Pattern Assessment Questionnaire for Identifying Seasonal Affective Disorders." *Journal of Affective Disorders* 41 (1996): 193–199.

Rosenthal, N. E., M. Genhart, F. M. Jacobsen, R. G. Skwerer, and T. A. Wehr. "Disturbances of Appetite and Weight Regulation in Seasonal Affective Disorder." *Annals of the New York Academy of Sciences* 499 (1987): 216–230.

Rosenthal, Norman E. *Winter Blues: Everything You Need to Know to Beat Seasonal Affective Disorder.* Rev. ed. New York: Guilford Press, 2006.

Thompson, Chris, Susan Thompson, and Rachel Smith. "Prevalence of Seasonal Affective Disorder in Primary Care: A Comparison of the Seasonal Health Questionnaire and the Seasonal Pattern Assessment Questionnaire." *Journal of Affective Disorders* 78 (2004): 219–226.

SECOND MESSENGERS. In the **nervous system**, **neurotransmitters** are "first messengers," conveying chemical messages from one cell to another. Second messengers are substances that pick up where the first messengers leave off, relaying messages from the receiving cell's outer membrane to its inner biochemical machinery. Some scientists believe that malfunctions in the second messenger system may play an important role in depression.

As an example of how second messengers work, consider what happens after the neurotransmitter **norepinephrine** delivers its message to a receiving cell. To do this, norepinephrine must bind to a specialized site, called a receptor, on the outside of the cell membrane—the cell's outer boundary. The activated receptor then binds with a particular type of protein, called a G protein, on the inside of the membrane. The activated G protein, in turn, converts adenosine triphosphate (ATP)—the chemical source of energy in cells—into a second messenger known as cyclic adenosine monophosphate (cAMP).

Within the cell, cAMP has a number of effects. For instance, it affects the opening and closing of ion channels—gates in the cell membrane through which electrically charged atoms, called ions, can pass. The flow of these ions creates an electrical current that produces tiny voltage changes across the cell membrane.

cAMP also affects the expression of genes in the cell's nucleus. Because it can act directly on genetic material, it may cause long-lasting changes in behavior. In addition, second messengers are involved in the production and release of neurotransmitters. Plus, they play a role in movements within the cell, carbohydrate metabolism, and processes of growth and development.

Link to Depression. Researchers have found evidence that the cAMP response is blunted in the brains of people with depression. This reduced response could interfere with neurotransmitter function even when neurotransmitters and **receptors** are present at normal levels.

To influence genetic material, cAMP affects another substance called cyclic AMP response element-binding protein (CREB). Then CREB binds with certain DNA sequences, thereby increasing or decreasing a gene's expression—the effects of the gene's instruction on the cells of the body. In animals with depression-like behavior, CREB is increased in some parts of the brain but decreased in others, indicating that the role of CREB in depression may depend on which part of the brain is involved.

In postmortem analyses of the human cortex—the brain's center of higher mental function and conscious experience—levels of CREB were reduced in depressed individuals who had not taken **antidepressants**. Conversely, other studies have shown that taking antidepressants long-term enhances CREB function, possibly depending on the type and dose of the medication.

See also: Neurons

Bibliography

Belmaker, R. H., and Galila Agam. "Major Depressive Disorder." *New England Journal of Medicine* 358 (2008): 55–68.

Brain Facts: A Primer on the Brain and Nervous System. 6th ed. Washington, DC: Society for Neuroscience, 2008.

SELECTIVE SEROTONIN REUPTAKE INHIBITORS. Selective serotonin reuptake inhibitors (SSRIs) are a very widely prescribed group of **antidepressants**. These medications increase the brain's available supply of **serotonin**, a chemical messenger that helps regulate mood, sleep, appetite, and sexual drive. One of the first drugs in this class, **fluoxetine** (better known by the brand name Prozac), was approved for sale in the United States in 1987. It quickly became the most talked about pharmaceutical of the day, and SSRIs were soon entrenched as the first-choice medication for depression.

Initially, Prozac was often portrayed by the media as a wonder drug that offered a quick, totally safe fix for depression. It sounded too good to be true—and in fact, that proved to be the case. Yet compared to previous antidepressants, Prozac and its fellow SSRIs still represented a major advance, as effective as their older counterparts but with generally milder side effects.

Five SSRIs—citalopram, escitalopram, fluoxetine, paroxetine, and sertraline—have now been approved by the Food and Drug Administration (FDA) specifically for treating depression. Each of these medications except citalopram has also been approved for treating one or more other conditions, such as **generalized anxiety disorder**, **obsessive-compulsive disorder** (OCD), **panic disorder**, **post-traumatic stress disorder**, social anxiety disorder, bulimia, or **premenstrual dysphoric disorder**. A sixth SSRI, fluvoxamine, is only formally approved for treating OCD. However, at a doctor's discretion, it may be prescribed for depression as well.

One way that SSRIs seem to affect mood is by blocking serotonin **reuptake**—in other words, reabsorption of serotonin by the cells that originally released it. Consequently, more serotonin is available for use by the brain, and that is thought to enhance the transmission of crucial chemical messages from one brain cell to another. SSRIs are called "selective" because they act primarily on serotonin. Most also have weak effects on other substances in the brain, however. These secondary effects help explain why some individuals improve more or have fewer side effects with one SSRI than with another.

Today, when a doctor writes a prescription for an antidepressant, it is more often than not for an SSRI. Over half of people with depression feel better after the first SSRI they try, although it may take several weeks to get the full benefits. For the rest, the doctor may boost the dose, add a second treatment, try a different SSRI, or switch to a non-SSRI approach.

SSRI Antidepressants

	Brand Names
Citalopram†	Celexa
Escitalopram†‡*	Lexapro
Fluoxetine†‡§*	Prozac, Sarafem
Fluvoxamine‡	Luvox
Paroxetine†‡§	Paxil, Pexeva
Sertraline†‡§	Zoloft
Combination Product	
Fluoxetine + olanzapine (an antipsychotic)†	Symbyax

† FDA approved for treating depression
‡ FDA approved for treating one or more anxiety disorders
§ FDA approved for treating premenstrual dysphoric disorder
* FDA approved as a depression treatment for children and/or adolescents

Use and Precautions. Depression is not like strep throat; people cannot just take their medicine and expect to feel better in a couple of days. Instead, people with depression may need to take an SSRI for four to eight weeks to feel the full benefits. Even after they are doing better, most need to stay on medication for at least six to nine months, and sometimes for years, to help keep symptoms from coming back.

SSRIs are taken by mouth as a capsule, extended-release capsule, tablet, or liquid. Most are taken once or twice daily. There is also a once-a-week version of fluoxetine called Prozac Weekly.

Although SSRIs are not considered addictive, stopping them abruptly or skipping several doses in a row can lead to withdrawal-like symptoms, called **antidepressant discontinuation syndrome**. Possible symptoms include nausea, vomiting, diarrhea, headache, dizziness, fatigue, sadness, irritability, and anxiety. To prevent this problem, it is important to take an SSRI exactly as prescribed. When it is time to stop the medication, a doctor can explain how to taper it off gradually and safely.

Risks and Side Effects. Although SSRIs generally cause fewer serious side effects than older-generation antidepressants, they are not risk-free. In fact, the majority of people taking an SSRI experience at least one side effect. Although many such effects are mild and short-lived, some are more bothersome and persistent. Possible side effects include nausea, sexual problems, dry mouth, headache, diarrhea, nervousness, rash, agitation, restlessness, sweating, weight gain, drowsiness, and insomnia.

Different SSRIs have slightly different side effect profiles. For example, weight gain is relatively more common among people taking paroxetine, and diarrhea is more likely among those taking sertraline. **Sexual dysfunction**—including problems such as loss of desire or inability to reach orgasm—tends to be one of the more troubling side effects for SSRI users. Sexual problems can occur with any SSRI, but they are particularly common with paroxetine.

Pregnancy raises other concerns. The American College of Obstetricians and Gynecologists (ACOG) has recommended that women who are pregnant or planning to become pregnant avoid paroxetine because it might increase the risk of heart birth defects. As far as other SSRIs go, their use late in pregnancy has been linked to short-term problems in newborns, including jitteriness, mild respiratory distress, rapid breathing, a weak cry, and poor muscle tone. The long-term implications of such problems are still unclear, however. Meanwhile, untreated depression poses serious risks of its own, including poor eating habits, smoking, alcohol or drug use, and suicidal behavior in expectant mothers and low birth weight in their babies. According to ACOG, the possible risks of SSRI use during pregnancy must be weighed carefully against the benefits.

Serotonin syndrome is a rare but potentially life-threatening drug reaction that can occur when serotonin levels build up to dangerously high levels in the body. This most often occurs when people combine two drugs that each raise serotonin levels. For example, it might happen if an SSRI is combined with another antidepressant or certain **migraine** medications (triptans), prescription pain relievers (meperidine), over-the-counter cough medicines (products containing dextromethorphan), or **dietary supplements (St. John's wort**, L-tryptophan). To prevent problems, it is especially important for people taking SSRIs to tell their doctor about any other medicines or supplements they are using.

Antidepressants, including SSRIs, may be literal lifesavers by reducing depression and thereby decreasing thoughts of **suicide**. Paradoxically, though, a small number of **children, adolescents**, and young adults may experience worsening mood symptoms or increased suicidal thoughts or behavior after taking antidepressants. Patients taking SSRIs—or parents of younger patients—should watch closely for any suicidal thoughts or actions, new or worsening signs of depression, or unusual changes in mood or behavior. If such symptoms occur, they should call their doctor right away.

See also: Antidepressants and Suicide; Anxiety Disorders; Treatment of Depression

Bibliography

American College of Obstetricians and Gynecologists Committee on Obstetric Practice. "ACOG Committee Opinion No. 354: Treatment with Selective Serotonin Reuptake Inhibitors During Pregnancy." *Obstetrics and Gynecology* 108 (2006): 1601–1603.

Antidepressant Medicines: A Guide for Adults with Depression. Agency for Healthcare Research and Quality, August 2007, http://effectivehealthcare.ahrq.gov/repFiles/AntidepressantsConsumerGuide .pdf.

Antidepressants: Comparing Effectiveness, Safety, and Price. Consumer Reports, 2009, http://www .consumerreports.org/health/resources/pdf/best-buy-drugs/Antidepressants_update.pdf.

Comparative Effectiveness of Second-Generation Antidepressants in the Pharmacologic Treatment of Adult Depression: Executive Summary. Agency for Healthcare Research and Quality, January 2007, http://effectivehealthcare.ahrq.gov/repFiles/Antidepressants_Executive_Summary.pdf.

Medication Information Sheet. Depression and Bipolar Support Alliance, May 4, 2006, http://www .dbsalliance.org/site/PageServer?pagename=about_treatment_medinfosheet.

Mental Health Medications. National Institute of Mental Health, July 28, 2009, http://www .nimh.nih.gov/health/publications/mental-health-medications/complete-index.shtml.

Moore, Anna. "Eternal Sunshine." *Guardian.co.uk* (May 13, 2007).

Revisions to Medication Guide: Antidepressant Medicines, Depression and Other Serious Mental Illnesses, and Suicidal Thoughts or Actions. Food and Drug Administration, http://www.fda.gov/ downloads/Drugs/DrugSafety/InformationbyDrugClass/ucm100211.pdf.

Selective Serotonin Reuptake Inhibitors (SSRIs). Mayo Clinic, December 10, 2008, http://www .mayoclinic.com/health/ssris/MH00066.

Serotonin Syndrome. Mayo Clinic, February 7, 2009, http://www.mayoclinic.com/health/ serotonin-syndrome/DS00860.

Stahl, Stephen M. *Not So Selective Serotonin Reuptake Inhibitors.* Clinical Neuroscience Research Center (San Diego) and University of California-San Diego, July 1998, http://www.psychiatrist .com/pcc/brainstorm/br5907.htm.

SELF-HELP.   Self-help refers to self-guided, rather than professionally guided, steps that people can take to cope with a problem or illness. For people struggling with depression, self-help strategies can make life easier and more enjoyable. Such strategies help manage symptoms of depression and maximize the benefits of professional treatment. By empowering people to be active participants in their own care, self-help approaches also may boost self-confidence and independence.

Several different approaches fall within this broad category. **Support groups** are gatherings of people with a common problem or interest who get together to share moral support and practical advice. Twelve-step programs are self-help groups that operate under a specific set of guiding principles for overcoming alcoholism or other forms of addiction. Self-advocacy groups focus on educating the public and lobbying lawmakers about relevant issues.

The more people inform themselves about depression, the better prepared they are to cope with it effectively. Asking a doctor or therapist about concerns is one route to self-education. Beyond that, millions of people read self-help books for information about managing an illness or solving a problem in daily life. Other educational resources include Web sites, television programs, and classes.

Self-help measures also include lifestyle changes that promote better mental health or help reduce depressive symptoms. Such measures include getting regular **exercise**, eating a healthful **diet**, and adopting good sleep habits. Because stress can set off a bout of depression or make it worse, practicing **relaxation techniques** and **stress management** strategies can be beneficial as well.

For a mild, transitory case of the blues, self-help alone may be all it takes to snap out of a low mood. Full-blown depression is another story. Professional treatment is generally needed, but self-help is still vitally important. Although therapy and medication can be invaluable—even lifesaving—they only work their best when the ill person plays an active role in his or her own recovery.

See also: Bibliotherapy; Psychoeducation

Further Information.   National Mental Health Consumers' Self-Help Clearinghouse, 1211 Chestnut Street, Suite 1207, Philadelphia, PA 19107, (800) 553-4539, www.mhselfhelp.org.

Bibliography

Depression (Major Depression): Lifestyle and Home Remedies. Mayo Clinic, February 14, 2008, http://www.mayoclinic.com/health/depression/DS00175/DSECTION=lifestyle-and-home -remedies.

How to Care: Support Groups/Self-Care. How to Care, 2000, http://www.howtocare.com/support _groups.htm.

SELIGMAN, MARTIN E. P. (1942–). Martin E. P. Seligman is a U.S. psychologist who is considered father of the positive psychology movement. This field of theory and research focuses on the positive emotions, individual traits, and social institutions that make life worth living. Seligman has also made major contributions to the understanding of **learned helplessness** and **pessimism**, concepts that have played an important role in modern theories of depression.

Over his wide-ranging career, Seligman's professional interests have expanded as he followed his research findings to their logical conclusions. Seligman started out doing animal research in a lab, where he first explored learned helplessness—a giving-up reaction that stems from exposure to unpleasant events that are beyond the individual's control. As Seligman began studying the same phenomenon in humans, he delved into attribution theory—the study of how people ascribe motives to their own and others' behavior. By relating helplessness to depression, Seligman ventured into clinical psychology. By studying how helplessness changes over the life span, he crossed into developmental territory. And by exploring how helplessness interacts with physical health, he contributed to health psychology.

Seligman's work on pessimism was an extension of his interest in learned helplessness and attribution theory. But given his propensity for seeing connections, it was not long before he began looking at pessimism's flipside: optimism. The study of optimism and other personal strengths and virtues soon led Seligman to propose the new field of positive psychology, and promoting this fast-growing field remains his primary mission today.

Early Career Highlights. Seligman was born in Albany, New York, in 1942. After high school, he earned his A.B. degree from Princeton University in 1964, followed by his Ph.D. from the University of Pennsylvania in 1967. His first professional posts were as an assistant professor of psychology at Cornell University and a visiting fellow in psychiatry at the University of London. But in 1976, Seligman returned as a psychology professor to the University of Pennsylvania, and he has remained there ever since. Currently, he is director of the university's Positive Psychology Center.

Seligman's first big discovery grew out of behavioral research on animals. In one research protocol, a dog was put into a cage divided by a low barrier in the middle, and small electric shocks were sent through the half of the floor where the dog stood. To escape the shocks, the dog had to jump the barrier to get to the other side of the floor, where there was no current. If the dog did not jump the first time, a researcher helped. After that, the dog would jump on its own.

Then Seligman added a new twist. He put the dog in a harness and delivered several more small shocks from which the dog could not escape. Afterward, Seligman placed the same dog back in the cage without a harness and once again delivered shocks through the floor. This time, though, the dog did not jump over the barrier to get away. Instead, it ran around yelping pathetically until the shock was turned off.

In the first part of the experiment, the dog found that it could stop the shock by jumping over the barrier. In other words, the dog learned to control its environment. But in the second part, the dog discovered just the opposite. After that experience, the dog stopped trying to change its environment. In other words, the dog learned to be helpless.

From these observations sprang an influential theory of human depression. Seligman noted that some people become depressed after being subjected to a traumatic or stressful situation, but others do not. One differentiating factor, according to Seligman, is the extent to which people believe they have control over the situation. Those who have some success at avoiding or easing the pain or at getting support from others are more likely to keep trying to escape the bad situation. Those who are unable to avoid the pain, in contrast, learn to feel helpless, hopeless, and depressed.

Pessimistic Explanatory Style. Seligman was clearly onto something. But many psychologists criticized the original theory of learned helplessness as being too simplistic to account for the complexity of human behavior. In response, the theory was reformulated to include the individual's view of why the unpleasant event was happening.

This new formulation drew on attribution theory, but it added some new elements. Instead of looking at an individual's explanation for a single event, it focused on a person's pattern of explanations across many situations—in other words, that person's explanatory style. Seligman explored three dimensions of explanatory style: permanence (how long the negative event or its cause will last), pervasiveness (how broad its effects are), and personalization (how much people blame themselves).

Seligman contrasted the opposing explanatory styles of optimism and pessimism. When confronted with one of life's hard knocks, optimists tend to believe it is just a temporary setback and one-time event, and it is not their fault. Pessimists, on the other hand, tend to see the same bad event as something that will last a long time and undermine everything they do, and they blame themselves. According to this view, pessimistic thinking engenders hopelessness, low self-esteem, and in some people, full-blown depression.

Seligman in Perspective. Seligman's influence has been felt across the whole spectrum of psychology. His bestselling books, such as *Authentic Happiness* (2002) and *Learned Optimism* (1990), have brought his ideas to the broader public as well. All told, Seligman's list of publications includes some 20 books and 200 articles.

Seligman served as president of the American Psychological Association (APA) in 1998, after being elected by the largest vote in modern history. His many other honors include two Distinguish`ed Scientific Contribution awards from the APA, two Fellow Awards from the American Psychological Society, and the Lifetime Achievement Award from the Society for Research in Psychopathology.

As APA president, Seligman's stated goal was to join practice and science together so that both might flourish. In his own career, he has realized this goal, and the field of psychology is much richer for it.

Further Information. University of Pennsylvania Positive Psychology Center, 3720 Walnut Street, Solomon Labs, Philadelphia, PA, (215) 898-7173, www.ppc.sas.upenn.edu, www.authentichappiness.sas.upenn.edu.

Bibliography

Peterson, Christopher, Steven F. Maier, and Martin E. P. Seligman. *Learned Helplessness: A Theory for the Age of Personal Control.* New York: Oxford University Press, 1993.

Schwartz, Arthur, and Ruth M. Schwartz. *Depression Theories and Treatments: Psychological, Biological, and Social Perspectives.* New York: Columbia University Press, 1993.

Seligman Bio. University of Pennsylvania Positive Psychology Center, http://www.ppc.sas.upenn .edu/bio.htm.

Seligman, Martin E. P. *Authentic Happiness: Using the New Positive Psychology to Realize Your Potential for Lasting Fulfillment.* New York: Free Press, 2002.

Seligman, Martin E. P. *Helplessness: On Depression, Development, and Death.* San Francisco: W. H. Freeman, 1975.

Seligman, Martin E. P. *Learned Optimism.* New York: Alfred A. Knopf, 1991.

Seligman, Martin E. P., Tracy A. Steen, Nansook Park, and Christopher Peterson. "Positive Psychology Progress: Empirical Validation of Interventions." *American Psychologist* 60 (2005): 410–421.

Seligman, Martin E. P., with Karen Reivich, Lisa Jaycox, and Jane Gillham *The Optimistic Child: A Proven Program to Safeguard Children Against Depression and Build Lifelong Resilience.* New York: Houghton Mifflin, 1995.

Sheehy, Noel, Antony J. Chapman, and Wendy Conroy, eds. "Seligman, Martin E. P.," in *Biographical Dictionary of Psychology.* New York: Routledge, 2002.

SEQUENCED TREATMENT ALTERNATIVES TO RELIEVE DEPRESSION.

The Sequenced Treatment Alternatives to Relieve Depression (STAR*D) study, funded by the **National Institute of Mental Health**, is the largest and longest **clinical trial** ever conducted to evaluate treatments for depression. The study was divided into four phases, each of which tested a different treatment or combination of treatments. If people did not become symptom-free after treatment in one phase, they could move on to the next. The research showed that even people with hard-to-treat depression often can get well after trying multiple treatment strategies.

The innovative design of the STAR*D study was intended to mirror real-world conditions. Study participants were allowed to choose the treatment strategies most acceptable to them, and random assignments to treatment groups for each participant were limited to just those options.

Study Design. The STAR*D study enrolled 4,041 volunteers with **major depression**, ages 18 through 75, over a seven-year period. They came from a range of ethnic and socioeconomic backgrounds. These volunteers were treated at 41 sites around the United States, including both private-practice and public clinics. Treatment was provided by both psychiatrists and primary care doctors. No prior study had ever looked at depression treatments in such a broad group of patients and treatment settings, reflecting the diversity found among adults with depression in the population at large.

Of the initial 4,041 participants, over a quarter were excluded because they either chose not to participate or did not have at least moderate depression. That left 2,876 people who completed the first phase of the study. The second phase included 1,439 people who did not become symptom-free in the first phase and chose to continue. The third phase included 377 people, and the fourth phase, 142 people.

Stepwise Approach to Treatment. Different treatments were offered at each step along the way. The various medications used were among the safest, easiest to take, and most frequently prescribed. The one type of **psychotherapy** offered also was a well-established approach. Treatment at each phase could continue for up to 14 weeks. After that point, people who were not symptom-free had the option of proceeding to the next phase, in which new treatment choices were available.

Level 1. All participants started out on **citalopram**, which is representative of a widely prescribed class of **antidepressants** called **selective serotonin reuptake inhibitors**. Those who still had symptoms after taking citalopram or who could not tolerate side effects from the medication were encouraged to move on to the next phase.

Results: About one-third of participants achieved full remission, meaning they were symptom-free after treatment. Another 10 percent to 15 percent were "responders" who did not reach full remission, but who had the severity of their symptoms decreased by at least half. These were good results in light of the fact that many study participants had **chronic depression** or **recurrent depression**, which tends to be challenging to treat.

Level 2. In this phase, people had the choice of either switching to a different medication or adding a second medication to the citalopram. Those in the switch group were randomly assigned to get sertraline, bupropion-SR, or venlafaxine-XR—three different types of antidepressants that act on different chemical messengers within the brain. Those in the add-on group added either bupropion-SR or buspirone. The latter is not an antidepressant itself but can boost an antidepressant's effects.

This phase also included a psychotherapy option. People could either switch to **cognitive therapy** instead of medication or add psychotherapy to citalopram. Cognitive therapy helps people identify distortions in their thoughts and learn more accurate and adaptive ways of thinking about the world. The 147 participants who switched to or added cognitive therapy took part in up to 16 therapy sessions over a 12-week period.

Results: About one-fourth of people in the medication switch group achieved full remission. All three switch medications were roughly equal in safety and effectiveness. About one-third of people in the medication add-on group became symptom-free. Those who added bupropion-SR did slightly better and had less troublesome side effects than those who added buspirone.

About one-fourth of people who switched to or added cognitive therapy experienced full remission—a result comparable to that seen in the medication-only groups. Those who switched to cognitive therapy also were spared the side effects of medication. But getting well took longer for people who added cognitive therapy to citalopram, compared to those who added a second medication.

Level 3. In this phase, people once again had the choice of either switching or adding on. Those in the switch group were randomly assigned to get either mirtazapine or nortriptyline—two types of antidepressants that work differently in the brain than the other medications previously used in the study. Those in the add-on group were randomly prescribed either **lithium**, a mood stabilizer used to treat bipolar disorder, or triiodothyronine, a medication used to treat thyroid conditions. These medications can enhance the effectiveness of antidepressants.

Results: From 12 percent to 20 percent of people in the switch group reached full remission, with the two medications faring about equally well in safety and effectiveness. About 20 percent of people in the add-on group became symptom-free. Triiodothyronine had fewer troublesome side effects than lithium.

Level 4. People who reached the final phase were taken off all previous medications and randomly switched to either tranylcypromine (yet another type of antidepressant) or the combination of venlafaxine-XR plus mirtazapine. These medications were chosen because previous research had indicated that they might be particularly helpful for people with highly **treatment-resistant depression**.

Results: From 7 to 10 percent of participants reached full remission, with those taking the venlafaxine-XR/mirtazapine combination showing a greater reduction in symptoms. People taking tranylcypromine were more likely to quit treatment, citing side effects as the reason.

What the Results Mean. The results of the STAR*D study underscore the value of tailoring depression treatment to each person's individual needs and preferences. The moral of the study: It is important to keep trying if the first treatment does not work, because the second—or third, or fourth—treatment might be more helpful.

Unless side effects become intolerable, it is also crucial to give a new medication enough time to work before concluding that it is not effective. In the first phase of the study, people who achieved full remission stayed on medication for an average of 12 weeks.

Another lesson learned is the benefit of working toward full remission. Not everyone will improve this much, but many people do. Those who reach the point of being symptom-free have a better chance of staying well than those who experience only a reduction in symptoms.

See also: Augmentation Therapy

Bibliography

Fava, Maurizio, A. John Rush, Stephen R. Wisniewski, Andrew A. Nierenberg, Jonathan E. Alpert, Patrick J. McGrath, et al. "A Comparison of Mirtazapine and Nortriptyline Following Two Consecutive Failed Medication Treatments for Depressed Outpatients: A STAR*D Report." *American Journal of Psychiatry* 163 (2006): 1161–1172.

In Second Try to Treat Depression, Cognitive Therapy Generally as Effective as Medication. National Institute of Mental Health, June 26, 2008, http://www.nimh.nih.gov/science-news/2007/in-second-try-to-treat-depression-cognitive-therapy-generally-as-effective-as-medication.shtml.

McGrath, Patrick J., Jonathan W. Stewart, Maurizio Fava, Madhukar H. Trivedi, Stephen R. Wisniewski, Andrew A. Nierenberg, et al. "Tranylcypromine Versus Venlafaxine Plus Mirtazapine Following Three Failed Antidepressant Medication Trials for Depression: A STAR*D Report." *American Journal of Psychiatry* 163 (2006): 1531–1541.

Nierenberg, Andrew A., Maurizio Fava, Madhukar H. Trivedi, Stephen R. Wisniewski, Michael E. Thase, Patrick J. McGrath, et al. "A Comparison of Lithium and T$_3$ Augmentation Following Two Failed Medication Treatments for Depression: A STAR*D Report." *American Journal of Psychiatry* 163 (2006): 1519–1530.

Rush, A. John, Madhukar H. Trivedi, Stephen R. Wisniewski, Jonathan W. Stewart, Andrew A. Nierenberg, Michael E. Thase, et al. "Bupropion-SR, Sertraline, or Venlafaxine-XR After Failure of SSRIs for Depression." *New England Journal of Medicine* 354 (2006): 1231–1242.

Thase, Michael E., Edward S. Friedman, Melanie M. Biggs, Stephen R. Wisniewski, Madhukar H. Trivedi, James F. Luther, et al. "Cognitive Therapy Versus Medication in Augmentation and Switch Strategies as Second-Step Treatments: A STAR*D Report." *American Journal of Psychiatry* 164 (2007): 739–752.

Trivedi, Madhukar H., A. John Rush, Stephen R. Wisniewski, Andrew A. Nierenberg, Diane Warden, Louise Ritz, et al. "Evaluation of Outcomes with Citalopram for Depression Using Measurement-Based Care in STAR*D: Implications for Clinical Practice." *American Journal of Psychiatry* 163 (2006): 28–40.

*Questions and Answers About the NIMH Sequenced Treatment Alternatives to Relieve Depression (STAR*D) Study: All Medication Levels.* National Institute of Mental Health, June 26, 2008, http://www.nimh.nih.gov/health/trials/practical/stard/questions-and-answers-about-the-nimh-sequenced-treatment-alternatives-to-relieve-depression-stard-study-all-medication-levels.shtml.

*Questions and Answers About the NIMH Sequenced Treatment Alternatives to Relieve Depression (STAR*D) Study: Background.* National Institute of Mental Health, June 26, 2008, http://www.nimh.nih.gov/health/trials/practical/stard/questions-and-answers-about-the-nimh-sequenced-treatment-alternatives-to-relieve-depression-stard-study-background.shtml.

SEROTONIN. Serotonin (also known as 5-HT, for 5-hydroxytryptamine) is a neurotransmitter—a chemical messenger within the brain—that helps regulate mood, sleep, appetite, and sexual drive. Serotonin deficits are thought to play a pivotal role in depression. **Selective serotonin reuptake inhibitors** (SSRIs), a widely prescribed group of

antidepressants, increase the brain's supply of this neurotransmitter. Most other types of antidepressants also boost serotonin's availability.

Research has linked serotonin deficiencies to severe depression and suicidal behavior. For instance, when researchers examined the cerebrospinal fluid of people with severe depression, they found that those with the lowest levels of serotonin were more likely to die by **suicide** than those with normal levels. Besides depres-

---

A Dose of Serotonin?

SSRIs and some other antidepressants work by blocking serotonin **reuptake**, the process by which serotinin is absorbed back into this cell that originally released it. This leaves more serotonin available for use by the brain, which may enhance the sending of nerve impulses and thereby improve a person's mood. But why not just take serotonin itself?

Serotonin cannot pass through the blood-brain barrier, a protective barrier formed by cells lining the small blood vessels that supply the brain. Some substances, such as serotonin and many drugs, are not allowed to pass from the bloodstream into the brain. Other substances, such as water and oxygen, are allowed to enter freely.

---

sion, other conditions that involve abnormalities in serotonin include **bipolar disorder**, **anxiety disorders**, autism, and schizophrenia. This chemical is clearly a key player in brain health.

Yet just as clearly, serotonin is only one link in a long chain of physiological events that underlie mental disorders. Today scientists are increasingly focused on the interplay between serotonin and other links in the chain. Take the tryptophan hydroxylase 2 (TPH2) gene, for example. This gene makes the TPH2 enzyme, which is involved in serotonin production. In human studies, a mutation in the gene has been linked to depression in some people. And in animal research, mice genetically engineered to have a comparable mutation showed a profound reduction in serotonin levels.

Transmitting a Message. Serotonin is produced by particular nerve cells, called serotonergic **neurons**. The cell bodies of these neurons are found in groups at several sites in the brainstem, the lower extension of the brain that connects it to the spinal cord. The sending branches of the serotonergic neurons project into many parts of the brain.

To convey a message from one brain cell to another, serotonin is first released by a sending cell into the synapse—the tiny gap between a cell and its neighbor. After crossing the gap, serotonin binds with a matching receptor on the receiving cell. After the message is delivered, serotonin is either absorbed back into the cell that originally released it or broken down by another molecule.

There are various types of serotonin receptors found in several different parts of the brain. Some serotonin receptors excite activity in the cell on which they are found, but others inhibit activity. This explains how the same chemical can have a variety of effects.

Tryptophan Depletion Studies. Until recently, it was not possible to measure serotonin in the brain directly, so scientists had to rely on indirect study methods, such as **tryptophan** depletion. Tryptophan is an amino acid that is a building block in serotonin production. In a tryptophan depletion study, people are given a drink loaded with amino acids except for tryptophan. Within hours, this causes a dramatic drop in blood tryptophan levels.

Tryptophan depletion studies have yielded interesting but complex results. Among depressed individuals who were being treated with serotonin-boosting antidepressants, most who had only partially recovered from depression suffered an immediate relapse after this procedure. The relapse was reversed by eating a tryptophan-rich meal.

In contrast, healthy volunteers with no family history of depression were unaffected by tryptophan depletion. Also, among people with untreated depression, depleting tryptophan did not make their symptoms worse. Researchers speculated that serotonin activity in these individuals might already have been as low as it could get.

Brain Imaging Studies. In a more recent line of research, scientists used a **brain imaging** technique called positron emission tomography (PET) to view the brain in action. When both depressed patients and healthy volunteers were given a drug to increase serotonin availability in the brain, only the healthy individuals showed a change in brain activity. This suggests that the depressed individuals had either a very blunted response to serotonin or a very low level of it even after receiving the drug.

A similar PET study looked at 25 depressed individuals who had previously attempted suicide. Individuals with a history of highly lethal suicide attempts showed less activity in certain brain regions than those who had made less lethal attempts. These brain regions were located in the **prefrontal cortex**, part of the brain involved in higher thought, problem solving, short-term memory, and emotion. The difference became even greater after people were given a serotonin-boosting drug.

Taken as a whole, serotonin research has produced a mixed bag of results. It is apparent that serotonin contributes to depression. But it is equally apparent that serotonin is only one of many biological factors that may be involved in causing a depressed mood.

See also: Genetic Factors; Glycogen Synthase Kinase 3 Beta; Monoamine Hypothesis; Neurotransmitters; Receptors; Serotonin Syndrome; Serotonin Transporter Gene; Tryptophan Hydroxylase Gene

Bibliography

Anderson, Amy D., Maria A. Oquendo, Ramin V. Parsey, Matthew S. Milak, Carl Campbell, and J. John Mann. "Regional Brain Responses to Serotonin in Major Depressive Disorder." *Journal of Affective Disorders* 82 (2004): 411–417.

Beaulieu, Jean-Martin, Xiaodong Zhang, Ramona M. Rodriguiz, Tatyana D. Sotnikova, Michael J. Cools, William C. Wetsel, et al. "Role of GSK3ß in Behavioral Abnormalities Induced by Serotonin Deficiency." *Proceedings of the National Academy of Sciences of the USA* 105 (2008): 1333–1338.

DePaulo, J. Raymond Jr. *Understanding Depression: What We Know and What You Can Do About It.* New York: John Wiley and Sons, 2002.

Mann, J. J., K. M. Malone, D. J. Diehl, J. Perel, T. B. Cooper, and M. A. Mintun. "Demonstration in Vivo of Reduced Serotonin Responsivity in the Brain of Untreated Depressed Patients." *American Journal of Psychiatry* 153 (1996): 174–182.

Medication Information Sheet. Depression and Bipolar Support Alliance, May 4, 2006, http://www.dbsalliance.org/site/PageServer?pagename=about_treatment_medinfosheet.

Neumeister, Alexander. "Tryptophan Depletion, Serotonin, and Depression: Where Do We Stand?" *Translational Neuroscience* 37 (2003): 99–115.

Oquendo, Maria A., Giovanni P. A. Placidi, Kevin M. Malone, Carl Campbell, John Keilp, Beth Brodsky, et al. "Positron Emission Tomography of Regional Brain Metabolic Responses to a Serotonergic Challenge and Lethality of Suicide Attempts in Major Depression." *Archives of General Psychiatry* 60 (2003): 14–22.

Selective Serotonin Reuptake Inhibitors (SSRIs). Mayo Clinic, December 10, 2008, http://www.mayoclinic.com/health/ssris/MH00066.

Serotonin and Judgment. Society for Neuroscience, http://www.sfn.org/index.cfm?pagename=brainBriefings_serotoninAndJudgment.

Serotonin and Other Molecules Involved in Depression: Beginner. Canadian Institute of Neurosciences, Mental Health and Addiction, http://thebrain.mcgill.ca/flash/d/d_08/d_08_m/d_08_m_dep/d_08_m_dep.html.

Serotonin and Other Molecules Involved in Depression: Intermediate. Canadian Institute of Neurosciences, Mental Health and Addiction, http://thebrain.mcgill.ca/flash/i/i_08/i_08_m/i_08_m_dep/i_08_m_dep_isrs.html.

Slattery, D. A., A. L. Hudson, and D. J. Nutt. "Invited Review: The Evolution of Antidepressant Mechanisms." *Fundamental and Clinical Pharmacology* 18 (2004): 1–21.

Tomorrow's Antidepressants: Skip the Serotonin Boost? National Institute of Mental Health, February 14, 2008, http://www.nimh.nih.gov/science-news/2008/tomorrows-antidepressants-skip-the-serotonin-boost.shtml.

SEROTONIN ANTAGONIST AND REUPTAKE INHIBITORS. Serotonin antagonist and reuptake inhibitors (SARIs) are antidepressant medications that affect key chemical messengers in the brain, including **serotonin**, in two different ways. First, they block the action of certain brain cell **receptors**. Second, they inhibit the **reuptake**, or reabsorption, of specific chemical messengers by the cells that originally released them. The net result is an increase in the availability of mood-boosting chemicals within the brain.

Two SARIs have been approved by the Food and Drug Administration: nefazodone and trazodone. The brand-name versions of these medications are no longer manufactured, but generic versions are still available. In the case of nefazodone, the brand-name version, called Serzone, was taken off the market in 2004 amid reports linking it to rare but life-threatening cases of liver failure. Studies to date have not conclusively established how great the risk might be. Until the safety issues are resolved, many doctors consider nefazodone a treatment of last resort.

Trazodone is another dual-action medication, but it has a different chemical structure from any other antidepressant in current use. Because it has a sedating effect and may lead to improved sleep, trazodone is often prescribed for insomnia, even in people without depression. For depressed individuals, it may be combined with another antidepressant that causes sleep problems to counter the other drug's sleep side effects.

SARI Antidepressants

	Brand Names*
Nefazodone†	Serzone
Trazodone†	Desyrel

† FDA approved for treating depression

* Some antidepressants are no longer sold as brand-name products, but are still available in generic form.

Use and Precautions. SARIs are taken by mouth, usually two or more times a day. For trazodone, the medication is generally taken along with a meal or light snack.

People may need a few weeks or longer to feel the full benefits of a SARI. Even after they start feeling better, most being treated for depression need to stay on medication for at least six to nine months, and sometimes for years, to help keep symptoms from coming back. People should not quit taking a SARI without talking to their doctor first.

Risks and Side Effects. Possible side effects of SARIs include drowsiness, dry mouth, dizziness, nervousness, nausea, constipation, weakness, vision problems, headache, and confusion. In males, trazodone occasionally causes painful, long-lasting erections unrelated to sexual arousal. Men should seek medical help immediately if this problem occurs. At times, surgery is required, and some of these cases result in permanent erectile dysfunction.

In rare cases, nefazodone may lead to severe liver damage, liver transplants, or even death. People taking this medication should be alert for symptoms of liver problems, such as yellowing of the skin or whites of the eyes, dark urine, loss of appetite, nausea, or stomach pain. They should contact their doctor immediately if such symptoms occur. Those who already have liver disease should avoid nefazodone.

Antidepressants may save lives by reducing depression and thus decreasing the risk of suicide. In a small number of **children**, **adolescents**, and young adults, however, taking antidepressants may actually lead to worsening mood symptoms or increased suicidal thoughts and behavior. Patients taking mirtazapine—or parents of younger patients—should be alert for any suicidal thoughts and actions or unusual changes in mood and behavior. If such symptoms occur, they should contact their doctor right away.

See also: Antidepressants and Suicide; Treatment of Depression

Bibliography

Antidepressant Medicines: A Guide for Adults with Depression. Agency for Healthcare Research and Quality, August 2007, http://effectivehealthcare.ahrq.gov/repFiles/AntidepressantsConsumerGuide .pdf.

Antidepressants: Comparing Effectiveness, Safety, and Price. Consumer Reports, 2009, http://www .consumerreports.org/health/resources/pdf/best-buy-drugs/Antidepressants_update.pdf.

Combined Reuptake Inhibitors and Receptor Blockers. Mayo Clinic, December 10, 2008, http:// effectivehealthcare.ahrq.gov/repFiles/AntidepressantsConsumerGuide.pdf.

Lamberg, Lynne. "Physicians Underprescribe Best Insomnia Treatments." *Psychiatric News* (September 2, 2005).

Medication Information Sheet. Depression and Bipolar Support Alliance, May 4, 2006, http://www.dbsalliance.org/site/PageServer?pagename=about_treatment_medinfosheet.

Nefazodone. National Library of Medicine, September 1, 2008, http://www.nlm.nih.gov/medlineplus/ druginfo/meds/a695005.html.

Shelton, Richard C., and Natalie Lester. "Selective Serotonin Reuptake Inhibitors and Newer Antidepressants." In *The American Psychiatric Publishing Textbook of Mood Disorders,* by Dan J. Stein, David J. Kupfer, and Alan F. Schatzberg, eds., 263–280. Washington, DC: American Psychiatric Publishing, 2006.

Trazodone. National Library of Medicine, August 1, 2009, http://www.nlm.nih.gov/medlineplus/ druginfo/meds/a681038.html.

SEROTONIN-NOREPINEPHRINE REUPTAKE INHIBITORS.

Serotonin-norepinephrine reuptake inhibitors (SNRIs) are antidepressant medications that increase the brain's available supply of two key chemical messengers: **serotonin** and **norepinephrine**. The medications work by blocking the **reuptake**, or reabsorption, of these chemicals back into the brain cells that originally released them. By boosting serotonin and norepinephrine, SNRIs enhance the sending of messages from one brain cell to another, and that is thought to help relieve depression.

The newest SNRI is desvenlafaxine, introduced in the United States in 2008. It is a modified version of an older SNRI, venlafaxine. The latter has been approved by the Food and Drug Administration (FDA) for treating not only depression, but also **generalized anxiety disorder**, **panic disorder**, and social anxiety disorder. A third medication in this class is duloxetine, which is FDA approved for the treatment of depression, **generalized anxiety disorder**, fibromyalgia, and diabetic nerve pain.

SNRIs are often compared to their more famous cousins, **selective serotonin reuptake inhibitors** (SSRIs). Both types of medication affect mood by inhibiting reuptake. But SSRIs target only one brain chemical: serotonin. SNRIs target two. Over half of people who take either an SNRI or an SSRI have their depression symptoms cut by at least 50 percent. And both SNRIs and SSRIs have relatively good safety profiles, so they may be used as first-choice treatments for depression.

SNRI Antidepressants

	Brand Names
Desvenlafaxine†	Pristiq
Duloxetine†‡	Cymbalta
Venlafaxine†‡	Effexor

† FDA approved for treating depression
‡ FDA approved for treating one or more anxiety disorders

Use and Precautions. SNRIs are taken by mouth one to three times a day. People with depression may need to take an SNRI for several weeks to feel the full benefits. Even after they are doing better, most need to stay on medication for at least six to nine months, and sometimes for years, to help keep symptoms from coming back.

Although SNRIs are not considered addictive, stopping them abruptly or skipping several doses in a row can lead to withdrawal-like symptoms, called **antidepressant discontinuation syndrome**. Possible symptoms include nausea, vomiting, diarrhea, headache, dizziness, fatigue, sadness, irritability, and anxiety. To prevent this problem, it is important to take an SNRI exactly as prescribed. When it is time to stop the medication, a doctor can explain how to taper it off gradually and safely.

"Depression Hurts"; Do Ads Hurt, Too?

"Depression hurts." This tagline from a series of commercials for Cymbalta (duloxetine) was among the more memorable ad campaigns of recent years. The commercials were prime examples of direct-to-consumer (DTC) advertising, a controversial practice in which pharmaceutical companies pitch their products directly to potential patients. Proponents claim that such ads combat undertreatment of neglected or stigmatized conditions, but critics claim that the ads promote overprescribing of unnecessary or inappropriate medications.

The FDA relaxed its policies on broadcast ads for prescription medications in 1997. By 2003, DTC advertising of prescription drugs in the United States had topped $3 billion a year. Antidepressants are one of the strongest DTC advertising categories. Advertisers like the category because depression is a common condition that is undertreated, so there is still room for substantial growth in sales. Also, due to regulations about risk disclosure in advertising, medications with relatively few side effects and contraindications are easier to promote directly to the public, and newer antidepressants fit the bill.

Research suggests that DTC advertising does indeed increase the total number of people receiving drug treatment for depression. However, it might not have as great an impact on the choice of a specific antidepressant, because physicians are still the gatekeepers to that decision. This explains why drug companies spend even larger sums on marketing to physicians.

Risks and Side Effects. Although all SNRIs have the same general mode of action, they vary in their chemical characteristics. As a result, a particular individual might have more side effects with one SNRI than with another. Although many such effects are mild and short-lived, others are more bothersome or persistent.

Venlafaxine is considerably more likely than many other antidepressants to cause nausea and vomiting. This problem may be reduced by taking the extended-release form of the medication. Other possible side effects of SNRIs include dizziness, trouble sleeping, abnormal dreams, sleepiness, constipation, sweating, dry mouth, yawning, shakiness, gas, anxiety, agitation, blurred vision, headache, and sexual problems.

SNRIs may raise blood pressure, and venlafaxine may lead to increased cholesterol levels, so people using these medications should keep close tabs on their cardiovascular health. People with certain eye conditions (narrow-angle glaucoma and increased intraocular pressure) should avoid SNRIs or use them cautiously. In addition, there have been reports linking duloxetine to liver problems. As a result, the medication is not recommended for people with chronic liver disease and those who drink large amounts of alcohol.

Serotonin syndrome is a rare but potentially life-threatening drug reaction that can occur when serotonin levels build up to dangerously high levels in the body. This most often occurs when people combine two drugs that each raise serotonin levels. For example, it might happen if an SNRI is combined with another antidepressant or certain **migraine** medications (triptans), prescription pain relievers (meperidine), over-the-counter cough medicines (products containing dextromethorphan), or **dietary supplements** (**St. John's wort**, L-tryptophan). To prevent problems, it is especially important for people taking SNRIs to tell their doctor about any other medicines or supplements they are using.

Antidepressants may save lives by reducing depression and thus decreasing the risk of suicide. In a small number of **children**, **adolescents**, and young adults, though, taking antidepressants may actually lead to worsening mood symptoms or increased suicidal thoughts and behavior. Patients taking SNRIs—or parents of younger patients—should be alert for any suicidal thoughts and actions or unusual changes in mood and behavior. If such symptoms occur, they should contact their doctor right away.

See also: Antidepressants and Suicide; Treatment of Depression

Bibliography

Antidepressant Medicines: A Guide for Adults with Depression. Agency for Healthcare Research and Quality, August 2007, http://effectivehealthcare.ahrq.gov/repFiles/AntidepressantsConsumerGuide.pdf.

Antidepressants: Comparing Effectiveness, Safety, and Price. Consumer Reports, 2009, http://www.consumerreports.org/health/resources/pdf/best-buy-drugs/Antidepressants_update.pdf.

Cymbalta (Duloxetine Hydrochloride) Oct 2005. Food and Drug Administration, October 5, 2005, http://www.fda.gov/Safety/MedWatch/SafetyInformation/SafetyAlertsforHumanMedicalProducts/ucm151091.htm.

Donohue, Julie M., and Ernst R. Berndt. "Effects of Direct-to-Consumer Advertising on Medication Choice: The Case of Antidepressants." *Journal of Public Policy and Marketing* 23 (2004): 115–127.

Kravitz, Richard L., Ronald M. Epstein, and Mitchell D. Feldman. "Influence of Patients' Requests for Direct-to-Consumer Advertised Antidepressants: A Randomized Controlled Trial." *JAMA* 293 (2005): 1995–2002.

Medication Information Sheet. Depression and Bipolar Support Alliance, May 4, 2006, http://www.dbsalliance.org/site/PageServer?pagename=about_treatment_medinfosheet.

Serotonin and Norepinephrine Reuptake Inhibitors (SNRIs). Mayo Clinic, December 10, 2008, http://www.mayoclinic.com/health/antidepressants/MH00067.

SEROTONIN SYNDROME.   Serotonin syndrome is a rare but potentially life-threatening drug reaction that can occur when **serotonin** levels build up to dangerously high levels in the body. Serotonin is a brain chemical that helps regulate mood, sleep, appetite, and sexual drive. Most **antidepressants**—including a popular group of medications called **selective serotonin reuptake inhibitors** (SSRIs)—increase the availability of serotonin in the brain. This is a good thing up to a point. Taken too far, though, excessive serotonin can cause serious problems.

Most cases of serotonin syndrome occur when people combine two drugs that each raise serotonin levels. For example, it might happen if two antidepressants are combined, or if an antidepressant is mixed with certain **migraine** medications (triptans), pain relievers (fentanyl, meperidine), over-the-counter cough medicines (products containing dextromethorphan), or **dietary supplements** (L-tryptophan, **St. John's wort**). Some illicit drugs (amphetamines, cocaine, Ecstasy, LSD) can boost serotonin and contribute to the problem as well.

Handle with Care

A number of prescription medications, over-the-counter medicines, dietary supplements, and illicit drugs boost serotonin levels. Below are some examples. Combining two or more of these products increases the chance of developing serotonin syndrome. At times, you and your doctor might still decide that the benefits of such a combination outweigh the risks. But to help you make an informed choice, your doctor needs to know about any medications, supplements, or other drugs you are taking.

Drug Category	**Serotonin-Boosting Drugs**
Antidepressants	
Monoamine oxidase inhibitors	Isocarboxazid, phenelzine, selegiline, tranylcypromine
Selective serotonin reuptake inhibitors	Citalopram, escitalopram, fluoxetine, fluvoxamine, paroxetine, sertraline
Serotonin-norepinephrine reuptake inhibitors	Desvenlafaxine, duloxetine, venlafaxine
Other Drugs	
Antibiotic	Linezolid
Cough and cold medicines	Over-the-counter products containing dextromethorphan
Dietary supplements	Ginseng, L-tryptophan, St. John's wort
HIV/AIDS medication	Ritonavir
Illicit drugs	Amphetamines, cocaine, Ecstasy, LSD
Migraine medications	Almotriptan, naratriptan, sumatriptan, zolmitriptan
Mood stabilizer	Lithium
Nausea medications	Granisetron, metoclopramide, ondansetron
Pain medications	Fentanyl, meperidine, pentazocine, tramadol

Less commonly, serotonin syndrome results from a large SSRI overdose. Because depression increases the risk of a **suicide** attempt, the possibility of an intentional overdose is always a concern. Statistically, though, the chance of dying from an SSRI overdose is quite low.

Getting Medical Help. Symptoms of serotonin syndrome typically appear within hours of starting a serotonin-boosting drug or increasing the dose. Possible symptoms include loss of coordination, muscle twitching, dilated pupils, heavy sweating, diarrhea, vomiting, headache, shivering, goose bumps, fever, seizures, confusion, hallucinations, and irregular heartbeat.

Severe serotonin syndrome can lead to unconsciousness or even death, so prompt action is critical. For mild symptoms, patients should call their doctor right away or go to an emergency room. For severe or rapidly worsening symptoms, they should call 911 immediately.

Treatment of serotonin syndrome depends on which symptoms develop and how severe they become. In mild cases, simply stopping the drug that caused the problem may be enough. Additional treatments—such as intravenous fluids, muscle relaxants, heart medications, or a breathing tube—may be prescribed for more serious symptoms. If necessary, medications that block serotonin production can be prescribed as well. Most symptoms of serotonin syndrome go away within 24 hours after starting treatment.

Bibliography

Antidepressant Medicines: A Guide for Adults with Depression. Agency for Healthcare Research and Quality, August 2007, http://effectivehealthcare.ahrq.gov/repFiles/AntidepressantsConsumerGuide.pdf.

Griffith, Gail. *Will's Choice.* New York: HarperCollins, 2005.

McKenzie, Mary S., and Bentson H. McFarland. "Trends in Antidepressant Overdoses." *Pharmacoepidemiology and Drug Safety* 16 (2007): 513–523.

Serotonin Syndrome. Mayo Clinic, February 7, 2009, http://www.mayoclinic.com/health/serotonin-syndrome/DS00860.

SEROTONIN TRANSPORTER GENE. The serotonin **transporter** gene (also known as SLC6A4 or 5-HTT) codes for a protein complex that carries a brain chemical called **serotonin** back into the cell that originally released it. Serotonin helps regulate mood, sleep, appetite, and sexual drive, and deficits in serotonin have been implicated in depression. By affecting the rate at which serotonin is absorbed back into the releasing cell, this gene influences how much serotonin is available for use by the brain.

The single best-studied genetic variant with regard to depression is a variation on the serotonin transporter gene. One study followed 847 individuals from ages 3 to 26. Researchers found that stressful life events between ages 21 and 25 increased the subsequent risk of being diagnosed with **major depression**, developing more depressive symptoms, and experiencing suicidal thoughts or attempts. Individuals with a variant of the serotonin transporter gene were especially likely to experience depression after stress. This variant was also associated with an increased likelihood of depression among people who had experienced childhood maltreatment.

Several other studies now support this finding. Taken together, they suggest that this particular gene variant may moderate the ability of **stress** to trigger or worsen depression. One possible mechanism is activation of the **amygdala**—a structure inside the brain that is involved in emotional learning and the fear response, and that tends to be unusually active in people with depression. In **brain imaging** studies, people with the gene variant show increased amygdala activity in response to stressful stimuli.

See also: Genetic Factors

Bibliography

Caspi, Avshalom, Karen Sugden, Terrie E. Moffitt, Alan Taylor, Ian W. Craig, HonaLee Harrington, et al. "Influence of Life Stress on Depression: Moderation by Polymorphism in the 5-HTT Gene." *Science* 301 (2003) 386–389.

Hariri, Ahmad R., Emily M. Drabant, Karen E. Munoz, Bhaskar S. Kolachana, Venkata S. Mattay, Michael F. Egan, et al. "A Susceptibility Gene for Affective Disorders and the Response of the Human Amygdala." *Archives of General Psychiatry* 62 (2005): 146–152.

Kim, Jae-Min, Robert Stewart, Sung-Wan Kim, Su-Jin Yang, Il-Seon Shin, Young-Hoon Kim, et al. "Interactions Between Life Stressors and Susceptibility Genes (5-HTTLPR and BDNF) on Depression in Korean Elders." *Biological Psychiatry* 62 (2007): 423–428.

Levinson, Douglas F. "Genetics of Major Depression." In *Handbook of Depression*. 2nd ed., by Ian H. Gotlib and Constance L. Hammen, eds., 165–186. New York: Guilford Press, 2009.

Zalsman, Gil, Yung-Yu Huang, Maria A. Oquendo, Ainsley K. Burke, Xian-zhang Hu, David A. Brent, et al. "Association of a Triallelic Serotonin Transporter Gene Promoter Region (5-HTTLPR) Polymorphism with Stressful Life Events and Severity of Depression." *American Journal of Psychiatry* 163 (2006): 1588–1593.

SEXUAL DYSFUNCTION.   Sexual dysfunction is a common symptom of depression as well as a side effect of certain **antidepressants**. The most frequent sexual complaint is low libido (sexual desire). Many with depression say decreased libido is among the most distressing consequences of their illness.

As a symptom of depression, reduced interest in sex is reported by up to 70 percent of those with the disorder. The more severe the depression, the less desire for sex people tend to feel. Depression leads to loss of interest in almost everything, lack of energy, low self-esteem, and social withdrawal. All these factors can interfere with intimate relationships and contribute to a low sex drive.

Other factors may link depression and sexuality as well. People with depression are at increased risk for **substance abuse**, and **alcohol** and narcotic drugs are known to interfere with libido, arousal, and orgasm. Moreover, certain brain chemicals, such as **serotonin**, affect both mood and sexual function.

Antidepressant Side Effects.   As a side effect of treatment, sexual problems are most often associated with a widely prescribed group of antidepressants called **selective serotonin reuptake inhibitors** (SSRIs). Possible side effects include reduced sexual desire and difficulty achieving orgasm. Men also may experience erectile dysfunction—difficulty getting or maintaining an erection that is hard enough for sexual intercourse. All SSRIs have a relatively high rate of sexual side effects. Some research suggests that an SSRI called paroxetine may be especially prone to causing sexual problems.

An older group of medications, known as **tricyclic antidepressants**, cause fewer sexual side effects than SSRIs. However, they may have other troubling effects—such as drowsiness, dry mouth, and blurred vision—that more than offset this advantage. Also, some studies indicate that two tricyclics—clomipramine and amoxapine—may be more likely to cause sexual side effects than other medications in this group.

Certain antidepressants that are neither SSRIs nor tricyclics seem to have the lowest rate of sexual side effects. These include bupropion, mirtazapine, nefazodone, and duloxetine.

Researchers still are not sure why some antidepressants interfere with sexual desire and performance. One theory is that these medications have a sedating effect, which puts a damper on libido. Other researchers speculate that antidepressants might affect key brain chemicals in parts of the brain that regulate sexual function. Complicating the picture is the role of depression itself in decreasing sexual interest.

Several options exist for managing antidepressant-related sexual dysfunction. In many cases, decreasing the dose of an antidepressant may improve libido while maintaining the drug's effectiveness against depression. If the lower dose does not adequately control depression, a second option is to switch antidepressants to one less likely to cause sexual problems. A third possibility is to add another medication—such as bupropion, mirtazapine, or the anti-anxiety drug buspirone—to counteract sexual side effects. Whatever option is chosen, it is important for people on antidepressants to talk to their doctor before stopping their medication or making any changes in how they take it.

Bibliography

Antidepressants: Which Cause the Fewest Sexual Side Effects? Mayo Clinic, January 15, 2008, http://www.mayoclinic.com/health/antidepressants/AN01739.

Baldwin, David S. "Depression and Sexual Dysfunction." *British Medical Bulletin* 57 (2001): 81–99.

Phillips, Robert L. Jr., and James R. Slaughter. "Depression and Sexual Desire." *American Family Physician* 62 (2000): 782–786.

SLEEP DISTURBANCES. Sleep disturbances and depression are closely intertwined. Depression may lead to sleep problems. In fact, disturbed sleep is one of the most common symptoms of **mood disorders** as well as a risk factor for worse outcomes in people with depression. Conversely, getting too little or poor quality sleep may trigger or worsen depressive symptoms. Research suggests that people with insomnia—difficulty falling or staying asleep—are 10 times more likely to develop depression than those who sleep well.

Depression is often associated with disturbances in vegetative functions—things the body does to keep itself alive, such as sleeping and eating. Typically, depression goes hand in hand with insomnia, lack of appetite, and weight loss. But depression also sometimes has the opposite effect, leading to oversleeping, increased appetite, and weight gain.

Poor sleep quality before treatment may increase the likelihood of a poor response to **psychotherapy** in people with depression. The same is true when people are treated with a combination of psychotherapy and **antidepressants**. Once people have recovered from an episode of depression, poor sleep quality is a risk factor for having a **recurrence**—and the first symptom to appear when depression returns is often insomnia.

Types of Sleep Disturbances. Depression may lead to insomnia, hypersomnia, or dream disturbances. These sleep problems, in turn, may worsen or prolong symptoms of depression.

Insomnia. More than 80 percent of people with depression suffer from insomnia, defined as difficulty falling asleep or staying asleep despite adequate opportunity for sleeping. The typical pattern involves waking up in the middle of the night and having trouble getting back to sleep, or waking up too early in the morning and not being able to go back to sleep at all. Depression is the most common cause of long-term insomnia.

Hypersomnia. Hypersomnia refers to sleeping longer than usual or excessive daytime sleepiness. The problem occurs in an estimated 7 to 15 percent of people with depression. It is more common in young adults, people with **seasonal affective disorder**, and individuals in the depression phase of **bipolar disorder**.

Dream Disturbances. Upsetting dreams and middle-of-the-night panic attacks also may occur in depressed individuals. Women with depression who often have distressing dreams report more suicidal symptoms than those without bad dreams.

The Depressed Brain at Sleep. Hundreds of studies over the past three decades have documented numerous changes in brain activity during sleep among people with depression. Some studies have monitored these changes with **electroencephalography** (EEG), a painless, non-invasive test that detects and records electrical activity in the brain. Others have used polysomnography—the recording of several physiological measures at once, such as brain electrical activity, eye movements, and heart rate.

Sleep studies have confirmed that, on average, depressed individuals take longer to fall asleep, wake up more often during the night, and spend less time asleep than those without depression. There are also key differences in the relative time spent in various sleep stages. For instance, people with depression tend to get an increased amount and percentage of REM (rapid eye movement) sleep, the stage during which EEG activity resembles that of wakefulness except that all physical movement other than coordinated eye movement is inhibited.

EEG sleep differences linked to depression tend to increase with age. Although such differences are seen in both sexes, they may be more pronounced in men. The more severe the sleep disturbance, the more severe other depressive symptoms are apt to be as well.

Good Night, Sleep Tight

When serious depression and chronic insomnia occur together, professional treatment is needed to relieve both problems. Good sleep habits, such as those described below, can help make the most of treatment and maintain better sleep for the long term.

Have a Soothing Bedtime Ritual
Set aside some time right before bed to do something relaxing. Soaking in a warm bath, doing some light reading, listening to soft music, or practicing meditation can help set aside the tensions of the day.

Keep a Regular Sleep Schedule
Go to bed and wake up around the same time every day. Stick to the schedule even on weekends.

Avoid Lying Awake in Bed
If you cannot fall asleep within 20 minutes, get up and do something relaxing until you feel sleepy. Otherwise, anxiety about not being able to sleep may make the insomnia worse.

Create a Restful Environment
Keep the bedroom dark, using light-blocking shades or a sleep mask, if necessary. Drown out other sounds with white noise, such as the sound of radio static or a fan. Set the thermostat at a comfortable temperature—not too hot, not too cold.

Use Sunlight to Advantage
Daylight is critical for regulating sleep patterns. Wake up with the sun, if possible, or use a very bright light in the morning. Get some natural light during the day.

Exercise Early in the Day
Daily physical activity promotes better sleep. But wind up the workout no less than five or six hours before bedtime.

Avoid Caffeine, Nicotine, and Alcohol
Nicotine and **caffeine** are stimulants that make it harder to sleep. Avoid **smoking**, and give caffeine at least eight hours to wear off. Also, avoid alcoholic drinks close to bedtime. **Alcohol** may cause drowsiness at first, but it interferes with deep sleep and causes middle-of-the-night waking.

Treatment Approaches.   There are several treatment options for depressed individuals who have insomnia. The most widely prescribed antidepressants are **selective serotonin reuptake inhibitors** (SSRIs). Many people who take SSRIs experience improvement in both their sleep and their overall mood. In some people, though, SSRIs can interfere with sleep.

For these individuals, an older group of medications, called **tricyclic antidepressants**, may be helpful. These medications are no longer first-choice treatments because they cause more side effects in general than SSRIs. But for people with insomnia, one of those side effects—a tendency to be sedating—can come in handy. Two other types of sleep-inducing antidepressants that may be helpful for insomnia are trazodone (from a group of medications known as **serotonin antagonist and reuptake inhibitors**) and mirtazapine (from a group of medications known as **noradrenergic and specific serotonergic antidepressants**).

In some cases, people may take both an SSRI and a low dose of a sedating antidepressant. In other cases, the SSRI may be combined with a short-acting sleeping pill. A final option is to combine an SSRI or psychotherapy for depression with behavioral treatment for insomnia. Strategies such as good sleep habits and **relaxation techniques** at bedtime can reduce anxiety over anticipated problems and encourage better sleep.

See also: Wake Therapy

Further Information.   American Academy of Sleep Medicine, One Westbrook Corporate Center, Suite 920, Westchester, IL 60154, (708) 492-0930, www.aasmnet.org, www.sleepeducation.com.

National Center on Sleep Disorders Research, 6701 Rockledge Drive, Bethesda, MD 20892, (301) 435-0199, www.nhlbi.nih.gov/about/ncsdr.

National Sleep Foundation, 1522 K Street N.W., Suite 500, Washington, DC 20005, (202) 347-3471, www.sleepfoundation.org.

Bibliography

American Psychiatric Association. *Diagnostic and Statistical Manual of Mental Disorders.* 4th ed., text rev. Washington, DC: American Psychiatric Association, 2000.

Ask the Sleep Expert: Sleep and Depression. National Sleep Depression, http://www.sleepfoundation.org/site/c.huIXKjM0IxF/b.2422615/k.238A/Ask_the_Sleep_Expert_Sleep_and_Depression.htm.

Buysse, Daniel J., Anne Germain, Eric A. Nofzinger, and David J. Kupfer. "Mood Disorders and Sleep." In *The American Psychiatric Publishing Textbook of Mood Disorders,* by Dan J. Stein, David J. Kupfer, and Alan F. Schatzberg, eds., 717–737. Washington, DC: American Psychiatric Publishing, 2006.

Depression and Sleep. National Sleep Foundation, http://www.sleepfoundation.org/site/c.huIXKjM0IxF/b.4815043/k.5315/Depression_and_Sleep.htm.

How to Get a Better Night's Sleep. Depression and Bipolar Support Alliance, http://www.dbsalliance.org/site/PageServer?pagename=about_sleep_better sleep.

Insomnia. National Heart, Lung and Blood Institute, March 2009, http://www.nhlbi.nih.gov/health/dci/Diseases/inso/inso_whatis.html.

Lamberg, Lynne. "Physicians Underprescribe Best Insomnia Treatments." *Psychiatric News* (September 2, 2005).

Your Guide to Healthy Sleep. National Heart, Lung and Blood Institute, November 2005, http://www.nhlbi.nih.gov/health/public/sleep/healthy_sleep.pdf.

SMOKING. Tobacco use is the leading preventable cause of disease, disability, and death in the United States. According to the Centers for Disease Control and Prevention, cigarette smoking accounts for more than 400,000 premature deaths each year—about one in five U.S. deaths. Smoking exacts an especially harsh toll among people with mental illness, who are almost twice as likely to smoke as the general population. Research has found a stronger link between **major depression** and heavy smoking, rather than lower levels of use.

The potential health consequences are severe. Smoking accounts for about one-third of all **cancer** cases, including 90 percent of lung cancers. It also increases the risk of **heart disease**, **stroke**, and chronic obstructive lung disease. In women of childbearing age, smoking is associated with infertility, premature delivery, stillbirth, and low-birth-weight babies. In women after menopause, it raises the risk of bone thinning and hip fracture.

Most people are aware by now that smoking is unhealthy. Yet once they pick up the habit, it can very tough to break. The reason: Tobacco contains nicotine, a highly addictive drug. Nicotine is readily absorbed into the bloodstream when a tobacco product is smoked or chewed. Once in the blood, it stimulates the adrenal glands to release epinephrine, a hormone that increases blood pressure, heart rate, and breathing rate.

Like cocaine and heroin, nicotine also increases levels of **dopamine**, a natural chemical that affects brain pathways involved in the experience of reward and pleasure. Certain other compounds in tobacco smoke, such as acetaldehyde, may heighten nicotine's effects in the brain.

For many smokers, long-lasting chemical changes in the brain caused by repeated nicotine exposure lead to addiction, a disease characterized by compulsive craving for and use of a drug despite negative consequences. When addicted smokers try to quit, they may have powerful cravings to smoke as well as withdrawal symptoms, such as irritability, trouble paying attention, sleep problems, and increased appetite. Quitting smoking also may worsen preexisting mental health problems, including depression. Because these effects are so unpleasant, it is tempting to resume smoking to relieve them, even though that only perpetuates the problem in the long run.

Fortunately, treatments such as counseling and medication can help people get through this difficult period and quit smoking for good. Studies show that the same types of treatments that are helpful for the general population can also help people with depression stub out their last cigarette.

The Depression Connection. The relationship between smoking and depression seems to be a two-way street. Depression may increase the risk of smoking, with people using nicotine in a misguided effort to take the edge off their mental pain. But smoking also may increase a person's susceptibility to depression, due to chemical changes in the brain caused by long-term nicotine exposure.

In addition to dopamine, nicotine may stimulate the release of two other brain chemicals, **serotonin** and **norepinephrine**. Current **antidepressants** work by boosting the activity of one or more of these three brain chemicals, and smoking may offer a temporary mood lift in much the same way. When people quit smoking, the enhanced release of these brain chemicals stops too, leaving them vulnerable to feelings of depression.

Smoking and depression also may be connected by common **genetic factors** that predispose people to both conditions. For instance, some studies indicate that variants of genes related to dopamine function affect the likelihood that a person with depression will smoke.

Behavioral factors may be important mediators. For example, people with depression may be at increased risk for **alcohol** abuse or alcoholism—and an alcohol problem may itself raise the risk of smoking.

Treatment Considerations.   Some smokers quit on their own, but many others need help. Research has shown that both telephone counseling programs and quit-smoking medications can double a person's chance of success.

Medications approved for this purpose include nicotine replacement products, such as gums and patches, as well as two non-nicotine medicines, bupropion and varenicline. Bupropion is sold as both an antidepressant (under the name Wellbutrin) and a quit-smoking medication (under the name Zyban). Due to its antidepressant action, it may be a good choice for many people with a history of depression who want to stop smoking.

In contrast, varenicline should be used with care. It has been linked to the development of a depressed mood, behavior changes, agitation, and suicidal thoughts and actions. Some people have reported these symptoms when they first began taking varenicline, and others developed them after several weeks of treatment or when they stopped the medication. It is difficult to tease out the side effects of varenicline from the withdrawal symptoms of giving up nicotine. But to be on the safe side, those who develop such symptoms while taking varenicline should stop the medication and call their doctor.

Incidentally, people who are already taking medication for another condition, such as an antidepressant for depression, should be sure to tell their doctor when they stop smoking. Some of the chemicals in tobacco affect how the body breaks down and uses various medications. Once people stop smoking, their medication dose may need to be adjusted.

Learning to Manage Stress.   Many smokers get into the habit of lighting up whenever they are feeling stressed, down, lonely, bored, or overwhelmed. During the transition to becoming ex-smokers, they need to find new ways of coping with stress and managing their feelings. A quit-smoking counselor may be able to offer general guidance on handling difficult situations or troubling emotions without turning to tobacco.

For those with full-fledged depression, though, more in-depth help might be needed. Antidepressants may be beneficial. In addition, **cognitive-behavioral therapy** (CBT), a form of **psychotherapy**, can help people learn to recognize and change the self-defeating thought and behavior patterns that are contributing to their depression. At the same time, CBT can help them learn new, more adaptive ways to manage stress and handle their feelings.

See also: Substance Abuse

Further Information.   American Cancer Society, 250 Williams Street N.W., Atlanta, GA 30303, (800) 227-2345, www.cancer.org.

American Legacy Foundation, 1724 Massachusetts Avenue N.W., Washington, DC 20036, (202) 454-5555, www.americanlegacy.org.

American Lung Association, 1301 Pennsylvania Avenue N.W., Suite 800, Washington, DC 20004, (800) 586-4872, www.lungusa.org, www.freedomfromsmoking.org.

Centers for Disease Control and Prevention, 1600 Clifton Road, Atlanta, GA 30333, (800) 232-4636, www.cdc.gov/tobacco.

National Cancer Institute, 6116 Executive Boulevard, Room 3036A, Bethesda, MD 20892, (877) 448-7848, (800) 784-8669, www.cancer.gov, 1800quitnow.cancer.gov, www.smokefree.gov.

National Institute on Drug Abuse, 6001 Executive Boulevard, Room 5213, Bethesda, MD 20892, (301) 443-1124, smoking.drugabuse.gov.

Bibliography

Dierker, Lisa C., Shelli Avenevoli, Marilyn Stolar, and K. R. Merikangas. "Smoking and Depression: An Examination of Mechanisms of Comorbidity." *American Journal of Psychiatry* 159 (2002): 947–953.

Double Your Chances of Quitting Smoking. American Cancer Society, November 14, 2008, http://www.cancer.org/docroot/PED/content/PED_10_3x_Double_Your_Chances.asp.

Hall, Sharon M., Janice Y. Tsoh, Judith J. Prochaska, Stuart Eisendrath, Joseph S. Rossi, Colleen A. Redding, et al. "Treatment for Cigarette Smoking Among Depressed Mental Health Outpatients: A Randomized Clinical Trial." *American Journal of Public Health* 96 (2006): 1808–1814.

Kern, Jennifer A. *Tobacco Use and Mental Health.* Mayo Clinic, November 19, 2008, http://www.mayoclinic.com/health/quit-smoking-blog/MY00401.

Medication Guide: Chantix. Pfizer, May 2008, http://www.fda.gov/CDER/Offices/ODS/MG/ChantixMG.pdf.

NIDA InfoFacts: Cigarettes and Other Tobacco Products. National Institute on Drug Abuse, September 2008. http://www.drugabuse.gov/infofacts/tobacco.html.

Quitting Tobacco: Handling Depression . . . without Smoking. National Cancer Institute, November 8, 2004, http://www.cancer.gov/cancertopics/factsheet/Tobacco/depression.

Smoking and Tobacco Use: Fact Sheet—Health Effects of Cigarette Smoking. Centers for Disease Control and Prevention, January 2008, http://www.cdc.gov/tobacco/data_statistics/fact_sheets/health_effects/health_effects.htm.

Tobacco/Nicotine. National Institute on Drug Abuse, http://www.drugabuse.gov/DrugPages/Nicotine.html.

Ziedonis, Douglas, Brian Hitsman, Jean C. Beckham, Michael Zvolensky, Lawrence E. Adler, Janet Audrain-McGovern, et al. "Tobacco Use and Cessation in Psychiatric Disorders: National Institute of Mental Health Report." *Nicotine and Tobacco Research* 10 (2008): 1691–1715.

SOCIAL SUPPORT. Social support refers to caring, comfort, and assistance offered by others. This type of emotional and practical support helps an individual cope with stressful situations and enjoy life to the utmost. Sources of interpersonal support include family, friends, neighbors, coworkers, helping professionals, and religious advisors. For those seeking to expand their social network further, **support groups** offer another valuable resource.

Not all relationships are created equal, however. Beneficial relationships help an individual work through personal problems, such as the breakup of a relationship, the loss of a job, or a serious illness. Others are there to offer advice, assistance, or a sympathetic ear. By decreasing **stress**, such relationships may prevent or reduce depression. By helping the person feel accepted and valued, they also may boost self-esteem.

In contrast, deleterious relationships actually do more harm than good, reinforcing thoughts of failure, hopelessness, and worthlessness. In such cases, others may be harshly critical or judgmental, or they may be overprotective or pessimistic themselves. By adding to the person's stress, such relationships may increase the risk of developing depression or make existing symptoms worse.

Some supporters have an especially powerful impact. For adults, supportive spouses can make a big difference. Research has shown that married individuals are less likely to be depressed than their separated, divorced, or widowed counterparts. For youngsters, parents are a major influence. A study of nearly 500 adolescent girls found that lack of parental support was predictive of future depression, but lack of peer support was not.

Social Isolation and Loneliness. Then there are individuals who lack enough social connections of any kind. Social isolation and loneliness are also very stressful, so it comes as no surprise that they are strong predictors of depression. A study of almost 1,300 Dublin residents, ages 65 and older, found that about a third described themselves as lonely, and about the same fraction also said they lacked a broad-based social network. Each of these factors was associated with a greater risk of depression. Between them, the two factors contributed to 70 percent of depression in the group.

Although this study focused on **older adults** in Ireland, other research has shown that the link between loneliness and depression cuts across age and cultural divides. Loneliness often goes along with low social support and high stress, and together these factors underlie many, if not most, cases of depression.

Once a person is depressed, withdrawal from others and loss of interest in social activities often lead to even greater isolation. It is a vicious cycle that can feed a sense of hopelessness and despair. To break this cycle, **psychotherapy** often includes training in social skills or discussion about social challenges. **Antidepressants** also can help people with depression regain the motivation and energy to become more socially involved.

See also: Relationship Issues

Bibliography

Cacioppo, John T., Mary Elizabeth Hughes, Linda J. Waite, Louise C. Hawkley, and Ronald A. Thisted. "Loneliness as a Specific Risk Factor for Depressive Symptoms: Cross-Sectional and Longitudinal Analyses." *Psychology and Aging* 21 (2006): 140–151.

Golden, Jeannette, Ronán M. Conroy, Irene Bruce, Aisling Denihan, Elaine Greene, Michael Kirby, et al. "Loneliness, Social Support Networks, Mood and Wellbeing in Community-Dwelling Elderly." *International Journal of Geriatric Psychiatry* (March 9, 2009): e-publication ahead of print.

Stice, Eric, Jennifer Ragan, and Patrick Randall. "Prospective Relations Between Social Support and Depression: Differential Direction of Effects for Parent and Peer Support?" *Journal of Abnormal Psychology* 113 (2004): 155–159.

Symister, Petra, and Ronald Friend. "The Influence of Social Support and Problematic Support on Optimism and Depression in Chronic Illness: A Prospective Study Evaluating Self-Esteem as a Mediator." *Health Psychology* 22 (2003): 123–129.

Williams, David R., and Harold W. Neighbors. "Social Perspectives on Mood Disorders." Nunes, Edward, Eric Rubin, Kenneth Carpenter, and Deborah Hasin. "Mood Disorders and Substance Use." In *The American Psychiatric Publishing Textbook of Mood Disorders,* by Dan J. Stein, David J. Kupfer, and Alan F. Schatzberg, eds., 145–158. Washington, DC: American Psychiatric Publishing, 2006.

SOCIOECONOMIC STATUS. Socioeconomic status (SES) refers to an individual's position on various social and economic measures, such as income, years of education, type of occupation, and place of residence. Low SES is associated with a higher-than-average risk of developing depression. Much of the increased risk may be due to the **stress** of living with financial pressure, lack of education, unemployment, and/or a poor standard of living.

One study of more than 1,000 Californians looked at income in 1965, 1974, and 1983, as well as mental health in 1994. Economic hardship was defined as a total household income of less than twice the federal poverty level. Individuals who experienced economic hardship at the first three study points had triple the rate of **clinical depression** at the last point, compared to those who had not suffered hardship.

Some of the heightened risk associated with low SES also may be attributable to decreased **social support**. A case in point: The risk of depression is greater among single mothers than married mothers, which may in part reflect having fewer financial and social resources.

In addition, people with fewer financial resources may not have access to high-quality mental health care. This makes it less likely that depression will be diagnosed promptly and treated appropriately.

The relationship between low SES and depression cuts both ways, however. Depression may contribute to a lower SES by making it harder to hold down a job or get along well in society. For depressed individuals who are also at a socioeconomic disadvantage, any lasting solution may need to address both their illness and their social and financial challenges.

See also: Environmental Factors

Bibliography

Beach, Steven R. H., Deborah J. Jones, and Kameron J. Franklin. "Marital, Family, and Interpersonal Therapies for Depression in Adults." In *Handbook of Depression.* 2nd ed., by Ian H. Gotlib and Constance L. Hammen, eds., 624–641. New York: Guilford Press, 2009.

Lynch, John W., George A. Kaplan, and Sarah J. Shema. "Cumulative Impact of Sustained Economic Hardship on Physical, Cognitive, Psychological, and Social Functioning." *New England Journal of Medicine* 337 (1997): 1889–1895.

Williams, David R., and Harold W. Neighbors. "Social Perspectives on Mood Disorders." Nunes, Edward, Eric Rubin, Kenneth Carpenter, and Deborah Hasin. "Mood Disorders and Substance Use." In *The American Psychiatric Publishing Textbook of Mood Disorders,* by Dan J. Stein, David J. Kupfer, and Alan F. Schatzberg, eds., 145–158. Washington, DC: American Psychiatric Publishing, 2006.

SPIRITUALITY AND RELIGION.   Spirituality refers to a sense of purpose and meaning in life that extends beyond material values and acknowledges the existence of a power greater than the individual self. Spiritual awareness may be expressed in many ways, including religion—a formal system of spiritual beliefs, practices, and rituals. Numerous studies have found a link between higher levels of spiritual or religious involvement and lower levels of depressive symptoms.

For example, one study included 130 **older adults** treated for **major depression**. The more often they took part in religious prayer or **meditation**, the less severe their hopelessness and depression tended to be. Another study included 131 rural, low-income mothers. The stronger their religious beliefs and greater their involvement in religious activities, the fewer symptoms of depression they were apt to have.

An analysis of 147 separate studies found that the protective nature of spirituality and religion cut across gender, age, and ethnic lines. The association between religious involvement and depression was particularly strong in people undergoing **stress** due to recent life events. Although stressful events can trigger or worsen depression in vulnerable individuals, religion may provide a buffer against such effects.

The Depression Connection.   There are several possible explanations for how spirituality and religion might be protective. Spiritual beliefs may inspire hope for the future and a positive view of the world—attitudes that are at odds with the hopelessness and negativity of a depressed mood. Some spiritual practices—such as prayer and meditation—also may promote relaxation.

Specific beliefs may have special relevance when people are in distress. For example, an altruistic attitude may help spiritually oriented individuals focus on others during times of crisis, reducing the self-focused **rumination** that is characteristic of depression. Beliefs about finding meaning in suffering may help people cope with tragedy or illness, and beliefs about an afterlife may help people come to terms with **grief**.

Spiritual Ennui

These days, depression is regarded as a brain disease, not a moral failing. For some early Christian theologians, however, a depression-like state was considered a deadly sin, especially when it distracted monks from their spiritual duties. The term *acedia* (also spelled *accidia*) referred to a state of spiritual malaise that involved despondency, discouragement, and disinterest. Scythian monk John Cassian (ca. 360–435) discussed acedia as a vice afflicting ascetics leading a solitary existence in the fifth century, but it could be argued that the problem of spiritual ennui is both universal and timeless.

Cassian's acedia is a specifically spiritual problem; it is not the same thing as depression, which is a mental disorder. Yet the similarities are strong enough that it is easy to see how the two could have become confused over the centuries, contributing to the notion of depression as a character flaw or moral failing.

Feeling part of a greater whole may help people realize that they are not personally responsible for everything bad that happens. A focus on forgiveness also may promote self-acceptance. These attitudes run counter to the **pessimism** and self-blame of depression.

People who are part of a religious community may reap the rewards of a large, close-knit social network. Studies have shown that highly religious individuals, compared to their less religious counterparts, also are more likely to be married and have stable family relationships—valuable sources of **social support** in stressful times. Plus, due to religious strictures, they may be less likely to engage in **substance abuse** when under stress, a choice that further reduces the risk for depression and **suicide**.

Toward Spiritual Wellness. Spiritual well-being rests in a positive relationship with oneself, other people, and the world as a whole. To develop greater self-understanding and draw on inner resources, many people meditate or keep a journal. To explore different spiritual paths, people often talk to others they admire, read inspirational books, or attend different types of religious services.

Volunteering is one way to reach out to others and the community at large. Research has shown that it also may promote better mental health and reduce the risk of depression. In addition, some individuals make a conscious choice to cultivate personal qualities such as altruism, compassion, optimism, gratitude, and forgiveness—all qualities associated with psychological well-being.

For those drowning in depression, however, it may not be that simple. It is very difficult to be a positive force in the world when awash in negative thoughts and feelings. Treatment for depression may help people recover the ability to nurture their own spirituality and connect with others in a life-affirming way.

See also: Pastoral Counselor

Further Information. Beliefnet, www.beliefnet.com.

Society for Spirituality, Theology and Health, Box 3825 Duke University Medical Center, Busse Building, Suite 0507, Durham, NC 27710, (919) 660-7556, www.societysth.org.

Bibliography

Ahern, Melissa M., and Michael Hendryx. "Community Participation and the Emergence of Late-Life Depressive Symptoms: Differences Between Women and Men." *Journal of Women's Health* 17 (2008): 1463–1470.

Altschule, Mark D. "Acedia: Its Evolution From Deadly Sin to Psychiatri Syndrome." *British Journal of Psychiatry* 111 (1965): 117–119.

Cruz, Mario, Richard Schulz, Harold A. Pincus, Patricia R. Houck, Salem Bensasi, and Charles F. Reynolds III. "The Association of Public and Private Religious Involvement with Severity of Depression and Hopelessness in Older Adults Treated for Major Depression." *American Journal of Geriatric Psychiatry* 17 (2009): 503–507.

Garrison, M. E., L. D. Marks, F. C. Lawrence, and B. Braun. "Religious Beliefs, Faith Community Involvement and Depression: A Study of Rural, Low-Income Mothers." *Women and Health* 40 (2004): 51–62.

Radden, Jennifer, ed. *The Nature of Melancholy: From Aristotle to Kristeva.* New York: Oxford University Press, 2000.

Smith, Timothy B., Michael E. McCullough, and Justin Poll. "Religiousness and Depression: Evidence for a Main Effect and the Moderating Influence of Stressful Life Events." *Psychological Bulletin* 129 (2003): 614–636.

Spirituality and Prayer. American Cancer Society, November 1, 2008, http://www.cancer.org/docroot/ETO/content/ETO_5_3X_Spirituality_and_Prayer.asp.

Spirituality and Stress Relief: Make the Connection. Mayo Clinic, July 23, 2008, http://www.mayoclinic.com/health/stress-relief/SR00035.

Williams, David R., and Harold W. Neighbors. "Social Perspectives on Mood Disorders." In *The American Psychiatric Publishing Textbook of Mood Disorders,* by Dan J. Stein, David J. Kupfer, and Alan F. Schatzberg, eds., 145–158. Washington, DC: American Psychiatric Publishing, 2006.

STIGMA.   Stigma refers to the negative attitude of society toward a personal characteristic that may be regarded as a flaw. It not uncommonly leads to prejudice and discrimination. Stigma attached to depression seems to be lessening somewhat, but it is still quite common. Unfortunately, fear of social disapproval may discourage some people with depression from seeking the treatment they need.

Great strides have been made in understanding depression in recent years. A vast body of scientific evidence now shows that it is rooted in a malfunctioning brain, not unlike many other **neurological disorders**. But although brain disorders such as **Alzheimer's disease**, **Parkinson's disease**, and **stroke** may be viewed with compassion, a **mental illness** such as depression is too often seen as a sign of personal weakness.

The media help perpetuate negative images of depression. For example, television news programs and newspapers may stress a history of mental illness in the background of violent criminals, even when there is no reason to believe the two things are connected. Comedians sometimes make fun of people with mental illness, and advertisers may present exaggerated images of mental illness to help sell their products.

Steps to Stop Stigma.   Ironically, the media are also powerful partners for eradicating stigma. Education is the antidote to inaccurate beliefs and unfair behavior. By presenting depression as just another illness—and a very common and treatable one at that—the media can have a major impact on public opinion.

Individuals with depression can be influential ambassadors for change as well. By sharing their own experiences, they let others know that depression is nothing to be embarrassed about. By spreading the truth about depression, they help counter the false and stigmatizing beliefs of others, which are very often rooted in ignorance rather than maliciousness.

Ultimately, the responsibility for stamping out stigma is shared by family, friends, coworkers, acquaintances—in short, each member of society. By learning about depression and passing the knowledge along, we can all help replace fear and rejection with understanding and respect.

Further Information. Active Minds, 2647 Connecticut Avenue N.W., Suite 200, Washington, DC 20008, (202) 332-9595, www.activeminds.org.

National Alliance on Mental Illness StigmaBusters, 2107 Wilson Boulevard, Suite 300, Arlington, VA 22201, (800) 950-6264, www.nami.org/stigma.

National Mental Health Awareness Campaign, P.O. Box 491608, Los Angeles, CA 90049, (800) 273-8255, www.nostigma.org.

SAMHSA Resource Center to Promote Acceptance, Dignity and Social Inclusion Associated with Mental Health, Substance Abuse and Mental Health Services Administration, 11420 Rockville Pike, Rockville, MD 20852, (800) 540-0320, www.stopstigma .samhsa.gov.

Bibliography

1 in 5: Overcoming the Stigma of Mental Illness. Saginaw County Community Mental Health Authority, http://www.sccmha.org/Anti-Stigma/SCCMHA%201in5_WBRG.pdf.

Stigma. National Mental Health Awareness Campaign, http://www.nostigma.org/stigma.php.

Stigma: Building Awareness and Understanding. Mental Health America, http://www.nmha.org/go/ information/get-info/stigma.

ST. JOHN'S WORT.   St. John's wort (*Hypericum perforatum*) is an herb that has been used for centuries to treat both psychological and physical disorders. In ancient times, herbalists used St. John's wort as a sedative, a treatment for malaria, and a balm for burns, wounds, and bug bites. Today the herb is widely prescribed as an antidepressant in Germany. In the United States, where St. John's wort is sold as a dietary supplement rather than a prescription medicine, it is one of the most popular **herbal remedies** for depression.

St. John's wort contains several chemical compounds, including hypericin and hyperforin, which may contribute to its effects. Scientists do not yet fully understand how these compounds affect the brain. However, preliminary studies suggest that St. John's wort might inhibit nerve cells from reabsorbing a brain chemical called **serotonin**. This chemical plays a major role in mood, and it also helps regulate sleep, appetite, and sexual drive.

Benefits for Depression.   Unlike many herbal remedies, St. John's wort has been investigated in well-controlled studies. However, results have been mixed in people who meet the criteria for **major depression**, which involves being in a low mood nearly all the time and/or losing interest or enjoyment in almost everything. For major depression to be diagnosed, these feelings must last for at least two weeks, be associated with several other symptoms, and lead to significant impairment in the ability to function in everyday life.

In a study sponsored by the National Institutes of Health, 340 adults with moderately severe major depression were randomly assigned to receive St. John's wort, an antidepressant, or a placebo (dummy pill) for eight weeks. The study found that St. John's wort was no more effective than the placebo. But the antidepressant also showed little difference from the placebo, suggesting that the failure to find an effect might have been partly due to problems with the study design.

In contrast, a six-week study of 332 people in Germany found that a particular extract of St. John's wort was more effective as a treatment for mild to moderate major depression than a placebo. This held true whether people took 600 mg daily in one dose or 1200 mg daily divided into two doses. One caveat: Products sold as herbal supplements in the United States may vary considerably in their strength and quality, so it is unclear whether the results from any given study apply to what is available in stores.

It is possible that St. John's wort might be more effective as a treatment for **minor depression**, a term sometimes used to describe an episode that is similar to major depression but involves fewer symptoms and less impairment in day-to-day functioning. Research is underway to test this possibility. For now, the best evidence suggests that St. John's wort works better than a placebo and about as well as **antidepressants** for treating relatively mild depressive symptoms. There is no evidence that the herb alone is sufficient for treating more severe depression.

St. John's Wort Supplements. St. John's wort is a long-lived plant with yellow flowers. Extracts from the plant are sold in capsule, tablet, tea, and liquid concentrate form. Many products are standardized to contain 0.3% hypericin or 2% to 5% hyperforin. But in fact, there is often wide variability in hypericin and hyperforin content from brand to brand, and within the same brand, from batch to batch.

The best dosage has yet to be determined. For adults, a starting dose of 900 mg daily (divided into three doses of 300 mg each) has sometimes been used. After the initial period, a dose of 300 mg to 600 mg daily may be adequate for maintenance, but this has not been well studied.

Side Effects and Cautions. Possible side effects of St. John's wort include dry mouth, dizziness, diarrhea, nausea, fatigue, and increased sensitivity to sunlight. When combined with certain antidepressants, St. John's wort may limit the antidepressant's effectiveness or increase side effects. The herb also may interact with other medications, including birth control pills, cyclosporine, digoxin, warfarin, and certain cancer medicines.

As with any herbal supplement, it is wise to talk to a health care provider before taking St. John's wort, especially when combining it with medication. Depression can get worse if not adequately treated, so anyone who develops symptoms that cause serious distress or interfere with the ability to get along in daily life should seek professional help rather than relying on self-care alone.

See also: Dietary Supplements

Bibliography

Hypericum Depression Trial Study Group. "Effect of *Hypericum perforatum* (St. John's Wort) in Major Depressive Disorder: A Randomized Controlled Trial." *JAMA* 287 (2002): 1807–1814.

Kasper, Siegfried, Ion-George Angheilescu, Armin Szegedi, Angelika Dienel, and Meinhard Kieser. "Superior Efficacy of St. John's Wort Extract WS 5570 Compared to Placebo in Patients with Major Depression: A Randomized, Double-Blind, Placebo-Controlled, Multi-center Trial. *BMC Medicine* 4 (2006): 14.

Mulrow, Linde K., M. Berner, and M. Egger. "St. John's Wort for Depression (Review)." *Cochrane Database of Systematic Reviews* 2 (2005): art. no. CD000448.

Natural Standard Research Collaboration. *St. John's Wort (Hypericum perforatum L.).* Mayo Clinic, May 1, 2006, http://www.mayoclinic.com/health/st-johns-wort/NS_patient-stjohnswort.

St. John's Wort and Depression. National Center for Complementary and Alternative Medicine, January 10, 2008, http://nccam.nih.gov/health/stjohnswort/sjwataglance.htm.

STRESS. Stress is the body's automatic, protective response to a perceived threat or challenge—any situation that requires a sudden behavioral adjustment. On a physiological level, stress involves changes in nearly every system of the body. On a psychological level, stress involves a heightened state of alertness, fear, or anxiety. Although the right amount of stress at the right time is helpful, stress that is excessive or prolonged can take a harsh toll on physical and mental well-being. Among other harmful effects, it may trigger or worsen depression.

There are two main types of stress: acute and chronic. Acute stress is immediate and intense—and sometimes exhilarating. It is the reaction to a current situation that is seen as threatening, frightening, or challenging. Examples include a big exam, fender bender, or black diamond ski run. Chronic stress stems from long-term exposure to acute stress. It is more subtle than acute stress, but also more prolonged. Examples include marital problems, financial woes, or medical illnesses that last for weeks, months, or years. Over time, chronic stress can gradually chip away at a person's physical and psychological health.

Warning Signs of Chronic Stress

Chronic stress can have wide-ranging effects on your body, mind, and behavior. Below are some common warning signs. Keep in mind that these symptoms can have other causes, too, including depression and other treatable illnesses. Talk to a health care provider if you develop new symptoms or if you have symptoms that are bad enough to cause serious distress or disrupt your daily life.

Physical Effects	Mental and Emotional Effects	Behavioral Effects
Chest pain	Anxiety	Accident proneness
Constipation or diarrhea	Boredom	Alcohol or drug abuse
Fatigue	Concentration issues	Chain smoking
Headaches	Forgetfulness	Crying spells
Muscle aches	Hopelessness	Impatient behavior
Sexual problems	Indecisiveness	Overeating
Skin breakouts	Insecurity	Productivity decline
Sleep problems	Irritability	Relationship conflicts
Upset stomach	Job burnout	Social isolation
Weight gain or loss	Pessimism	Temper outbursts

Two Physiological Pathways. When a person experiences stress, two different communication systems in the body are activated: the sympathetic-adrenal medullary (SAM) system and the hypothalamic-pituitary-adrenal (HPA) axis.

SAM System. This pathway is the first line of defense in an emergency. It works through the sympathetic **nervous system**—the branch of the nervous system that mobilizes the body's energy and marshals its resources for an immediate response. The sympathetic nervous system stimulates the adrenal medulla, the inner part of the adrenal glands, to release a hormone called epinephrine (also known as adrenaline). Meanwhile, another hormone called **norepinephrine** (also known as noradrenaline) is secreted by the adrenal medulla and sympathetic nerve endings.

These **hormones** activate receptors in blood vessels and other structures, preparing the heart and muscles for action. Among other effects, they increase the heart rate, strengthen the force of heart contractions, and raise the level of glucose (blood sugar). SAM hormones start revving up the body in a matter of seconds.

HPA Axis. This pathway originates in part of the brain called the **hypothalamus**, which serves as a joint command center for the nervous system and **endocrine system**. In a stressful situation, the hypothalamus secretes **corticotropin-releasing hormone** (CRH). This hormone travels to the pituitary gland, where it triggers the release of adrenocorticotropic hormone (ACTH). ACTH, in turns, travels to the adrenal cortex, the outer part of the adrenal glands, where it triggers the release of a powerful hormone called **cortisol**. Some people with depression produce too much CRH and cortisol. The pituitary gland

and adrenal cortex are sometimes enlarged as well, another sign of overactivity in the HPA system.

Cortisol belongs to the family of hormones called glucocorticoids, so named because they affect glucose metabolism. Although SAM hormones start acting within seconds, glucocorticoids kick in over a period of minutes to hours. At first, they mobilize glucose, the body's main source of energy, moving it

---

The Serotonin Connection

Serotonin is a chemical messenger in the brain that is thought to play an important role in depression. Glucocorticoids interact with serotonin **receptors**, specialized sites on brain cells that receive and react to the chemical's messages. In rats, chronic stress and high levels of glucocorticoids have been shown to produce changes in certain serotonin receptors. Researchers have found similar changes in the brains of humans who died by **suicide** or suffered from diseases that cause overproduction of stress hormones.

---

from storage sites into the bloodstream. The hormones also increase cardiovascular tone to ready the body for action, and they delay long-term body processes that are not essential in a crisis, such as digestion, growth, and reproduction. Later, glucocorticoids help the body recover from stress and return to its normal state. At this point, they promote glucose replenishment and efficient cardiovascular function.

Overactive Stress Response. The body's stress system is designed to keep things on an even keel most of the time, only shifting into high gear when it is really necessary. But some people have an overactive stress response that causes them to react strongly to the slightest provocation. Dysfunction in genes controlling the stress response may be one source of this problem. In addition, an exaggerated stress response in adulthood may be rooted in extreme stress during early childhood, when critical brain pathways are still developing.

The latter connection could help explain why children who have experienced severe stress or trauma—such as physical or sexual abuse or the loss of a parent—are at increased risk for depression as adults. The early life stress may shape their developing nervous system in a way that leaves them super-sensitive to even mild threats or minor challenges. Over time, the strain of living in an exaggerated state of high alert may lead to the development of depression.

See also: Diathesis-Stress Model; Hypothalamic-Pituitary-Adrenal Axis; Relaxation Techniques; Serotonin Transporter Gene; Stress Management

Further Information. American Institute of Stress, 124 Park Avenue, Yonkers, NY 10703, (914) 963-1200, www.stress.org.

Bibliography

Andrews, Linda Wasmer. *Stress Control for Peace of Mind.* New York: Main Street, 2005.
Belmaker, R. H., and Galila Agam. "Major Depressive Disorder." *New England Journal of Medicine* 358 (2008): 55–68.
Gillespie, Charles F., and Charles B. Nemeroff. "Hypercortisolemia and Depression." *Psychosomatic Medicine* 67 (2005): S26-S28.
Heim, Christine, D. Jeffrey Newport, Stacey Heit, Yolanda P. Graham, Molly Wilcox, Robert Bonsall, et al. "Pituitary-Adrenal and Autonomic Responses to Stress in Women After Sexual and Physical Abuse in Childhood." *JAMA* 284 (2000): 592–597.

Serotonin and Other Molecules Involved in Depression: Advanced. Canadian Institute of Neurosciences, Mental Health and Addiction, http://thebrain.mcgill.ca/flash/a/a_08/a_08_m/a_08_m_dep/a_08_m_dep.html.

Society for Neuroscience. *Brain Facts: A Primer on the Brain and Nervous System.* 6th ed. Washington, DC: Society for Neuroscience, 2008.

Stress Management: Understand Your Sources of Stress. Mayo Clinic, July 23, 2008, http://www.mayoclinic.com/health/stress-management/SR00031.

Stress: Win Control Over the Stress in Your Life. Mayo Clinic, September 12, 2008, http://www.mayoclinic.com/health/stress/SR00001.

The Stress Response. Benson-Henry Institute for Mind Body Medicine, 2006, http://www.mbmi.org/basics/whatis_stress_response.asp.

STRESS MANAGEMENT.   Stress management refers to a group of strategies that help prevent or reduce the body's **stress** response. This response makes it possible to react quickly to a perceived threat or challenge—in short, any situation that requires a sudden behavioral adjustment. In the right amount and at the right time, stress is a helpful, healthful thing. But when stress is excessive or prolonged, the strain can take a toll on the mind and body. Among other adverse effects, stress may trigger or worsen depression, so developing stress management skills may help decrease depressive symptoms as well.

Stress management training is often incorporated into **cognitive-behavioral therapy**. It also may be offered by itself to help prevent or relieve stress, depression, and other stress-related problems. **Relaxation techniques**, such as **meditation** or progressive muscle relaxation, are core components of most stress management programs. Other strategies that may be taught include monitoring and changing stressful thoughts, scheduling pleasant activities, seeking **social support**, reorganizing work demands, managing time efficiently, and adopting a healthy lifestyle.

Education about stress is another critical component of most stress management programs. Participants learn how to identify their personal sources of stress. Some sources can be avoided, and others can be controlled more effectively. In addition, participants learn how to recognize the physiological and psychological signs that they are becoming stressed out, so they can take steps to keep the stress response in check.

Research shows that stress management training may help reduce depressive symptoms in people at high risk for depression. One study included 100 women who had recently been diagnosed with early-stage breast cancer. Half were randomly chosen to take part in a 10-week stress management program, in which women met as a group to learn skills for coping with cancer-related stress. Participation in the program reduced the rate of moderate depression. It also boosted optimism and increased women's belief that they had gotten something positive from the cancer experience.

See also: Behavioral Therapy

Further Information.   Benson-Henry Institute for Mind Body Medicine, 151 Merrimac Street, Boston, MA 02114, (617) 643-6090, www.mbmi.org.

Center for Mindfulness in Medicine, Health Care, and Society, University of Massachusetts Medical School, 55 Lake Avenue North, Worcester, MA 01655, (508) 856-2656, www.umassmed.edu/Content.aspx?id=41252.

Bibliography

Andrews, Linda Wasmer. *Stress Control for Peace of Mind.* New York: Main Street, 2005.

Antoni, Michael H. *Stress Management Intervention for Women with Breast Cancer.* Washington, DC: American Psychological Association, 2003.

Antoni, Michael H., Jessica M. Lehman, Kristin M. Kilbourn, Amy E. Boyers, Jenifer L. Culver, Susan M. Alferi, et al. "Cognitive-Behavioral Stress Management Intervention Decreases the Prevalence of Depression and Enhances Benefit Finding Among Women Under Treatment for Early-Stage Breast Cancer." *Health Psychology* 20 (2001): 20–32.

STROKE. A stroke occurs when blood flow to part of the brain is interrupted, depriving brain tissue of vital oxygen and nutrients. In the most common type of stroke, a blood vessel in the brain is blocked by a clot. In another type, a blood vessel breaks and bleeds into the brain. Depending on which part of the brain is affected, damage caused by a stroke can lead to emotional problems, paralysis, mental impairment, or speech difficulties.

About one-third of stroke survivors have serious problems with depressive symptoms at some point after their stroke. In part, this may be a psychological reaction. A stroke can cause disabilities that range from mild to severe and are sometimes permanent. The **stress** produced by such losses may trigger or worsen depression in susceptible individuals.

Physiological factors related to the brain injury may play a role as well. Post-stroke changes in brain chemicals may interfere with the ability to feel positive emotions. Research also indicates that post-stroke depression is related to stroke damage in particular areas of the brain. In fact, this research offers some of the most compelling evidence to date for depression that is the direct physiological result of a general illness.

Left untreated, depression is associated with increased physical and mental impairment. Successful rehabilitation after a stroke often calls for focused, repetitive practice of skills, and depression makes it hard to muster up the necessary concentration and motivation. On the other hand, when stroke survivors receive treatment for their depression, it may not only lift their mood, but also boost their mental and physical recovery.

Diagnostic Challenges. Unfortunately, post-stroke depression often goes undiagnosed and untreated. Survivors and even doctors may dismiss the symptoms of depression as a "normal" response to the aftermath of a stroke. To complicate matters further, some stroke survivors have speech problems that make it hard for them to communicate about how they feel.

The symptoms of post-stroke depression are the same as those for any **major depression**. Some of the symptoms—such as slowed-down movements and speech, loss of interest, lack of appetite, and trouble sleeping—can result from the stroke itself. Among health care professionals, there is ongoing debate about how much weight to give such symptoms when diagnosing depression.

Treatment Considerations. Each year in the United States, about 780,000 strokes occur, causing more serious long-term disability than any other disease. During the recovery period afterward, rehabilitation can help survivors relearn lost skills as well as learn new ways to compensate for any residual disabilities. The components of a rehab program vary depending on the skills affected. Members of the rehab team may include a rehabilitation doctor, nurse, dietitian, physical therapist, occupational therapist, speech therapist, social worker and psychiatrist, psychologist, or counselor.

Antidepressants and **psychotherapy** are the mainstays of treatment for depression. In people who have suffered a stroke, the strongest evidence is for the benefits of antidepressant medication. Some doctors are reluctant to prescribe antidepressants to stroke survivors because of concerns about possible side effects. With careful medical monitoring, though, the benefits of treating depression generally outweigh the risks and lead to better overall recovery.

Focus on Prevention

Because depression is so common in the months right after a stroke, researchers have looked for ways to stop the problem before it starts. Some have tried giving antidepressants or psychotherapy to stroke survivors right away, without waiting for depressive symptoms to appear. The idea is that by keeping depression from occurring in the first place, people can better focus on their post-stroke recovery. But a recent review of the scientific literature found only limited evidence that psychotherapy might help in this regard, and no evidence to justify the preventive use of antidepressants. More research is needed, however, because the review was hampered by a dearth of well-designed studies.

See also: Folate; Heart Disease; Mood Disorder Due to a General Medical Condition; Neurological Disorders; Physical Illness; Vitamin B12

Further Information. American Stroke Association, 7272 Greenville Avenue, Dallas, TX 75231, (888) 478-7653, www.strokeassociation.org.

National Institute of Neurological Disorders and Stroke, P.O. Box 5801, Bethesda, MD 20824, (800) 352-9424, www.ninds.nih.gov.

National Stroke Association, 9707 E. Easter Lane, Building B, Centennial, CO 80112, (800) 787-6537, www.stroke.org.

Bibliography

American Heart Association. *Heart Disease and Stroke Statistics.* Dallas, TX: American Heart Association, 2008.

Boland, Robert. "Depression in Medical Illness (Secondary Depression)." In *The American Psychiatric Publishing Textbook of Mood Disorders,* by Dan J. Stein, David J. Kupfer, and Alan F. Schatzberg, eds., 639–652. Washington, DC: American Psychiatric Publishing, 2006.

Chemerinski, Eran, and Steven R. Levine. "Neuropsychiatric Disorders Following Vascular Brain Injury." *Mount Sinai Journal of Medicine* 73 (2006): 1006–1014.

Depression Trumps Recovery. American Stroke Association, http://www.strokeassociation.org/presenter.jhtml?identifier=3027315.

Hackett, Maree L., Chaturangi Yapa, Varsha Parag, and Craig S. Anderson. "Frequency of Depression After Stroke: A Systematic Review of Observational Studies." *Stroke* 36 (2005): 1330–1340.

Hackett, Maree L., Craig S. Anderson, Allan House, and Christina Halteh. "Interventions for Preventing Depression After Stroke." *Cochrane Database of Systematic Reviews* 3 (2008): art no. CD003689.

Hackett, Maree L., Craig S. Anderson, Allan House, and Jun Xia. "Interventions for Treating Depression After Stroke." *Cochrane Database of Systematic Reviews* 4 (2008): art. no. CD003437.

Kimura, Mahito, Robert G. Robinson, and James T. Kosier. "Treatment of Cognitive Impairment After Poststroke Depression: A Double-Blind Treatment Trial." *Stroke* 31 (2000): 1482–1486.

Narushima, K., J. T. Kosier, and R. G. Robinson. "A Reappraisal of Poststroke Depression, Intra- and Inter-hemispheric Lesion Location Using Meta-analysis." *Journal of Neuropsychiatry and Clinical Neuroscience* 15 (2003): 422–430.

NINDS Stroke Information Page. National Institute of Neurological Disorders and Stroke, September 22, 2008, http://www.ninds.nih.gov/disorders/stroke/stroke.htm.

Post-stroke Rehabilitation Fact Sheet. National Institute of Neurological Disorders and Stroke, August 20, 2008, http://www.ninds.nih.gov/disorders/stroke/poststrokerehab.htm.

Stroke. Mayo Clinic, July 3, 2008, http://www.mayoclinic.com/health/stroke/DS00150.

What You Need to Know About Stroke. National Institute of Neurological Disorders and Stroke, September 11, 2007, http://www.ninds.nih.gov/disorders/stroke/stroke_needtoknow.htm.

STYRON, WILLIAM (1925–2006).

U.S. author William Styron is best known for his novels *Lie Down in Darkness, The Confessions of Nat Turner,* and *Sophie's Choice.* However, he also wrote a short but deeply moving memoir of his personal experience with severe depression that became the bestselling book *Darkness Visible* (1990). The critical and popular success of Styron's book opened the door for numerous other memoirs of depression that followed.

In 1985, at the age of 60, Styron became depressed after giving up a longtime **alcohol** habit. The medication he was prescribed led to side effects that just worsened his mental condition, and he sank into a deep, suicidal depression that only lifted when he was hospitalized from December of that year through February 1986.

Darkness Visible began as a 1989 lecture Styron gave at a symposium on mood disorders at Johns Hopkins University School of Medicine. Expanded versions of that text were published first as an essay in *Vanity Fair* magazine and later as a book.

Styron continued to struggle with depression for years afterward and was hospitalized several more times. Building upon his own experiences, he became an ardent advocate for other sufferers. Although he was certainly not the first celebrated writer to pen a personal account of his battles with depression, he was one of the most eloquent. Styron's book also was published at a time when public awareness and acceptance of depression were starting to grow, and his memoir struck a chord. It helped usher in a new era of greater frankness about this all-too-common illness.

"Gray Drizzle of Horror"

In *Darkness Visible,* Styron provides a harrowing account of his personal struggles with debilitating depression:

> What I had begun to discover is that, mysteriously and in ways that are totally remote from normal experience, the gray drizzle of horror induced by depression takes on the quality of physical pain. But it is not an immediately identifiable pain, like that of a broken limb. It may be more accurate to say that despair, owing to some evil trick played upon the sick brain by the inhabiting psyche, comes to resemble the diabolical discomfort of being imprisoned in a fiercely overheated room. And because no breeze stirs this cauldron, because there is no escape from this smothering confinement, it is entirely natural that the victim begins to think ceaselessly of oblivion.

Bibliography

Casey, Nell. "William Styron, 1926–2006—Unlikely Bard of Depression." *Slate* (November 7, 2006).

Lehmann-Haupt, Christopher. "William Styron, Novelist, Dies at 81." *New York Times* (November 2, 2006).

Styron, William. *Darkness Visible: A Memoir of Madness.* New York: Random House, 1990.

SUBSTANCE ABUSE. Substance abuse refers to a pattern of misusing chemical substances, such as **alcohol**, illicit drugs, or prescription medications. Although this pattern of behavior leads to serious adverse consequences, the person keeps repeating it. The result is often a downward spiral, in which substance-related problems at home, work, or school get progressively worse over time. Eventually, substance abuse may lead to addiction—a long-lasting, relapsing disease characterized by compulsive drug craving, seeking, and abuse as well as by persistent chemical changes in the brain. About one-third of people who are starting treatment for **major depression** have a recent history of substance abuse or addiction.

Depression and substance abuse can cause many of the same symptoms, and even for mental health professionals, disentangling the two can be a challenge. Yet getting a correct diagnosis and proper treatment for both conditions is critical. Failure to treat coexisting substance abuse or addiction may jeopardize a person's **recovery** from depression, and vice versa.

Left untreated, depression and substance abuse can cause needless suffering and lead to tragic consequences. The despair and loss of inhibition associated with getting drunk or high may set the stage for impulsive and self-destructive acts, sometimes culminating in **suicide**.

Criteria for Diagnosis. The symptoms of substance abuse, dependence, intoxication, and withdrawal are defined by the ***Diagnostic and Statistical Manual of Mental Disorders, Fourth Edition, Text Revision*** (*DSM-IV-TR*), a diagnostic guidebook published by the American Psychiatric Association and widely used by mental health professionals from many disciplines. Collectively, these are often referred to as substance use disorders. The diagnostic criteria are summarized below.

Substance Abuse. The core feature of substance abuse is a pattern of substance use that leads to serious adverse consequences. This pattern occurs repeatedly or continuously for at least a year, and it causes significant distress or disruption in daily life. The result is one or more of the following symptoms: (1) repeated failure to live up to important obligations at home, work, or school (such as neglecting children, missing work, or skipping class), (2) repeated substance use in situations where it is physically dangerous (such as driving under the influence), (3) substance-related legal problems (such as arrests for disorderly conduct), or (4) continued substance use despite serious social or relationship fallout (such as physical fights or divorce).

Substance Dependence. As substance abuse starts to cause multiple physical, mental, and behavioral symptoms, it may escalate to substance dependence. One common feature of dependence is tolerance, in which it takes more and more of the substance to produce the same effect. Another common feature is withdrawal, in which someone who has recently quit using a substance experiences unpleasant symptoms as a result. When dependence includes both physiological and psychological symptoms, it can be equated with addiction.

Like substance abuse, dependence is typified by a pattern of substance use leading to serious distress or disruption in daily life. In addition, over the course of a year, the person has three or more of the following symptoms: (1) tolerance, (2) withdrawal, (3) taking the substance in larger amounts, or over a longer period than intended, (4) wanting or unsuccessfully trying to cut down on substance use, (5) spending considerable time on obtaining, using, or recovering from the substance, (6) giving up or cutting back on other important activities, or (7) continuing to use the substance despite recognizing that it causes problems.

Substance Intoxication. Intoxication is the medical term for getting drunk or high. It is characterized by a set of specific, reversible symptoms caused by the recent ingestion of or exposure to a substance. The symptoms include maladaptive psychological or behavioral changes—such as mood swings, belligerence, or impaired judgment—that are due to the substance's effects on the central **nervous system**. The exact symptoms vary from substance to substance.

Substance Withdrawal. Withdrawal is characterized by specific, maladaptive effects caused by stopping or reducing use of a substance after a period of heavy, prolonged use. These mental, physical, and behavioral effects cause significant distress or problems at home, work, or school. Different substances produce different withdrawal symptoms. As a rule of thumb, though, most withdrawal symptoms are the opposite of those caused by intoxication with the same substance.

Because withdrawal can be intense, people may be tempted to go back to using the substance to relieve the symptoms. Treatment can help a person get through this stage safely and successfully. Detoxification (detox, for short) is the first step in the treatment process, during which a substance is eliminated from the body and the person goes through medically supervised withdrawal.

The Depression Connection. Having depression and substance abuse or addiction at the same time can make each problem worse. People with depression who also have a substance use disorder generally have a higher risk of suicide, more personal and relationship problems, and an increased risk of anxiety disorders. These individuals also tend to be hospitalized more frequently and have harder to treat symptoms, compared to those with depression alone.

Depression may lead to substance abuse, if people turn to drugs or alcohol in an attempt to cope with their feelings. Unfortunately, such attempts to "self-medicate" tend to backfire badly. Although substance use may initially reduce symptoms, it typically deepens depression in the long run, and it also creates its own set of stressful personal and social problems.

Substance abuse may lead to depression, if it unmasks a previously hidden tendency to develop the condition. Scientists theorize that, in people with a genetic predisposition to depression, certain substances may trigger changes in critical brain chemicals or signaling pathways.

The two disorders also may be related through a third factor they have in common. Depression and substance abuse each have a genetic component, and some of the underlying genetic variations may contribute to the risk for both diseases. Nearly half of people with depression have a close relative who suffers from substance abuse or addiction. In this group, depression generally starts younger, lasts longer, and leads to more depressive episodes and suicide attempts.

Diagnostic Challenges. Symptoms of substance abuse sometimes mimic those of depression. For instance, some substances—such as alcohol, benzodiazepines (anti-anxiety medications), and barbiturates (sedatives)—are central **nervous system** (CNS) depressants. At low doses, they depress the inhibitory centers of the brain. At higher doses, they can depress other nervous system functions, slow reaction times, and reduce breathing and heart rates. Long-term use of these substances can lead to depressive symptoms, such as inability to feel pleasure, poor concentration, and trouble sleeping.

Other substances—such as cocaine and amphetamines—are CNS stimulants. They stimulate the brain in a way that temporarily increases feelings of well-being, energy, and alertness. Repeated use can lead to feelings of hostility or paranoia in some people, and even a single high dose can produce dangerously high body temperatures and an irregular heartbeat. Withdrawal from stimulants can give rise to depressive symptoms, such as inability to feel pleasure and suicidal thoughts.

If a person's depressive symptoms seem typical of intoxication or withdrawal from a particular substance, that may be all they are, especially if the person has no previous history of depression. Such symptoms generally go away in a matter of days. On the other hand, if someone has depressive symptoms that are more intense, long-lasting, or varied than what is usually seen with that substance, a diagnosis of depression may be considered. Other clues that a person with a substance use disorder might also be depressed include a family history of depression, mood symptoms that preceded the substance use, and mood symptoms that continue even after a lengthy abstinence.

Substance Abuse or Depression?

Several substances can cause symptoms during intoxication or withdrawal that are similar to those caused by depression. A thorough, professional evaluation is needed to determine whether the problem is substance abuse, depression, or both.

	Intoxication Symptoms	Withdrawal Symptoms
Alcohol, Barbiturates, or Benzodiazepines	Impaired attention or memory* Slurred speech Poor coordination Unsteady walking Involuntary, rapid movements of the eyeballs Passing out or coma	Trouble sleeping* Restless activity accompanied by inner tension* Anxiety* Nausea or vomiting Sweating or a rapid pulse Shaky hands Transitory hallucinations Seizures
Amphetamines or Cocaine	Weight loss* Behavior that seems slowed down or speeded up* Muscle weakness, slow and shallow breathing, chest pain, or irregular heart rhythms Rapid or slow heartbeat Dilated pupils High or low blood pressure Sweating or chills Nausea or vomiting Confusion, seizures, spasms, or coma	Fatigue* Sleeping too much or too little* Increased appetite* Behavior that seems speeded up or slowed down* Vivid, unpleasant dreams
Opioids (opium-related compounds, such as morphine, codeine, and heroin)	Impaired attention or memory* Slurred speech Drowsiness or coma	Sadness, irritability, or anxiety* Crying* Trouble sleeping* Dilated pupils, sweating, or goose bumps Diarrhea Nausea or vomiting Muscle aches Yawning Fever

* Symptoms that resemble or are often associated with depression.

Treatment Considerations. Psychological approaches play a central role in the treatment of coexisting substance abuse and depression. **Cognitive-behavioral therapy**—a form of **psychotherapy** that helps people recognize and change maladaptive patterns of thinking and behaving—has been shown to be effective for both conditions.

Active participation in **self-help** programs such as Alcoholics Anonymous and Narcotics Anonymous also can enhance recovery from substance abuse. These so-called 12-step programs offer a set of guiding principles for overcoming alcoholism or other forms of addiction. More recently, some self-help programs have been designed especially for people with a **dual diagnosis** of substance abuse and depression or other mental disorders. Examples include Double Trouble in Recovery and Dual Recovery Anonymous. Although this approach seems promising, more research is needed to determine its effectiveness.

Antidepressant Medications. Antidepressant medications also may be helpful. An analysis of well-controlled studies that used **antidepressants** to treat combined depression and substance use disorders found a modest beneficial effect. In studies that found a decrease in depression, antidepressant treatment also helped reduce substance abuse. However, the authors concluded that antidepressants should be combined with therapy for addiction, not used as a stand-alone treatment in this group.

In someone getting inpatient care for addiction, antidepressants may not be started until after the person has completed detox. Several common symptoms of withdrawal—anxiety, agitation, drowsiness, nausea, and headache—also can occur as side effects of antidepressants. Waiting to start antidepressants ensures that treatment providers do not confuse the two types of symptoms. Nevertheless, if the depression is severe and does not begin improving within the first few days of abstinence, antidepressants may be initiated at that time.

Some antidepressant are safer than others for people with substance use disorders. **Monoamine oxidase inhibitors** (MAOIs), an older group of antidepressants, are usually avoided. The combination of an MAOI and alcohol can lead to a dangerous spike in blood pressure, potentially causing a stroke. But whatever antidepressant a person is taking, mixing medication with unprescribed drugs or alcohol is discouraged.

See also: Caffeine; Comorbidity; Smoking; Substance-Induced Mood Disorder

Further Information. Alcoholics Anonymous, P.O. Box 459, New York, NY 10163, (212) 870-3400, www.aa.org.

Double Trouble in Recovery, P.O. Box 245055, Brooklyn, NY 11224, (718) 373-2684, www.doubletroubleinrecovery.org.

Dual Recovery Anonymous, P.O. Box 8107, Prairie Village, KS 66208, (877) 883-2332, www.draonline.org.

Narcotics Anonymous, P.O. Box 9999, Van Nuys, CA 91409, (818) 773-9999, www.na.org.

National Clearinghouse for Alcohol and Drug Information, P.O. Box 2345, Rockville, MD 20847, ncadi.samhsa.gov.

National Council on Alcoholism and Drug Dependence, 244 E. 58th Street, 4th Floor, New York, NY 10022, (212) 269-7797, www.ncadd.org.

National Institute on Alcohol Abuse and Alcoholism, 5635 Fishers Lane, MSC 9304, Bethesda, MD 20892, (301) 443-3860, www.niaaa.nih.gov.

National Institute on Drug Abuse, 6001 Executive Boulevard, Room 5213, Bethesda, MD 20892, (301) 443-1124, www.drugabuse.gov, teens.drugabuse.gov.

Partnership for a Drug-Free America, 405 Lexington Avenue, Suite 1601, New York, NY 10174, (212) 922-1560, www.drugfree.org.

Bibliography

American Psychiatric Association. *Diagnostic and Statistical Manual of Mental Disorders.* 4th ed., text rev. Washington, DC: American Psychiatric Association, 2000.

Antidepressants and Alcohol: What Is the Concern? Mayo Clinic, July 24, 2007, http://www.mayoclinic.com/health/antidepressants-and-alcohol/AN01653.

Comorbidity: Addiction and Other Mental Illnesses. National Institute on Drug Abuse, December 2008, http://www.drugabuse.gov/PDF/RRComorbidity.pdf.

Davis, Lori, Akihito Uezato, Jason M. Newell, and Elizabeth Frazier. "Major Depression and Comorbid Substance Use Disorders." *Current Opinion in Psychiatry* 21 (2008): 14–18.

NIDA for Teens: Glossary. National Institute on Drug Abuse, http://teens.drugabuse.gov/utilities/glossary.php.

Nunes, Edward V., and Frances R. Levin. "Treatment of Depression in Patients with Alcohol or Other Drug Dependence: A Meta-analysis." *JAMA* 291 (2004): 1887–1896.

Quello, Susan B., Kathleen T. Brady, and Susan C. Sonne. "Mood Disorders and Substance Use Disorder: A Complex Comorbidity." *Science and Practice Perspectives* 3 (2005): 13–24.

Stimulants. National Institute on Drug Abuse, http://teens.drugabuse.gov/facts/facts_stim1.php.

SUBSTANCE-INDUCED MOOD DISORDER. A substance-induced mood disorder is a pronounced and persistent disturbance in **mood** that is due to the direct physiological effects of an abused drug, a medication, or a toxin. The disorder may take the form of depression (an overly low mood), **mania** (an overly high mood), or a mixture of both. Many substances cause some mood symptoms. This diagnosis is reserved for cases in which such symptoms are especially prominent.

A substance-induced mood disorder caused by an abused drug can be associated with either intoxication or withdrawal. Intoxication refers to the reversible physical, mental, and behavioral effects caused by the recent ingestion of a particular substance. Withdrawal refers to symptoms caused by a halt or reduction in prolonged, heavy substance use.

Timing is everything when it comes to diagnosing a substance-induced mood disorder. If a person's mood symptoms seem typical of intoxication or withdrawal from a particular substance, that is probably all they are, especially if the person has no previous history of depression or mania. Such symptoms generally go away in a matter of days.

In contrast, someone with a substance-induced mood disorder has mood symptoms caused by lingering physiological effects of substance use. The symptoms begin during or within four weeks after the last use, and they are more severe than those typical of intoxication or withdrawal from that substance. When a medication or toxin is involved, the symptoms must have a similarly close temporal relationship to taking the medicine or being exposed to the toxic substance. Once the mood symptoms start, they cause enough distress or disruption to warrant treatment.

If a person's depression seems to be caused by substance use, it is vital to get at the root of the problem. For a drug of abuse, treatment for **substance abuse** may be needed. For a medication, the doctor may be able to adjust the dosage or switch to a different medicine. For a toxin, identification and elimination of the source of exposure is critical. In addition to taking these steps, treating the mood disorder itself is also important.

Substances that Can Cause Mood Disorders

Below are just some of the substances that can cause symptoms of either depression or mania that are serious enough to warrant treatment. Such symptoms lead to significant distress or disruption in daily life.

Substance Intoxication	**Alcohol**
	Amphetamines
	Cocaine
	Hallucinogens
	Inhalants
	Opioids
	Sedatives

Substance Withdrawal	Alcohol
	Amphetamines
	Cocaine
	Sedatives
Medications	Anesthetics
	Anticonvulsants
	Antidepressants
	Antipsychotics
	Birth control pills
	Blood-pressure lowering drugs
	Heart medications
	Muscle relaxants
	Pain relievers
	Parkinson's disease medications
	Steroids
	Ulcer medications
Toxins	Carbon monoxide
	Gasoline
	Organophosphate insecticides
	Paint

See also: Mood Disorders

Bibliography

American Psychiatric Association. *Diagnostic and Statistical Manual of Mental Disorders.* 4th ed., text rev. Washington, DC: American Psychiatric Association, 2000.

Frances, Allen, Michael B. First, and Harold Alan Pincus. *DSM-IV Guidebook.* Washington, DC: American Psychiatric Press, 1995.

Quello, Susan B., Kathleen T. Brady, and Susan C. Sonne. "Mood Disorders and Substance Use Disorder: A Complex Comorbidity." *Science and Practice Perspectives* 3 (2005): 13–24.

SUBSTANCE P.　Substance P is a neurotransmitter—a chemical messenger in the **nervous system**—that transmits and amplifies pain signals to and from the brain. It belongs to a family of **neurotransmitters** called neurokinins. Research indicates that excessive amounts of neurokinins, including substance P, may be released during states of emotional distress.

Substance P is found in areas of the brain associated with depression and emotional behavior, including the **hypothalamus**, **hippocampus**, **amygdala**, and **prefrontal cortex**. It is also found near brain cells for which **dopamine**, **norepinephrine**, and **serotonin** serve as the primary neurotransmitters. These other neurotransmitters are thought to be involved in depression, and substance P might have an indirect effect on depressive behavior by modulating them.

Neurokinin-1 Receptor Antagonists.　Brain cells affected by substance P have specialized sites, called neurokinin-1 (NK-1) **receptors**, which bind to and react with the substance. Mice that have been genetically engineered to inactivate the gene for NK-1 receptors are unusually active when put in a situation where they can try to swim their way out of water. Their response is similar to how normal mice behave in the same situation when given a traditional antidepressant.

Spurred on by these findings, several drug companies have tried to develop new **antidepressants** that would work by blocking the action of NK-1 receptors. In animal studies, these drugs looked promising. But studies in humans have so far been less encouraging. Nevertheless, this is still an active area of research as companies race to find the next big thing in depression treatment.

Bibliography

Alvaro, G., and R. Di Fabio. "Neurokinin-1 Receptor Antagonists: Current Prospects." *Current Opinion in Drug Discovery and Development* 10 (2007): 613–621.

DeVane, C. Lindsay. "Substance P: A New Era, a New Role." *Pharmacotherapy* 21 (2001): 1061–1069.

Hafizi, Sepehr, Prakash Chandra, and Philip J. Cowen. "Neurokinin-I Receptor Antagonists as Novel Antidepressants: Trials and Tribulations." *British Journal of Psychiatry* 191 (2007): 282–284.

Rosenkranz, Melissa A. "Substance P at the Nexus of Mind and Body in Chronic Inflammation and Affective Disorders." *Psychological Bulletin* 133 (2007): 1007–1037.

Stahl, Stephen M. *Peptides and Psychiatry, Part 3: Substance P and Serendipity—Novel Psychotropics Are a Possibility.* Clinical Neuroscience Research Center (San Diego) and University of California-San Diego, http://www.psychiatrist.com/pcc/brainstorm/br6003.htm.

SUICIDE. Suicide—the intentional taking of one's own life—is the eleventh-leading cause of death in the United States, occurring in people of both genders, all ages, and every ethnic group. About 30 percent to 40 percent of people who die by suicide suffer from **major depression**. Adding other disorders that cause depressive symptoms—such as **dysthymia**, **bipolar disorder**, and **adjustment disorder with depressed mood**—raises the percentage much higher.

Depression can lead to suicidal thoughts, just as any other illness leads to symptoms. These thoughts let up as treatment for depression takes hold. In the meantime, though, people are at risk for suicide. The risk is especially high if they do not realize that the hopelessness they are experiencing is a symptom of a treatable disorder. During a severe episode of depression, people may feel as if they have no control over disturbing thoughts and painful emotions. If they believe there is no escape from the mental suffering, they may see suicide as the only way out.

It is critical for people who are having suicidal thoughts to recognize them for what they are: symptoms of a brain disorder that can be treated and overcome. If the thoughts are intense or persistent, or if they progress beyond passing thoughts to the planning or action stage, it is crucial to seek professional help immediately.

If You Feel Depressed and Suicidal

If you are thinking about suicide, remind yourself that such thoughts are classic—and treatable—symptoms of depression. Although you may feel as if there is no hope and believe that suicide is the only option, such feelings and thoughts are distorted by your illness. They are not accurate reflections of the way things really are.

Depression also can make you want to pull away from others, but try to resist that impulse. Share your thoughts and feelings about death with someone else—a trusted family member, friend, or other support person. In addition, reach out for professional help by talking to a doctor or mental health professional or calling a suicide hotline. This is one battle you do not need to fight alone.

Once treatment has begun, it is important for people to remember that different individuals respond differently to **antidepressants** and **psychotherapy**. Finding the best treatment plan for a particular person may take some time. But there are many different medications and therapies available. Eventually, almost everyone with depression gets some relief, and the majority experience substantial improvement.

Warning Signs. Family and friends of those with depression should take any mention of death or suicide seriously. Four out of five suicidal individuals give some advance sign of their intentions. People who talk about suicide or call a **suicide crisis center** are 30 times more likely than average to die by their own hand.

When someone talks about suicide, discussing the situation in a calm, rational, nonjudgmental way may encourage the person to seek professional help. It is not necessary to tiptoe around the subject. Merely asking a few caring questions will not make matters worse. In fact, experts recommend asking direct questions about how, when, and where the person plans to act, because that can help determine whether he or she is in immediate danger.

Keep in mind, however, that severely depressed individuals often become withdrawn, self-absorbed, and uncommunicative, so the signs that they are considering suicide may be more subtle than an open declaration of intent. Following are some other common warning signs.

Talking about Unbearable Feelings. Depression can lead to extremely painful feelings of hopelessness, despair, worthlessness, and guilt. When people perceive such feelings as being more than they can bear, the risk of suicide is increased.

Putting Affairs in Order. People who are contemplating suicide may settle up business matters, prepare a will, take out life insurance, or give away valued possessions. They also may talk about what others will do after they are gone.

Abusing Alcohol or Drugs. Experts estimate that **substance abuse** may be involved in half of all suicides. When people with depression also have a drug or **alcohol** problem, both conditions need to be professionally treated.

Rehearsing a Suicide Scenario. Discussing specific suicide methods, purchasing a gun, and hoarding medication are all signs that suicidal thoughts may have progressed to the planning stage.

If Someone You Know Is Suicidal

If someone you know might be thinking about suicide, open a dialogue about your concerns. Describe the specific behaviors that worry you and lead you to suspect that the person may be in trouble, and offer reassurance that you are there to help. Remind the person how important he or she is to you and to others. Let the person know that feeling guilty about being depressed or ashamed over not being good enough is a symptom of the illness, not a true reflection of his or her worth. Be understanding, but never promise confidentiality, because you might need to involve others to protect the person.

Encourage the person to get professional care, and offer to lend a hand in any way you can. For instance, you might help by suggesting treatment resources or driving the person to the first appointment with a treatment provider. Resist the temptation to take responsibility for making the person well, though, because that is more than you can possibly do.

Although it is a great thing to be supportive, do not try to handle a crisis alone. If a person is actively threatening to take his or her life, or if you believe that danger is imminent, call a suicide hotline or contact the individual's doctor or therapist. If necessary, call 911.

At this point, it is time to intervene and get help for the person, rather than waiting to see if the thoughts simply pass on their own.

Seeming Suddenly Calmer. People may be especially vulnerable to suicide right after the lowest point in an episode of depression. An abrupt shift from seeming very distressed and hopeless to seeming very calm and settled might indicate that a decision about suicide has been made. Genuine **recovery** from deep depression is a gradual process. A drastic, overnight change may signal trouble.

Risk Factors. Suicide affects people of all ages and from every walk of life. Some individuals are at higher-than-average risk, however. One strong predictor is a history of mental disorders. More than 90 percent of those who die by suicide have a mental illness or an alcohol or drug problem.

A history of prior suicide attempts is another major predictor. It is estimated that somewhere between eight and 25 suicide attempts occur for every suicide death. Such attempts should never be brushed off lightly, because up to 40 percent of those who eventually complete suicide have attempted it previously.

Gender and age can be risk factors as well. Almost four times as many males as females die by suicide, although women attempt suicide two to three times as often as men. For young people ages 10 to 24, suicide is the third-leading cause of death. For **older adults**, the suicide rate is disproportionately high. Although people ages 65 and up comprise only 12 percent of the total U.S. population, they make up 16 percent of suicide deaths.

Suicide Prevention. Suicide is the most severe—and most irrevocable—complication of depression. The key to preventing suicide is to the treat depression and any other mental health or substance use disorders the person may have. As the depressed mood begins to lift, thoughts of suicide usually start to go away as well.

Research shows that the rate of repeat suicide attempts can be cut in half by **cognitive therapy**, a form of **psychotherapy** that helps people identify and change distorted thoughts. For those who have attempted suicide in the past, cognitive therapy may help them consider alternative courses of action if thoughts of self-harm ever come up again.

When someone seems to be in imminent danger of suicide, getting immediate help from a treatment provider or the nearest hospital emergency room may avert a life-threatening situation. If necessary, psychiatric **hospitalization** can keep a person safe and under 24-hour supervision until the individual's mental condition has stabilized.

See also: Antidepressants and Suicide

Further Information. American Association of Suicidology, 5221 Wisconsin Avenue N.W., Washington, DC 20015, (202) 237-2280, www.suicidology.org.

Jed Foundation, 220 Fifth Avenue, 9th Floor, New York, NY 10001, (212) 647-7544, www.jedfoundation.org.

Kristin Brooks Hope Center, (800) 784-2433, www.hopeline.com.

National Strategy for Suicide Prevention, Substance Abuse and Mental Health Services Administration, (800) 789-2647, mentalhealth.samhsa.gov/suicideprevention.

National Suicide Prevention Lifeline, (800) 273-8255, www.suicidepreventionlifeline.org.

Suicide Awareness Voices of Education, 8120 Penn Avenue S., Suite 470, Bloomington, MN 55431, (952) 946-7998 www.save.org.

Suicide Prevention Action Network USA, 1010 Vermont Avenue N.W., Suite 408, Washington, DC 20005, (202) 449-3600, www.spanusa.org.

Bibliography

Depression and Mood Disorders. National Strategy for Suicide Prevention, http://mentalhealth.samhsa
   .gov/suicideprevention/rates.asp.
Factsheet: Suicide. Mental Health America, http://www.nmha.org/go/information/get-info/suicide.
Older Adults: Depression and Suicide Facts. National Institute of Mental Health, May 18, 2009.
   http://www.nimh.nih.gov/health/publications/older-adults-depression-and-suicide-facts-fact
   -sheet/index.shtml.
Someone You Know Is Suicidal. Suicide Awareness Voices of Education, http://www.save.org/index
   .cfm?page_id=705E1907-C4DD-5D32–2C7087CE5924CCA4.
Suicide. Centers for Disease Control and Prevention, Summer 2008, http://www.cdc.gov/
   ViolencePrevention/pdf/Suicide-DataSheet-a.pdf.
Suicide and Depression. Suicide Awareness Voices of Education, http://www.save.org/index.cfm
   ?fuseaction=home.viewPage&page_id=705C8CB8–9321-F1BD-867E811B1B404C94.
Suicide in the U.S.: Statistics and Prevention. National Institute of Mental Health, May 18, 2009,
   http://www.nimh.nih.gov/health/publications/suicide-in-the-us-statistics-and
   -prevention/index.shtml.
Understanding Suicidal Thinking. Depression and Bipolar Support Alliance, May 4, 2006,
   http://www.dbsalliance.org/pdfs/suicidefinalweb04.pdf.

SUICIDE CRISIS CENTER.

A suicide crisis center is a facility designed to help individuals who are having suicidal thoughts or experiencing severe emotional distress. Such centers are staffed by mental health professionals, paraprofessionals, and volunteers who are specially trained to deal with suicidal emergencies in person or over the phone. Services may include counseling, referrals, and community education.

The National Suicide Prevention Lifeline (800–273-TALK) is a free, confidential, 24-hour hotline funded by the Substance Abuse and Mental Health Services Administration. Callers are routed to the nearest facility in a network of more than 130 crisis centers around the United States. These centers provide crisis counseling and mental health referrals over the phone day and night. One study of 1,085 suicidal callers to eight centers found that they reported decreased hopelessness, distress, and intent to die during the course of the phone call.

Further Information. Kristin Brooks Hope Center, (800) 784-2433, www.hopeline .com.

National Suicide Prevention Lifeline, (800) 273-8255, www.suicidepreventionlifeline.org.

Bibliography

Gould, Madelyn S., John Kalafat, Jimmie Lou HarrisMunfakh, and Marjorie Kleinman. "An Evaluation of Crisis Hotline Outcomes Part 2: Suicidal Callers." *Suicide and Life-Threatening Behavior* 37 (2007): 338-352.
National Suicide Prevention Lifeline: About. National Suicide Prevention Lifeline, http://www .suicideprevention.org/About/Default.aspx.

SUPPORT GROUPS.

A support group is a gathering of people with a common problem or interest who get together to share moral support and practical advice. For people with depression, joining a support group that focuses on the illness can be a valuable addition to professional treatment. Being part of a group lets people know they are not alone with their depression.

Virtual Support

If you don't have access to an in-person support group, online groups are another option. These may take the form of message boards, chat rooms, or e-mail lists. One advantage to online groups is that they are available anywhere, anytime. The anonymity also can be appealing, but the downside is that it is difficult to know who is reading your posts, what their motives might be, and how reliable their information is. Never give out personal contact information, such as your last name, street address, or phone number. Also, to cut down on inappropriate or abusive messages, look for a group that is moderated by an expert or hosted by a reputable organization.

Group members typically share coping tips and recommend helpful resources. They understand each other's challenges and concerns, because they have been there themselves. Those who are doing well serve as beacons of inspiration and hope to the others. In addition, some groups offer educational activities, such as lectures by mental health experts or structured discussions on specific topics.

Support groups may be formed by interested individuals, nonprofit organizations, or mental health clinics. The leader may be either a group member or a trained facilitator. But whatever the format, the goal is to offer information and encouragement rather than to provide formal treatment. This differentiates support groups from **group therapy**, which brings together several individuals with similar diagnoses for formal treatment under the guidance of a mental health professional.

Local mental health providers often can provide referrals to support groups in the area. In addition, the **Depression and Bipolar Support Alliance** offers more than 1,000 peer-run support groups around the United States.

See also: Social Support

Further Information. Depression and Bipolar Support Alliance, 730 N. Franklin Street, Suite 501, Chicago, IL 60610, (800) 826-3632, www.dbsalliance.org.

HealthyPlace, www.healthyplace.com.

National Mental Health Consumers' Self-Help Clearinghouse, 1211 Chestnut Street, Suite 1207, Philadelphia, PA 19107, (800) 553-4539, www.mhselfhelp.org.

Bibliography

Find a Support Group in Your Community. Depression and Bipolar Support Alliance, May 9, 2006, http://www.dbsalliance.org/site/PageServer?pagename=support_supportgroups.

Support Groups: Find Information, Encouragement and Camaraderie. Mayo Clinic, December 1, 2007, http://www.mayoclinic.com/print/support-groups/MH00002.

Support Groups: Share Experiences About Depression, Other Mental Conditions. Mayo Clinic, August 14, 2007, http://www.mayoclinic.com/print/support-groups/MH00044.

SUPPORTIVE THERAPY.   Supportive therapy offers emotional sustenance to people in distress without probing for deeper conflicts or directly working to change their thinking style or personality. The approach relies on general methods that are not specific to any one school of **psychotherapy**, such as reassurance, advice, encouragement, and persuasion. In research on depression treatments, supportive therapy sometimes is included as a treatment option against which the more specific methods of another form of therapy can be compared.

In clinical settings, supportive techniques are widely used in everyday practice. They may be incorporated into many other forms of psychotherapy. In addition, supportive therapy alone may be sufficient for treating depressive symptoms that are mild or limited to particular problems. For instance, there is evidence that supportive therapy can help reduce emotional distress and depression in people with **cancer**.

See also: Treatment of Depression

Bibliography

Arnold, Winston. *Introduction to Supportive Psychotherapy.* Arlington, VA: American Psychiatric Publishing, 2004.

Jacobsen, Paul B., and Heather S. Jim. "Psychosocial Interventions for Anxiety and Depression in Adult Cancer Patients: Achievements and Challenges." *CA: A Cancer Journal for Clinicians* 58 (2008): 214–230.

Markowitz, John C., James H. Kocsis, Paul Christos, Kathryn Bleiberg, and Alexandra Carlin. "Pilot Study of Interpersonal Psychotherapy Versus Supportive Psychotherapy for Dysthymic Patients with Secondary Alcohol Abuse or Dependence." *Journal of Nervous and Mental Disease* 196 (2008): 468–474.

SUSTO. *Susto* ("soul loss") is a folk illness resembling depression that is prevalent among some Latino groups in the United States as well as in Mexico, Central America, and South America. Other names for susto include *espanto, pasmo, tripa ida, perdida del alma,* and *chibih.* The condition is thought to occur when a terrifying event causes the soul to leave the body. The resulting unhappiness and illness make it hard to get along in everyday life.

The first signs of susto may appear at any time from days to years after the frightening event. Many symptoms of susto are similar to those of depression, including sadness, lack of motivation to do anything, appetite disturbances, sleep problems, and feelings of low self-worth. Physical symptoms of susto include muscle aches and pains, headaches, stomachaches, and diarrhea. In extreme cases, it is believed that susto can lead to death.

Curanderismo as Therapy. *Curanderismo* is a Latino system of folk medicine that includes healing rituals, prayer, **herbal remedies**, and massage. People may seek help from specially trained healers, known as *curanderos* (men) or *curanderas* (women), whose knowledge of healing methods has been passed down from relatives or learned through apprenticeships. Many attribute their healing ability to divine energy channeled through their bodies.

Curanderismo maintain that humans are physical, mental, emotional, and spiritual beings. The spiritual self, in the form of an energetic aura surrounding the body, is especially vulnerable to trauma. When the soul is lost due to a great fright, this aura is violated. The healing process aims to restore strength, health, and resilience to the damaged spirit. The techniques used may include ritual healings to call the soul back to the body. *Barridas* (ritual cleansings) may be performed to rebalance the body and soul.

Curanderismo exists outside mainstream medicine, so its effectiveness has not been established in scientific studies. However, proponents claim that it reduces symptoms and relieves **stress**. Believers who choose to use curanderismo along with, rather than instead of, conventional treatments may be getting the best of both worlds. They should inform their health care providers about any herbal remedies they are using, however, because some herbs can cause side effects or interact harmfully with medications.

See also: Cultural Factors

Bibliography

American Psychiatric Association. *Diagnostic and Statistical Manual of Mental Disorders.* 4th ed., text rev. Washington, DC: American Psychiatric Association, 2000.

Avila, Elena with Joy Parker. *Woman Who Glows in the Dark: A Curandera Reveals Traditional Aztec Secrets of Physical and Spiritual Health.* New York: Jeremy P. Tarcher, 1999.

Curanderismo. American Cancer Society, March 26, 2007, http://www.cancer.org/docroot/ETO/content/ETO_5_3X_Curanderismo.asp.

T

TEMPERAMENT. Temperament is one of the two main parts of personality. It is the innate component that first appears early in life and includes such characteristics as emotional responsiveness, willingness to explore, and energy level. The other main part of personality is character, the acquired component that is rooted in socialization and learning. Both temperament and character affect people's susceptibility to depression.

Different theorists have used different terminology to describe fundamental aspects of temperament. However, one common thread running through many theories is the concept of negative or positive emotionality. Negative emotionality reflects sensitivity to unpleasant stimuli, which leads to **emotions** such as **sadness**, fear, anxiety, guilt, and anger. In contrast, positive emotionality reflects sensitivity to pleasant stimuli, which leads to emotions such as joy and enthusiasm as well as characteristics such as sociability and energy. Research has shown that both high negative emotionality and low positive emotionality are associated with depression.

Another common theme in research on temperament is behavioral inhibition or activation. Behavioral inhibition reflects sensitivity to threat cues, resulting in a tendency to show fear and withdrawal in unfamiliar situations. In contrast, behavioral activation reflects sensitivity to reward cues, resulting in a tendency to approach new situations and have feelings of energy and vigor. Research has linked depression to low behavioral activation, and to a lesser extent, high behavioral inhibition.

Negative emotionality and behavioral inhibition often go hand in hand. One study of 289 children followed their development from birth to fifth grade. Children who were high in "withdrawal negativity"—a combination of negative emotionality and the tendency to avoid or dislike new situations—were more likely than other children to adopt an overly negative thinking style when faced with a stressful event. This type of thinking style is closely linked to depression.

Although temperament is rooted in the genes, it affects how people think, feel, and interact with their environment. It is a point where nature and nurture intersect to help decide how vulnerable a particular person is to depression.

See also: Personality Factors

Bibliography

Clark, Lee Anna, David Watson, and Susan Mineka. "Temperament, Personality, and the Mood and Anxiety Disorders." *Journal of Abnormal Psychology* 103 (1994): 103–116.

Compas, Bruce E., Jennifer Connor-Smith, and Sarah S. Jaser. "Temperament, Stress Reactivity, and Coping: Implications for Depression in Childhood and Adolescence." *Journal of Clinical Child and Adolescent Psychology* 33 (2004): 21–31.

Kasch, Karen L., Jonathan Rottenberg, Bruce A. Arnow, and Ian H. Gotlib. "Behavioral Activation and Inhibition Systems and the Severity and Course of Depression." *Journal of Abnormal Psychology* 111 (2002): 589–597.

Klein, Daniel N., Emily Durbin, and Stewart A. Shankman. "Personality and Mood Disorders." In *Handbook of Depression*. 2nd ed., by Ian H. Gotlib and Constance L. Hammen, eds., 93–112. New York: Guilford Press, 2009.

Mezulis, Amy H., Janet Shibley Hyde, and Lyn Y. Abramson. "The Developmental Origins of Cognitive Vulnerability to Depression: Temperament, Parenting, and Negative Life Events in Childhood as Contributors to Negative Cognitive Style." *Developmental Psychology* 42 (2006): 1012–1025.

TRADITIONAL CHINESE MEDICINE.   Traditional Chinese medicine (TCM) is a system of healing that originated thousands of years ago in China. The ancient view of health and healing, which still permeates TCM, is closely tied to Taoist philosophy. The body is thought to reflect natural elements and energies that can be observed and experienced in the environment. Depression is one of the conditions addressed by TCM. In fact, the first-known Chinese medical text, *The Yellow Emperor's Classic of Medicine* (ca. 100 BC), offers theories on the origins of depression.

In TCM, health represents a delicate balance between two opposing yet inseparable forces: yin and yang. Yin stands for the cold, slow, or passive principle; yang, for the hot, excited, or active principle. Disease is seen as the result of an imbalance in these forces. Such an imbalance blocks the flow of vital energy, called qi, along internal energy pathways, called meridians. Depression is attributed to a depletion of yang qi, leading to an overly yin state.

Three major therapeutic approaches used in TCM are **herbal remedies**, massage, and **acupuncture**, a procedure in which specific points along the meridians are stimulated by various means, including the insertion of hair-thin needles. The goal is to unblock qi in order to restore harmony and wellness within the body. **Diet** also is considered important for promoting health, and certain foods—such as daikon radish, sesame seeds, soybeans, and kelp—are thought to be beneficial for depression.

Treatment of Depression.   Several small studies have looked at the treatment of depression with acupuncture. Taken as a whole, these studies suggest that acupuncture might help reduce the severity of symptoms. For instance, some have found that electroacupuncture, which uses tiny electrical charges to stimulate acupuncture points, may be as effective as an antidepressant for treating moderate depression. Large, well-controlled studies are needed before any firm conclusions can be drawn, however.

TCM practitioners often combine multiple herbs in preparations known as formulas. One classic formula called Mood Smooth (*Jia Wei Xiao Yao Wan*) has been used for six centuries to treat depression. It combines several herbs, including mint, peony, angelica, licorice, ginger, and gardenia. Scientific evidence for its effectiveness is lacking, however. Factors such as geographic location, harvest season, and post-harvest processing and storage can have a significant effect on the numerous chemically active compounds found in such formulas, making it especially hard to evaluate how well they work.

Further Information.   American Association of Acupuncture and Oriental Medicine, P.O. Box 162340, Sacramento, CA 95816, (866) 455-7999, www.aaaomonline.org.

Bibliography

Smith, C. A., and P. P. J. Hay. "Acupuncture for Depression." *Cochrane Database of Systematic Reviews* 3 (2004): art. no. CD004046.

Stone, Michael H. "Historical Aspects of Mood Disorders." In *The American Psychiatric Publishing Textbook of Mood Disorders,* by Dan J. Stein, David J. Kupfer, and Alan F. Schatzberg, eds., 3–15. Washington, DC: American Psychiatric Publishing, 2006.

Thie, Julia. "Chinese Medical Treatments." In *Complementary and Alternative Treatments in Mental Health Care,* by James H. Lake and David Spiegel, eds., pp. 169–194. Washington, DC: American Psychiatric Publishing, 2007.

Traditional Chinese Medicine for Depression. American Academy of Acupuncture and Oriental Medicine, http://www.aaaom.org/HPDEPRESSION.htm.

Wang, Hao, Hong Qi, Bai-song Wang, Yong-yao Cui, Liang Zhu, Zheng-xing Rong, et al. "Is Acupuncture Beneficial in Depression? A Meta-analysis of 8 Randomized Controlled Trials." *Journal of Affective Disorders* (June 10, 2008): e-publication ahead of print.

Whole Medical Systems: An Overview. National Center for Complementary and Alternative Medicine, March 2007, http://nccam.nih.gov/health/backgrounds/wholemed.htm.

TRANSCRANIAL MAGNETIC STIMULATION. Transcranial magnetic stimulation (TMS) is a treatment that uses rapid pulses of magnetic fields to stimulate brain cells in an area of the brain thought to affect mood. So far, one TMS device has been cleared by the Food and Drug Administration for treating individuals with depression when standard antidepressant treatment has not worked.

TMS is noninvasive, meaning no surgery is required. It is also nonsystemic, meaning its effects are localized. **Antidepressants**, in contrast, circulate around the whole body in the bloodstream, so they can cause unwanted side effects, such as weight gain, upset stomach, sexual problems, or dry mouth. TMS is less likely to cause such whole-body effects, so it may be especially helpful for individuals with severe depression who cannot tolerate antidepressants. It may also be appealing to women with **postpartum depression** who do not want to take medication while breastfeeding.

On the other hand, TMS is a relatively new option, so it has not been as well studied as antidepressants. Because TMS induces changes in brain function, it is possible it could have long-term health effects that have not yet been identified. Also, some studies have shown a change in brain structure after TMS, the significance of which is still unclear. Until more is known about the safety and effectiveness of TMS, it is currently used only when other, more established treatments have failed to provide relief.

Treatment Procedure. TMS is an outpatient procedure that can be performed at a doctor's office. A typical course of treatment involves five sessions per week for four to six weeks. Each treatment session takes about 40 minutes.

During the procedure, a special electromagnetic coil is placed against the patient's scalp near the forehead. Because the device makes loud clicking sounds, the patient wears earplugs. The electromagnet produces very rapid pulses of highly concentrated magnetic fields, which pass through the hair, skin, and skull and penetrate two to three centimeters (about an inch) into the brain. These magnetic fields are similar in type and strength to those produced by a magnetic resonance imaging (MRI) machine. They are focused on a brain region that is thought to be involved in mood regulation.

The magnetic pulses produce tiny, painless electrical currents, which cause brain cells in this region to become active. The activated cells, in turn, may release **neurotransmitters**— naturally occurring chemicals that carry messages from one brain cell to another.

Depression involves abnormalities in various neurotransmitters, and normalizing levels of these brain chemicals is believed to help alleviate symptoms of the disorder.

Benefits for Depression. Direct stimulation of the brain with various devices is the new frontier of depression treatment. Magnetic stimulation is less invasive than methods requiring surgery, so it is a more appealing option to many people.

Most studies have found that TMS decreases symptoms of depression when compared to sham TMS, which looks like the real thing but does not actually produce magnetic fields. However, some researchers have found only small improvements, and others have found more substantial effects, comparable to those seen with medication. The TMS method used by the researchers may account for this difference, with newer methods showing larger effects than older ones. As researchers continue to refine the treatment procedure, the effectiveness may keep improving as well.

The results of TMS are temporary and may only last days or weeks. Also, like other treatments, TMS works better for some people than for others. Research suggests that it may be less effective for **older adults**, people with very long-lasting depression, and those with a coexisting anxiety disorder. It is still unclear whether TMS can be continued long term, or once depression has lifted, whether periodic booster treatments can keep the symptoms from returning.

Risks and Side Effects. Researchers are still trying to determine the optimal site in the brain for TMS and the best amount of stimulation. The stimulation may be adjusted over time, depending on a person's symptoms of depression or side effects of treatment.

The most common side effect of TMS is scalp discomfort at the stimulation site. Other possible effects include headache, lightheadedness, tingling or twitching of facial muscles, and discomfort from noise made by the TMS device. In rare cases, TMS also may cause seizures, hearing problems, or **mania** (a dangerously high or irritable mood). More research is needed to study the long-term effects of TMS.

See also: Brain Stimulation; Magnetic Seizure Therapy; Treatment of Depression; Treatment-Resistant Depression

Bibliography

Baldauf, Sarah. "Brain Stimulation: Transcranial Magnetic Stimulation." *U.S. News and World Report* (July 15, 2009).

Demitrack, M. A., and M. E. Thase. "Clinical Significance of Transcranial Magnetic Stimulation (TMS) in the Treatment of Pharmacoresistant Depression: Synthesis of Recent Data." *Psychopharmacology Bulletin* 42 (2009): 5–38.

Fitzgerald, Paul B., Timothy L. Brown, Natasha A. U. Marston, Z. Jeff Daskalakis, Anthony de Castella and Jayashri Kulkarni. "Transcranial Magnetic Stimulation in the Treatment of Depression." *Archives of General Psychiatry* 60 (2003): 1002–1008.

Gross, M., L. Nakamura, A. Pascual-Leone, and F. Fregni. "Has Repetitive Transcranial Magnetic Stimulation (rTMS) Treatment for Depression Improved? A Systematic Review and Meta-analysis Comparing the Recent vs. the Earlier rTMS Studies." *Acta Psychiatrica Scandinavica* 116 (2007): 165–173.

Lisanby, Sarah H., Mustafa M. Husain, Peter B. Rosenquist, Daniel Maixner, Rosben Gutierrez, Andrew Krystal, et al. "Daily Left Prefrontal Repetitive Transcranial Magnetic Stimulation in the Acute Treatment of Major Depression: Clinical Predictors of Outcome in a Multisite, Randomized Controlled Clinical Trial." *Neuropsychopharmacology* 34 (2009): 522–534.

NeuroStar TMS Therapy. Neuronetics, 2009, http://www.neurostartms.com.

O'Reardon, John P., H. Brent Solvason, Philip G. Janicak, Shirlene Sampson, Keith E. Isenberg, Ziad Nahas, et al. "Efficacy and Safety of Transcranial Magnetic Stimulation in the Acute Treatment of

Major Depression: A Multisite Randomized Controlled Trial." *Biological Psychiatry* 62 (2007): 1208–1216.

Transcranial Magnetic Stimulation. Mayo Clinic, July 26, 2008, http://www.mayoclinic.com/health/transcranial-magnetic-stimulation/MY00185.

TRANSPORTER.   A transporter is a protein complex that spans a cell membrane and ferries **neurotransmitters**, ions, and other substances between the outside and inside of the cell. Transporters play a critical role in regulating how much of a neurotransmitter, or chemical messenger, is available for use by the brain at any given time.

When two brain cells communicate, the message is carried across the tiny gap between them, called a synapse, by a neurotransmitter. Once the message is delivered, the neurotransmitter remains in the synapse, waiting to be disposed of. One way the brain can do this is by returning the neurotransmitter to the sending cell for reuse.

That is where the transporter comes in. Spanning the membrane of the sending cell, its job is to recognize and bind with neurotransmitter molecules. It then carries the molecules back into the cell that originally released them, a process known as **reuptake**.

One type of transporter that has been studied with regard to depression is the serotonin transporter, which serves as a conduit for serotonin, a neurotransmitter thought to play a key role in mood. In particular, research has linked depression to a variation on the **serotonin transporter gene**, which encodes for this particular protein complex. Research has shown that people with the genetic variation are especially likely to develop depression after experiencing a stressful life event.

Bibliography

Caspi, Avshalom, Karen Sugden, Terrie E. Moffitt, Alan Taylor, Ian W. Craig, HonaLee Harrington, et al. "Influence of Life Stress on Depression: Moderation by Polymorphism in the 5-HTT Gene." *Science* 301 (2003) 386–389.

Impacts of Drugs on Neurotransmission. National Institute on Drug Abuse, October 2007, http://www.nida.nih.gov/NIDA_notes/NNvol21N4/Impacts.html.

VandenBos, Gary R., ed. "Transporter," in *APA Dictionary of Psychology.* Washington, DC: American Psychological Association, 2007.

TRAUMATIC EVENTS.   Psychological traumas are events that threaten death or injury to oneself or others and that give rise to intense feelings of fear, horror, or helplessness. Exposure to a traumatic event at least once in a lifetime is not uncommon. Research shows that more than 50 percent of females and 60 percent of males experience a trauma at some point. Trauma exposure is a risk factor for a wide range of mental health disorders, including depression.

Examples of events that can be traumatic include child physical or sexual abuse, physical assault, rape, serious accidents, natural disasters, terrorist attacks, or the sudden, unexpected death of a loved one. People who experience a trauma firsthand are more likely to develop lasting psychological aftereffects than those who just witness or hear about it. Also, the more intense the trauma, the greater the risk of long-term psychological fallout.

One way trauma may have a prolonged effect on feelings, thoughts, and behavior is by changing how the brain itself functions. **Brain imaging** studies show that the **amygdala** and other closely related brain structures are often unusually reactive well after a traumatic event has passed. The amygdala, which is involved in emotional learning and the fear response, also tends to be overactive in people with depression.

Disasters in the News

In the modern world, traumatic events are witnessed not only by those on the scene, but also by television viewers and Internet users all over the world. Plus, they may be seen not just once, but over and over. How many Americans have never watched the disturbing images of people falling from the World Trade Center after the 9/11 terrorist attacks?

Such media images do not have the same visceral impact as firsthand experience, but they can still be very distressing. For adults directly affected by the event, studies suggest that reliving it through media reports may contribute to depression or PTSD. For example, a phone survey of people living near the World Trade Center found that those who frequently watched images of people falling or jumping from the towers were twice as likely to be depressed weeks later as those who did not watch frequently.

It is still unclear whether media reports lead to more depression, or depression leads to watching more trauma-related news. But many experts suggest that survivors of a traumatic event limit their viewing of media reports about the incident. Children seem to be particularly impressionable, so it may be wise to limit their exposure to media reports about any traumatic event, even if they were not personally affected.

Aftermath of Hurricane Katrina. A large-scale disaster, whether natural or manmade, gives researchers a unique window into the effects of trauma on large numbers of people. One review of the psychological literature identified 225 samples of disaster survivors. Depression was the second-most common psychological problem reported in these samples—second only to **post-traumatic stress disorder** (PTSD), an anxiety disorder that occurs specifically in response to trauma.

Hurricane Katrina, which led to the flooding of New Orleans in 2005, was the costliest and among the five deadliest hurricanes ever to strike the United States. In one study, about half of New Orleans residents continued to have mental health problems more than a year later.

Some of these problems may have been due to the trauma of the storm, and others may have been triggered or perpetuated by the ongoing **stress** of rebuilding. Depression was a prominent issue among those with poor mental health.

Another study included 93 Katrina survivors who had been relocated to Colorado after losing their homes. The survivors were interviewed within six months of the hurricane and then again six months later. Those with long-term depression or PTSD symptoms were characterized by low levels of adaptive coping and self-perceived coping ability. But another group of hurricane survivors, characterized by high levels of these coping skills, proved to be more resilient. They bounced back emotionally soon after the storm and continued to do well months later. This difference in coping ability may partly explain why some people develop long-term depression after a trauma but others recover from the psychological blow more quickly.

Child Abuse and Adult Depression. A large body of research now shows that trauma experienced early in life can have particularly lingering effects even decades later. Interestingly, many current researchers in the field have a biological orientation that is quite different from the psychoanalytic views of **Sigmund Freud** (1856–1939). Yet their results back up one of Freud's major contentions: that childhood trauma or loss can play a central role in shaping later experiences.

One rigorously designed study included 676 adults with a court-substantiated history of child abuse or neglect before age 11. The average age at the time of the study was 29. This group was compared with a matched group of adults who had no such history. Researchers found that child physical abuse or neglect was associated with an increased risk for **major depression** later in life. Among former abuse or neglect victims who became depressed, there was also a heightened risk for other mental health problems, such as PTSD, drug addiction, antisocial personality, and **dysthymia** (less intense but very persistent depression).

According to one hypothesis, early trauma may affect a child's developing stress response system, rendering it super-sensitive to even mild threats or minor challenges in the future. Over time, the strain of living with an overactive stress response may lead to depression. Specific genetic variations may help determine who is most susceptible to this effect.

Taken as a whole, research on the link between trauma and depression indicates a complex relationship. Biology, genetics, and learned coping skills all may have an important part to play.

See also: Corticotropin-Releasing Hormone; Environmental Factors

Further Information. International Society for Traumatic Stress Studies, 111 Deer Lake Road, Suite 100, Deerfield, IL 60015, (847) 480-9028, www.istss.org.

National Center for Child Traumatic Stress, University of California-Los Angeles, 11150 W. Olympic Blvd., Suite 650, Los Angeles, CA 90064, (310) 235-2633, www.nctsnet.org.

Bibliography

Bradley, Rebekah G., Elisabeth B. Binder, Michael P. Epstein, Yilang Tang, Hemu P. Nair, Wei Liu, et al. "Influence of Child Abuse on Adult Depression: Moderation by the Corticotropin-Releasing Hormone Receptor Gene." *Archives of General Psychiatry* 65 (2008): 190–200.

Foa, Edna B., and Linda Wasmer Andrews. *If Your Adolescent Has an Anxiety Disorder: An Essential Resource for Parents.* New York: Oxford University Press, 2006.

Ganzel, Barbara, B. J. Casey, Gary Glover, Henning U. Voss, and Elise Temple. "The Aftermath of 9/11: Effect of Intensity and Recency of Trauma on Outcome." *Emotion* 7 (2007): 227–238.

Kim, Son Chae, Ruth Plumb, Quynh-Nga Gredig, Larry Rankin, and Barbara Taylor. "Medium-Term Post-Katrina Health Sequelae Among New Orleans Residents: Predictors of Poor Mental and Physical Health." *Journal of Clinical Nursing* 17 (2008): 2335–2342.

Knabb, Richard D., Jamie R. Rhome, and Daniel P. Brown. *Tropical Cyclone Report: Hurricane Katrina, 23–30 August 2005.* National Hurricane Center, December 20, 2005, http://www.nhc.noaa.gov/pdf/TCR-AL122005_Katrina.pdf.

Norris, Fran H. *Range, Magnitude, and Duration of the Effects of Disasters on Mental Health: Review Update 2005.* Research Education Disaster Mental Health, March 2005, http://www.redmh.org/research/general/REDMH_effects.pdf.

Wadsworth, M. E., C. D. Santiago, and L. Einhorn. "Coping with Displacement from Hurricane Katrina: Predictors of One-Year Post-Traumatic Stress and Depression Symptom Trajectories." *Anxiety, Stress, and Coping* (April 3, 2009): e-publication ahead of print.

Widom, Cathy Spatz, Kimberly DuMont, and Sally J. Czaja. "A Prospective Investigation of Major Depressive Disorder and Comorbidity in Abused and Neglected Children Grown Up." *Archives of General Psychiatry* 64 (2007): 49–56.

TREATMENT FOR ADOLESCENTS WITH DEPRESSION STUDY. The Treatment for Adolescents with Depression Study (TADS), funded by the **National Institute of Mental Health**, was a major **clinical trial** that looked at options for treating **major depression** in **adolescents** ages 12 to 17. The $17 million study was carried out at 13 academic and community clinics across the United States. The results showed that a combination of **antidepressants** and **psychotherapy** was the most effective option, working better than either treatment used alone.

Findings from the first 12 weeks of the study were published in 2004 in the *Journal of the American Medical Association* (*JAMA*). Data from the full 36-week study period were published in 2007 in the *Archives of General Psychiatry.*

Study Design. The study enrolled 439 adolescents with major depression. It included a mix of younger and older adolescents from various parts of the country. The participants also represented both sexes and a variety of racial, ethnic, and socioeconomic backgrounds. As a result, the study's findings can be generalized to the broader adolescent population.

The treatments evaluated in the study were **fluoxetine, cognitive-behavioral therapy** (CBT), and a combination of the two. Fluoxetine is a widely prescribed antidepressant from the group known as **selective serotonin reuptake inhibitors**. CBT is a well-studied form of psychotherapy that helps people identify and change patterns of thought and behavior that may be contributing to their symptoms.

Stage 1. For the first 12 weeks of the study, participants were randomly assigned to one of four treatment groups: fluoxetine alone, a placebo (sugar pill) alone, CBT alone, or a combination of floxetine and CBT.

Results: After 12 weeks, 71 percent of those in the combination treatment group were improved. This was better than the improvement rates for fluoxetine alone (61 percent), CBT alone (43 percent), and the placebo (35 percent).

Stage 2. Participants in the combination, fluoxetine, and CBT groups who had improved during Stage 1 continued with their assigned treatment for six more weeks. Those taking a placebo who had not improved were allowed to choose any of the other three treatments in the study. Those on a placebo who had gotten better were followed for another 12 weeks and offered treatment if their depression worsened during that time.

Results: After 18 weeks, improvement with combination treatment (85 percent) still outpaced that seen with fluoxetine alone (69 percent) and CBT alone (65 percent).

Stage 3. Participants who continued to do well in Stage 2 moved on to Stage 3, which lasted for 18 more weeks, for a total of 36 weeks in the study.

Results: After 36 weeks, the greatest improvement was still seen with combination treatment (86 percent). The improvement rate for CBT alone (81 percent) had caught up to that for fluoxetine alone (81 percent).

What the Results Mean. The TADS results suggest that combining an antidepressant and psychotherapy is the most effective treatment overall for adolescents with depression. Of course, each person is different, and the decision about which treatment is best for a particular individual still must be made on a case-by-case basis.

In the study, fluoxetine was more effective than CBT during the first several weeks of treatment. Although CBT eventually caught up, adding fluoxetine may have prevented some unnecessary suffering early on.

Suicidal thinking decreased in all the treatment groups. Nevertheless, participants who took fluoxetine alone had higher rates of new and alarming suicidal thoughts and behavior than those who received CBT or combination treatment. Thus, adding CBT may have lessened the risk of **suicide**.

Bibliography

Questions and Answers About the NIMH Treatment for Adolescents with Depression Study (TADS). National Institute of Mental Health, June 26, 2008, http://www.nimh.nih.gov/health/trials/

practical/tads/questions-and-answers-about-the-nimh-treatment-for-adolescents-with
-depression-study-tads.shtml.

TADS Team. "The Treatment for Adolescents with Depression Study (TADS): Long-Term Effective-ness and Safety Outcomes." *Archives of General Psychiatry* 64 (2007): 1132–1144.

Treatment for Adolescents with Depression Study (TADS) Team. "Fluoxetine, Cognitive-Behavioral Therapy, and Their Combination for Adolescents with Depression: Treatment for Adolescents with Depression Study (TADS) Randomized Controlled Trial." *JAMA* 292 (2004): 807–820.

Treatment for Adolescents with Depression Study (TADS). National Institute of Mental Health, April 4, 2008, http://www.nimh.nih.gov/health/trials/practical/tads/index.shtml.

Treatment for Adolescents with Depression Study. Duke University, 2005, https://trialweb .dcri.duke.edu/tads/manuals.html.

TREATMENT OF DEPRESSION.   Depression is one of the most treatable of all men-tal disorders. The mainstays of treatment are **psychotherapy** (talk therapy), **pharma-cotherapy** (drug therapy), or a combination of both. Often, the initial treatment provider is a family doctor. But for full-blown depression, it is usually best to ask for a referral to a doctor or therapist who is a specialist in mental health care.

It may take some trial and error to find the best therapy and/or medication for a particu-lar individual. But eventually, most people, even those with severe depression, respond well to these two treatment approaches. For the minority who do not, other somatic treatments—which, like medication, target the physiological roots of depression in the brain—may be helpful. Eventually, almost everyone with depression can gain some relief from symptoms.

For people with mild to moderate depression, either psychotherapy or medication may be used as a solo treatment. The choice of which one to try first is based on factors such as patient preference and access to skilled therapists. In some cases, both treatments might be combined right from the start, even when depression is relatively mild. For example, this might happen for people with a history of poor treatment compliance or response, and there is also some evidence that it may be the best approach for **adolescents**.

For those with more severe depression, medication is usually required, either by itself or along with psychotherapy. **Antidepressants** are the primary class of medication used to treat depression.

Depression does not go away overnight, so it is important to give any treatment enough time to work before concluding that it is ineffective. In general, that means allowing at least four to eight weeks to see what benefits may accrue. During this period, the treatment provider monitors the patient closely, watching for signs of improvement and any side effects.

If the patient still is not feeling better after several weeks, the treatment provider might suggest increasing the dose of medication or intensity of therapy, switching to a new med-ication or therapy, or combining the two approaches. If the patient is already on an anti-depressant, adding a second type of medication to boost the antidepressant's effectiveness is another possibility.

Other Treatment Approaches.   Psychotherapy and medication are by far the most common treatments for depression, but they are not the only ones. **Electroconvulsive therapy** (ECT), which involves passing a carefully controlled electrical current through a person's brain to induce a brief seizure, is an established option for people with severe, per-sistent, or urgent symptoms. It has proved to be very effective for treating depression, even in many cases where other treatments have failed.

Light therapy involves daily exposure to a very bright light from an artificial source. It is a well-validated treatment for **seasonal affective disorder**, a form of depression in which symptoms start and stop around the same time each year, typically beginning in fall or winter and subsiding in spring.

Brain stimulation uses electrical current or magnetic fields to bring about desirable changes in brain function. ECT is the only form of brain stimulation that is currently considered a standard treatment for depression. But newer brain stimulation methods have been recently approved or are currently being tested, including **transcranial magnetic stimulation**, **vagus nerve stimulation**, **deep brain stimulation**, and **magnetic seizure therapy**.

St. John's wort is a popular herbal supplement. Research suggests it may be helpful for treating mild forms of depression. However, anyone who develops symptoms that cause serious distress or interfere with daily life should seek professional help rather than relying on self-care alone.

See also: Acute Treatment; Augmentation Therapy; Continuation Treatment; Maintenance Treatment

Bibliography

American Psychiatric Association Work Group on Major Depressive Disorder. *Practice Guideline for the Treatment of Patients with Major Depressive Disorder.* 2nd ed. Washington, DC: American Psychiatric Publishing, 2000.

Depression. American Psychiatric Association, http://www.healthyminds.org/Main-Topic/Depression.aspx.

Depression: Treatment and Drugs. Mayo Clinic, February 14, 2008, http://www.mayoclinic.com/health/depression/DS00175/DSECTION=treatments-and-drugs.

Fochtmann, Laura J., and Alan J. Gelenberg. "Guideline Watch: Practice Guideline for the Treatment of Patients with Major Depressive Disorder, 2nd Edition." *APA Practice Guidelines.* American Psychiatric Association, September 2005, http://www.psychiatryonline.com/content.aspx?aid=148217.

How Is Depression Detected and Treated? National Institute of Mental Health, January 30, 2009, http://nimh.nih.gov/health/publications/depression/how-is-depression-detected-and-treated.shtml.

Treatment for Adolescents with Depression Study (TADS) Team. "Fluoxetine, Cognitive-Behavioral Therapy, and Their Combination for Adolescents with Depression: Treatment for Adolescents with Depression Study (TADS) Randomized Controlled Trial." *JAMA* 292 (2004): 807–820.

TREATMENT-RESISTANT DEPRESSION. Treatment-resistant depression refers to the situation in which people receive at least one treatment for depression at an adequate dose or intensity and for a sufficient time, yet their symptoms do not go away. In some cases, people continue to have symptoms despite trying three or four—or even more—different treatments.

Of course, many people with depression feel better and get back to their usual selves after the first treatment they try. Studies have found that a little over half of depressed people who are treated with a first type of medication or psychotherapy have the severity of their symptoms cut by at least 50 percent. Out of that group, about two-thirds become symptom-free. But that still leaves a sizable fraction of people for whom the first treatment is not adequate.

The good news is that a wide range of effective treatments now exist for depression. If the first—or second or third—one tried does not work, the next one may do the job. Research shows that complete relief from all symptoms is a realistic goal for many people with treatment-resistant depression. Those who achieve a complete **recovery** are less likely to have their symptoms come back later than those who have only a **partial remission**. But even those whose recovery is incomplete often feel substantially better.

Causes and Risk Factors. Several factors may contribute to treatment-resistant depression. In general, the more severe depression is and the longer it lasts, the more difficult it is to treat. When people don't take their medication as prescribed or skip their therapy appointments, they may miss out on the full benefits of treatment.

At times, the problem may actually be a case of mistaken identity. In particular, **bipolar disorder** sometimes is misdiagnosed as **major depression** when the depressive phases are more pronounced than the manic ones. Coexisting mental and physical health problems—such as thyroid disease, chronic pain, heart disease, **anxiety disorders,** and **substance abuse**—also can mimic or worsen depression. For the best results, it is crucial to treat these other conditions.

Ongoing **stress** may intensify or prolong symptoms of depression as well. In such cases, **psychotherapy** can help people learn coping skills and **stress management** techniques that help them make the most of treatment.

Treatment of Resistant Depression. Finding the right treatment for depression can involve some trial and error. For people who have already tried one or more treatments without success, it pays to keep trying. There is a good chance they will eventually find the right treatment for them, although some patience may be required.

The **Sequenced Treatment Alternatives to Relieve Depression** (STAR*D) study, funded by the National Institute of Mental Health, is the largest and longest study ever done to evaluate treatments for depression. The study was divided into four phases, each of which tested a different treatment or combination of treatments. If people did not become symptom-free after treatment in one phase, they could move on to the next.

The STAR*D study showed that many people with depression who do not get enough relief from the first medication they try eventually get better by either switching to a different medication or adding a new medication to the current one. The add-on strategy can take two forms: combination or augmentation. Combination therapy involves combining **antidepressants** of two different types to heighten their effect. **Augmentation therapy** involves combining an antidepressant with a medication that was not originally intended to treat depression, but which may boost the antidepressant's action.

Although it has not been studied as systematically, a stepwise strategy for finding the right form of psychotherapy also makes sense. People who tried psychotherapy unsuccessfully in the past might consider trying a new therapist or different approach, such as **family therapy**, **group therapy**, **cognitive behavioral analysis system of psychotherapy**, or **dialectical behavior therapy**. Also, when it has been a while since the last attempt, people sometimes find that their attitude has changed, leading to better results this time around.

Hope Through Technology. When several types of medication and psychotherapy have been tried without success, other options are available. **Electroconvulsive therapy** (ECT) involves passing a carefully controlled electrical current through the person's brain, which induces a brief seizure that is thought to alter some of the electrochemical processes involved in brain functioning.

Although ECT has been around for decades, newer treatments are available, too. **Vagus nerve stimulation** uses a small implanted device, similar to a pacemaker, to deliver mild electrical pulses to the vagus nerve. This nerve then transmits the pulses to the brain, targeting areas that affect mood and other symptoms of depression. **Transcranial magnetic**

stimulation uses short pulses of magnetic fields to stimulate brain cells in an area of the brain thought to affect mood.

Experimental options include **magnetic seizure therapy**, in which powerful magnetic fields induce a mild seizure, and **deep brain stimulation**, in which electrodes are surgically implanted in the brain. For the minority of people who are not helped by any standard treatments, these investigational approaches provide fresh hope.

See also: Brain Stimulation; Chronic Depression

Bibliography

Fava, Maurizio, and Katharine G. Davidson. "Definition and Epidemiology of Treatment-Resistant Depression." *Psychiatric Clinics of North America* 19 (1996): 179–200.

McGrath, Patrick J., Jonathan W. Stewart, Maurizio Fava, Madhukar H. Trivedi, Stephen R. Wisniewski, Andrew A. Nierenberg, et al. "Tranylcypromine Versus Venlafaxine Plus Mirtazapine Following Three Failed Antidepressant Medication Trials for Depression: A STAR*D Report." *American Journal of Psychiatry* 163 (2006): 1531–1541.

Next Steps: Getting the Treatment You Need to Reach Real Recovery. Depression and Bipolar Support Alliance, 2006, http://www.dbsalliance.org/pdfs/NextSteps.pdf.

Nierenberg, Andrew A., Maurizio Fava, Madhukar H. Trivedi, Stephen R. Wisniewski, Michael E. Thase, Patrick J. McGrath, et al. "A Comparison of Lithium and T$_3$ Augmentation Following Two Failed Medication Treatments for Depression: A STAR*D Report." *American Journal of Psychiatry* 163 (2006): 1519–1530.

*Questions and Answers About the NIMH Sequenced Treatment Alternatives to Relieve Depression (STAR*D) Study: All Medication Levels.* National Institute of Mental Health, June 26, 2008, http://www.nimh.nih.gov/health/trials/practical/stard/questions-and-answers-about-the-nimh-sequenced-treatment-alternatives-to-relieve-depression-stard-study-all-medication-levels.shtml.

*Questions and Answers About the NIMH Sequenced Treatment Alternatives to Relieve Depression (STAR*D) Study: Background.* National Institute of Mental Health, June 26, 2008, http://www.nimh.nih.gov/health/trials/practical/stard/questions-and-answers-about-the-nimh-sequenced-treatment-alternatives-to-relieve-depression-stard-study-background.shtml.

Treatment-Resistant Depression: Explore Options When Depression Won't Go Away. Mayo Clinic, August 29, 2007, http://www.mayoclinic.com/health/treatment-resistant-depression/DN00016.

TRICYCLIC ANTIDEPRESSANTS. Tricyclic antidepressants—named for their three-ring molecular structure—are an older group of antidepressant medications, dating back to the 1950s. The original first-line **antidepressants**, they remain in use today. They are closely related to tetracyclic antidepressants, which have a four-ring molecular structure, but which are otherwise generally similar. The two types of antidepressants are discussed together here, and the abbreviation TCA is inclusive for both.

Although TCAs are comparable in effectiveness to newer antidepressants, they tend to cause more side effects. But because different individuals respond differently to specific medications, TCAs may still be helpful for some people.

TCAs work by blocking the **reuptake**, or reabsorption, of three important brain chemicals: **serotonin**, **norepinephrine**, and **dopamine**. In most cases, serotonin and norepinephrine are affected far more than dopamine. By inhibiting reuptake, TCAs increase the availability of these chemicals in the brain, which is thought to reduce depression. But TCAs also affect other types of cell **receptors**, which can lead to a wide range of unwanted effects.

Despite the potential for adverse effects, TCAs may help some individuals with depression when first-choice antidepressants do not work. For those who have trouble sleeping, the sedating effects of TCAs may come in handy. Also, for some **chronic pain** sufferers with depression, TCAs may help not only improve their mood, but also control their pain.

In addition to the impact on depression, some TCAs also affect anxiety. Clomipramine is approved by the Food and Drug Administration (FDA) as a treatment for **obsessive-compulsive disorder**, an anxiety disorder characterized by recurrent, uncontrollable thoughts (obsessions) and actions (compulsions). Doxepin is also FDA-approved for treating general anxiety.

TCA Antidepressants

	Brand Names*
Tricyclic Antidepressants	
Amitriptyline†	Elavil
Clomipramine‡	Anafranil
Desipramine†	Norpramin
Doxepin†‡	Sinequan
Imipramine†	Tofranil
Nortriptyline†	Aventyl, Pamelor
Protriptyline†	Vivactil
Trimipramine†	Surmontil
Tetracyclic Antidepressants	
Amoxapine†	Asendin
Maprotiline†‡	Ludiomil
Combination Products	
Amitriptyline + chlordiazepoxide (an anti-anxiety medication)†‡	Limbitrol
Amitriptyline + perphenazine (an antipsychotic)†‡	Etrafon, Triavil

† FDA approved for treating depression

‡ FDA approved for treating anxiety or a specific anxiety disorder

* Some antidepressants are no longer sold as brand-name products, but are still available in generic form

Use and Precautions. People with depression may need to take a TCA for several weeks to feel the full benefits. Even after they are doing better, most need to stay on medication for at least six to nine months, and sometimes for years, to help keep symptoms from coming back.

People just starting a TCA usually begin on a low dose, which may be gradually increased until the doctor finds the optimal dosage. The medication is taken by mouth one to four times daily. It should be taken as directed around the same time every day—often at bedtime, because drowsiness is a common side effect.

Although TCAs are not considered addictive, stopping them abruptly can lead to withdrawal-like symptoms called **antidepressant discontinuation syndrome**. To prevent this problem, it is important to take the medication exactly as prescribed. When it is time to stop, a doctor can explain how to taper it off a little at a time.

Risks and Side Effects. Potential side effects of TCAs include drowsiness, dry mouth, blurred vision, constipation, dizziness, nausea, trouble urinating, sexual problems, faster heart rate, low blood pressure, confusion, headache, sensitivity to sunlight, increased appetite, weight gain, and weakness. TCAs should generally be avoided by people with **heart disease**, **diabetes**, narrow-angle glaucoma, or an enlarged prostate.

Coping with Side Effects

Side effects and safety concerns are the major downside to TCAs. People taking these medications should talk to their doctor about strategies for minimizing adverse effects. In some cases, measures such as those below can make problems more manageable. In other cases, the doctor may change the dose or switch the medication.

Dry Mouth

TCAs block the action of a chemical messenger in the nervous system called acetylcholine, and that in turn reduces saliva. To counter this problem, it may help to frequently sip water, eat ice chips, chew sugarless gum, or suck on sugarless hard candy. Your doctor or dentist may also recommend an artificial saliva product or oral rinse.

Blurred Vision

TCAs can dry out the eyes too, causing blurred vision. Ask your doctor about artificial tears, gels, gel inserts, and ointments that help keep the eyes moist. A checkup by an eye doctor can rule out other medical conditions that might be causing the vision problem.

Constipation

Blocking the action of acetylcholine also disrupts the workings of the digestive tract, which can lead to constipation. To counter this problem, drink plenty of fluids and eat a diet rich in high-fiber foods, such as whole grains, bran cereal, beans, and fresh fruits and vegetables. If needed, ask your doctor about fiber supplements and stool softeners.

Dizziness

TCAs can cause blood pressure to drop, leading to dizziness. The problem is particularly common in **older adults**. If you develop this side effect, avoid driving or operating dangerous machinery. Get up slowly after sitting or lying down, and use rails or sturdy furniture for support. Your doctor might also recommend taking the TCA at bedtime.

Call Your Doctor

Contact your doctor right away about severe or unusual side effects.

Because depression increases the risk of a **suicide** attempt, the possibility of an intentional overdose is always a concern. A TCA overdose can be dangerous or even lethal, especially when combined with alcohol or other drugs. Possible consequences of taking too much of a TCA include seizures and abnormal heart rhythms.

Antidepressants may save lives by reducing depression and thus decreasing the risk of suicide. In a small number of **children**, **adolescents**, and young adults, however, taking antidepressants may actually lead to worsening mood symptoms or increased suicidal thoughts and behavior. Patients taking TCAs—or parents of younger patients—should be alert for any suicidal thoughts and actions or unusual changes in mood and behavior. If such symptoms occur, they should contact their doctor right away.

See also: Antidepressants and Suicide; Treatment of Depression

Bibliography

Antidepressants: Get Tips to Cope with Side Effects. Mayo Clinic, December 9, 2008, http://www.mayoclinic.com/health/antidepressants/MH00062.

Clomipramine. National Library of Medicine, September 1, 2008, http://www.nlm.nih.gov/medlineplus/druginfo/meds/a697002.html.

Constipation. National Digestive Diseases Information Clearinghouse, July 2007, http://digestive.niddk.nih.gov/ddiseases/pubs/constipation.

Dry Eye. National Eye Institute, September 2009, http://www.nei.nih.gov/health/dryeye/dryeye.asp.

Dry Mouth. American Dental Association, http://www.ada.org/public/topics/dry_mouth.asp.

Flanagan, Robert J. "Fatal Toxicity of Drugs Used in Psychiatry." *Human Psychophamacology* 23 (2008): 43–51.

Imipramine. National Library of Medicine, September 1, 2008, http://www.nlm.nih.gov/medline plus/druginfo/meds/a682389.html.

Maprotiline. National Library of Medicine, September 1, 2008, http://www.nlm.nih.gov/medline plus/druginfo/meds/a682158.html.

Medication Information Sheet. Depression and Bipolar Support Alliance, May 4, 2006, http://www.dbsalliance.org/site/PageServer?pagename=about_treatment_medinfosheet.

Mental Health Medications. National Institute of Mental Health, July 28, 2009, http://www.nimh .nih.gov/health/publications/mental-health-medications/complete-index.shtml.

Protriptyline. National Library of Medicine, September 1, 2008, http://www.nlm.nih.gov/medline plus/druginfo/meds/a604025.html.

Taylor, D. "Antidepressant Drugs and Cardiovascular Pathology: A Clinical Overview of Effectiveness and Safety." *Acta Psychiatrica Scandinavica* 188 (2008): 434–442.

Tricyclic Antidepressants (TCAs). Mayo Clinic, December 10, 2008, http://www.mayoclinic.com/ health/antidepressants/MH00071.

TRYPTOPHAN. Tryptophan is an essential amino acid, a building block of protein that must be obtained from the diet, because the body cannot produce it. Once consumed, tryptophan is used by the body to help make niacin (a B vitamin) and **serotonin** (a brain chemical that helps regulate sleep and mood). A deficiency in serotonin is thought to be a key factor in causing depression. And because tryptophan is a precursor of serotonin, it is another link in the chain of events that lead up to depressive symptoms.

Tryptophan is found in protein foods, such as turkey, chicken, milk, cheese, fish, eggs, tofu, seeds, nuts, and peanuts. Only a small amount of tryptophan is needed, and the typical Western diet contains more than enough.

L-tryptophan, a form of the amino acid, also is sold as a dietary supplement. A couple of decades back, the Food and Drug Administration (FDA) restricted the availability of L-tryptophan supplements in the United States after they were linked to a 1989 outbreak of eosinophilia-myalgia syndrome (EMS), a debilitating disorder affecting multiple organ systems. Symptoms of EMS include fatigue, muscle pain and weakness, joint pain, anxiety, depression, tight-feeling skin, and trouble concentrating. More than 1,500 cases of EMS, including at least 37 deaths, were reported to the Centers for Disease Control and Prevention in connection with the outbreak.

It later came to light that most of these cases could be traced to supplements from one Japanese lab, implying that the EMS-causing supplements might have been contaminated. In 2001, the FDA loosened the reins on marketing L-tryptophan supplements, and they are once again widely available. But questions linger about whether EMS is caused by L-tryptophan itself, supplement impurities, or a combination of the two, perhaps acting in concert with other environmental or genetic factors. Until such questions are finally resolved, caution is still recommended.

Connection to Depression. Tryptophan played a prominent role in early research on the link between serotonin and depression. Before it was possible to measure serotonin in the brain directly, scientists had to rely on indirect study methods. One popular study protocol, called tryptophan depletion, involved giving people a drink loaded with amino acids except for tryptophan. Within hours, this caused a dramatic drop in blood tryptophan levels.

Tryptophan depletion studies yielded interesting but complex results. Among depressed individuals who were being treated with serotonin-boosting **antidepressants**, most who had only partially recovered from depression suffered an immediate relapse after this procedure. The relapse was reversed by eating a tryptophan-rich meal. On the other hand, relapse after tryptophan depletion was rare in people who had already fully recovered from depression. Relapse was also uncommon in those taking antidepressants that primarily boost a brain chemical other than serotonin.

Healthy volunteers with no family history of depression were unaffected by tryptophan depletion. Also, among people with untreated depression, depleting tryptophan did not make their symptoms worse. Taken together, these studies indicate that tryptophan does indeed affect depression via serotonin, but in complicated ways.

Tryptophan + Antidepressant.   Researchers have wondered whether adding tryptophan to an antidepressant might lead to greater benefits than the antidepressant alone. Some studies have found an added benefit, but others have not.

In one study of **major depression** conducted by Toronto researchers, a low dose of the antidepressant **fluoxetine** was combined with 2 grams or 4 grams daily of tryptophan, which is sold by prescription in Canada. At 4 grams, tryptophan produced daytime drowsiness. But the combination of fluoxetine and 2 grams daily of tryptophan was well tolerated, and it led to faster relief of symptoms—an important benefit, because it can take weeks for the effects of a standard antidepressant to kick in.

Any additive effect may be due to the complementary ways in which tryptophan and fluoxetine work. Serotonin is a chemical messenger that carries information between brain cells. Tryptophan increases the amount of serotonin before it is released by a sending cell, and fluoxetine blocks its reabsorption after it has been released. But this was a small study, so more research is needed before firm conclusions are drawn.

Although tryptophan might possibly increase an antidepressant's benefits, it also could increase the side effects. Anyone on an antidepressant should consult a physician before taking tryptophan.

See also: Tryptophan Hydroxylase Gene

Bibliography

"Current Trends Eosinophilia-Myalgia Syndrome: Follow-Up Survey of Patients—New York, 1990–1991." *MMWR* 40 (1991): 401–403.

Information Paper on L-Tryptophan and 5-Hydroxy-L-Tryptophan. Food and Drug Administration, February 2001, http://www.cfsan.fda.gov/~dms/ds-tryp1.html.

Levitan, Robert D., Jian-Hua Shen, Ripu Jindal, Helen S. Driver, Sidney H. Kennedy, and Colin M. Shapiro. "Preliminary Randomized Double-Blind Placebo-Controlled Trial of Tryptophan Combined with Fluoxetine to Treat Major Depressive Disorder: Antidepressant and Hypnotic Effects." *Journal of Psychiatry and Neuroscience* 25 (2000): 337–346.

Moore, Polly, Hans-Peter Landolt, Erich Seifritz, Camellia Clark, Tahir Bhatti, John Kelsoe, et al. "Clinical and Physiological Consequences of Rapid Tryptophan Depletion." *Neuropsychopharmacology* 23 (2000): 601–622.

Neumeister, Alexander. "Tryptophan Depletion, Serotonin, and Depression: Where Do We Stand?" *Translational Neuroscience* 37 (2003): 99–115.

Slattery, D. A., A. L. Hudson and D. J. Nutt. "Invited Review: The Evolution of Antidepressant Mechanisms." *Fundamental and Clinical Pharmacology* 18 (2004): 1–21.

Tryptophan. National Library of Medicine, May 1, 2006, http://www.nlm.nih.gov/medlineplus/ency/article/002332.htm.

TRYPTOPHAN HYDROXYLASE GENE. The tryptophan hydroxylase (TPH) gene makes the TPH enzyme. This enzyme is involved in the production of **serotonin**, a brain chemical that is thought to play a central role in depression. Scientists searching for the genetic roots of depression have often focused on genes related to serotonin, and TPH is among the ones that have been singled out for study.

The TPH enzyme transforms a dietary amino acid called **tryptophan** into 5-hydroxytryptophan (5-HTP). Then 5-HTP is converted in the brain to 5-hydroxytryptamine—the chemical name for serotonin.

The conversion of tryptophan into 5-HTP is the rate-limiting step in the production of serotonin. In other words, it is the slowest step in the process, and thus the one that determines how quickly serotonin is made. The rate at which this conversion takes place is affected by levels of tryptophan in the brain as well as by levels of activity in the brain cells that use serotonin as a chemical messenger.

It is easy to see why scientists have focused on the TPH gene, which sets this whole chain of events in motion. Variations in the gene may lead to dysfunction in the serotonin-production process. That dysfunction could be a contributing factor in the development of depression.

Two Types of TPH Gene. There are two different types of TPH gene, known as TPH1 and TPH2. In human studies, a mutation in the TPH2 gene has been linked to depression in some people. In animal research, mice genetically engineered to have a comparable mutation showed a profound reduction in serotonin levels.

The TPH1 gene also influences serotonin. Research has shown that variation in that gene is associated with a higher risk for suicidal behavior. It also is linked to an increased risk for **bipolar disorder**, a mental disorder in which people alternate between overly high and overly low moods.

See also: Genetic Factors

Bibliography

Chen, C., S. J. Glatt, and M. T. Tsuang. "The Tryptophan Hydroxylase Gene Influences Risk for Bipolar Disorder but Not Major Depressive Disorder: Results of Meta-analyses." *Bipolar Disorders* 10 (2008): 816–821.

Galfalvy, Hanga, Yung-Yu Huang, Maria A. Oquendo, Dianne Currier, and J. John Mann. "Increased Risk of Suicide Attempt in Mood Disorders and TPH1 Genotype." *Journal of Affective Disorders* (October 30, 2008): e-publication ahead of print.

Tomorrow's Antidepressants: Skip the Serotonin Boost? National Institute of Mental Health, February 14, 2008, http://www.nimh.nih.gov/science-news/2008/tomorrows-antidepressants-skip-the-serotonin-boost.shtml.

VandenBos, Gary R., ed. "Tryptophan Hydroxylase" and "5-Hydroxytryptophan," in *APA Dictionary of Psychology.* Washington, DC: American Psychological Association, 2007.

U

UNIPOLAR DEPRESSION. Unipolar depression is an umbrella term that refers to any mood disorder in which there are episodes of depression (an overly low mood), but no alternating episodes of **mania** (an overly high mood). This stands in contrast to **bipolar disorder**, in which people cycle back and forth between the two mood extremes.

When people talk about unipolar depression, they often mean **major depression**, a mood disorder that involves being in a low mood nearly all the time and/or losing interest or enjoyment in almost everything. In major depression, these feelings last for at least two weeks, are associated with several other symptoms, and lead to serious problems getting along in everyday life.

Unipolar depression also can include **dysthymia**, a form of depression that involves being mildly depressed most of the day. These feelings occur more days than not for at least two years and are associated with other symptoms. In both dysthymia and major depression, the abnormal mood goes in just one direction. There are excessively low dips, but never excessively high peaks.

Bibliography

American Psychiatric Association. *Diagnostic and Statistical Manual of Mental Disorders.* 4th ed., text rev. Washington, DC: American Psychiatric Association, 2000.

V

VAGUS NERVE STIMULATION. Vagus nerve stimulation (VNS) is a relatively new treatment that uses a small implanted device, similar to a pacemaker, to deliver mild electrical pulses to the vagus nerve. This nerve then transmits the pulses to the brain, targeting areas that affect mood and other symptoms of depression. VNS was originally introduced as a treatment for **epilepsy**. In 2005, the Food and Drug Administration approved its use as a long-term, add-on therapy for people with chronic or recurrent **major depression** who have unsuccessfully tried at least four other treatments, such as four different **antidepressants**.

The vagus nerve is a primary communication pathway from the brain to the body's major organs. There is one vagus nerve on each side of the body; VNS targets the one on the left. This nerve runs from the brainstem, through the left side of the neck, and into the chest and abdomen. By sending electrical signals back up this pathway to the brain, VNS aims to create a reaction that will improve mood and reduce depressive symptoms.

Studies of the treatment's effectiveness have yielded mixed results, however. If the treatment works as intended, symptoms of depression decrease or go away, although it might take several months to see noticeable improvement. Not everyone gets better, though. And in some cases, depression may even get worse with VNS.

Clearly, VNS is not for everyone. Yet for those with hard-to-treat depression who have exhausted other options, it offers fresh hope. To maximize the benefits, VNS is usually combined with standard treatments, such as antidepressants or **psychotherapy**.

Treatment Procedure. VNS requires surgery to implant the pacemaker-like device, called a pulse generator. The surgery takes one to two hours. It can be done on either an outpatient basis, where the patient goes home that same day, or an inpatient basis, where the patient stays in the hospital overnight. Either general or local anesthesia may be used.

During the surgery, the pulse generator is implanted through a small incision in the upper left side of the chest. This battery-powered device is about the size of a stopwatch. A thin, flexible wire connected to the pulse generator is guided under the skin to the left side of the neck. There, the wire is attached to the left vagus nerve through a second small incision.

A few weeks after surgery, the pulse generator is turned on during a visit to the doctor's office. The device is typically set to deliver stimulation that lasts for 30 seconds and occurs every five minutes around the clock. But the duration, frequency, and current can be adjusted by the doctor depending on a particular person's symptoms and side effects.

Periodic doctor visits are needed to make sure the device is working properly and has not shifted out of position.

Side effects, such as a raspy voice or shortness of breath upon exertion, sometimes occur during the stimulation periods. Such unwanted effects, even if mild, may be troublesome at certain times; for example, during public speaking, while singing, or when exercising. Patients are given a magnetic controller that can be held over the pulse generator to temporarily stop stimulation at such times.

Benefits for Depression. VNS targets areas of the brain that affect the production or activity of two brain chemicals, **norepinephrine** and **serotonin**. These chemicals are thought to be involved in depression, and many antidepressants increase the availability of one or both. The vagus nerve carries sensory information from the body to the locus coeruleus, an area in the brainstem that is a major source of norepinephrine, and the raphe nuclei, the main source of serotonin.

VNS therapy may sometimes succeed when other treatments for depression do not help or have stopped working. Although some people start feeling better within a few weeks of starting VNS, many take several months for the benefits to kick in. After a year of treatment, about one person in three is feeling better, and research shows that most of these individuals maintain their improvement through the second year. For some people, long-term VNS may decrease the need for medication over time.

Risks and Side Effects. Although VNS is generally safe, there are some risks associated with the initial surgery as well as possible side effects of the **brain stimulation**. Potential surgical complications include pain, infection, damage to the vagus nerve, heart or lung problems, nausea, and scarring.

Possible side effects of the brain stimulation include voice changes, cough, neck or chest pain, breathing problems during exercise, difficulty swallowing, tingling of the skin, and tickling in the throat. Less commonly, VNS might actually lead to worsening of depression or suicidal thoughts and behavior. There is also a chance that the pulse generator could malfunction or move out of place, necessitating further surgery.

Most side effects are mild to moderate, and many can be minimized by having the doctor adjust the timing or strength of the electrical pulses. If the side effects become too bothersome, the device can be shut off temporarily or permanently.

See also: Treatment of Depression

Bibliography

George, Mark S., A. John Rush, Lauren B. Marangell, Harold A. Sackeim, Stephen K. Brannan, Sonia M. Davis, et al. "A One-Year Comparison of Vagus Nerve Stimulation with Treatment as Usual for Treatment-Resistant Depression." *Biological Psychiatry* 58 (2005): 364–373.

Marangell, L. B., M. Martinez, R. A. Jurdi, and H. Zboyan. "Neurostimulation Therapies in Depression: A Review of New Modalities." *Acta Psychiatric Scandinavica* 116 (2007): 174–181.

Rush, A. John, Harold A. Sackeim, Lauren B. Marangell, Mark S. George, Stephen K. Brannan, Sonia M. Davis, et al. "Effects of 12 Months of Vagus Nerve Stimulation in Treatment-Resistant Depression: A Naturalistic Study." *Biological Psychiatry* 58 (2005): 355–363.

Sackeim, Harold A., Stephen K. Brannan, A. John Rush, Mark S. George, Lauren B. Marangell, and John Allen. "Durability of Antidepressant Response to Vagus Nerve Stimulation (VNS™)." *International Journal of Neuropsychopharmacology* 10 (2007): 817–826.

Vagus Nerve Stimulation. Mayo Clinic, July 31, 2008, http://www.mayoclinic.com/health/vagus-nerve-stimulation/MY00183.

Vagus Nerve Stimulation Therapy. Cyberonics, 2007, http://www.vnstherapy.com.

VETERANS.   Few situations offer greater opportunity for exposure to chronic **stress** and **traumatic events** than wartime military service—and stress and trauma frequently trigger mental health problems. Of veterans who seek mental health care through the Department of Veterans Affairs (VA), 30 percent have depression. Other common problems among veterans include **post-traumatic stress disorder**, shorter-term stress reactions, and **substance abuse**.

In a recent survey of 312,000 U.S. military veterans in their twenties and thirties, nine percent reported having at least one episode of **major depression** within the past year—a slightly higher rate than in the population as a whole. But over half said they had experienced some significant problems that affected their ability to get along at home, at work, in personal relationships, or in social life. Other studies have shown that such problems tend to increase for at least several months after coming home from Iraq or Afghanistan. Returning National Guard and Reserve soldiers may have particular trouble readjusting to their civilian jobs and life outside the military.

For veterans who develop full-blown depression, getting prompt, appropriate treatment can help heal the wounds of war and ease the transition back to everyday life. The VA offers readjustment counseling services for veterans and their families as well as mental health outpatient services and inpatient psychiatric care at facilities around the country. In addition, a special **suicide** prevention hotline (800–273-TALK; press "1") for veterans provides 24/7 crisis counseling by phone.

Further Information.   Department of Veterans Affairs, (800) 827-1000, www.mentalhealth.va.gov.

Bibliography

Major Depressive Episode and Treatment for Depression Among Veterans Aged 21 to 39. Substance Abuse and Mental Health Services Administration Office of Applied Studies, November 6, 2008, http://oas.samhsa.gov/2k8/veteransDepressed/veteransDepressed.htm.

Milliken, Charles S., Jennifer L. Auchterlonie, and Charles W. Hoge. "Longitudinal Assessment of Mental Health Problems Among Active and Reserve Component Soldiers Returning From the Iraq War." *JAMA* 298 (2007): 2141–2148.

Returning From the War Zone: A Guide for Families of Military Members. National Center for Posttraumatic Stress Disorder, http://www.mentalhealth.va.gov/ptsd/files/FamilyGuide.pdf.

Seal, Karen H., Daniel Bertenthal, Christian R. Miner, Saunak Sen, and Charles Marmar. "Bringing the War Back Home: Mental Health Disorders Among 103 788 US Veterans Returning From Iraq and Afghanistan Seen at Department of Veterans Affairs Facilities." *Archives of Internal Medicine* 167 (2007): 476–482.

Veterans FAQs. National Suicide Prevention Lifeline, http://www.suicidepreventionlifeline.org/Veterans/FAQs.aspx.

VITAMIN B12.   Vitamin B12 is a vitamin that helps maintain healthy nerve and red blood cells. It is also needed to help make DNA, the genetic material inside every cell of the body. One possible symptom of vitamin B12 deficiency is depression. A study of 700 physically disabled women over age 65 found that those who were deficient in the vitamin were twice as likely to be severely depressed as those who were not deficient. An association between lack of the vitamin and depression also has been reported in older men.

Researchers are still studying how vitamin B12 might affect mood. Vitamin B12 and other B vitamins help break down an amino acid called homocysteine in the body. Homocysteine is then converted into **S-adenosyl-L-methionine** (SAMe), a compound that helps form chemical messengers in the brain. These brain chemicals include **serotonin** and **dopamine**, both of which are thought to play important roles in depression.

When B vitamin levels are low, homocysteine can build up in the blood. High blood levels of homocysteine are associated with an increased risk of stroke. Stroke-related damage in certain areas of the brain may be one reason for the high rate of depression seen in stroke survivors.

Therefore, lack of vitamin B12 may contribute to depression—but depression may contribute to vitamin deficiencies as well. People with depression might fail to get enough B12 due to loss of appetite and unhealthy food choices.

When a Deficiency Occurs.   A vitamin B12 deficiency can lead to symptoms of nerve damage, including mood changes, memory loss, confusion, difficulty walking, and numbness and tingling of the limbs. These symptoms are sometimes permanent if the deficiency is left untreated for a long time.

The cause of such symptoms is not fully understood. However, it is known that a vitamin B12 deficiency can damage the nerves' myelin sheath, a fatty covering that protects nerve fibers.

Most people in the United States get the recommended amount of vitamin B12 in their **diet**. But because the vitamin is naturally found in foods that come from animals, some strict vegetarians may not consume enough. More commonly, though, a deficiency occurs when people have a stomach or intestinal condition that keeps them from absorbing the vitamin normally. Such conditions include celiac disease, Crohn's disease, and surgical procedures in which part of the stomach or intestines is removed.

Up to 30 percent of adults over age 50 have atrophic gastritis, an inflammation of the stomach that reduces the secretion of gastric juices. People with this disorder may be unable to absorb natural B12 as well as they once did. However, they can still absorb the synthetic B12 that is added to fortified foods and found in **dietary supplements**.

Sources of Vitamin B12.   The Recommended Dietary Allowance (RDA) for vitamin B12 is 2.4 micrograms for adults of both sexes, except during pregnancy and breastfeeding, when the daily requirement rises. Good food sources include fish, meat, poultry, eggs, milk, dairy products, and fortified cereals.

Daily Vitamin B12 Requirement

Age	Micrograms (μg)
Birth–6 months	0.4*
7–12 months	0.5*
1–3 years	0.9
4–8 years	1.2
9–13 years	1.8
14 years and up	2.4
Pregnancy	2.6
Breastfeeding	2.8

* For infants, the Institute of Medicine has set "Idequate Intake levels" rather than RDAs. This is done when the scientific evidence is insufficient to set a firm RDA, so guidelines instead give the nutrient intake that is assumed to be adequate based on the best available information.

Doctors may recommend vitamin B12 supplements or an increased intake of fortified foods for vegetarians and **older adults**. To avoid a deficiency, some doctors advise older adults to take 100 to 400 micrograms of supplemental B12 daily, an amount found in many vitamin B-complex supplements. Once someone has developed a B12 deficiency, however, raising vitamin levels back to normal may require special pills or shots.

Others who might need supplements include people with stomach and intestinal disorders, those with pernicious anemia (a condition in which the body does not make enough red blood cells), and those taking medications that decrease vitamin B12 absorption (such as some heartburn, ulcer, and diabetes medicines). In addition, it is very important that breastfeeding women who follow strict vegetarian diets talk to a pediatrician about the proper use of vitamin B12 supplements for their babies, because an undetected and untreated B12 deficiency in infants can lead to severe, permanent neurological damage.

Safety Considerations. The Institute of Medicine of the U.S. National Academies is the scientific body that establishes dietary guidelines for nutrients, such as the RDA and the Tolerable Upper Intake Level (UL)—the maximum daily intake that is unlikely to lead to harmful health effects. The institute did not set a UL for vitamin B12, because there is very little potential for adverse effects caused by consuming too much of the vitamin.

See also: Folate

Bibliography

Dietary Supplement Fact Sheet: Vitamin B12. National Institutes of Health Office of Dietary Supplements, April 26, 2006, http://ods.od.nih.gov/factsheets/vitaminb12.asp.

Folstein, Marshal, Timothy Liu, Inga Peter, Jennifer Buel, Lisa Arsenault, Tammy Scott, et al. "The Homocysteine Hypothesis of Depression." *American Journal of Psychiatry* 164 (2007): 861–867.

Higdon, Jane. *Vitamin B$_{12}$.* Oregon State University Linus Pauling Institute, March 2003, http://lpi.oregonstate.edu/infocenter/vitamins/vitaminB12.

Penninx, Brenda W. J. H., Jack M. Guralnik, Luigi Ferrucci, Linda P. Fried, Robert H. Allen, and Sally P. Stabler. "Vitamin B$_{12}$ Deficiency and Depression in Physically Disabled Older Women: Epidemiologic Evidence From the Women's Health and Aging Study." *American Journal of Psychiatry* 157 (2000): 715–721.

Tiemeier, Henning, H. Ruud van Tuijl, Albert Hofman, John Meijer, Amanda J. Kiliaan, and Monique M. B. Breteler. "Vitamin B$_{12}$, Folate, and Homocysteine in Depression: The Rotterdam Study." *American Journal of Psychiatry* 159 (2002): 2099–2101.

Vitamin B-12 and Depression: Are They Related? Mayo Clinic, February 9, 2007, http://www.mayoclinic.com/health/vitamin-b12-and-depression/AN01543.

Vitamin B-12. American Academy of Family Physicians, June 2007, http://familydoctor.org/online/famdocen/home/articles/765.html.

WAKE THERAPY. Wake therapy is an experimental treatment for depression that involves controlled sleep deprivation, either for one whole night or for the second half only. In the early 1970s, researchers made a surprising discovery: Keeping people awake in a sleep clinic overnight sometimes led to a very rapid and dramatic, if short-lived, improvement in their mood. Wake therapy is the outgrowth of that discovery.

It is still unclear exactly how wake therapy might work. But the answer seems to lie in its effect on **circadian rhythms**, the body's internal system for regulating physiological and behavioral cycles that repeat daily, such as the sleep-wake cycle. Circadian rhythms are controlled by the body's internal "clock," located in a pair of tiny brain structures called the suprachiasmatic nucleus. A disruption in these rhythms may play a role in many types of depression.

Animal research suggests that sleep deprivation may temporarily weaken the body's internal clock as well as decrease cyclic variations in many brain chemicals. In this state, the internal clock may be easier to reset so that it is better synchronized with the external 24-hour day. More in-sync body cycles, in turn, may result in a better modulated mood.

Benefits for Depression. In studies of wake therapy, about 60 percent of people with **major depression** felt significantly better within hours. This is a big advantage over psychotherapy and medication, which can take weeks to have their full impact. The catch is that the benefits of wake therapy usually disappear as soon as the person goes back to sleep. To overcome this limitation, researchers are now combining wake therapy with **light therapy**, **antidepressants**, or gradual changes in the person's bedtime.

With the right combination of treatments, benefits may last for weeks or months. To date, the most striking results have been seen in people who are in the depressed phase of **bipolar disorder**, a condition in which people go back and forth between very low and very high moods. But other types of depression have been treated successfully as well.

Wake therapy may add to the benefits of more-established treatments for those who do not get enough relief from psychotherapy or antidepressants alone. It is also an attractive option for pregnant or breastfeeding women and others who prefer not to use medication. Results so far are encouraging. The future will tell whether wake therapy lives up to its promise and takes its place among the standard treatments for depression.

Bibliography

Wirz-Justice, Anna, Francesco Benedetti, Mathias Berger, Raymond W. Lam, Klaus Martiny, Michael Terman, et al. "Chronotherapeutics (Light and Wake Therapy) in Affective Disorders." *Psychological Medicine* 35 (2005): 939–944.

Wirz-Justice, Anna. "Chronobiology and Psychiatry." *Sleep Medicine Reviews* 11 (2007): 423–427.

WOMEN.   Women are about twice as likely as men to develop depression at some point during their lifetime. This gender discrepancy holds true for both **major depression** and its milder but very persistent cousin, **dysthymia**. The gender gap is found in all cultural and socioeconomic groups within the United States, and it also has been observed in countries around the world.

During childhood, boys and girls seems to have about the same risk for depression. After age 14, however, incidence rates diverge sharply. By late **adolescence**, the two-to-one ratio is established, and it lasts throughout adulthood. Several possible explanations for this gender difference have been advanced.

Female Risk Factors.   **Hormones** seem to be at least part of the explanation. Female hormones fluctuate dramatically around the time of puberty, childbirth, and **menopause**. It is probably no coincidence that these are also occasions when depression is more likely to occur. Some women also experience a severe but short-lived mood disturbance right before their menstrual periods—a condition known as **premenstrual dysphoric disorder** (PMDD). The symptoms of PMDD have been linked to cyclic changes in hormones that occur during the course of each menstrual cycle.

Genetic factors may help determine how hormonal changes across the menstrual cycle and over the life span affect a particular woman. All healthy young women have menstrual cycles and many give birth, but most remain depression-free. Researchers think normal hormonal changes may only trigger depression in women with an underlying genetic vulnerability to the disorder.

Personality factors have been implicated as well. Study after study has shown that women are more likely to feel strong emotional ties to many people and to see their relationships with others as central to their identity. In general, women also tend to care more about what others think about them and be strongly emotionally affected by events in the lives of those around them. When all goes well, this interpersonal orientation can be a source of great satisfaction and support. But when a problem occurs, those who are overly invested in their relationships or dependent on the approval of others may be susceptible to depression.

Cognitive factors also may play a role. **Rumination** refers to thinking about negative feelings, distressing symptoms, and the dark side of life in a passive, repetitive manner, rather than in an active, problem-solving way. Research has shown that people who ruminate when they are sad or blue are prone to higher levels of depression over time than people who don't ruminate. This pattern of thinking is more common in women than men.

Stress and Trauma.   The factors mentioned above may create the potential for depression. But a stressful or traumatic event is often what sets an episode of depression in motion, especially early in the course of the disease. Women may be at particular risk for certain types of **stress** and trauma.

For example, women's greater orientation toward others opens the door to increased stress when relationship problems occur. Also, women who work outside the home and still handle most of the household chores may feel overburdened. In addition, some women find themselves overwhelmed by caregiving responsibilities for children, aging parents, or disabled family members. When low **socioeconomic status** is added to the mix, it only intensifies the pressure—and single mothers have one of the highest poverty rates of any demographic group in the United States.

Certain **traumatic events**, including domestic violence and sexual assault, also affect women disproportionately. Both physical and sexual assault have been linked to depression.

For women, it might seem as if the deck is stacked against them. Yet it is worth remembering that, in any given year, 90 percent of women do not experience major depression. For the other 10 percent, effective treatments are available to help them build on their strengths and overcome challenges at every stage of life.

See also: Estrogen; Postpartum Depression; Pregnancy

Further Information. American College of Obstetricians and Gynecologists, P.O. Box 96920, Washington, D.C. 20090, (202) 638-5577, www.acog.org.

National Women's Health Information Center, U.S. Department of Health and Human Services, 8270 Willow Oaks Corporate Drive, Fairfax, VA 22031, (800) 994-9662, www.womenshealth.gov.

Bibliography

Depression in Women: Understanding the Gender Gap. Mayo Clinic, September 6, 2008, http://www.mayoclinic.com/health/depression/MH00035.

McBride, Carolina, and R. Michael Bagby. "Rumination and Interpersonal Dependency: Explaining Women's Vulnerability to Depression." *Canadian Psychology* 47 (2006): 184–194.

Nolen-Hoeksema, Susan, and Lori M. Hilt. "Gender Differences in Depression." In *Handbook of Depression.* 2nd ed., by Ian H. Gotlib and Constance L. Hammen, eds., 386–404. New York: Guilford Press, 2009.

The NSDUH Report: Major Depressive Episode and Treatment Among Adults. Substance Abuse and Mental Health Services Administration Office of Applied Studies, May 14, 2009, http://www.oas.samhsa.gov/2k9/149/MDEamongAdults.pdf.

Wise, Dana D., Angela Felker, and Stephen M. Stahl. "Tailoring Treatment of Depression for Women Across the Reproductive Lifecycle: The Importance of Pregnancy, Vasomotor Symptoms, and Other Estrogen-Related Events in Psychopharmacology." *CNS Spectrums* 13 (2008): 647–655, 658–662.

Women and Depression: Discovering Hope. National Institute of Mental Health, April 2, 2009, http://www.nimh.nih.gov/health/publications/women-and-depression-discovering-hope/index.shtml.

WORKPLACE ISSUES. One hallmark of **clinical depression** is having symptoms that are serious enough to interfere with life in everyday settings, such as the workplace. The degree of impairment depends not only on how severe the depression is, but also on the demands of the job. Work that involves impersonal and mechanical tasks may be easier to keep up. In contrast, work that requires considerable social interaction or mental focus may suffer more.

Depression is a major problem in the workforce. In fact, it is the third-most common problem that brings workers to an **employee assistance program** (EAP)—a confidential program offering information, support, and referral services to employees and family members who are having problems with daily living or emotional well-being. As an EAP issue, depression is outranked only by family crises and **stress**.

The **economic impact** of lost workdays and decreased job performance due to depression is massive. Experts peg the annual toll on U.S. businesses at about $70 billion, factoring in absenteeism, lost productivity, and health care costs. Economic costs that high reverberate throughout society. The good news is that treatment makes a big difference. When symptoms improve, work performance generally rebounds as well.

On-the-Job Stress. Depression can affect work, but the reverse is also true. Some workers experience a high level of job stress, which in turn may trigger or worsen depression in susceptible individuals. Researchers define job stress as harmful physical and psychological responses that occur when the requirements of a job do not match the abilities, skills, resources, or needs of the worker. Below are some examples of workplace conditions that are common sources of stress.

Job Demands. A heavy workload, infrequent rest breaks, long work hours, or shift work may contribute to stress. So may hectic or repetitive tasks that provide little sense of control or do not make good use of a worker's abilities.

Management Style. Poor communication within the organization is a common stressor. Others include lack of family-friendly policies and lack of employee participation in decision-making.

Coworker Relationships. Inadequate help and support from coworkers can give rise to stress. One study of 3,347 workers in Finland found that lack of team spirit was associated with increased worker depression and use of antidepressants.

Work Roles. Some workers become stressed out trying to meet conflicting job demands; for example, trying to satisfy both the boss and a customer. Others have to contend with unclear job expectations or too many responsibilities.

Career Concerns. Overly rapid change at work and insufficient opportunity for growth and advancement can be stressful. So can job insecurity, which also increased the risk for onset of depression in a study of 3,707 Dutch workers.

Environmental Factors. Unpleasant or dangerous physical conditions also put workers under stress. Examples include crowding, noise, poor workstation design, and exposure to toxic substances.

Crash and Burnout

Job burnout refers to a state of physical, mental, and emotional exhaustion caused by long-term work stress. The problem is especially common among workaholics and individuals in helping professions, such as nurses, therapists, teachers, and police officers. If ignored, job burnout can lead not only to a career crash, but also to problems such as depression, anxiety, and **alcohol** or **substance abuse.**

Following are some warning signs of job burnout. But keep in mind that these signs can indicate other health problems as well. A doctor, therapist, counselor, or EAP advisor can help sort out the cause of a particular problem.

Physical Signs	Mental and Emotional Signs	Behavioral Signs
Lacking enough energy to do your job.	Feeling as if you have to drag yourself to work.	Making critical or sarcastic remarks to coworkers.
Experiencing a change in sleep habits or appetite.	Feeling cynical or disillusioned about your job.	Being cranky and impatient with customers.
Having unexplained aches and pains.	Getting little joy or satisfaction from your achievements.	Using alcohol or drugs to feel better—or not to feel at all.

Less Stress at Work. Stress at work is associated not only with depression, but also with a host of other problems, such as **heart disease**, back pain, and workplace accidents. It is in the best interests of everyone—from top management down—to lower the stress level so workers are happier and healthier on the job.

For individual employees, it may help to learn **stress management** and **relaxation techniques** that can be used at work. For employers, it may help to restructure jobs that are overly stressful. Examples of workplace changes that reduce job stress include keeping the workload and hours at a reasonable level, clearly defining responsibilities, including workers in decision-making, and providing opportunities for social interaction.

See also: Americans with Disabilities Act

Further Information. Job Accommodation Network, P.O. Box 6080, Morgantown, WV 26506, (800) 526-7234, www.jan.wvu.edu.

National Disability Rights Network, 900 Second Street N.E., Suite 211, Washington, DC 20002, (202) 408-9514, www.napas.org.

National Institute for Occupational Safety and Health, 1600 Clifton Road, Atlanta, GA 30333, (800) 232-4636, www.cdc.gov/niosh.

Bibliography

Andrea, Helene, Ute Bültmann, Ludovic G. P. M. van Amelsvoort, and Ymert Kant. "The Incidence of Anxiety and Depression Among Employees: The Role of Psychosocial Work Characteristics." *Depression and Anxiety* (February 25, 2009): e-publication ahead of print.

DePaulo, J. Raymond Jr. *Understanding Depression: What We Know and What You Can Do About It.* New York: John Wiley and Sons, 2002.

Factsheet: Depression in the Workplace. Mental Health America, http://www.mentalhealthamerica .net/go/information/get-info/depression/depression-in-the-workplace.

Job Burnout: Understand the Symptoms and Take Action. Mayo Clinic, October 2, 2008, http://www .mayoclinic.com/health/burnout/WL00062.

Sinokki, M., K. Hinkka, K. Ahola, S. Koskinen, T. Kiaukka, M. Kivimäki, et al. "The Association Between Team Climate at Work and Mental Health in the Finnish Health 2000 Study." *Occupational and Environmental Medicine* (April 9, 2009): e-publication ahead of print.

Statistics on Depression. Depression and Bipolar Support Alliance, January 30, 2009, http://www .dbsalliance.org/site/PageServer?pagename=about_statistics_depression.

Stress . . . at Work. National Institute for Occupational Safety and Health, 1999, http://www.cdc .gov/niosh/stresswk.html.

Wang, Philip S., and Ronald C. Kessler. "Global Burden of Mood Disorders." In *The American Psychiatric Publishing Textbook of Mood Disorders,* by Dan J. Stein, David J. Kupfer, and Alan F. Schatzberg, eds., 55–67. Washington, DC: American Psychiatric Publishing, 2006.

Y

YOGA. Yoga is a mind-body practice, rooted in the ancient traditions of India, which combines physical postures, breathing techniques, and **meditation**. It has become a very popular form of **exercise** in the United States. In the 2007 National Health Interview Survey, more than 13 million U.S. adults said they had used yoga for health purposes within the past year. One reason for doing yoga is to relieve depression, and there is evidence that it may indeed help boost a low mood, improve well-being, and counteract **stress**.

The oldest-known yoga text, *The Yoga Sutras,* was written more than 2,000 years ago. However, many historians think yoga may have been practiced for as long as five millennia. The discipline of yoga was originally intended to help people attain spiritual enlightenment.

Hatha yoga, the form most widely practiced in the United States today, emphasizes postures (called *asanas*) and breathing exercises (called *pranayama*). There are several styles of hatha yoga, including Iyengar, Astanga, Kundalini, Bikram, and Vini. For most Westerners, the goal of yoga is to enhance fitness, promote relaxation, and improve health.

One small study looked at the benefits of yoga for depressed individuals who were already taking **antidepressants**, but whose symptoms had not fully lifted. The 17 people who completed the study took 20 classes on Iyengar yoga, a form that employs props, such as blankets and ropes, to help even beginners learn poses gradually and accurately. Two-thirds of these individuals saw their depression go away by the study's end.

Although such results are promising, more research is needed to confirm them. In the meantime, for those who choose to try yoga, there are generally few risks when it is taught by a qualified instructor. People with certain medical conditions may need to avoid some postures. For example, people with high blood pressure or a detached retina should avoid some head-down poses. A good instructor should ask about health concerns before the first class and offer modified poses for those who require them.

See also: Relaxation Techniques

Further Information. Yoga Alliance, 1701 Clarendon Boulevard, Suite 110. Arlington, VA 22209, (888) 921-9642, www.yogaalliance.org.

Bibliography

About Yoga. National Center for Complementary and Alternative Medicine, http://nccam.nih .gov/health/yoga.

Shapiro, David, Ian A. Cook, Dmitry M. Davydov, Cristina Ottaviani, Andrew F. Leuchter, and Michelle Abrams. "Yoga as a Complementary Treatment of Depression: Effects of Traits and Moods on Treatment Outcome."

Yoga for Health: An Introduction. National Center for Complementary and Alternative Medicine, May 2008, http://nccam.nih.gov/health/yoga/introduction.htm.

Z

ZUNG SELF-RATING DEPRESSION SCALE. The Zung Self-Rating Depression Scale (ZSDS) is a self-report questionnaire designed to measure the severity of depression symptoms in adults. The scale originally was developed in 1965 by U.S. psychiatrist William W. K. Zung. Although numerous other scales for measuring depression have been developed in the intervening decades, the ZSDS has stood the test of time. It is still used to screen for depression in people who might have the illness as well as to assess how well treatment is working in those who have already been diagnosed.

The ZSDS, which usually takes about five minutes to complete, is composed of 20 items describing various symptoms of depression. People use a four-point scale to indicate how frequently they have experienced each symptom. Half of the items are worded positively (for example, "I feel down-hearted and blue") and half negatively (for example, "I feel that I am useful and needed").

Pros and Cons of the ZSDS. Relatively few studies have looked at the reliability of the ZSDS—that is, the extent to which results of the test are consistent and repeatable. But the evidence that is available shows good consistency in the degree to which all items on the test are measuring the same thing.

Research on the validity of ZSDS—that is, the extent to which it actually measures what it purports to measure—has shown that it does a good job of discriminating people with several types of depression from those who are not depressed. However, the test does not ask about certain symptoms of **atypical depression**, such as increased appetite and oversleeping, so it may not be as helpful for assessing this depression subtype.

The ZSDS can be used a screening tool for identifying people in need of a full diagnostic workup and as a clinical tool for tracking the success of treatment. As a screening test, the ZSDS performs about as well as other popular tests of depression. But as a clinical tool, when the test is given periodically to see how well treatment is working, the ZSDS is less sensitive to a change in symptoms over time than many other measures.

See also: Diagnosis of Depression; Screening Tests

Bibliography

Yonkers, Kimberly A., and Jacqueline A. Samson. "Mood Disorders Measures." In *Handbook of Psychiatric Measures,* 2nd ed., by A. John Rush Jr., Michael B. First, and Deborah Blacker, eds., 499–528. Washington, DC: American Psychiatric Publishing, 2008.

Zung, W. W. "The Role of Rating Scales in the Identification and Management of the Depressed Patient in the Primary Care Setting." *Journal of Clinical Psychiatry* 51 suppl. (1990): 72–76.

Zung, W. W. K. "A Self-Rating Depression Scale." *Archives of General Psychiatry* 12 (1965): 63–70.

Zung, William W. K. *This Week's Citation Classic.* June 11, 1979, http://www.garfield.library .upenn.edu/classics1979/A1979HZ25800001.ppd.

Appendix: Organizations

Support Resources

Child and Adolescent Bipolar Foundation, 1000 Skokie Boulevard, Suite 570, Wilmette, IL 60091, (847) 256-8525, www.bpkids.org.

Depression and Bipolar Support Alliance, 730 N. Franklin Street, Suite 501, Chicago, IL 60610, (800) 826-3632, www.dbsalliance.org, www.peersupport.org, www.facingus.org.

Dual Recovery Anonymous, P.O. Box 8107, Prairie Village, KS 66208, (877) 883-2332, www.draonline.org.

Families for Depression Awareness, 395 Totten Pond Road, Suite 404, Waltham, MA 02451, (781) 890-0220, www.familyaware.org.

HealthyPlace, www.healthyplace.com.

Mental Health America, 2000 N. Beauregard Street, 6th Floor Alexandria, VA 22311, (800) 969-6642, www.nmha.org, www.depression-screening.org.

National Alliance on Mental Illness, 2107 Wilson Boulevard, Suite 300, Arlington, VA 22201, (800) 950-6264, www.nami.org.

National Mental Health Consumers' Self-Help Clearinghouse, 1211 Chestnut Street, Suite 1207, Philadelphia, PA 19107, (800) 553-4539, www.mhselfhelp.org.

Postpartum Support International, P.O. Box 60931, Santa Barbara, CA 93160, (800) 944-4773, www.postpartum.net.

Information Resources

Agency for Healthcare Research and Quality, Office of Communications and Knowledge Transfer, 540 Gaither Road, Suite 2000, Rockville, MD 20850, (301) 427-1364, www.ahrq.gov.

Annenberg Foundation Trust at Sunnylands, www.copecaredeal.org.

Bazelon Center for Mental Health Law, 1101 15th Street, NW, Suite 1212, Washington, DC 20005, (202) 467-5730, www.bazelon.org.

Center for Mental Health Services, National Mental Health Information Center, P.O. Box 2345, Rockville, MD 20847, (800) 789-2647, mentalhealth.samhsa.gov.

CenterWatch, 100 North Washington Street, Suite 301, Boston, MA 02114, (866) 219-3440, www.centerwatch.com.

Dana Foundation, 745 Fifth Avenue, Suite 900, New York, NY 10151, (212) 223-4040, www.dana.org.

Food and Drug Administration, 10903 New Hampshire Avenue, Silver Spring, MD 20993, (888) 463-6332, www.fda.gov.

IDEA Partnership, 1800 Diagonal Road, Suite 320, Alexandria, VA 22314, (877) 433-2463, www.ideapartnership.org.

Job Accommodation Network, P.O. Box 6080, Morgantown, WV 26506, (800) 526-7234, www.jan.wvu.edu.

Mayo Clinic, www.mayoclinic.com.

National Alliance for Research on Schizophrenia and Depression, 60 Cutter Mill Road, Suite 404, Great Neck, New York 11021, (516) 829-0091, www.narsad.org.

National Asian American Pacific Islander Mental Health Association, 1215 19th Street, Suite A, Denver, CO 80202, (303) 298-7910, www.naapimha.org.

National Center for American Indian and Alaska Native Mental Health Research, Mail Stop F800, Nighthorse Campbell Native Health Building, 13055 E. 17th Avenue, Aurora, CO 80045, (303) 724-1414, aianp.uchsc.edu.

National Center for Complementary and Alternative Medicine, 9000 Rockville Pike, Bethesda, MD 20892, (888) 644-6226, nccam.nih.gov.

National Disability Rights Network, 900 Second Street N.E., Suite 211, Washington, DC 20002, (202) 408-9514, www.napas.org.

National Institute of Mental Health, 6001 Executive Boulevard, Room 8184, MSC 9663, Bethesda, MD 20892, (866) 615-6464, www.nimh.nih.gov.

National Institutes of Health, 9000 Rockville Pike, Bethesda, MD 20892, (301) 496-4000, www.nih.gov.

National Library of Medicine, 8600 Rockville Pike, Bethesda, MD 20894, (888) 346-3656, www.clinicaltrials.gov, www.medlineplus.gov, www.pubmed.gov.

National Mental Health Awareness Campaign, P.O. Box 491608, Los Angeles, CA 90049, (800) 273-8255, www.nostigma.org.

National Women's Health Information Center, U.S. Department of Health and Human Services, 8270 Willow Oaks Corporate Drive, Fairfax, VA 22031, (800) 994-9662, www.womenshealth.gov.

Nemours Foundation, www.kidshealth.org.

Office of Minority Health, U.S. Department of Health and Human Services, P.O. Box 37337, Washington, D.C. 20013, (800) 444-6472, www.omhrc.gov.

SAMHSA Resource Center to Promote Acceptance, Dignity and Social Inclusion Associated with Mental Health, Substance Abuse and Mental Health Services Administration, 11420 Rockville Pike, Rockville, MD 20852, (800) 540-0320, www.stopstigma.samhsa.gov.

Society for Neuroscience, 1121 14th Street N.W., Suite 1010, Washington, DC 20005, (202) 962-4000, www.sfn.org.

U.S. Department of Justice, Disability Rights Section, 950 Pennsylvania Avenue N.W., Washington, DC 20530, (800) 514-0301, www.ada.gov.

World Health Organization, www.who.int.

Zero to Three, National Center for Infants, Toddlers and Families, 2000 M Street N.W., Suite 200, Washington, DC 20036, (202) 638-1144, www.zerotothree.org.

Treatment Resources

Academy of Cognitive Therapy, 260 South Broad Street, 18th Floor, Philadelphia, PA 19102, (267) 350-7683, www.academyofct.org.

Albert Ellis Institute, 45 East 65th Street, New York, NY 10065, (800) 323-4738, www.albertellisinstitute.org.

American Academy of Child and Adolescent Psychiatry, 3615 Wisconsin Avenue N.W., Washington, D.C.20016, (202) 966-7300, www.aacap.org.

American Association for Geriatric Psychiatry, 7910 Woodmont Avenue, Suite 1050, Bethesda, MD 20814, (301) 654-7850, www.aagponline.org, www.gmhfonline.org.

American Association for Marriage and Family Therapy, 112 S. Alfred Street, Alexandria, VA 22314, (703) 838-9808, www.aamft.org.

American Association of Children's Residential Centers, 11700 W. Lake Park Drive, Milwaukee, WI 53224, (877) 332-2272, www.aacrc-dc.org.

American Association of Pastoral Counselors, 9504A Lee Highway, Fairfax, VA 22031-2303, (703) 385-6967, www.aapc.org.

American Counseling Association, 5999 Stevenson Avenue, Alexandria, VA 22304, (800) 347-6647, www.counseling.org.

American Group Psychotherapy Association, 25 East 21st Street, 6th Floor, New York, NY 10010, (877) 668-2472, www.agpa.org.

American Hospital Association, One North Franklin, Chicago, IL 60606, (312) 422-3000, www.aha.org.

American Medical Association, 515 North State Street, Chicago, IL 60654, (800) 621-8335, www.ama-assn.org.

American Mental Health Counselors Association, 801 N. Fairfax Street, Suite 304, Alexandria, VA 22314, (800) 326-2642, www.amhca.org.

American Nurses Association, 8515 Georgia Avenue, Suite 400, Silver Spring, MD 20910, (800) 274-4262, www.nursingworld.org.

American Psychiatric Association, 1000 Wilson Boulevard, Suite 1825, Arlington, VA 22209, (888) 357-7924, www.psych.org, www.dsmivtr.org, www.dsm5.org.

American Psychiatric Nurses Association, 1555 Wilson Boulevard, Suite 602, Arlington, VA 22209, (866) 243-2443, www.apna.org.

American Psychoanalytic Association, 309 East 49th Street, New York, NY 10017, (212) 752-0450, apsa.org.

American Psychological Association, 750 First Street N.E., Washington, DC 20002, (800) 374-2721, www.apa.org, www.apahelpcenter.org, www.psychologymatters.org.

Asian American Psychological Association, PMB 527, 5025 N. Central Avenue, Phoenix, AZ 85012, www.aapaonline.org.

Association for Behavioral and Cognitive Therapies, 305 7th Avenue, 16th Floor, New York, NY 10001, (212) 647-1890, www.abct.org.

Association for Contextual Behavioral Science, www.contextualpsychology.org.

Association of Black Psychologists, P.O. Box 55999, Washington, D.C. 20040, (202) 722-0808, www.abpsi.org.

Beck Institute for Cognitive Therapy and Research, One Belmont Avenue, Suite 700, Bala Cynwyd, PA 19004, 610) 664-3020, www.beckinstitute.org.

Behavioral Tech, 2133 Third Avenue, Suite 205, Seattle, WA 98121, (206) 675-8588, www.behavioraltech.org.

Center for Environmental Therapeutics, www.cet.org.

Cognitive Behavioral Analysis System of Psychotherapy, www.cbasp.org.

Emotion-Focused Therapy, www.emotionfocusedtherapy.org.

International Neuromodulation Society, 2000 Van Ness Avenue, Suite 402, San Francisco, CA 94109, (415) 683-3237, www.neuromodulation.com.

International Society for Interpersonal Psychotherapy, www.interpersonalpsychotherapy .org.

Mindfulness-Based Cognitive Therapy, www.mbct.com.

National Association of Cognitive-Behavioral Therapists, P.O. Box 2195, Weirton, WV 26062, (800) 853-1135, www.nacbt.org.

National Association of Psychiatric Health Systems, 701 13th Street N.W., Suite 950, Washington, DC 20005, (202) 393-6700, www.naphs.org.

National Association of School Psychologists, 4340 E. West Highway, Suite 402, Bethesda, MD 20814, (301) 657-0270, www.nasponline.org.

National Association of Social Workers, 750 First Street N.E., Suite 700, Washington, DC 20002, (202) 408-8600, www.socialworkers.org, www.helpstartshere.org.

National Association of Therapeutic Schools and Programs, 5272 River Road, Suite 600, Bethesda, MD 20816, (301) 986-8770, www.natsap.org.

Screening for Mental Health, One Washington Street, Suite 304, Wellesley Hills, MA 02481, (781) 239-0071, mentalhealthscreening.org.

Society for Light Treatment and Biological Rhythms, www.sltbr.org.

Society of Clinical Child and Adolescent Psychology, clinicalchildpsychology.org.

Suicide Resources

American Association of Suicidology, 5221 Wisconsin Avenue N.W., Washington, DC 20015, (202) 237-2280, www.suicidology.org.

Jed Foundation, 220 Fifth Avenue, 9th Floor, New York, NY 10001, (212) 647-7544, www.jedfoundation.org.

Kristin Brooks Hope Center, (800) 784-2433, www.hopeline.com.

National Suicide Prevention Lifeline, (800) 273-8255, www.suicidepreventionlife line.org.

Suicide Awareness Voices of Education, 8120 Penn Avenue S., Suite 470, Bloomington, MN 55431, (952) 946-7998, www.save.org.

Suicide Prevention Action Network USA, 1010 Vermont Avenue N.W., Suite 408, Washington, DC 20005, (202) 449-3600, www.spanusa.org.

FURTHER READING

General Reading

Burns, David D. *Feeling Good: The New Mood Therapy.* New York: Avon Books, 1999.

DePaulo, J. Raymond Jr. *Understanding Depression: What We Know and What You Can Do about It.* New York: John Wiley and Sons, 2002.

Ellis, Albert. *How to Stubbornly Refuse to Make Yourself Miserable about Anything (Yes, Anything!).* Rev. ed. New York: Kensington Publishing, 2006.

Evans, Dwight L., and Linda Wasmer Andrews. *If Your Adolescent Has Depression or Bipolar Disorder: An Essential Resource for Parents.* New York: Oxford University Press, 2005.

Jamison, Kay Redfield. *Night Falls Fast: Understanding Suicide.* New York: Vintage Books, 1999.

Jamison, Kay Redfield. *Touched with Fire: Manic-Depressive Illness and the Artistic Temperament.* New York: Free Press, 1993.

Kramer, Peter D. *Against Depression.* New York: Viking, 2005.

Kramer, Peter D. *Listening to Prozac.* New York: Viking Penguin, 1993.

Lewinsohn, Peter M., Ricardo F. Muñoz, Mary Ann Youngren, and Antonette M. Zeiss. *Control Your Depression.* Rev. ed. New York: Fireside, 1992.

Maisel, Eric. *The Van Gogh Blues: The Creative Person's Path through Depression.* Novato, CA: New World Library, 2002.

Marra, Thomas. *Depressed and Anxious: The Dialectical Behavior Therapy Workbook for Overcoming Depression and Anxiety.* Oakland, CA: New Harbinger, 2004.

Mondimore, Francis Mark. *Adolescent Depression: A Guide for Parents.* Baltimore: Johns Hopkins University Press, 2002.

Radden, Jennifer, ed. *The Nature of Melancholy: From Aristotle to Kristeva.* New York: Oxford University Press, 2000.

Rosenthal, Norman E. *Winter Blues: Everything You Need to Know to Beat Seasonal Affective Disorder.* Rev. ed. New York: Guilford Press, 2006.

Seligman, Martin E.P. *Learned Optimism.* New York: Alfred A. Knopf, 1991.

Seligman, Martin E.P., with Karen Reivich, Lisa Jaycox and Jane Gillham. *The Optimistic Child: A Proven Program to Safeguard Children against Depression and Build Lifelong Resilience.* New York: Houghton Mifflin, 1995.

Shenk, Joshua Wolf. *Lincoln's Melancholy: How Depression Challenged a President and Fueled His Greatness.* Boston: Houghton Mifflin, 2005.

Society for Neuroscience. *Brain Facts: A Primer on the Brain and Nervous System.* 6th ed. Washington, DC: Society for Neuroscience, 2008.

Solomon, Andrews. *The Noonday Demon: An Atlas of Depression.* New York: Scribner, 2001.

Somers, Elizabeth. *Food and Mood: The Complete Guide to Eating Well and Feeling Your Best.* 2nd ed. Owl Books: New York, 1999.

Thase, Michael E., and Susan S. Lang. *Beating the Blues: New Approaches to Overcoming Dysthymia and Chronic Mild Depression.* New York: Oxford University Press, 2004.

U.S. Department of Health and Human Services. *Culture, Race, and Ethnicity: A Supplement to Mental Health: A Report of the Surgeon General.* Rockville, MD: U.S. Department of Health and Human Services, 2001.

U.S. Department of Health and Human Services. *Mental Health: A Report of the Surgeon General.* Rockville, MD: U.S. Department of Health and Human Services, 1999.

Wilens, Timothy E. *Straight Talk about Psychiatric Medications for Kids.* Rev. ed. New York: Guilford Press, 2004.

Williams, Mark, John Teasdale, Zindel Segal, and Jon-Kabat Zinn. *The Mindful Way through Depression: Freeing Yourself from Chronic Unhappiness.* New York: Guilford Press, 2007.

First-Person Memoirs

Casey, Nell, ed. *Unholy Ghost: Writers on Depression.* New York: Perennial, 2001.

Griffith, Gail. *Will's Choice.* New York: HarperCollins, 2005.

Irwin, Cait, with Dwight L. Evans and Linda Wasmer Andrews. *Monochrome Days: A Firsthand Account of One Teenager's Experience with Depression.* New York: Oxford University Press, 2007.

Manning, Martha. *Undercurrents: A Life beneath the Surface.* San Francisco: Harper SanFrancisco, 1994.

Osmond, Marie with Marcia Wilkie and Judith Moore. *Behind the Smile: My Journey Out of Postpartum Depression.* New York: Warner Books, 2001.

Shields, Brooke. *Down Came the Rain: My Journey through Postpartum Depression.* New York: Hyperion, 2005.

Styron, William. *Darkness Visible: A Memoir of Madness.* New York: Random House, 1990.

Thompson, Tracy. *The Beast: A Journey through Depression.* New York: Plume, 1995.

Wurtzel, Elizabeth. *Prozac Nation: Young and Depressed in America—A Memoir.* New York: Riverhead Books, 1994.

Professional Resources

American Psychiatric Association Work Group on Major Depressive Disorder. *Practice Guideline for the Treatment of Patients with Major Depressive Disorder.* 2nd ed. Washington, DC: American Psychiatric Publishing, 2000.

American Psychiatric Association. *Diagnostic and Statistical Manual of Mental Disorders.* 4th ed., text rev. Washington, DC: American Psychiatric Association, 2000.

Beck, Aaron, T., A. John Rush, Brian F. Shaw and Gary Emery. *Cognitive Therapy of Depression.* New York: Guilford Press, 1979.

Blatt, Sidney J. *Experiences of Depression: Theoretical, Clinical, and Research Perspectives.* Washington, DC: American Psychological Association, 2004.

Bowlby, John. *Attachment and Loss (Volume 3): Loss, Sadness and Depression.* London: Hogarth, 1980.

Burton, S.W., and H.S. Akiskal, eds. *Dysthymic Disorder.* London: Gaskell, 1990.

Busch, Frederic N., Marie Rudden and Theodore Shapiro. *Psychodynamic Treatment of Depression.* Washington, DC: American Psychiatric Publishing, 2004.

Clarke, Gregory, Peter Lewinsohn, and Hyman Hops. *Leader's Manual for Adolescent Groups: Adolescent Coping with Depression Course.* Portland, OR: Kaiser Permanente Center for Health Research, 1990.

First, Michael B., Allen Frances, and Harold Alan Pincus. *DSM-IV Handbook of Differential Diagnosis.* Washington, DC: American Psychiatric Press, 1995.

Frances, Allen, Michael B. First, and Harold Alan Pincus. *DSM-IV Guidebook.* Washington, DC: American Psychiatric Press, 1995.

Gilbert, Paul. *Psychotherapy and Counselling for Depression*. 3rd ed. Los Angeles: Sage Publications, 2007.

Gotlib, Ian H., and Constance L. Hammen, eds. *Handbook of Depression*. 2nd ed. New York: Guilford Press, 2009.

Greenberg, Leslie S., and Jeanne C. Watson. *Emotion-Focused Therapy for Depression*. Washington, DC: American Psychological Association, 2006.

Joiner, Thomas, and James C. Coyne, eds. *The Interactional Nature of Depression: Advances in Interpersonal Approaches*. Washington, DC: American Psychological Association, 1999.

Klerman, Gerald L., Myrna M. Weissman, Bruce J. Rounsaville, and Eve S. Chevron. *Interpersonal Psychotherapy of Depression*. New York: Basic Books, 1984.

Lake, James H., and David Spiegel, eds. *Complementary and Alternative Treatments in Mental Health Care*. Washington, DC: American Psychiatric Publishing, 2007.

Levenson, Hanna, Stephen F. Butler, Theodore A. Powers, and Bernard D. Beitman. *Concise Guide to Brief Dynamic and Interpersonal Therapy*. 2nd ed. Washington, DC: American Psychiatric Publishing, 2002.

McCullough, James P. Jr. *Treating Chronic Depression with Disciplined Personal Involvement: Cognitive Behavioral Analysis System of Psychotherapy (CBASP)*. New York: Springer, 2006.

McCullough, James P. Jr. *Treatment for Chronic Depression: Cognitive Behavioral Analysis System of Psychotherapy (CBASP)*. New York: Guilford Press, 2003.

Mynors-Wallis, Laurence. *Problem-Solving Treatment for Anxiety and Depression*. New York: Oxford University Press, 2005.

Papageorgiou, Costas, and Adrian Wells, eds. *Depressive Rumination: Nature, Theory and Treatment*. Hoboken, NJ: John Wiley and Sons, 2004.

Persons, Jacqueline B., Joan Davidson, and Michael A. Tompkins. *Essential Components of Cognitive-Behavior Therapy for Depression*. Washington, DC: American Psychological Association, 2001.

Peterson, Christopher, Steven F. Maier, and Martin E.P. Seligman. *Learned Helplessness: A Theory for the Age of Personal Control*. New York: Oxford University Press, 1993.

Plutchik, Robert. *Emotions and Life: Perspectives from Psychology, Biology, and Evolution*. Washington, DC: American Psychological Association, 2003.

Qualls, Sara H. and Bob G. Knight, eds. *Psychotherapy for Depression in Older Adults*. Hoboken, NJ: John Wiley and Sons, 2006.

Rush, A. John Jr., Michael B. First and Deborah Blacker, eds. *Handbook of Psychiatric Measures*, 2nd ed. Washington, DC: American Psychiatric Publishing, 2008.

Schwartz, Arthur and Ruth M. Schwartz. *Depression Theories and Treatments: Psychological, Biological, and Social Perspectives*. New York: Columbia University Press, 1993.

Segal, Zindel V., J. Mark G. Williams, and John D. Teasdale. *Mindfulness-Based Cognitive Therapy for Depression: A New Approach to Preventing Relapse*. New York: Guilford Press, 2002.

Seligman, Martin E.P. *Helplessness: On Depression, Development, and Death*. San Francisco: W.H. Freeman, 1975.

Shaffer, David, and Bruce D. Waslick, eds. *The Many Faces of Depression in Children and Adolescents*. Washington, DC: American Psychiatric Publishing, 2002.

Stein, Dan J., David D. Kupfer and Alan F. Schatzberg, eds. *The American Psychiatric Publishing Textbook of Mood Disorders*. Washington, DC: American Psychiatric Publishing, 2006.

VandenBos, Gary R., ed. *APA Dictionary of Psychology*. Washington, DC: American Psychological Association, 2007.

Watson, Jeanne C., Rhonda N. Goldman, and Leslie S. Greenberg. *Case Studies in Emotion-Focused Therapy of Depression: A Comparison of Good and Poor Outcome*. Washington, DC: American Psychological Association, 2007.

Weissman, Myrna M., John C. Markowitz, and Gerald L. Klerman. *Comprehensive Guide to Interpersonal Psychotherapy*. New York: Basic Books, 2000.

Zettle, Robert D. *ACT for Depression: A Clinician's Guide to Using Acceptance and Commitment Therapy in Treating Depression*. Oakland, CA: New Harbinger, 2007.

INDEX

Note: An italicized *b* following a page number indicates a box. Page numbers in **bold font** refer to main entries in this encyclopedia.

ABOUT THE AUTHOR

LINDA WASMER ANDREWS, M.S., has been writing about psychology and health since the early 1980s. She is the author or coauthor of 13 previous books for children, teens, and adults, including *If Your Adolescent Has Depression or Bipolar Disorder* (Oxford University Press, 2005) and *Monochrome Days* (Oxford University Press, 2007). Her work also appears regularly in national magazines, such as *Self, Figure, Heart-Healthy Living,* and *American Profile*. Linda lives in Albuquerque, New Mexico; visit her online at www.lindaandrews.com.